Lecture Notes in Computer Scier

Edited by G. Goos, J. Hartmanis, and J. van I

T0238300

Springer
Berlin
Heidelberg
New York
Hong Kong
London
Milan
Paris
Tokyo

Henk Blanken   Torsten Grabs
Hans-Jörg Schek   Ralf Schenkel
Gerhard Weikum (Eds.)

Intelligent Search on XML Data

Applications, Languages, Models,
Implementations, and Benchmarks

Springer

Series Editors

Gerhard Goos, Karlsruhe University, Germany
Juris Hartmanis, Cornell University, NY, USA
Jan van Leeuwen, Utrecht University, The Netherlands

Volume Editors

Henk Blanken
University of Twente, Faculty of EEMCS
Department of Computer Science
P.O. Box 217, 7500 AE Enschede, The Netherlands
E-mail: blanken@cs.utwente.nl

Torsten Grabs
Hans-Jörg Schek
Institute of Information Systems, ETH Zürich
8092 Zürich, Switzerland
E-mail: {grabs;schek}@inf.ethz.ch

Ralf Schenkel
Gerhard Weikum
Saarland University, Department of Computer Science
P.O. Box 151150, 66041 Saarbrücken, Germany
{schenkel;weikum}@cs.uni-sb.de

Cataloging-in-Publication Data applied for

A catalog record for this book is available from the Library of Congress.

Bibliographic information published by Die Deutsche Bibliothek
Die Deutsche Bibliothek lists this publication in the Deutsche Nationalbibliografie;
detailed bibliographic data is available in the Internet at <http://dnb.ddb.de>.

CR Subject Classification (1998): H.3, H.2, H.4, C.2, F.2, J.1

ISSN 0302-9743
ISBN 3-540-40768-5 Springer-Verlag Berlin Heidelberg New York

Springer-Verlag Berlin Heidelberg New York
a member of BertelsmannSpringer Science+Business Media GmbH

http://www.springer.de

© Springer-Verlag Berlin Heidelberg 2003
Printed in Germany

Typesetting: Camera-ready by author, data conversion by PTP Berlin GmbH
Printed on acid-free paper   SPIN: 10950050   06/3142   5 4 3 2 1 0

Preface

Recently, we have seen a significant increase in popularity and adoption of XML, the eXtensible Markup Language of the World Wide Web Consortium (W3C). XML is used to represent information in many areas such as traditional databases, e-business, the scientific environment, and on the Web. Also metadata characterizing the contents of, for instance, digital libraries can be described with XML. Query languages have been developed to handle XML documents. These languages exploit Boolean retrieval and often produce too many or too few results. They lack the concept of semantic similarity and have no means to produce ranked retrieval results. To improve the quality of the results, manipulation of text data within XML documents can be helpful. This introduces the scientific field of information retrieval (IR) where, on one hand, keyword search is exploited but, on the other hand, the structure of documents is not taken into account at all. An important challenge is to combine these two areas leading us to content- and structure-based querying, or, put in another way, to *intelligent search in XML data*. When trying to tackle this challenge, many problems arise. This book reports on research efforts, mainly European, aimed at solving some of these problems.

To appreciate the book, an introductory knowledge of traditional database technology, information retrieval, and XML is needed. As such, the book provides very suitable material for courses at graduate or senior level, and also for upgrading the skills of computer scientists working on Web applications, digital libraries, database systems, and information retrieval.

The chapters of the book are grouped into five parts; each part starts with a brief introduction explaining the aim and content of the part.

Part I is called "Applications" and contains the description of an e-health and a video library application. This part is a motivation for the rest of the book. Many aspects of intelligent searching in huge collections of information are considered. Attention is paid to clarifying query terms using ontologies, to the structuring or labeling of documents, to keyword searching, and to the ranking of answers to obtain the best results.

Part II is called "Query Languages" and presents IR extensions to query languages for XML. It consists of three chapters. Certain elements in the XML documents contain free text to which IR techniques can be applied. The first of the three chapters gives a state-of-the-art description of the W3C standardization activity to extend the XML query language XQuery. In subsequent chapters definition efforts are described to extend query languages for XML. One effort comes from a commercial and another from a university environment.

Part III is called "Retrieval Models" and consists of six chapters. In this part we will use the term modeling in different meanings. The first meaning concerns the definition of the concept of relevance that is used to rank documents for a given query. To this end graph-based ontologies with edge weights reflecting the strength of relationships between concepts can be helpful. Another approach is to take into account the place in a document where a searched keyword occurs. For instance, a title may be a more relevant place than a footnote.

A second meaning occurs when modeling is related to the formulation of a user's information need. It is important to capture these needs to the best possible extent. Several techniques, including ontologies and relevance feedback, can be used to better capture the user's request for information.

Last but not least, modeling may refer to text documents. Here modeling aims to automatically derive XML documents from free text documents or to organize documents into topic categories by automatic classification.

Part IV is called "Implementing Intelligent XML Systems" and consists of six chapters. Topics discussed in this part are system architecture, query processing, and access paths. Mapping XML documents and index terms to underlying structures can be done in several ways. One way is to exploit existing off-the-shelf DBMSs and to store subtrees of the documents as one unit.

Another method uses a two level system; the lower level being a binary relational system, the higher level providing nested object structures. Both mapping and query handling are explained.

XML documents can also be stored on the Web and handling intelligent search queries for the Web offers many problems and possibilities. Web-based query processing systems are characterized using several features. Query processing may concern XML documents containing multimedia information, e.g. images. Automatically derived metadata can be used to enhance the quality of the results. Moreover, concepts in different XML documents may be related. Also this fact can be exploited to improve performance.

Finally, access structures may speed up query processing. A special role is reserved for tree structures. Query processing, think of handling path expressions and joins, can strongly benefit from these structures.

Part V is called "Evaluation" and contains only two chapters. Evaluating (object-relational) database systems normally concerns efficiency. Often benchmarks are used to compare the speed, resource consumption, and so on, with competitive systems. Evaluation of information retrieval systems is, on the other hand, mainly related to effectiveness: how good are the answers obtained by a system in a certain setting compared to other IR systems? One of the two chapters addresses efficiency, the other one effectivness.

Acknowledgements

In December 2002, a workshop on "Intelligent Search in XML Data" was held at Schloss Dagstuhl (Germany). During this workshop participants presented their state-of-the-art work. This book documents those presentations.

The participants played a great part in writing and subsequently reviewing chapters of the book. They had, without exception, a high work load. We thank them for their productive and pleasant cooperation.

Several research projects described in this book have been (partially) supported by the following agencies: Deutsche Forschungsgemeinschaft (German Science Foundation), the Netherlands Organisation for Scientific Research, the DELOS Network of Excellence for Digital Libraries[1], the IEEE Computer Society[2], Deutscher Akadmischer Austausch Dienst (DAAD)[3], and the British Council[4] under the Academic Research Collaboration (ARC) Programme.

September 2003

Henk M. Blanken
Torsten Grabs
Hans-Jörg Schek
Ralf Schenkel
Gerhard Weikum

---

[1] http://delos-noe.org/
[2] http://computer.org/
[3] http://www.daad.de/
[4] http://www.britishcouncil.org/

Contents

List of Contributors

Editors

Henk Blanken
Department of Computer Science
Faculty of EEMCS
University of Twente
P.O. Box 217
7500 AE Enschede
The Netherlands
blanken@cs.utwente.nl

Hans-Jörg Schek
ETH Zürich
Database Research Group
Institute of Information Systems
8092 Zürich
Switzerland
schek@inf.ethz.ch

Gerhard Weikum
Universität des Saarlandes
Fachrichtung 6.2 Informatik
Postfach 151150
66041 Saarbrücken
Germany
weikum@cs.uni-sb.de

Torsten Grabs
ETH Zürich
Database Research Group
Institute of Information Systems
8092 Zürich
Switzerland
grabs@inf.ethz.ch

Ralf Schenkel
Universität des Saarlandes
Fachrichtung 6.2 Informatik
Postfach 151150
66041 Saarbrücken
Germany
schenkel@cs.uni-sb.de

Authors

Giuseppe Amato
Istituto di Scienza e Tecnologie
dell'Informazione
"Alessandro Faedo"
Area della Ricerca CNR di Pisa
Via G. Moruzzi 1
56124 Pisa
Italy
Giuseppe.Amato@isti.cnr.it

Mohammad Abolhassani
Informationssysteme
Institut für Informatik und Interaktive Systeme
Universität Duisburg-Essen
47048 Duisburg
Germany
mohasani@is.informatik.
uni-duisburg.de

Henk Ernst Blok
Department of Computer Science
Faculty of EEMCS
University of Twente
P.O. Box 217
7500 AE Enschede
The Netherlands
blokh@cs.utwente.com

Ling Feng
Department of Computer Science
Faculty of EEMCS
University of Twente
P.O. Box 217
7500 AE Enschede
The Netherlands
ling@cs.utwente.nl

Norbert Fuhr
Informationssysteme
Institut für Informatik und Inter-
aktive Systeme
Universität Duisburg-Essen
47048 Duisburg
Germany
fuhr@uni-duisburg.de

Claudio Gennaro
Istituto di Scienza e Tecnologie
dell'Informazione
"Alessandro Faedo"
Area della Ricerca CNR di Pisa
Via G. Moruzzi 1
56124 Pisa
Italy
claudio.gennaro@isti.cnr.it

Georg Göbel
University of Innsbruck
Institut für Biostatistik und Doku-
mentation
Schöpfstrasse 41
6020 Innsbruck
Austria
georg.goebel@uibk.ac.at

Norbert Gövert
University of Dortmund
Department of Computer Science
44221 Dortmund
Germany
goevert@ls6.cs.uni-dortmund.
de

Kai Großjohann
Informationssysteme
Institut für Informatik und Interaktive Systeme
Universität Duisburg-Essen
47048 Duisburg
Germany
kai.grossjohann@
uni-duisburg.de

Djoerd Hiemstra
Department of Computer Science
Faculty of EEMCS
University of Twente
P.O. Box 217
7500 AE Enschede
The Netherlands
hiemstra@cs.utwente.nl

Gabriella Kazai
Department of Computer Science
Queen Mary University of London
England, E1 4NS
gabs@dcs.qmul.ac.uk

Maurice van Keulen
Faculty of EEMCS
Department of Computer Science
Faculty of EEMCS
University of Twente
P.O. Box 217
7500 AE Enschede
The Netherlands
vankeulen@cs.utwente.nl

Mounia Lalmas
Department of Computer Science
Queen Mary University of London
England, E1 4NS
mounia@dcs.qmul.ac.uk

Torsten Grust
Department of Computer and
Information Science
University of Konstanz
P.O. Box D188
78457 Konstanz
Germany
Torsten.Grust@uni-konstanz.
de

Willem Jonker
Department of Computer Science
Faculty of EEMCS
University of Twente
P.O. Box 217
7500 AE Enschede
The Netherlands
jonker@cs.utwente.nl

Martin Kersten
Centre for Mathematics and Computer Science (CWI)
Kruislaan 413
1098 SJ Amsterdam
The Netherlands
martin.kersten@cwi.nl

Sascha Kriewel
Informationssysteme
Institut für Informatik und Interaktive Systeme
Universität Duisburg-Essen
47048 Duisburg
Germany
kriewel@is.informatik.
uni-duisburg.de

Karin Leitner
University of Innsbruck
Institut für Biostatistik und Dokumentation
Schöpfstrasse 41
6020 Innsbruck
Austria
karin.leitner@uibk.ac.at

Johan A. List
Centre for Mathematics and Computer Science (CWI)
Kruislaan 413
1098 SJ Amsterdam
The Netherlands
johan.list@acm.org

Karl P. Pfeiffer
University of Innsbruck
Institut für Biostatistik und Dokumentation
Schöpfstrasse 41
6020 Innsbruck
Austria
karl-peter.pfeiffer@uibk.ac.at

Michael Rys
Microsoft Corporation
Redmond (WA)
USA
rys@acm.org

Albrecht Schmidt
Department of Computer Science
Aalborg University
Fredrik Bajers Vej 7E
9220 Aalborg Øst
al@cs.auc.dk

Marko Smiljanić
Department of Computer Science
Faculty of EEMCS
University of Twente
P.O. Box 217
7500 AE Enschede
The Netherlands
markosm@cs.utwente.nl

Stefan Manegold
Centre for Mathematics and Computer Science (CWI)
Kruislaan 413
1098 SJ Amsterdam
The Netherlands
stefan.manegold@cwi.nl

Fausto Rabitti
Istituto di Scienza e Tecnologie dell'Informazione
"Alessandro Faedo"
Area della Ricerca CNR di Pisa
Via G. Moruzzi 1
56124 Pisa
Italy
fausto.rabitti@isti.cnr.it

Pasquale Savino
Istituto di Scienza e Tecnologie dell'Informazione
"Alessandro Faedo"
Area della Ricerca CNR di Pisa
Via G. Moruzzi 1
56124 Pisa
Italy
pasquale.savino@isti.cnr.it

Harald Schöning
Software AG
Uhlandstr. 12
64297 Darmstadt
Germany
Harald.Schoening@softwareag.com

Anja Theobald
Universität des Saarlandes
Fachrichtung 6.2 Informatik
Postfach 151150
66041 Saarbrücken
Germany
theobald@cs.uni-sb.de

Martin Theobald
Universität des Saarlandes
Fachrichtung 6.2 Informatik
Postfach 151150
66041 Saarbrücken
Germany
mtheobald@cs.uni-sb.de

Florian Waas
Microsoft Corporation
Redmond (WA)
USA
florianw@microsoft.com

Menzo Windhouwer
Centre for Mathematics and Computer Science (CWI)
P.O. Box 94079
1090 GB Amsterdam
The Netherlands
Menzo.Windhouwer@cwi.nl

Roelof van Zwol
Utrecht University
Institute for Information and Computing Sciences
Centre for Content and Knowledge Engineering
PO Box 80.089
3508 TB Utrecht
The Netherlands
roelof@cs.uu.nl

Arjen P. de Vries
Centre for Mathematics and Computer Science (CWI)
Kruislaan 413
1098 SJ Amsterdam
The Netherlands
arjen@acm.org

Roger Weber
ETH Zürich
Database Research Group
Institute of Information Systems
8092 Zürich
Switzerland
weber@inf.ethz.ch

Pavel Zezula
Faculty of Informatics
Masaryk University of Brno
Botanicka 68a
602 00 Brno
Czech Republic
zezula@fi.muni.cz

Part I

Applications

Introduction

XML – short for the W3C eXtended Markup Language – is highly successful as a format for representing data with regular structure. This explains the high interest by database researchers XML has received recently focusing mainly on so-called *data-centric* settings. Data-centric settings are characterized by rigidly structured information where queries have precise semantics and yield exact matches as answers. Important results of this stream of research are various proposals for XML query languages which have lead to the development of XPath and XQuery by the W3C. Other important work has, for instance, addressed representing database content in XML format in order to ease data interchange between different repository systems over the internet.

However, many of the aforementioned settings exploit only little of XML's flexibility. Important future application domains require more flexibility and benefit largely from the semistructured data model underlying XML. Text documents are a prominent example of such settings which has lead to the notion of so-called *document-centric* settings for this class of applications. An important characteristics of these applications is that they may cover various different sorts of content or media. Moreover, they might be loosely coupled and distributed across the Internet. Consequently, they require much more flexible data structures than data-centric settings. In addition, it might be difficult to find a clear distinction between structure (schema) and contents (data) which is in turn essential for data-centric settings. Clearly, querying techniques from data-centric approaches cannot be sensibly transferred to document-centric settings. Hence, these applications require *intelligent search*, i.e., functionality for predicates with a vague interpretation and result ranking from information retrieval. The first part of this book is devoted to exemplary applications that require functionality for intelligent search, namely *digital libraries for video content* and *electronic support of medicine and health care*. Subsequent chapters will come back to the requirements introduced here and explain how intelligent search on XML addresses them.

Chapter 1 by Pfeiffer, Göbel and Leitner discusses the demand for intelligent search in medicine and health care. Currently, there is only little functionality for intelligent search that supports patients and health-care professionals. In particular, automatically or semi-automatically finding up-to-date medical information or newest evidence and relating it to a particular case is difficult or even impossible. This is in sharp contrast to billing and accounting in the health-care context which is already completely automated by computer systems. The chapter investigates in depth the requirements for intelligent search in health-care and medicine, and outlines the benefits of XML standardization efforts in this context for representing data, information and knowledge.

Chapter 2 by Gennaro, Rabitti and Savino investigates using XML in the context of digital libraries. The chapter focuses on digital libraries with audio and, in particular, video content. XML is well-suited to represent the metadata of video digital libraries since it facilitates interoperability and eases indexing and query processing. The chapter reports in detail how XML has been successfully used in the ECHO digital library project funded by the European Commission.

1

Demand for Intelligent Search Tools in Medicine and Health Care

Karl P. Pfeiffer, Georg Göbel, and Karin Leitner

1.1 Introduction

The high demand for medical knowledge poses a big challenge for information technology to offer user-friendly systems which help healthy citizens, patients and health professionals to find proper data, information and knowledge.

Medicine has a long history in structured or semi-structured documentation. On the one hand medical documentation of diagnoses has been performed using the ICD-10 (International Classification of Diseases, 10th revision [294]) or other coding systems; on the other hand indexing of scientific literature has been done using key words from MeSH (Medical Subject Headings [213]). Coding systems like ICD, classifications and medical thesauri have been available for years. Scientifically validated terminologies like SNOMED (Standardized Nomenclature in Medicine [291]) and standardised messaging standards like HL7 (Health Level 7 [155]) and DICOM (Digital Imaging and Communication in Medicine [99]) have been facilitating communications between computer systems and different modalities and have achieved a broad market acceptance within the healthcare industry. Medical queries are among the most popular topics people are searching for in different databases and knowledge sources. Due to the early development of medical domain knowledge sources, most of the coding systems are only available in proprietary, non standardised structures or schemes.

Although there might be no specific field of domain knowledge which has been more penetrated with thesauri, classifications etc, it has taken a long time to accept XML technologies as a standard to meet challenges of medical content management, data communication and medical knowledge representation.

In March 2003 the BMJ (British Medical Journal) Publishing Group started the first excerpt from BestTreatments, a website built for patients and their doctors that looks at the effectiveness of treatments for chronic medical conditions, based officially on "Clinical Evidence", which is recognised internationally as a gold standard for evidence-based information [226]. From

H. Blanken et al. (Eds.): Intelligent Search on XML Data, LNCS 2818, pp. 5–18, 2003.

Table 1.1.

	Citizen, Patient	Medical Professional
General Medical Knowledge Facts & Figures	Health Information System Patient Information System	Health Professional Information Systems EBM - Sources
Personalised Medical Information	Personal Health Record	Electronic Health Care Record, Electronic Patient Record

Table 1.1 it can easily be deduced that health professionals and patients need the same evidence-based information, served up in parallel, drawn from the same sources. Additionally, personalised medical and health information on patients – allergies, medications, health plans and emergency contacts should be accessible online from any location via the internet, always being aware of data safety and security. Sharing this information in case of emergency with doctors and processing it with powerful health tools (e.g. immunization planner, health risk appraisal, personal health plan) are fascinating challenges for scientists and industrial vendors.

1.2 Medical Knowledge Representation: Status Quo

Medical knowledge bases *contain all the knowledge and experience to be invoked by a reasoning program to produce advice that supports a decision* [301]. Generally, medical knowledge is retrievable from

- the medical literature (documented knowledge)
- experts in a specific domain (clinical experience).

Some authors distinguish between knowledge about terminology – conceptual knowledge – and more general (medical) knowledge – general inferential knowledge [246]. Neither current medical literature nor experiences from experts today are usually being processed in a comprehensive form which supports medical decisions. One mechanism to transfer experiences from one person to another is the creation of knowledge bases, which can potentially provide health care workers with access to large bodies of information. Knowledge, the next step of complexity, must then be expressed in the terminology and semantics of the knowledge base and several methods must be designed to acquire knowledge from experts. V. Bemmel [301] defines a medical knowledge base as *a systematically organised collection of medical knowledge that is accessible electronically and interpretable by the computer. ... Usually medical knowledge bases include a lexicon (vocabulary or allowed terms) and specific relationships between the terms.*

This definition does not specify a detailed formalism of how relationships can express expert knowledge. Thus long term research projects like UMLS

(Unified Medical Language Systems) [168] or GALEN (Generalised Architecture for Languages, Encyclopaedias and Nomenclatures in Medicine) [130] showed the necessity of methodologies to map medical knowledge to machine-readable information sources in different languages.

1.2.1 UMLS

The UMLS project [168] is a long-term NLM (National Library of Medicine) research and development effort to facilitate the retrieval and integration of information from multiple machine-readable biomedical information sources. The goal is to make it easier to develop systems that link information from patient record systems, bibliographic databases, factual databases, expert systems etc. The UMLS can also facilitate the development of data creation and indexing applications. It consists of three parts:

- The Metathesaurus contains semantic information about biomedical concepts, their various names, and the relationships among them. It is built from thesauri, classifications, coding systems and lists of controlled terms that are developed and maintained by many different organisations. It includes many concepts from a broad multilingual range of vocabularies and classifications (e.g. SNOMED, ICD, MeSH).
- The Semantic Network is a network of general categories or semantic types to which all concepts in the Metathesaurus have been assigned.
- The specialist lexicon contains syntactic information about biomedical terms and may cover the majority of component terms in the concept names presented in the meta-thesaurus.

1.2.2 GALEN

In Europe a consortium of universities, agencies and vendors has formed the GALEN project to develop standards for representing coded patient information from 1992 to 1995 [130]. This initiative is based on a conceptual knowledge formalism, which categorises conceptual knowledge (knowledge about terminology) into three subtypes (conventional knowledge, descriptive knowledge, formal knowledge). To address the problems of clinical terminologies, GALEN is constructing a semantically sound model of clinical terminology - the GALEN Coding reference (GALEN CORE) model. This model comprises

- elementary clinical concepts such as 'fracture', 'bone', 'left', and 'humerus';
- relationships such as 'fractures can occur in bones', that control how these may be combined;
- complex concepts such as 'fracture of the left humerus' composed from simpler ones. This compositional approach allows for detailed descriptions while preserving the structure provided by the individual components.

1.3 Challenges for Information and Knowledge Management in Medicine

Hospital information (health care) systems are usually composed of a distributed set of heterogeneous applications. The efficient management of a patient may involve the exchange of information and the co-operation among diverse applications [324]. Most of the contents of medical databases today are designed for humans to read, not for computer programs to manipulate the data in a sensible way.

The electronic health care record (EHCR) will play a key role in the development of future health care systems. Patient-centred storage of data and communication between different health care providers using different information systems requires not only a well-defined communication standard but also precise definition of the data in order to further use it, for example in decision support or personalized search for medical knowledge.

Computers can adeptly parse information for layout and routine processing – here a header, there a link to other information – but in general, computers have no reliable way to process the semantics: this content deals with Morbus Parkinson (MP), and MP can be linked to several information sources, but also this content may constitute information contained in an EHCR of the MP patient called *John Smith*, who *has been visiting* the hospital *monthly* due to his condition, always on *Friday*. Instead, these semantics were encoded by clinical nurses or doctors. In future, intelligent agents will "know" how to perform this task and will also be able to find out the meaning of semantic data by following hyperlinks to definitions of key terms and rules for reasoning about them logically.

From the technical viewpoint, two important technologies are already in place: XML and RDF (Resource Description Framework). XML is used by RDF, which provides the technology for expressing the meaning of terms and concepts in a way that enables computers to process and "understand" this information. RDF uses XML for its syntax and URIs to specify entities, concepts, properties and relations.

If a program wants to compare or combine information across two records or databases, it has to know that two different terms may be used to designate the same concept (e.g. LARGE BOWEL – COLON), they may be synonyms. But in other situations the same word may have different meanings in different contexts (e.g. CERVICAL may refer to the cervix – an anatomical part of the womb, or to the neck). They are so-called homonyms. Ideally, the program must have a way to discover such common meanings for whichever database it encounters. For this purpose, ontologies within a domain field must be built. Usually these types of ontologies include a taxonomy and a set of inference rules. The taxonomy defines classes of objects and relations among them [30]. Inference rules in ontologies enable computers to manipulate the terms much more effectively for the human user: an ontology may express the rule: "If a patient is associated with a social insurance number of a certain insurance, and a prescription contains this insurance number, then the patient receives drugs based on guidelines of that specific insurance."

An example from the clinical environment shall be given that illustrates the potential use of search agents supporting physicians in routine patient care. The search agent uses heterogeneous databases, automatically makes inferences from the EHCR and advises the physician regarding specific medical issues. This scenario demonstrates the use of a search agent during a consultation with a woman experiencing typical symptoms of menopause who is concerned about hormone replacement therapy (HRT), one option to successfully treat these symptoms.

Mary Jones is 49 years old. For the past 4 years she has been noticing variations in the length of her monthly cycle and pattern of bleeding. Moreover, she has been experiencing hot flushes, night sweats, vaginal dryness, as well as joint pains. She suffers from unpredictable mood swings. Mary has heard of HRT, but usually in the context of its associated risk of breast cancer. On the other hand Anne, her neighbour, has told her that she should start HRT, as it would greatly alleviate her suffering, prevent her bones from fracturing in her old age and protect her from cardiovascular disease. Moreover, Anne said that, according to the latest research, HRT reduces the risk of Alzheimer's disease. Anne feels quite confused and decides to see Dr. Eleanor Trevor, her local GP, about this issue. Dr. Trevor understands Mary's concerns, as HRT has been the subject of ongoing debate for many years. She knows that the fear of breast cancer is one of the prime reasons for rejection or discontinuation of HRT. And even though HRT had been promoted for many years in relation to several health issues such as prevention of osteoporosis and cardiovascular disease, Dr. Trevor is aware that recent research suggests not to use HRT for prevention of osteoporosis and that it may actually increase the risk of cardiovascular disease. She knows that in addition there are several other organs affected by the hormonal constituents used in HRT such as the endometrium, colon and central nervous system. Moreover, it depends very strongly on the individual person receiving HRT whether it is useful or may actually be harmful. She wonders about Mary's physical constitution (her age, body mass index, parity, her age when Tim, her first child was born, etc.) and risk factors (Mary is overweight and smokes). Dr. Trevor lets her search agent support her in this issue. She is glad she has this tool available because it is near-impossible to stay up to date with the latest results in medical research. Before she had her agent, she would have had to look for best evidence in databases such as CDSR (Cochrane Database of Systematic Reviews [77]) or DARE (Database of Abstracts of Reviews of Effects [88]), search biomedical databases such as Medline or Embase [106], search the internet or even hand search the literature. She was glad she had done a course in searching for evidence, as she knew from a colleague who didn't even try to treat according to best practice, as he didn't know how to find the evidence. After finding the evidence herself she would have had to apply it to the individual patient. She would have had to go through all the patient notes, call the hospital and other specialists for any additional information needed, and the decisions would have been based mainly on her own expertise and experience, weighing risks and benefits of a particular treatment. This whole process became much more convenient with her agent. Basically, the search agent performs all tasks of information retrieval, integration with patient information, and knowledge representation automatically, in a speedy, comprehensive, reliable and safe manner. Dr. Trevor feels that it provides her with many benefits such as saving her time, supporting her in her decisions, and ultimately enabling her to offer better patient care. When she lets the agent run over Mary's particular case, it automatically searches for the best evidence currently available in the field of HRT, retrieves Mary's online health record (a health record pulling information together from all medical facilities Mary had been visiting), detects that Mary also has high blood pressure and a positive family history of breast cancer, which Dr. Trevor hadn't been aware of, and independently determines the overall risks (breast cancer, blood clots, stroke and coronary heart disease) and benefits (fracture reduction and reduced risk of colorectal cancer) HRT would have in Mary's case. The agent presents its findings to Dr. Trevor who is very satisfied with the feedback, comments and helpful decision support. She tells Mary that firstly she should try to alter her lifestyle – eat healthy, exercise regularly and quit smoking. She also lets her know that there are several alternative therapies around that may or may not be helpful in relieving menopausal symptoms but that in general, there is more research needed in that area. She remarks that herbal therapies may have adverse side effects or exhibit harmful interactions with other medications. She tells Mary that HRT should be considered only a short-term option, as in the long run, according to the best evidence currently available and in consideration of Mary's status the risks do outweigh the benefits.

Software Agents in medicine run without direct human control or constant supervision to accomplish goals provided by medical experts. Agents typically collect, filter and process information found in distributed heterogeneous data sources, sometimes with the assistance of other agents. It will be a big challenge in the future to train these agents to find the appropriate and very specific information for a patient with certain symptoms, diagnoses or treatments.

1.4 Data, Information, and Knowledge in Medicine

Data management in the medical field will be expanded by information processing techniques using different heterogeneous data sources like Hospital IS, Laboratory IS etc. Data will be compiled to information as well as prior and explicit knowledge. Knowledge acquisition, modelling, storage and processing methods will offer users new possibilities to access global medical knowledge bases [293]. Bibliographic databases like PubMed [240] will evolve to become global knowledge sources offering *up-to-date, relevant, high-quality, multimedia* and *multilingual* knowledge to consumers all over the world. From the viewpoint of medical experts and based on the experiences with decision support systems and expert systems, *content* and *data / information representations* are key challenges for knowledge engineers.

1.4.1 Medical Content

Relevance, context-based personalisation, links to related topics, integration of EPHR-data are viewed as challenging issues for architects of Medical IS in the future.

Structuring and 'semantic labelling' of medical topics constitute an increasingly important focus of interest [21]. These tasks must be performed in an efficient way at the point of information acquisition and storage even though context-based personalisation of contents is of interest to users only at medical content retrieval. By adding structure where there is none, users can query and re-use knowledge. The usefulness of existing resources can be extended if they are represented within a structured knowledge framework.

Information, knowledge and experience existing only in people's minds can be connected with data. This creates intelligent resources that can be stored, navigated, re-used and expanded. Term- or word based linkage of information will be extended by dynamic multidirectional semantic linkage of topics to powerful link engines, which improve their functionality and scope automatically and autonomously.

Medical knowledge bases face an increasingly important issue: considering the increase of information available and the rise of the users' demand for personalised content, why should a customer be satisfied with contents from knowledge bases if they are not suited to their particular requirements? Content managers need to be able to find flexible ways of structuring the content and delivering it to different users according to their individual requirements. This will even lead to the integration of personal clinical data gathered from the customers' individual electronic health care records.

In future, users' individual behaviour will affect not only representation of knowledge, but knowledge acquisition- and structuring strategies based on retrieval agents will be customised and influenced by user (inter-)actions as well. Within the scope of learning curves, domain-specific knowledge will be separated from process-oriented knowledge. In this context, customers' interactions will be recognised and processed as well as behavioural patterns of user groups.

XML technologies enable managing semi-structured documents and structured data in a uniform way. Hence, it should be possible to mix data and documents in order to build *virtual health related documents issued from several sources.*

1.4.2 Knowledge Representation

Future targets of Knowledge Representation and Visualisation are the "representation of complex information for discovery of hypothesis and illustration of results and coherences" [234].

1.4.3 Independence from Modalities

It is commonly recognized in work on multimodal information presentation that much of the true value of modality-independent representation lies in appropriate presentation of non-identical but overlapping information. Textual representations and graphical visualisation have different strengths and weaknesses and so their combination can achieve powerful synergies. Conversely, simply placing textual and graphical information together is no guarantee that one view is supportive of another: if the perspective on the information taken in a graphical and in a text representation have no relation (or worse, even clash), then the result is incoherence rather than synergy.

Despite these problems, independence from modalities is one of the key issues for users working within the medical field. Especially health professionals must have access to their knowledge bases via different modalities like TV or computer screens, table PCs, handheld devices, shutter glasses etc.

1.4.4 Interactivity

Interactive multimedia can be used to provide information, to train, educate, entertain, store collections of audiovisual material, as well as distribute multimedia and allow for user input. The range of tools, including the well-known PC-mouse or keyboard, will be extended by new interaction tools (e.g. haptic or vocal tools). Nonlinear media structures will challenge the development of powerful knowledge browsers controlled via voice interfaces.

1.4.5 Process Representation

One key issue in representing medical knowledge is the organisation of process-oriented knowledge ('How-to knowledge'). Formal methods like UML (Unified Modeling Language) extend production rules, semantic networks and frame-technology (terminology-based knowledge) in order to describe medical procedures, processes, treatment protocols etc. in a reusable, system-independent way.

1.4.6 Pro-activity

Electronic guides assist users during their work and try to detect and solve problems beforehand. Additionally, users may receive notifications on updates or new documents according to specified criteria. Already today there are several rule based systems which perform an automatic analysis of drug prescription to avoid drug interaction or just look for cheaper drugs or produce automatic warnings in the case of allergies.

1.5 Expectations from an Intelligent Search Engine

As medical environments become increasingly electronic, clinical databases are continually growing, accruing masses of patient information. This wealth of data is an invaluable source of information to researchers, serving as a test bed for the development of new information technologies and as a repository of real-world data for data mining and population-based studies or clinical epidemiology. However, the real value of this information is not fully taken advantage of, in part because of issues concerning security and patient confidentiality, but also due to the lack of an effective infrastructure to access the data. Users want to query and retrieve data from multiple clinical data sources, automatically de-identifying patient data so it can be used for research purposes. Key aspects may be XML-based querying of existing medical databases, easy inclusion of new information resources, minimal processing impact on existing clinical systems via a distributed cache, and flexible output representation (e.g. via XSL(T)).

Despite the fact that several authors distinguish between fact retrieval and information retrieval, many authors are noticing that all these methods are used to manage knowledge *between* people. Therefore, aspects of human knowledge processing, including problems and methods from cognitive psychology, psycholinguistics and psycho-mnemonics, must be considered. It is widely accepted that human information processing problems can not be fully explained or solved using well-known models like deductive logic or neural networks.

Concept systems enable the representation of complex clinical states or procedures through relational links between concepts, expressing e.g. negation, quantification, temporal relations, localisations and precise or fuzzy time spans. The concept ABDOMINAL PAIN, for example, could have the LOCALISATION 'RIGHT UPPER QUADRANT' and 'RADIATING TO RIGHT SHOULDER'. It could have the QUALITY 'EPISODIC' and 'SEVERE'. It could have its ONSET 'AFTER FATTY MEAL'. Further, it could have a DURATION of 'SEVERAL HOURS'.

ENV 1828 [107] provides a categorical structure and combinatorial rules to support the exchange of surgical procedure information between different national and international coding systems and languages within Europe.

It covers surgical procedures of all surgical disciplines and includes definitions and examples of concepts (e.g. ENDOSCOPE), different types of relations (e.g. INTERVENTIONAL EQUIPMENT is a super-ordinate concept to ENDOSCOPE in a generic relation;, HEAD, FACE, NECK, CHEST are sub-ordinate concepts to HUMAN BODY in a partitive relation), semantic links (e.g. BY MEANS OF; FROM), modifiers (e.g. RIGHT; LEFT; TWO; THREE) and combinatorial rules (e.g., removal of the kidney for cancer: cancer is not necessary, it is a removal of a kidney). In order to enable health information systems architects to use well-known IR techniques like (semantic) query expansion, text classification algorithms etc., this standard needs to be integrated into their system. Thus, new requirements may challenge traditional DB techniques (e.g. relational or object-oriented data modelling, SQL query formulation) which might, in fact, prove insufficient in this new context.

The complexity and diversity of medical information and knowledge representation goes far beyond the scope of the traditional information sources. A library, for example, does not provide quality rankings of the works in the collection. Because of the greater volume of networked information, Internet users want guidance about where to spend the limited amount of time they have to research a subject.

They may need to know the three "best" documents for a given purpose. They want this information without paying the costs of employing humans to critique the myriad of Web sites. One solution that again calls for human involvement is to share judgments about what is worthwhile. Software-based rating systems have to let users describe the quality of particular Web sites.

1.6 Search Functionalities from the Viewpoint of Users

Communication between users and the source applications is usually managed by mediator applications [324] which encapsulate the communication APIs of the various systems and are responsible for the interpretation of information (its structure, syntax and semantics). Thus, a 'medical search angel' may consist of a *communication manager* encapsulating the communication API of the system, a *syntax manager*, which may itself be associated with coding modules for the various types of syntax used in different systems, such as ICD-10, HL7, etc. and a *semantics manager*, which carries out "semantic mapping" between the terms of the different vocabularies used in the different systems and converts the data.

Virtual Case Managers (VCM) must be able to interact with users and determine their personal backgrounds. Up until now, websites have generally been developed separately for patients and doctors. A VCM derives information about the individual background from the vocabulary used by and interactions with the person or by posing additional questions.

1.7 Presentation of Search Results

- *Personalisation*: if a doctor is seeking an effective treatment for heart failure, the search results must be customised according to his needs and may depend on previous queries and interactions. Drill-down from top level overviews to specific topics may lead to different search results depending on several parameters like regional, cultural or temporal circumstances and the professional background.
- *Aggregation / Navigation*: 'Search results' will imply a new meaning: because medical documents may be virtual and – as they contain structured information – can be considered databases, future search results will not be static links but link-traverse triggers (re)calling the search (web) service based on relevant feedback algorithms.
- *Ranking*: Due to its implications, medical information must be as reliable as possible. Quality assurance strategies like HON [156], MedCertain [214] etc. are based on optional cooperation of content providers. Within this context, XML-based indexing and rating services offer technical access and rating controls. The majority of current retrieval engines are using term or link frequencies as ranking criteria, which doesn't include assessments on semantic or 'common sense' level.

1.8 Search Functionalities from the Viewpoint of a Search System

Medical search engines will include "Medical Knowledge" for better understanding and processing of user queries. Linking information sources on a supra-sentential level goes far beyond ordinary text-linking on a syntactic or morphological level. XML plays a key role in different layers of knowledge engineering (see Table 1.2): searching heterogeneous knowledge sources is a domain of multi-agent system applications as well as representing and linking semi-structured information. Within all layers, XML technology is used to increase independency from specific models and application systems.

1.9 Integration of Semantic Intelligence

If retrieval systems are supposed to interact with their users in an 'intelligent way' the systems have to include semantic intelligence in addition to text repositories, lexica, hit lists and search indices. Besides technical issues on lexical and morphological levels (see Table 1.2), which concern user interfaces, four levels of interest can be identified which can be separated from other aspects like medical natural language processing, information modelling, and user interface design [100].

Table 1.2.

	Medical Application/Challenge	(XML) Application (Examples)/Current projects
Phonological level	Free Text Speech Recognition	VoiceML
Lexical level	Medical Term Recognition	HL7-XML, ICD-10, MeSH
Morphological level	Stemming, Compound analysis Linking of medical terms	
Syntactical level	Medical Grammars	SNOMED
Semantic level	Knowledge Representation, linking of medical concepts	UMLS, RDF(S), DAML-OIL, GALEN
Discourse level	Linking of medical topics	Topic Maps
Common Sense level	Health Agents	Intelligent Web Services

- The *Syntactical Level* concerns medical grammars and syntactic rules.
- The *Semantic Level* includes linking between different coding schemes and classifications. On this level, trans-lingual problems can be targeted.
- On the *Discourse Level*, a medical topic is identified and may be linked to other knowledge sources. At this point, the integration of additional sources (e.g. figures about morbidity or resource statistics) may be appropriate. Applications working on a discourse level are able to identify relevant related data sources and search them automatically.
- The *Common Sense Level* is a level of abstraction comparable to the 'general medical knowledge' of a medical specialist.

Intelligent functionalities are a key issue in medical information retrieval systems even if the availability of data in XML format enables conversion of human readable data to machine readable data. Challenges of intelligent semantic integration concern, for example, the description of the health status of patients whose data could be used for different queries according to various contexts.

1.10 Conclusions

The medical discipline is currently moving from data representation towards information and knowledge representation. Hospital and clinical information systems are changing from database to multimedia information- and knowledge-based systems and may evolve into pro-active, self-learning systems. Health care has a long-standing tradition of standardized documentation, using different catalogues for diagnoses and procedures. The main purpose of this type of documentation has been administration or financing rather than medical documentation. The complexity of medical contents and the need for representing time-dependent relations, detailed descriptions of symptoms, findings and therapies etc. make it necessary to have the main documents available in free text, in order to achieve the precision and granularity required for personal communication. In recent years a lot of work has been done to extend structured documentation to replace free text and set up concepts for the representation of complex medical situations and processes.

This also applies to the representation of health related knowledge for patients and health professionals. The ever-increasing amount of scientific medical literature available via the internet as well as the countless web pages with health related information for patients necessitate very special tools to achieve specific and precise search results. One precondition for a successful search is to have a certain extent of structure in the data, e.g. using object-attribute-value triples and standardized terminologies. Standardized, controlled medical terminologies like the ICD-code, SNOMED or MeSH may constitute a starting point for the identification of key words in free text, but are not sufficient to represent the dynamic relationships between different objects, making modifiers and semantic links necessary.

There is also a long-standing tradition of standardized communication of data in medicine using e.g. HL7. Nevertheless, the next generation of health care information systems must not only allow exchange of data between heterogeneous systems, but must enable the representation of complex medical contents as well. Intelligent search engines, virtual agents and very specific data analysis tools will process semi-structured data and will help make the latest, quality assured information available for health care professionals, financiers and patients. Health information generators will search for individual person-centred information in the web using person-specific information from the EHCR and will design health promotion programs based on the latest evidence-based, quality-assured knowledge. Structured routine data in a hospital or clinical information system will be analysed for clinical studies looking at e.g. long-term side effects, epidemiology, quality standards, cost effectiveness, outcomes etc.

The expected functionalities from intelligent search engines in medicine can be summarized by the following points:

- Extraction of the most important facts from an electronic health care record or personal health care record, which may be distributed across various types of databases at different locations, using a master patient index
- Expressing these facts as medical concepts and linking them using ontologies and specific medical grammar to represent the complex health status of a patient in a semi-structured way
- Searching in quality-assured information systems for the latest information, relevant specifically to the individual person
- Searching for the state-of-the-art treatment for a certain disease analysing the outcomes of the latest clinical studies and using evidence-based medicine databases

- Transforming patient queries expressed in a common, non-medical language into queries using standardized medical terminology
- Identifying synonyms or homonyms and interpreting them correctly via their medical context
- The mathematical models of the search are multi-dimensional similarity or distance functions, taking the uncertainty and imprecision of medical terms into account
- Pro-active generation of health information and creation of prevention, treatment, rehabilitation and wellness programs for the individual consumer, presented in lay terminology.

Data, information and knowledge stored in different information systems will form one lifelong, virtual electronic health care record and will help improve efficiency, effectiveness and safety of the health care system.

2

The Use of XML in a Video Digital Library

Claudio Gennaro, Fausto Rabitti, and Pasquale Savino

2.1 Introduction

Video can be considered today as a primarily mean of communication, due to its richness in informative content and to its appeal. Indeed, the combination of audio and video is an extremely important communication channel: it is considered that approximately 50% of what is seen and heard simultaneously is retained. Due to all these considerations, audio/video is particularly important in many different application sectors, such as TV broadcasting, professional applications (e.g. medicine, journalism, advertising, education, etc.), movie production, historical video archives. Furthermore, most of the video material produced is extremely difficult to access, due to several limitations: video documents are extremely large in size, so that archiving and transmission are expensive; video document's content, even if extremely rich, is difficult to extract in order to support an effective content-based retrieval.

The necessity to effectively and efficiently manage such types of information will become more important with the forthcoming commercialization of interactive digital television. In coming years, the use of digital technology will promote a significant change in the television world, where the viewer will move from a passive role to using the interactive facilities increasingly offered by the providers. Digital technology allows to mix traditional audio-visual contents with data, enabling the transmission of multimedia software applications to be executed in a digital television or in an analog television equipped with a powerful decoder or Set-Top Box. These applications can be synchronized with traditional content and provide interactivity to the user, together with a return channel for communication with the provider. There will be an excellent opportunity for television to become a privileged vehicle for the development of a connected society.

In this chapter, we want to show how the role of XML is becoming a key choice in the management of audio/video information, which is becoming of paramount importance in applications such as interactive digital television. The role of XML spans different levels, from the specification of metadata (e.g.,

H. Blanken et al. (Eds.): Intelligent Search on XML Data, LNCS 2818, pp. 19–33, 2003.

MPEG-7 [222]) to the specification of mixed audio/video and data/program structures for digital TV decoders [104] [154].

To illustrate the new role of XML, we focus here on Video Digital Libraries(video DLs for short), where different aspects of the management of audio-visual information are addressed, with particular emphasis on access by content. As specific example of video DL, we refer to the ECHO system (European CHronicoles On-line). The ECHO system assists the user during the indexing and retrieval of A/V documentaries. Multiple speech recognition modules, for different European languages are included. Likewise, video and image analysis techniques are used for extracting visual features and segmenting video sequences by automatically locating boundaries of shots, scenes, and conversations. Metadata are then manually associated with film documentaries in order to complete their classification. Search and retrieval via desktop computers and wide area networks is performed by expressing queries on the audio transcript, on metadata or by image similarity retrieval. Retrieved documentaries or their abstracts are then presented to the user. By the collaborative interaction of image, speech and manually associated metadata, the system compensates for problems of interpretation and search in the error-full and ambiguous data sets. A fundamental aspect of the ECHO system is the metadata model (based on the IFLA/FRBR [239]) used for representing the audio-visual contents of the archive. XML is used as an internal representation of video metadata, as well as an interchange format with other systems.

In particular, the chapter includes a first section that describes the functionality and the characteristics of a video DL, followed by a section that illustrates the advantage of a representation of video metadata through XML. The third section presents the ECHO DL and the fourth section focuses on the management of XML metadata in the ECHO Audio-Video Metadata Editor.

2.2 The Functionality of an Audio/Video Digital Library

A DL is characterized by the possibility of organizing, distributing, preserving, and retrieving collections of digital works in a way that makes them easily accessible to specific communities of users. Typically, these services are offered in an open and distributed environment, where the "openness" means that different DL Systems can be accessed by users in a transparent way. Video digital libraries[1] can be considered the proper solution to enable the access and the effective use of audio/video documents.

A video DL has the same functionality of any DL; the most relevant are the following:

---

[1] In the following we will refer to digital libraries containing collections of audio/video documents as "video digital libraries"

Library creation. In traditional digital libraries, the library creation requires to store the text documents, extract the text and index it. Simple metadata models are used to describe the document content, such as Dublin Core [101] which consists of a simple list of fields. This process is well–known and many different techniques have been developed to support it. The same process, repeated for video documents is more complex and requires the integrated use of several techniques: video storage is more complex than text storage, due to the dimension of video material; it is difficult to perform automatic video indexing, so that user intervention is necessary. In many cases, the approach consists of the integration of automatic content extraction techniques (e.g. speech recognition, key frame extraction and analysis) and manual indexing.

Library exploration. In traditional digital libraries, exploration is quite simple: the document dimension is limited, so that their transmission is not expensive; retrieval involves only text content and simple metadata fields. On the contrary, the exploration of a video DL requires the support to transmit large amounts of data in a limited time; it also requires to support the formulation of complex queries involving different data types (e.g. text, images, moving objects) plus metadata values. However, metadata models of video are usually structured, in order to capture the complex nature of video.

Regarding the support for content-based retrieval, which is the most relevant service offered by a DL, we must observe that video DLs are much more complex than traditional DLs due to complexity and the richness in content of video. Video can be viewed at two different levels: the video structure, i.e. how a video is composed into different pieces, and the content of the video. Video structure is typically hierarchical: in general, a video is composed of a number of frames which can be grouped into shots. The shot boundaries are determined by physical changes in the video. Moreover, groups of shots, possibly non contiguous, can be grouped together to form a scene. A scene has a specific meaning in the video (e.g. the description of a specific event). The problem is complicated by the fact that shots can also overlap. Video content description is structured according to the video structure, since a description can be associated to the entire video but also to its components. All these different types of information must be associated to the video in order to support a powerful content-based retrieval. This is made possible through the adoption of a metadata model that allows to provide a complete and detailed description of the video, through the integration of different technologies supporting automatic feature extraction, and through the integration of manual and automatic indexing.

Furthermore, we need to support complex queries on video metadata: queries that may involve the values associated to some metadata fields, as well as queries that involve the structure of the metadata (for example we may search all videos directed by Fellini and played by Mastroianni; or we may search all videos having in the first scene a description of Rome composed of shots giving a panoramic view plus shots that describe in detail some monuments).

Another important functionality of DLs in general and of video DLs in particular, consists in the possibility of allowing the interoperability with other digital libraries. This means that it should be possible to exchange documents (composed of data + metadata) among different libraries, and it should be possible to query different DLs in a transparent way (the user should be able to issue a query to several different DLs, even if they are using different metadata formats).

Finally, in many cases it is necessary to exchange metadata among different modules of the DL. For example, the module responsible for the storage of metadata and the metadata editor, need to exchange metadata frequently.

The approach to management of video in existing DL systems is extremely differentiated. The simplest approach consists in the management of video as an unstructured data type. Indexing is exclusively based on metadata manually associated to the entire video. This approach supports simple retrieval based on these metadata values. More advanced video archiving and retrieval systems, such as Virage [307] and Informedia [312] base indexing mainly on automatic processing techniques. Typical metadata automatically extracted are the transcript speeches present in the documents, key frames, faces and objects recognized in the video. Retrieval is based on this information. A third category consists of systems that offer all typical services of a DL plus a sophisticated video indexing, based on the integration of automatic processing techniques with manual indexing. A single metadata model is used for features automatically extracted and for information provided manually. The metadata model may also support a description of video structure.

2.3 The Use of XML in a Video Digital Library

In a DL metadata are the primary source to process, organize, retrieve and exchange information related to the archived documents. As underlined in the previous section, metadata associated to an audio/video document have a complex structure that reflects the complexity and the richness in content of the documents. The metadata format used to describe the content of audio/video documents must support the structuring of information and it must be flexible enough to support a description at different levels of detail. All these characteristics are present in the XML format that is well suited to represent this complex and hierarchical structure, and its adoption is expected to provide a number of benefits. Main advantages in the use of XML are expected in at least three different areas:

- XML can be used as an internal format for the representation of metadata. Indeed, metadata are exchanged among different modules of the same

DL. A typical example is the exchange of metadata between the module responsible for the storage of the metadata and the metadata editor. In case a standard format (such as XML) is used to represent metadata, a simple interface can be defined in order to exchange entire video metadata files or part of video metadata. This allows to develop the two components independently with a limited effort.

- XML can be used to support the interoperability with other DLs. Interoperability is related with the possibility of exchanging metadata among systems with the same characteristics, and the possibility of exchanging metadata among systems with different characteristics. The use of XML to represent metadata within the same organization permits the definition and adoption of uniform metadata schemas. Also the interoperability with other DL systems can be improved, because the development of wrappers used to convert metadata in different formats is simplified by the adoption of a standard format.
- XML can be used to simplify the automatic and manual indexing processes and to support effective and efficient processing of queries. Existing DLs either store the metadata in a DBMS or use ad-hoc storage and retrieval functionality. The use of XML allows to retrieve metadata by using the XML search facilities.

2.4 The ECHO Digital Library System

In the following sections, we illustrate the functionality of the ECHO[2] DL system with particular emphasis on the description of the characteristics of the ECHO Metadata Model and the support for editing metadata in ECHO. The objective of the ECHO project has been to develop and experiment a DL system for historical documentaries owned by four different European audio-visual archives. The ECHO services allow users to search and access all these documentary film collections and exploit the content for their own particular requirements, whether commercial, educational, leisure, or whatever. This means that the ECHO services have to operate over linguistic, cultural and national boundaries, while respecting the requirements of international standards.

The ECHO DL system supports interoperability over distributed, heterogeneous digital collections and services. Achieving interoperability in the DL setting is facilitated by conformance to an open architecture as well as agreement on items such as formats, data types and metadata conventions.

An adequate support of retrieval and management of documents requires a correspondingly adequate description of document content. This is enabled by

---

[2] ECHO has been funded by the IST programme of the European Commission under the V Framework; the project began in February 2000 and will be completed in March 2003 [109].

the adoption of a suitable metadata model to represent the documents: in the ECHO project a new metadata model [9] for audiovisual contents has been defined and adopted. The model that has been implemented is an adaptation of the IFLA model, a general conceptual framework used to describe heterogeneous digital media resources [239]. The ECHO system supports semiautomatic video indexing: a number of metadata information, such as the scenes composing the video, key-frames that describe each scene, image features describing each key frame, spoken dialog (automatically transformed into text through a speech recognition process), faces, specific objects, are automatically extracted. Later on, the user can complete the indexing by specifying metadata that cannot be automatically extracted. Search and retrieval via desktop computers and wide area networks is performed by expressing queries on the audio transcript, on the metadata, or by image similarity retrieval. Furthermore, retrieval over multiple languages is supported by using cross-language retrieval techniques. Retrieved films or their abstracts are then presented to the user. By the collaborative interaction of image, speech and natural language understanding technology, the system compensates for problems of interpretation and search that arise when handling the error-full and ambiguous data sets. The project has also developed techniques to produce visual summaries. The creation of visual summaries is based on the use of a number of video features, such as the different scenes recognized, faces, text, objects, and action scenes detected. After this initial analysis, the more relevant clips are determined and assembled in order to maintain the flow of the story.

In the following sections we provide more details on the management of metadata in the ECHO DL system.

2.5 Managing XML Metadata in ECHO

In this section we present the ECHO Metadata Model. We first give an abstract view of the proposed model and illustrate how it has been implemented using XML Schema. We then present the Metadata Editor functionality: a tool used for browsing and editing the audio/video metadata. Since the metadata database of the DL is implemented in XML, at the end of this chapter we present two example queries and how they are processed by the system.

2.5.1 The Metadata Model

The ECHO Metadata Model [9] has been defined as an extension to the IFLAFRBR model. This IFLAFRBR model is composed of four levels describing different aspects of intellectual or artistic endeavour: work, expression, manifestation, and item. The entities of the model are organized in a structure that reflects the hierarchical order of the entities from the top level

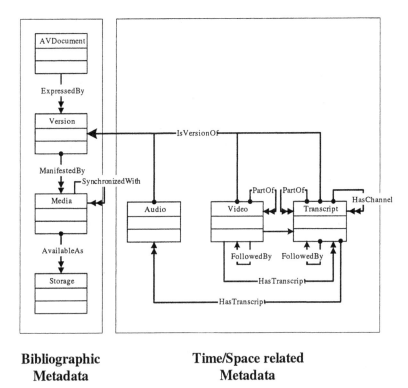

Bibliographic Metadata   **Time/Space related Metadata**

Fig. 2.1. Schematic representation of the ECHO Metadata Model.

(work) to the bottom (item). Figure 2.1 shows a schematic representation of the ECHO Metadata Model.

The AVDocument entity is the most abstract one; it provides the general intellectual or artistic view of the document. For instance, let us suppose we want to describe a document about the "Berlin Olympic Games in 1936". An AVDocument object will represent the abstract idea of the documentary film on the games. A number of objects, of the abstract entity Version, could represent different language version of the same film, e.g., versions in Italian or in German. The Italian version could have three different objects that belong to the entity Version: a Video object, a Transcript object and an Audio object (called Expressions). Moreover, Expression objects can be also part of other Expression objects. For example, the Video object representing the Italian version of the whole documentary film can have other Video objects representing specific scenes of the film.

However, the Version entity does not represent any specific implementation of the film. This aspect can be represented by means of the manifestation level. For instance, a Media object could represent a digital realization of the document in MPEG format. More than one manifestation of the same Version, e.g. MPEG, AVI, etc., may exist.

Nevertheless, the Media object does not refer to any physical implementation. For instance, the MPEG version of the Italian version of the games can be available on different physical supports, each one represented by a different Storage object (e.g., videoserver, DVD, etc).

It is worth noting that the entities of the model are grouped in two sets called "Bibliographic metatada" and "Time/Space related metadata". The entities of the former set concern pure cataloguing aspects of the document, without going into the peculiarity of the type of the multimedia object described. More in general, from the perspective of the "Bibliographic metatada" the object catalogued is a black box. The latter set of entities concerns the nature of the catalogued object. In particular in our model we focused on the time/space aspect of the multimedia object, i.e., how the audio/video objects are divided in scene, shots, etc. However, in general, any kind of metadata which can help the user to identify and retrieve the object can be used. For instance, if the object is computer video game, there could be entities for describing the saved games, the characters of the players, etc.

2.5.2 Lifecycle of the Documents

Since the metadata model is relatively complex, the design of the metadata editor is of primary importance. The editor is intended to be used by the cataloguers of the archive, that insert new audiovisual documents and that specify the metadata of the documents. The typical cataloguer workflow is the following:

1. A new audiovisual document is digitalized or transformed from one digital format into another.
2. The document is archived by the system in the videoserver.
3. The document is processed for automatic indexing (extraction of scene cuts, speech recognition, etc.)
4. When the automatic indexing has been completed, the user is informed by the system and the manual indexing can start.
5. The user typically edits the textual description for typos or factual content, reviews or sets values of the metadata fields, adjusts the bounds of the document segments, removes unwanted segments and merges multiple documents. This phase is usually performed starting from the top level of the model (the AVDocument), and continuing by modifying/editing the lower-level objects connected to the AVDocument (i.e., Version, Media and Storage objects).

2.5.3 The Metadata Editor

The metadata editor communicates with the middleware of the Echo system in order to obtain the metadata of the A/V documents from the database.

In particular, once the user has found a relevant document, by means of the video retrieval tool, the URI (Uniform Resource Identifier) of the document is obtained and passed to the metadata editor. This URI is sent to the data manager which returns the document metadata. The format chosen for exchanging document metadata is XML.

An important feature of the metadata editor is that it not hard wired with a particular metadata attributes set, indeed the metadata schema is defined in the W3C XML Schema Definition (XSD) used by the editor as configuration file for the metadata model. The advantage of this choice is that it is possible to add/remove fields in the schema of the metadata of the audiovisual document (see Figure 2.2). This is achieved by giving the editor the ability of recognizing a subset of the types available for the XSD schemas, such as: strings, boolean, dates, integers, etc.

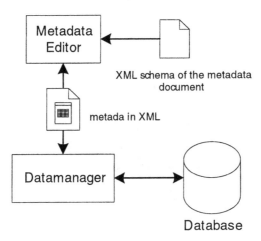

Fig. 2.2. The architecture of the Metadata Editor.

In Figure 2.3, an illustration of the schema definition schema is given.

Inside the tag <sequence> (see the XSD documentation for more details [111]) a metadata field for the AVDocument entity can be defined by means of the tag <**xsd:element**>. The tag <**xsd:annotation**> is useful for the reader in order to better understand the meaning of the field and it is used also by the editor as a ToolTip when the mouse pointer is moved over the form's input control related to field.

Eventually, the instance of an A/V document based on the presented schema could be as illustrated in Figure 2.4.

By means of the XML schema it also possible to describe tags which contain a closed list of strings. This feature is used to aid the cataloguer during the metadata ingestion phase, but it is useful also during the retrieval

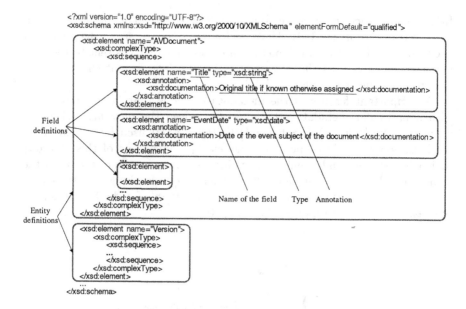

Fig. 2.3. Illustration of the schema definition of the Metadata Model.

```
<AVDocument xmlns:xsi="http://www.w3.org/2000/10/XMLSchema-instance "
            xsi:schemaLocation="http:///EchoServer.it/Echo.xsd>

<Title> Olympic Games on 1936 </Title>
<Genre>Documentary</Genre>
<Description>Documentary on 193 Berlin Olympic Games </Description>
<Person_names >
    <string_item>Jesse Owens</string_item>
    <string_item>Hendrika Mastenbroek </string_item>
</Person_names >

...

</AVDocument>
```

Fig. 2.4. Illustration of the AVDocument instance.

phase, since this tag cannot contain misspelled words. In Figure 2.5 following an example of a XML schema closed list type definition is given.

The closed lists are automatically recognized by the editor and represented in the editing interface as ComboBox controls.

Since entity instances are memorized as individual XML documents, the references among them are achieved by using URI pointers.

The interface of the editor is designed in such a way that it is possible to browse the tree structure of an audio/video document. Figures 2.6 shows the screenshot of the main window of the editor: it displays a document like a folder navigation tool. On the top level of the tree, there is an icon representing an AVDocument object (the work of the "Olympic Games on 1936" in our

```
<xsd:simpleType name="CutType">
    <xsd:restriction base="xsd:string">
        <xsd:enumeration value="HardCut"/>
        <xsd:enumeration value="FadeIn"/>
        <xsd:enumeration value="FadeOut "/>
        <xsd:enumeration value="FadeInFadeOut "/>
    </xsd:restriction>
</xsd:simpleType>
```

Fig. 2.5. Illustration of a Closed List Type definition.

example). Connected to the work object the editor presents the three main Versions that belong to the AVDocument. Moreover, selecting an icon representing a Version (the English Version in the figure), it is possible to see the Media instances of the Version and, hence, the corresponding Storage objects.

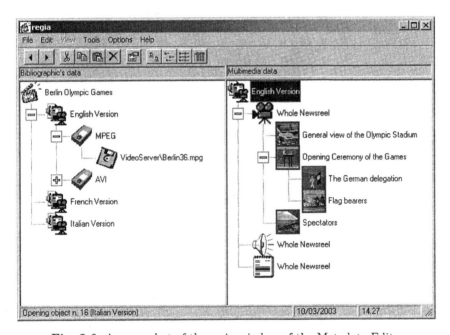

Fig. 2.6. A screenshot of the main window of the Metadata Editor

The navigation tool shows only the main expressions belonging to a document (i.e., the expression which correspond to the whole audio/video document). The editor allows to browse a single Version (one at a time) by using a second frame on the right side of the window. In this way it is possible to see the existing Video, Audio and Transcript Expressions (at least one of them must exist) of the document and, for each Expression, to browse their segmentation in scenes, shots, etc.

Fig. 2.7. A screenshot of the Expression Tool of the Metadata Editor

By clicking on the icon corresponding to a metadata object, it is possible to modify, in a separated window, the metadata fields of the object. Particular attention has been paid to the expression window design, i.e, the Expression Tool (Figure 2.7). Besides the textual fields, the Expression Tool allows access to the metadata relative to the video segmentation, and allows to modify them. More precisely, the user can view the video, hear the audio and read the transcript. The window shows also an overview of the video segmentation, by means of a timeline control (see the bottom of the Expression Tool window). These slides are subdivided in partitions that represent the media segmentation. By selecting a segment, the Expression Tool shows the sub-Expression corresponding to the segment of the media (for instance, a scene or a shot). For convenience, the same segments are also represented by their Keyframes, allowing the user to see the video content of the sub-Expressions.

XML Searching

As illustrated above, since the schema of the metadata model is complex, it can be hard to search the metadata documents. In particular, the structure of the Temporal/Spatial part has an undefined depth.

In order to understand the search complexity of possible queries, we present two examples of queries on the Echo database about 20th century events:

Example 1 *Search all mpeg videos about the fall of the Berlin wall.*
Example 2 *Search all video scenes where the word "jeep" is said.*

The first query involves only the bibliographic metadata, indeed the words "fall", "Berlin", and "wall", can be searched in the AVDocument title and its description, and then it is possible to check if it contains video in mpeg. Figure 2.8 depicts the possible result of this search, where the AVDocument retrieved has two Video implementations: one in mpeg format and one in AVI format.

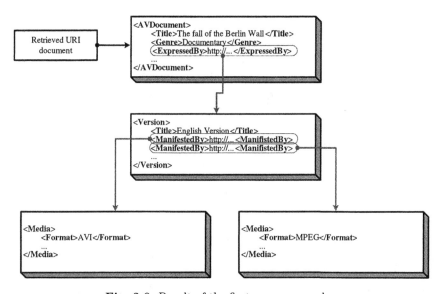

Fig. 2.8. Result of the first query example.

The second query is much more complex. We first have to scan all the Transcript entities and search for those which contain the word "jeep". Subsequently, we must save the URI of these found Transcipt XML documents. Since we would like to select all the scenes connected to these Transcripts we have to save also the time code where the word "jeep" is spoken. The result of this first query phase is a list of Transcript URIs associated with a list of timecodes. For convenience this result could be temporary stored in an XML file such as the following.

```
<QueryResult1>
    <Transcript URI="http://EchoServer.it/tran25.xml">
        <timecode>122424</timecode>
    </Transcript>
    <Transcript URI="http://EchoServer.it/tran128.xml">
        <timecode>556332</timecode>
        <timecode>223422</timecode>
    </Transcript>
</QueryResult1>
```

In the second phase of the search we have to scan for all the Video XML documents which have in the field <HasTranscript> one of the URIs contained in the QueryResult1.xml and which are identified as scenes. This last check can be done looking at the tag <IndicationVideoUnit>. This field indicates the granularity of the Video object. If it contains the closed list item "Scene" ("Shot"), it means that the Video object is actually a scene (shot) of the whole video. If this check is positive we have to select all the Video XML documents which contain the timecode of one of the timecodes in the found Transcript. The result is a list of Video URIs corresponding to XML files describing the scenes where the word "jeep" is said. These URIs are then shown in the retrieval interface and can be selected by the user and opened by means of the Metadata Editor. The Editor is able to open the selected scene and show the video and its associated metadata. Figure 2.9 illustrates the elaboration and the possible result of this query, where two Video documents are retrieved.

2.6 Conclusions

In this chapter we have shown how XML is becoming a key choice in the management of audio/video information, in the context of video digital libraries. These advantages have been exemplified in the implementation of the ECHO Video DL system.

Moreover, XML is gaining a key role in new audio-visual applications of increasing importance such as interactive digital television. Consider, for example, the role of XML in the effort of standardization of the Multimedia Home Platform protocol (MHP) of Digital Video Broadcasting (DVB) [104], in the standardization of video metadata information in MPEG-7 [222], and the standardization of mixed audio/video and data/program structures at the implementation level [154].

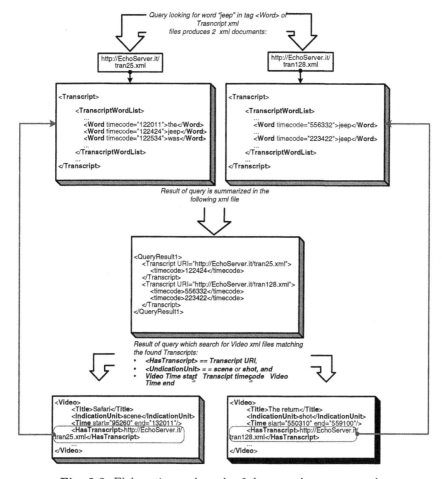

Fig. 2.9. Elaboration and result of the second query example.

Part II

Query Languages

Introduction

XML is used to represent all kinds of documents in data repositories, and across the Web. Current XML query languages such as XPath and XQuery are inspired by SQL and provide Boolean retrieval.

In order to be successful, however, XML query languages have to be extended to allow keyword searching in (text parts of) documents. In other words, they need to provide additional functionality for relevance-oriented search. Combining current XML query languages with searching for keywords poses major challenges.

The term *relevance* comes from the information retrieval community and can be explained as follows. To perform a certain task, a user may need information and information is called relevant if it fullfils this need. Although the concept of relevance is inherently subjective and vague, reliable indicators have been developed in the past. These indicators exploit e.g., word statistics, proximity and linguistic tools like stemmers. However, unlike the database community, wich has developed several standard data models and query languages (most notably the relational model and SQL), the information retrieval community has not developed standards for relevance-oriented querying. There have been numerous suggestions for information retrieval models, but each vendor of information retrieval systems uses its own proprietary relevance function and query language. It will be a major step forward if the XML community is able to provide standards for relevance-oriented search that are acceptable to both the database and the information retrieval community.

This part consists of three chapters. The first chapter describes requirements for extensions of XQuery and XPath for relevance-oriented search. The other two chapters describe practical examples of such query languages.

Chapter 3 by Rys describes in detail the W3C XQuery and XPath full-text requirements. Extensions of XQuery/XPath should for instance support operators that work on relative positions of words (e.g., proximity operators), operators that work on the words themselves (e.g., wildcards, stemming) and score functions reflecting the relevance of documents. The chapter presents the advantages and disadvantages of three approaches to extend XQuery/XPath: sublanguage approaches, function approaches, and syntactic approaches.

Chapter 4 by Fuhr, Großjohann, and Kriewel presents an extension of XPath for intelligent XML retrieval. The extension provides constructs for weighting the elements in XML documents, relevance-oriented search, and vague predicates over a variety of data types. Since XIRQL (and other extensions to XPath and XQuery) are not intended to be end user languages, the chapter presents a graphical user interface that supports the user in identifying relevant elements from the XML data.

Chapter 5 by Schöning describes the integration of text retrieval with search conditions on structured parts of XML data within the commercial system Tamino, one of the leading native XML database engines. Tamino has had XML-aware text retrieval support from its very beginning. It was based on an extended version of XPath, and has further extended these capabilities in the context of XQuery. It also has flexible linguistic analysis techniques like stemming and phonetic similarity for a variety of natural languages.

3

Full-Text Search with XQuery: A Status Report

Michael Rys

3.1 Introduction

XML [45] has become one of the most important data representation formats. One of the major reasons for this success is that XML is well-suited not only for representing marked-up documents – as its heritage based on SGML indicates – but also highly-structured hierarchical data such as object hierarchies or relational data and semistructured data (see Fig. 3.1). Even data that traditionally has been represented in binary format such as graphics is now being represented using XML (e.g., SVG).

We will use the following definitions for the terms structured, semistructured and marked-up data. Note that these definitions are somewhat different to the definitions of data-centric XML and document-centric XML given in other locations in that they focus less on the use and more on the actual structure. Often, data-centric XML represents some form of structured or semistructured data, while document-centric XML often represents semistructured or marked-up data, although sometimes it may be representing structured data.

Definition 1. Structured data *is data that easily fits into a predefined, homogeneous type structure such as relations or nested objects.*

Definition 2. Semistructured data *is data that is mainly structured but may change its structure from instance to instance. For example, it has some components that are one-off annotations that only appear on single instances or that are of heterogeneous type structure (e.g., once the address data is a string, once it is a complex object).*

Definition 3. Marked-up data *is data that represents mainly free-flowing text with interspersed markup to call out document structure and highlighting.*

The most important aspect of XML as a data representation format is that it allows combining the different data formats in one single document, thus providing a truly universal data representation format.

H. Blanken et al. (Eds.): Intelligent Search on XML Data, LNCS 2818, pp. 39–57, 2003.
© Springer-Verlag Berlin Heidelberg 2003

```
<PatientRecord pid="P1">
    <FirstName>Janine</FirstName>
    <LastName>Smith</LastName>
    <Address>
        <Street>1 Broadway Way</Street>
        <City>Seattle</City>
        <Zip>WA 98000</Zip>
    </Address>
    <Visit date="2002-01-05">
        Janine came in with a <symptom>rash</symptom>. We identified a
        <diagnosis>antibiotics allergy</diagnosis> and <remedy>changed her
        cold prescription</remedy>.
    </Visit>
</PatientRecord>
<PatientRecord>
    <pid>P2</pid>
    <FirstName>Nils</FirstName>
    <LastName>Soerensen</LastName>
    <Address>
        23 NE 40th Street, New York
    </Address>
</PatientRecord>
```

Fig. 3.1. XML fragment representing structured data (the FirstName and Last-Name properties of the PatientRecord), semistructured data (the pid and Address properties), and marked-up data (Visit)

Since more and more data is making use of XML's capability to combine different formats, being able to query and search XML documents becomes an important requirement. Existing query languages such as SQL or OQL are well-suited to deal with structured, hierarchical data, but are not directly appropriate for semistructured data or even marked-up documents. The SQL standard for example provides an interface to a sublanguage called SQL/MM to perform searches over documents, mainly because the documents and their markup are not part of the fundamental data model of SQL. This is in contrast to XML, where markup is the primary structural component of the data model. Thus, a new query language needed to be developed that can be used to query XML data.

In order to understand the query requirements, one also needs to understand a fundamental difference between marked-up data on one side and structured and semistructured data on the other side. In the case of marked-up data, the basic information content of the data is being preserved, even if the XML markup has been removed from the document. In the case of structured and semistructured data, removing one of the most important information of the data, the semantic association, would often lose too much information to still be able to make use of the data.

For example, while removing the markup of the Visit element of Fig. 3.1 loses some information, the bare text still contains enough useful information for the reader to understand the data. On the other hand, the markup in the structured and semistructured parts of the PatientRecord provides the necessary semantic information to interpret the raw data. Removing the markup would leave us with data that has lost most of its meaning.

Thus a query language that queries data represented in XML needs the capability to extract information from both the markup and the data itself. This means that the language needs a normal navigational component to deal with structured data as well as a text retrieval component to deal with marked-up data.

In addition, the markup structure can be provided adhoc without a schema (so called well-formed XML) or it can be described using a schema language such as the W3C XML Schema definition and validation language [310]. This means that the query language needs to be able to query well-formed documents besides being able to utilize possibly available schema information.

XQuery [34] is a declarative query language for querying XML documents. It is currently being designed by a working group of the Worldwide Web Consortium [W3C] and is expected to be released as a recommendation late 2003/early 2004. It is based on the functional programming paradigm with a type system based on the W3C XML Schema definition and validation language [310]. The first version of XQuery will provide a SQL-like language that combines the XPath [12] document navigation capabilities with a sequence iterator commonly referred to as a FLWR expression, XML like constructors and an extensive function library. For example, the following XQuery expression finds all patient visits that belong to people with first name Nils and have New York in their address (could be as street or as city) and order them by visit date:

```
for $p in /PatientRecord, $v in $p/Visit
where $p/FirstName = "Nils"
and   fn:contains(fn:string($p/Address), "New York")
order by $v/@date
return
  <Visit date="{$v/@date}"
         Name="{$p/FirstName} {$p/LastName}">{
  $v/*
  }</Visit>
```

While the first version of XQuery does not support full-text search or information retrieval capabilities, such functionality is slated to be added as an extension to XQuery 1.0. The XQuery working group has formed a task force that has published a requirement document [58] and a set of use cases [10] and is currently reviewing a couple of language proposals. Such full-text capabilities allow us to search the marked-up part or the structured and semistructured parts of XML documents using information retrieval technology.

In the following, we will be reviewing the requirements and some of the use cases and will discuss some possible approaches on how such a language could be designed and integrated with XQuery and how they can provide intelligent searching over XML data.

3.2 XQuery Full-Text Requirements

The XQuery Full-Text requirements document [58] is a work in progress, and may be revised in subsequent versions. Therefore the document and the assumptions made in this chapter cannot not be considered to be fully stable. However they show, where the working group focuses for the design of the first version of the full-text language.

This section reviews the full-text specific requirements and provides some additional insight about the requirements. The section takes the liberty to arrange some of the requirements differently to the requirement document and leaves the less interesting requirements for this discussion out.[1]

3.2.1 Definitions

Before we start looking at the requirements, let's repeat some definitions used by the requirement document.

Definition 4. Full-Text Search *[...] is an extension to the XQuery/XPath language. It provides a way to query text which has been tokenized, i.e. broken into a sequence of words, units of punctuation, and spaces. Tokenization enables functions and operators which work with the relative positioning of words (e.g., proximity operators). Tokenization also enables functions and operators which operate on a part or the root of the word (e.g., wildcards, stemming).*

Definition 5. Score *reflects relevance of matched material.*

It is interesting to note that the definition of score does not refer to full-text search itself. The wider understanding of score and relevance will be an important aspect in making XQuery the language for intelligent retrieval from XML documents (see below).

The requirement document also defines the terms *must*, *should* and *may* that describe the priority and importance of the requirements for the first version of the language.

The following are some definitions that we use:

---

[1] The requirements themselves are Copyright © 2003 World Wide Web Consortium, (Massachusetts Institute of Technology, European Research Consortium for Informatics and Mathematics, Keio University). All Rights Reserved. http://www.w3.org/Consortium/Legal/2002/copyright-documents-20021231.

Definition 6. XQuery/XPath Full-Text Language *(or short: Full-Text Language) is the extension to the XQuery/XPath language that provides the Full-Text Search capabilities.*

The following section discusses the requirements. We will number the requirements in order to reference them.

3.2.2 Language Design

This section covers the fundamental requirements for XQuery/XPath Full-Text language design.

The Data Model

(R1) XQuery/XPath Full-Text functions *must* operate on instances of the XQuery/XPath Data Model [115].

This requirement says that the Full-Text Language needs to operate on the data that is available in the data model. Since the Full-Text Language operates on tokenized text, this means that the text in the data model will have to be tokenized for the purpose of Full-Text Search. Since the W3C XQuery/XPath specifications are not describing implementation strategies such as indices, it is assumed that implementations will take care of the tokenization in an implementation-defined way. A specific implementation may provide an indexing mechanism that needs to be applied before one even can perform Full-Text Search on the data, or another one may perform it dynamically at query time. Obviously the later will not scale with the size of the data or the complexity of the query, but may be appropriate if it operates on non-persistent data such as data arriving over a stream.

Side-Effects on the Data

(R2) XQuery/XPath Full-Text *must not* introduce or rely on side-effects.

The language should not introduce side-effects such as modifying the data model or depend on such side-effects. This requirement is important in order to keep the language within the functional framework of XQuery and XPath and to keep it optimizable and scalable. It is especially important in the context of full-text search, since it is for example tempting to just annotate every visited node with attributes containing relevance information.

Score Function and Full-Text Predicates

(R3) XQuery/XPath Full-Text *must* allow Full-Text predicates and Score functions independently.

(R4) XQuery/XPath Full-Text *must* either use the same language for Full-Text predicates and Score functions or use a language for Full-Text predicates that is a proper subset of the language for Score functions.

These two requirements provide the relationship between the Boolean and relevance-based Full-Text Search. Unlike systems that only provide for scoring expressions and then define a certain relevance value (normally 0) to represent false and anything greater to denote true, the XQuery/XPath Full-Text language provides a Boolean language that then also can be used in the context of score expressions. For example, the Boolean language searches for specific tokens. A Boolean search expression then is used in a score expression that functions as second-order operation to determine the relevance of the data w.r.t. search expression. The design of the language also allows for other expressions to be used in the context of score expressions.

Score Algorithm

The following is a list of requirements on the algorithm used to determine the relevance used by score and its exposition inside XQuery/XPath.

(R5) XQuery/XPath Full-Text *must* allow the user to return Score.

(R6) XQuery/XPath Full-Text *must* allow the user to sort by Score.

(R7) XQuery/XPath Full-Text *must* define the type and range of Score values. The Score should be a float, in the range 0-1.

(R8) XQuery/XPath Full-Text *must not* require an explicit definition of the global corpus statistics (statistics, such as word frequency, used in calculating Score).

(R9) XQuery/XPath Full-Text *may* partially define the semantics of Score.

(R10) XQuery/XPath Full-Text *must* be able to generate a Score for a combination of Full-Text predicates.

(R11) The algorithm to produce combined Scores *must* be vendor-provided.

(R12) The algorithm to produce combined Scores *should* be overridable by users.

(R13) Users *must* be able to influence individual components of complex score expressions.

The requirements above mean that the algorithm to determine relevance will be mostly implementation-defined, however the language should provide some parameterization – such as weighting – and the standard may define some semantics – such as a relevance value of 0 being the same as no match.

Important is the requirement that the implementation-provided scoring algorithm needs to combine scores. This allows users to concentrate on writing the correct scoring expression without having to write their own score-combining expressions. Together with requirements (R3) and (R4), this means that the score algorithm works as a second-order function on the Full-Text Language. A Full-Text Language expression is passed to the score algorithm, which then investigates the expression itself to determine the relevance of each search predicate term and how to combine the individual relevance values based on the overall expression.

Extensibility

The following requirements deal with the ability of the Full-Text Language to evolve. The first requirement will allow implementers (not only vendors) to add additional functionality. This is especially important in order to use the standardized part of the language as the foundation for research into extending information retrieval over XML data beyond the current state.

(R14) XQuery/XPath Full-Text *must* be extensible by vendors.

(R15) XQuery/XPath Full-Text *may* be extensible by users.

The ability to extend the relevance algorithms and the linguistic search functionality is often requested by the advanced user community. The may-requirement above makes this a low priority for this version, but will keep it as a possibilty for future versions. Future versions of the language should be built within the framework given by the first version as requirement (R16) requires:

(R16) The first version of XQuery/XPath Full-Text *must* provide a robust framework for future versions.

As a result of this requirement, we hope that the design of the Full-Text Language will take possible future functionality into account and thus will be designed in an extensible way.

End User Language

(R17) It is not a requirement that XQuery/XPath Full-Text be designed as an end-user user interface language.

This non-requirement is important, since it clearly communicates that the language-like XQuery and XPath-should not be seen as an end-user language but a language that is used by implementers to build applications. It also indicates, that the language to be designed is not the language exposed by end-user search engines such as Google.

3.2.3 XPath/XQuery Integration

This section specifies requirements for the integration of the XQuery/XPath Full-Text Language with XQuery and XPath. The important requirements are:

XPath

(R21) Part, but not necessarily all, of XQuery/XPath Full-Text *must* be usable as part of an XPath expression.

This requirement acknowledges that not every expression may be usable in the context of XPath, since XPath itself made certain design decisions that may end up being in contradiction to some of the functionality of the Full-Text Language. For example, XPath currently does not allow expressions to generate new elements.

Extensibility Mechanisms

(R22) XQuery/XPath Full-Text *should* use the extensibility mechanisms that exist in XQuery and XPath for integration into XQuery and XPath.

This requirement basically says that the design of the Full-Text Language should be based on the primary mechanism of XQuery and XPath, which consist of functions, built-in operators and expressions.

(R23) XQuery/XPath Full-Text *must* use the extensibility mechanisms that exist in XQuery and XPath for it's own extensibility.

By making the Full-Text language part of XQuery and/or XPath, it should not change these languages in any fundamental way. This means that it should not introduce its own way to extend the language.

Composability

(R24) XQuery/XPath Full-Text *must* be composable with XQuery, and should be composable with itself.

This requirement makes the Full-Text Language a normal component of XQuery. It also means that the Full-Text Language can use XQuery expressions, access variables and compose with the normal XQuery operators such as the Boolean operators. This is an important requirement to judge different Full-Text Language proposals, since certain approaches may be limited in their composability with XQuery and XPath.

3.2.4 Functionality and Scope

This section defines requirements for the functionality in the XQuery/XPath Full-Text Language, and the scope of XQuery/XPath Full-Text queries.

Functionality

(R27) XQuery/XPath Full-Text *must* provide, in the first release, a minimum set of Full-Text functionality that is useful. It consists of single-word search, phrase search, support for stopwords, single character suffix, 0 or more character suffix, 0 or more character prefix, 0 or more character infix, proximity searching (unit: words), specification of order in proximity searching, combination using AND, combination using OR, combination using NOT, word normalization, diacritics, and ranking, relevance.

The interesting term used here is "useful". The "usefulness" was determined by reviewing the use cases and by polling the membership of the working group members.

(R28) Additional functionality represented in the XQuery and XPath Full-Text Use Cases *must* be considered, but *may* be left to a future release.

(R29) Additional functionality from other Full-Text search contexts such as SQL/MM Full-Text [170] *must* be considered, but *should* be left to a future release.

An interesting use case/requirement in the Full-Text Use Case document is the case of ignoring substructures for full-text searching. This use case covers an important scenario in searching marked-up data: searching main text while disregarding inlined annotations.

For example, the following text contains a footnote:

```
<chapter>
    <p>Users can be tested at any computer
    workstation <footnote>They may be most
    comfortable at their own workstation.
    </footnote> or in a lab.</p>
</chapter>
```

Normal full-text search for the token "comfortable" inside chapters will find the chapter above. However, one may want to exclude footnotes and other annotations when searching for a phrase or token. Thus being able to ignore subtrees inside marked-up text seems like an important use case.

Search Scope

(R30) XQuery/XPath Full-Text *must* allow search within an arbitrary structure (an arbitrary XPath expression).

The important aspect here is that the language needs to allow search within any arbitrary structure returned by an XPath expression. However, an implementation may still have an implementation restriction on what can be searched. It may for example require, that the data has to be indexed and tokenized apriori.

(R31) XQuery/XPath Full-Text *must* NOT preclude Full-Text search within structures constructed during a query.

Again, the language should allow searching within an arbitrary structure constructed by an XQuery expression. However, since such a search requires the data to be tokenized dynamically, the requirement does not mandate the functionality.

(R32) XQuery/XPath Full-Text *must* allow a query to return arbitrary nodes.

This requirement can of course be easily achieved if the Full-Text Language is being composed with XPath and XQuery.

(R33) XQuery/XPath Full-Text *must* allow the combination of predicates on different parts of the searched document 'tree'.

This requirement means that different predicates on different parts of the XML data can be correlated. For example, it can be used to get all books where the title contains stemmed tokens corresponding to the stemmed forms of "XQuery" and the abstract has the term "Full-Text" within 2 tokens of "XQuery".

Attributes

XML provides two ways to represent text data: Either in form of element content or as attribute values. Marked-up data rarely uses attributes for representing data; they are mainly used for representing meta-information. Nevertheless, Full-Text Search should be able to search within attribute values:

(R34) XQuery/XPath Full-Text *must* support Full-Text search within attributes.

(R35) XQuery/XPath Full-Text *may* support Full-Text search within attributes in conjunction with Full-Text search within element content.

The combination of searches in attributes and separate searches in element content is covered by requirement (R33). This requirement can be interpreted as allowing searches that span element and attribute boundaries. This is somewhat problematic since attributes are not ordered in XML, therefore the notion of proximity would have to be adopted to the presence of attributes.

Markup

(R36) If XQuery/XPath Full-Text supports search within names of elements and attributes, then it *must* distinguish between element content and attribute values and names of elements and attributes in any search.

Searching on XML documents still needs to heed the structure given by the data model. This means that the Full-Text Language needs to clearly identify where to find the data.

Element Boundaries

(R37) XQuery/XPath Full-Text *must* support search across element boundaries, at least for NEAR.

Since XML markup can be adding structure and split contiguous text into separate parts, it becomes important for the Full-Text Search capabilities to search across the element boundaries, especially in the context of marked-up data.

(R38) XQuery/XPath Full-Text *must* treat an element as a token boundary. This *may* be user-defined.

This requirement is in my opinion not correctly motivated. Given our understanding of the different nature of XML markup for structured/semistructured and marked-up data, the requirement should really be "XQuery/XPath Full-Text *should* provide an option to treat element markup as a token boundary or to treat it as having no impact on tokenization." When tokenizing marked-up data, which most likely represents the major use case for Full-Text Search, the element markup should not impact tokenization because the markup may be used within a single token. In the case of structured and semistructured data, the element markup indeed should become a token boundary, because each markup represents a semantic unit.

For certain use cases, it may be even necessary to distinguish on an element level. For example, the data in Fig. 3.1 should use the markup as token boundary for the structured and semistructured data and should not use it as token boundary for the marked-up data.

Score

Finally, we have a couple of score related requirements. They relate to the accessability and scoping of the relevance value (R39), its impact on the result ordering (R40) and its extensibility in a future version (R41).

(R39) Score *must* be accessible anywhere in the scope of the query.

(R40) Score *should* not be used for implicit ordering.

(R41) Score *may* be extendable to a general distance-measure.

Since the relevance value can be accessed by the user and can be used explicitly for ordering, relevance ordering or ranking is still possible. The two requirements (R39) and (R40) are motivated by use cases where one wants to retrieve a score value, but order the data according to other criteria including a score value over different relevance criteria.

(R41), while only a may requirement for this version of XQuery is one of the most interesting from both a research, and future extensibility support. Designing the Full-Text Language in a way that the score algorithm can understand the relevance of other expressions is an important foundation for developing XQuery into THE declarative query language for intelligent retrieval of XML data. For more details on this aspect, see the future section.

3.3 XQuery Use Cases

The XQuery Use-Case Document provides a collection of interesting use cases that cover a variety of areas of full-text searching. Instead of repeating all the use cases here, the reader is referred to [10]. The following gives a list of some of the main aspects that the use cases cover. Note that the use case document differentiates between use cases that are considered for this version of the language and use cases that are considered for future versions.

The use cases start out with simple word and phrase queries and make sure that they cover the universality requirement in providing examples in non-IndoEuropean based languages. The use cases progress to take markup components such as elements and attributes into account for the search and provide more complex word and phrase queries.

Another batch of use cases deals with stop words. They provide examples to ignore words and even override provided stop words, although the later case will not be considered for this version of the language. Other use cases cover linguistic aspects such as collation information and stemming in addition to more syntactic aspects such as wildcards. The use cases also provide for use of thesauri.

Furthermore they provide scenarios that cover distance measures such as proximity and relevance queries using score. An important aspect of the use cases is to combine full-text search expressions using logical operators and compose them with XQuery and XPath expressions and even combining several full-text search operators.

Several of the provided use cases will pose interesting challenges to implementations and will also require additional research into providing efficient and scalable implementation strategies. Many of these use cases – such as the overriding stop words – are fortunately marked for consideration for later versions of the language, to give more time to research the challenges they pose.

3.4 Some Language Approaches

So far we have reviewed the published W3C working drafts on full-text search in XQuery. In this section we would like to look at some language approaches that can be taken to provide the necessary full-text search capabilities to XQuery and XPath.

The requirements basically identify two kinds of "full-text" retrieval capabilities: Boolean search and relevance search. Boolean search will most likely be represented in XQuery and XPath using functions in a special namespace that return Boolean results. The question is how these functions will be providing the search functionality. Relevance search algorithms utilize not only the data and the relevance associated to it, but also the search expression's influence on the relevance. Thus relevance search is inherently a so-called second-order functionality.

Second-order functions are functions that instead of taking the resulting value of an argument expression take the expression itself as the argument. For example, the function f in the expression $f(1+2)$ is a first order function if it is equivalent to $f(3)$ but a second order function if it takes the expression $1+2$ as its argument. Neither XPath 2.0 nor XQuery 1.0 has currently support for second-order functions. XQuery has one second order expression so far that is expressed in syntax: the FLWOR-expression (for-let-where-orderby-return).

Another important design requirement is that the actual relevance search algorithms are not part of the standard but instead are left to implementations. This is to assure that the standard does not hamper innovation on finding better relevance algorithms. This of course comes at the cost of smaller short-term interoperability.

Finally, another important aspect of providing "full-text" language support in XQuery is that in the future, one may want to use the language's framework to provide support for other type of relevance-based searches such as image or sound retrieval or even relevance-based searches using the existing XQuery exact match predicates. It seems to me that a good language design would provide a general relevance operator in the language that can be used to combine full-text relevance searches with relevance searches on multi-media data or even over exact match expressions.

Given these design requirements, there are still many different approaches that can be taken to satisfy the requirements. We would like to look at the following approaches in a bit more details:

Sublanguage approach: Provide a minimal XQuery/XPath functional interface to an existing full-text language such as SQL/MM. Especially for relevance searches, the whole search expression is expressed in that sublanguage.

Function approach: Add XQuery functions that provide the required functionality. A full text search expression is composed from these functions with the normal XQuery operators such as and and or.

Syntactic approach: Add full-text functionality to the language by adding many new statement operators to the XQuery and XPath languages.

These three approaches are of course not fully orthogonal but can be combined. For example, one may choose the functional approach for the Boolean Search functionality and add syntax to provide the second order functionality of calculating the relevance score.

The following subsections give my critique of the different approaches. A good language design needs to find a balance between the following dimensions: number of functions, number of arguments, complexity of arguments, number of additional operators. One of the tasks of the W3C working groups will be weighting the benefits and cost and placing the final design in these 4 dimensions.

3.4.1 Sublanguage Approach

The so-called sublanguage approach could be represented by the two functions:

```
ft:text-contains($n as node, $query as xs:string)
        as xs:boolean
ft:text-score($n as node, $query as xs:string) as xs:double
```

which take the full-text sublanguage and apply it to the tokenized string value of the subtree rooted at the provided node. For example:

```
ft:text-contains($n, 'contains "food" or "meal"')
```

which returns true if the subtree rooted at $n contains a tokenized string that matches the terms food or meal. This is obviously very easy to map to existing full-text search engines, assuming that the string sublanguage easily maps to the language provided by that engine. If the sublanguage is well-defined, it is also easy to read. However it has several important drawbacks with respect to the requirements:

1. Parameterization: It is not possible to use the standard XQuery variable mechanism to parameterize the full-text query. You have to either dynamically create the string using string concatenation or the full-text language part has to implement its own variable reference mechanism.

2. Composability (R24): Every XQuery/XPath expression that you want to compose with has to be replicated in the sublanguage. For example, if you want to allow a query that checks for tokens in different subtrees such as:

```
ft:text-contains($n, 'chapter/title contains "food"
               or chapter/p contains "meal"')
```

has to provide navigational access (and thus will duplicate XPath) and the Boolean operators.

3. Extensibility: Extending the string language becomes harder since you have to change the syntax of the sublanguage with every extension. And any extension in XQuery or XPath cannot be leveraged. Thus it clearly violates (R22) and (R23).

4. Future intelligent retrieval: The specific use of the string sublanguage to calculate the score makes it impossible to provide a more comprehensive relevance search capability using the same framework. It thus seems to violate (R16) in this regard.

While I think this approach is a good way for a specific implementation to utilize existing architecture to provide full-text search capability in XQuery, I find it not an acceptable solution for the problem of providing long-term, standards-based full-text capabilities in XQuery/XPath.

3.4.2 Function Approaches

These approaches provide a set of XQuery/XPath functions that provide the base-functionality of the full-text search language. These functions then are being used in normal XQuery expressions and use XQuery functionality wherever possible.

For example, an approach may provide the following functions:

```
ft:text-contains($n as node*, $terms as xs:string*)
        as xs:boolean
ft:proximity-contains($n as node*, $terms as xs:string*,
                      $distance as xs:int) as xs:boolean
ft:thesaurus($terms as xs:string*, $thesaurus as xs:string)
        as xs:string*
ft:score($e as expression) as xs:double
```

and a bunch of other functions (note: for the purpose of this presentation, the functions and their signatures have been simplified). For example, ft:contains would return true if at least one node would contain a token that matches at least one term (which could be a phrase), ft:proximity-contains would return true at least one node would contain tokens that matches the terms within the given proximity distance, ft:thesaurus would return the looked up terms in the given thesaurus, and ft:score would be a second order function that takes any suitably restricted XQuery/XPath expression consisting of mainly full-text functions, XQuery/XPath Boolean and navigational operators and returns the relevance score.

For example, the expression that searches for the term 'food' in the chapter title or the term 'meal' in the chapters' paragraphs would be using the XPath navigation:

```
ft:text-contains($n/chapter/title, 'food') or
ft:text-contains($n/chapter/p, 'meal')
```

and the following expression calculates the relevance factor of the same search:

```
ft:score(ft:text-contains($n/chapter/title, 'food') or
         ft:text-contains($n/chapter/p, 'meal'))
```

Note that the parameterization of the relevance algorithm will be out of scope of the language itself. If a user wants to use different weights, then the functions will have to add weight parameters.

Finding the best functional approach is difficult. For example, if too many functions are being added, even the simplest full-text search predicates will be very verbose and hard to read and write. Also, linguistic functionality such as the language to be used, whether the term contains a wildcard, whether stemming should be performed, what collation should be used for the comparison should be provided in some form. Often this cannot be provided as a separate function, or the function would not be very efficient. For example, a collation function that provides all case varieties for each term would increase the number of passed values tremendously and is very inefficient, however providing the collation as a parameter will provide a more efficient way to search based on the case. Providing linguistic options as function parameters on the other hand makes the functions very unwieldy, since every function call will have 5 additional parameters. Often these parameters do not need to be set, and users have to remember, whether the 7th or 8th parameter denotes the collation argument. So another option is to provide a single option string that contains a simple name/value pair or provide an XML tree that conveys the same information. The XML tree approach is problematic if the language should be usable from XPath however, since XPath currently does not have any built-in functionality that generates new XML nodes and generating the tree is more complex than generating the option string.

Another design point that needs to be considered is the notion of the relevance search function. Since it is a second-order function and XQuery/XPath currently does not provide second-order functions, adding such a function would be a considerable extension to XQuery/XPath. Alternatively, one could provide a syntactic option for the relevance search (see Section 3.4.3 below for more detail). Another advantage of the syntactic approach for relevance search would be that it can be used for a variety of relevance searches, whereas a function that belongs to the full-text namespace should probably only operate on full-text expressions.

The functional approaches on the other hand have none of the drawbacks of the sublanguage approaches. They are easily parameterizable and composable. They can easily reuse the XPath and XQuery expressions and can easily be composed with other relevance search expressions, even though the actual relevance function may have to be different from the full-text relevance function.

3.4.3 Syntactic Approaches

The syntactic approaches extend the XQuery/XPath language by adding additional operators. These operators may be designed to define a separate language that can be used in XQuery/XPath as subexpressions but themselves only allow a limited subset of the XQuery/XPath operations as subexpressions. For example, one could envision a search-score-where-return equivalent to the XQuery FLWOR expression that would allow a limited set of XQuery expressions in its search, score and where clauses, but that could be used in any XQuery expression. Alternatively, one could extend the existing FLWOR clause with a score clause in the following way:

```
[1] FLWRExpr    ::=
    ((ForClause |  LetClause)+ ScoreClause* WhereClause?
    OrderByClause? "return")* QuantifiedExpr
[2] ScoreClause ::= Score (Variable "as")? Expr
[3] Score ::= "score"
```

which would allow expressions such as:

```
for $x in $nodeset
let $tok1 := "XML", $tok2 := "XQuery"
score $score as ft:text-contains($x/title, $tok1)
      or ft:text-contains($x/title, $tok2)
return
  <result><score>{ $score }</score>
          <text>{ $x/title/text() }</text>
  </result>
```

In either case, additional built-in operators such as NEAR-WITHIN to express a proximity search will need to be added to provide the full-text search capabilities. They may be modeled on an existing full-text search language such as SQL/MM like in the sublanguage case.

On the positive side, a syntactic approach for adding relevance search such as the score clause above avoids the problem of having to introduce the general concept of second-order functions into XQuery and XPath. Adding built-in operators for the full-text search capabilities may still provide language composability, although adding additional language constructs at the level of the FLWOR-expression that provides limited composability seems like a less preferable route. Furthermore, extending the full-text language becomes

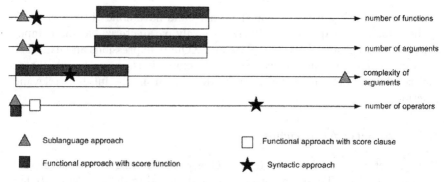

Fig. 3.2. Different language approaches and their syntactic dimensions

harder since it means that any extension will change the grammar of XQuery and XPath. Finally, the parameterization of the operators with the linguistic information becomes a non-trivial undertaking, since the large amount of parameters possible leads to a complex grammar.

3.4.4 Comparing the Approaches

Figure 3.2 gives the placement on the dimensional axes of some of the approaches discussed in this investigation.

The investigation of the three main approaches above clearly shows that the sublanguage approaches are less suited for adding the full-text search capabilities to XQuery/XPath than either a functional or syntactic approach. A functional approach seems to be more flexible and less brittle in the long-term than a syntactic approach, although the functional approaches have the problem of finding the right balance between number of functions, number or arguments and complexity of arguments.

It is my believe that the best course of action for XQuery is to take a functional approach towards adding the Boolean full-text search capabilities with either a functional or syntactic approach along the line of the outlined score-clause to provide the second-order functionality of relevance search.

3.4.5 Some General Implementation Issues

Regardless of the syntactic approach, every implementation will need to provide clever full-text indexes and understand how to perform even full-text queries over data that has not been indexed a priori. The relevance algorithms are considered "secret sauce" and thus highly implementation specific and non-interoperable. Implementations need to understand how to efficiently and effectively provide relevance on queries over a variety of XML data and XQuery systems will need to provide a clear way to provide users with ways to parameterize and tune the relevance algorithms. None of these aspects will be covered by the W3C standards work, but will be the most important aspects of enabling intelligent information retrieval from XML documents.

3.5 Conclusions

We made the case that finding and extracting information from XML documents is an important aspect of future information discovery and retrieval and that XQuery for structural queries, extended with full-text capabilities for information retrieval queries, is an important and appropriate tool to facilitate this functionality. We then gave an overview of the current publicly available state of the XQuery working group's work on full-text search. In particular, we reviewed the requirements document and took a look at the use cases. Finally, we reviewed some of the possible language approaches and investigated some of the issues that any language proposal will have to address.

The work in the W3C XQuery working group will continue along the lines outlined in the requirements and use cases document. We can expect that the next step will be to review proposals and to investigate the language issues to find the right language – at least in the opinion of the working group – to satisfy the requirements in the context of XQuery and XPath.

Even more interesting will be, how the full-text search framework provided by the working group will be used to extend XQuery for other approximate query functionality over the structural parts and types of data (such as binary image data in base64- or hex-encoding).

It is my believe that the best course of action for XQuery is to take a functional approach towards adding the Boolean full-text search capabilities with either a functional or syntactic approach along the line of the outlined score-clause to provide the second-order functionality of relevance search.

Finally, there are several interesting research areas that need more investigation. They range from implementation problems such as performance and scaling aspects of the dynamic processing provided by the generality of several of the possible language approaches over the design of the right APIs to provide external parameterization of the scoring algorithms to how to combine both full-text and XQuery optimization techniques to benefit both the structural and full-text queries.

4

A Query Language and User Interface for XML Information Retrieval

Norbert Fuhr, Kai Großjohann, and Sascha Kriewel

4.1 Introduction

As XML is about to become the standard format for structured documents, there is an increasing need for appropriate information retrieval (IR) methods. Since classical IR methods were developed for unstructured documents only, the logical markup of XML documents poses new challenges.

Since XML supports logical markup of texts both at the macro level (structuring markup for chapter, section, paragraph and so on) and the micro level (e.g., MathML for mathematical formulas, CML for chemical formulas), retrieval methods dealing with both kinds of markup should be developed. At the macro level, fulltext retrieval should allow for selection of appropriate parts of a document in response to a query, such as by returning a section or a paragraph instead of the complete document. At the micro level, specific similarity operators for different types of text or data should be provided (such as similarity of chemical structures, phonetic similarity for person names).

Although a large number of query languages for XML have been proposed in recent years, none of them fully addresses the IR issues related to XML; especially, the core XQuery proposal of the W3C working group [34] offers no support for IR-oriented querying of XML sources; the discussion about extensions for text retrieval has started only recently (see the requirements document by [34] and the use cases by [10]). There are only a few approaches that provide partial solutions to the IR problem, namely by taking into account the intrinsic imprecision and vagueness of IR; however, none of them are based on a consistent model of uncertainty (see section 4.5).

In this chapter, we present the query language XIRQL which combines the major concepts of XML querying with those from IR. XIRQL is based on XPath, which we extend by IR concepts. We also provide a consistent model for dealing with uncertainty.

For building a complete IR system, the query language and the model are not enough. One also needs to deal with user interface issues. On the

H. Blanken et al. (Eds.): Intelligent Search on XML Data, LNCS 2818, pp. 59–75, 2003.
© Springer-Verlag Berlin Heidelberg 2003

input side, the question of query formulation arises: the query language allows for combining structural conditions with content conditions, and the user interface needs to reflect this. On the output side, we observe two kinds of relationships between retrieval results. In traditional document retrieval, the retrievable items (i.e., documents) are considered to be independent from each other. This means that the system only needs to visualize the ordering imposed by the ranking. But in the case of retrieval from XML documents, two retrieved items may have a structural relationship, if they come from the same document: One could be the ancestor of another, or a sibling, and so on.

So in addition to the query language XIRQL, we describe graphical user interfaces for interactive query formulation as well as for result presentation.

This chapter is structured as follows. In the following section, we discuss the problem of IR on XML documents (section 4.2). Then we present the major concepts of our new query language XIRQL (section 4.3). Our graphical user interfaces are described in section 4.4. A survey on related work is given in section 4.5, followed by the conclusions and the outlook.

4.2 Requirements for an XML IR Query Language

From an IR point of view, the combination of content with logical markup in XML offers the following opportunities for enhancing IR functionality in comparison to plain text:

- Queries referring to content only should retrieve relevant document parts according to the logical structure, thus overcoming the limitations of passage retrieval. The FERMI model by [70] suggests the following strategy for the retrieval of structured (multimedia) documents: A system should always retrieve the most specific part of a document answering the query.
- Based on the markup of specific elements, high-precision searches can be performed that look for content occurring in specific elements (e.g., distinguishing between the sender and the addressee of a letter, finding the definition of a concept in a mathematics textbook). On the other hand, the intrinsic uncertainty and vagueness of IR should also be considered when interpreting structural conditions; thus, a vague interpretation of this type of conditions should be supported.
- The concept of *mixed content* allows for the combination of high precision searches with plain text search. An element contains mixed content if both subelements and plain text (#PCDATA) may occur in it. Thus, it is possible to mark up specific items occurring in a text. For example, in an arts encyclopedia, names of artists, places they worked, and titles of pieces of art may be marked up (thus allowing for example, to search for Picasso's paintings of toreadors, avoiding passages mentioning Picasso's frequent visits to bull-fights).

With respect to these requirements, XPath seems to be a good starting point for IR on XML documents. However, the following features should be added to XPath:

Weighting. IR research has shown that document term weighting as well as query term weighting are necessary tools for effective retrieval in textual documents. So comparisons in XPath referring to the text of elements should consider index term weights. Furthermore, query term weighting should also be possible, by introducing a weighted sum operator (allowing conditions like 0.6· "XML" +0.4· "retrieval"). These weights should be used for computing an overall retrieval status value for the elements retrieved, thus resulting in a ranked list of elements.

Relevance-oriented search. The query language should also support traditional IR queries, where only the requested content is specified, but not the type of elements to be retrieved. In this case, the IR system should be able to retrieve the most relevant elements; following the FERMI multimedia model cited above, this should be the most specific element(s) that fulfill(s) the query. In the presence of weighted index terms, the tradeoff between these weights and the specifity of an answer has to be considered, possibly by an appropriate weighting scheme.

Data types and vague predicates. The standard IR approach for weighting supports vague searches on plain text only. XML allows for fine grained markup of elements, and thus, there should be the possibility to use special search predicates for different types of elements. For example, for an element containing person names, similarity search for proper names should be offered; in technical documents, elements containing measurement values should be searchable by means of the comparison predicates $>$ and $<$ operating on floating point numbers. Thus, there should be the possibility to have elements of different data types, where each data type comes with a set of specific search predicates. In order to support the intrinsic vagueness of IR, most of these predicates should be vague (search for measurements that were taken at about 20 °C, for instance).

Structural vagueness. XPath is closely tied to the XML syntax, but it is possible to use syntactically different XML variants to express the same meaning. For example, a particular information could be encoded as an XML attribute or as an XML element. As another example, a user may wish to search for a value of a specific data type in a document (a person name, say), without bothering about the element names. Thus, appropriate generalizations should be included in the query language.

4.3 XIRQL Concepts

In this section, we describe concepts for integrating the features listed in the previous section in XIRQL. These are: weighting, relevance-oriented search, data types and vague predicates, and structural vagueness.

4.3.1 Weighting

At first glance, extending XPath by a weighting mechanism seems to be a straightforward approach. Assuming probabilistic independence, the combination of weights according to the different Boolean operators is obvious, thus leading to an overall weight for any answer. However, there are two major problems that have to be solved first: 1) How should terms in structured documents be weighted? 2) What are the probabilistic events, i.e., which term occurrences are identical, and which are independent? Obviously, the answer to the second question depends partly on the answer to the first one.

As we said before, classical IR models have treated documents as atomic units, whereas XML suggests a tree-like view of documents. One possibility for term weighting in structured documents would be the development of a completely new weighting mechanism. Given the long experience with weighting formulas for unstructured documents, such an approach would probably take a big effort to obtain good retrieval quality. As an alternative, we suggest to generalize the classical weighting formulas. Thus, we have to define the "atomic" units in XML documents that are to be treated like atomic documents. The benefit of such a definition is twofold:

1. Given these units, we can apply some kind of tf · idf formula for term weighting.
2. For relevance-oriented search, where no type of result element is specified, only these units can be returned as answers, whereas other elements are not considered as meaningful results.

We start from the observation that text is contained in the leaf nodes of the XML tree only. So these leaves would be an obvious choice as atomic units. However, this structure may be too fine-grained. (It could be the markup of each item in an enumeration list, or markup of a single word in order to emphasize it.) A more appropriate solution is based on the concept of *index nodes* from the FERMI multimedia model: Given a hierarchic document structure, only nodes of specific types form the roots of index objects. In the case of XML, this means that we have to specify the names of the elements that are to be treated as index nodes. This definition can be part of the XML Schema (see below).

From the weighting point of view, index objects should be disjoint, such that each term occurrence is considered only once. On the other hand, we should allow for retrieval of results of different granularity: For very specific queries, a single paragraph may contain the right answer, whereas more general questions could be answered best by returning a whole chapter of a book. Thus, nesting of index objects should be possible. In order to combine these two views, we first start with the most specific index nodes. For the higher-level index objects comprising other index objects, only the text that is not contained within the other index objects is indexed. As an example, assume that we have defined section, chapter and book elements as index nodes in our example document; the corresponding disjoint text units are marked as dashed boxes in Figure 4.1.

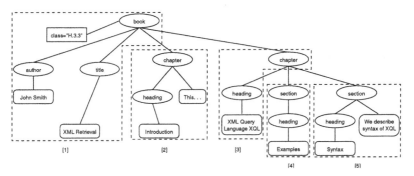

Fig. 4.1. Example XML document tree. Dashed boxes indicate index nodes; bracketed numbers serve as identifiers.

So we have a method for computing term weights, and we can do relevance based search. Now we have to solve the problem of combining weights and structural conditions. For the following examples, let us assume that there is a comparison predicate cw (contains word) which tests for word occurrence in an element. Now consider the query //section[heading cw "syntax"] and assume that this word does not only occur in the heading, but also multiple times within the same index node (i.e., section). Here we first have to decide about the interpretation of such a query: Is it a content-related condition, or does the user search for the occurrence of a specific string? In the latter case, in would be reasonable to view the filter part as a Boolean condition, for which only binary weights are possible. We offer this possibility by providing data types with a variety of predicates, where some of them are Boolean and others are vague (see below).

In the content-related interpretation, we use the weight from the corresponding index node. The major justification for this strategy is the fact that the meaning of a term depends heavily on its context, and this context should never be ignored in content-oriented searches — even when structural conditions are specified. These conditions should only work as additional filters. So we take the term weight from the index node. Thus the index node determines the significance of a term in the context given by the node.

With the term weights defined this way, we have also solved the problem of independence/identity of probabilistic events: Each term in each index node represents a unique probabilistic event, and all occurrences of a term within the same node refer to the same event. (Both occurrences of the word "syntax" in the last section of our example document represent the same event, for example.) Assuming unique node IDs, events can be identified by event keys that are pairs [node ID, term]. Given the node IDs shown in square brackets in Figure 4.1, the occurrence of the word "syntax" in the last section is represented by the event [5, syntax]. For retrieval, we assume that different events are independent. That is, different terms are independent of each other. Moreover, occurrences of the same term in different index nodes are also independent of each other. Following this idea, retrieval results correspond to Boolean combinations of probabilistic events which we call event expressions. For example, a search for sections dealing with the syntax of XQL could be specified as //section[.//* cw "XQL" and .//* cw "syntax"]. Here, our example document would yield the conjunction [5, XQL] ∧ [5, syntax]. In contrast, a query searching for this content in complete documents would have to consider the occurrence of the term "XQL" in two different index nodes, thus leading to the Boolean expression ([3, XQL] ∨ [5, XQL]) ∧ [5, syntax].

For dealing with these Boolean expressions, we adopt the idea of event keys and event expressions described by [129]. With the method described there, we can compute the correct probability for any combination of independent events (see also [128]). Furthermore, the method can be extended to allow for query term weighting. Assume that the query for sections about XQL syntax would be reformulated as //section[0.6 · .//* cw "XQL" + 0.4 · .//* cw "syntax"]. For each of the conditions combined by the weighted sum operator, we introduce an additional event with a probability as specified in the query (the sum of these probabilities must not exceed 1). Let us assume that we identify these events as pairs of an ID referring to the weighted sum expression, and the corresponding term. Furthermore, the operator '·' is mapped onto the logical conjunction, and '+' onto disjunction. For the last section of our example document, this would result in the event expression $[q_1, \text{XQL}] \wedge [5, \text{XQL}] \vee [q_1, \text{syntax}] \wedge [5, \text{syntax}]$. Assuming that different query conditions belonging to the same weighted sum expression are disjoint events, this event expression is mapped onto the scalar product of query and document term weights: $P([q_1, \text{XQL}]) \cdot P([5, \text{XQL}]) + P([q_1, \text{syntax}]) \cdot P([5, \text{syntax}])$.

4.3.2 Relevance-Oriented Search

Above, we have described a method for combining weights and structural conditions. In contrast, relevance-based search omits any structural conditions; instead, we must be able to retrieve index objects at all levels. The index weights of the most specific index nodes are given directly. For retrieval of the higher-level objects, we have to combine the weights of the different text units contained therein. For example, assume the following document structure, where we list the weighted terms instead of the original text:

```
<chapter> 0.3 XQL
  <section> 0.5 example </section>
  <section> 0.8 XQL 0.7 syntax </section>
</chapter>
```

A straightforward possibility would be the OR-combination of the different weights for a single term. However, searching for the term "XQL" in this example would retrieve the whole chapter in the top rank, whereas the second section would be given a lower weight. It can be easily shown that this strategy always assigns the highest weight to the most general element. This result contradicts the structured document retrieval principle mentioned before. Thus, we adopt the concept of augmentation from [127]. For this purpose, index term weights are downweighted (multiplied by an augmentation weight) when they are propagated upwards to the next index object. In our example, using an augmentation weight of 0.6, the retrieval weight of the chapter with respect to the query "XQL" would be $0.3 + 0.6 \cdot 0.8 - 0.3 \cdot 0.6 \cdot 0.8 = 0.636$, thus ranking the section ahead of the chapter.

For similar reasons as above, we use event keys and expressions in order to implement a consistent weighting process (so that equivalent query expressions result in the same weights for any given document). [127] introduce augmentation weights (i.e., probabilistic events) by means of probabilistic rules. In our case, we can attach them to the root element of index nodes. Denoting these events as index node number, the last retrieval example would result in the event expression $[1, \text{XQL}] \vee [3] \wedge [3, \text{XQL}]$.

In the following, paths leading to index nodes are denoted by 'inode()' and recursive search with downweighting is indicated via '...'. As an example, the query /document//inode()[... cw "XQL" and ... cw "syntax"] searches for index nodes about "XQL" and "syntax", thus resulting in the event expression $([1, \text{XQL}] \vee [3] \wedge [3, \text{XQL}]) \wedge [2] \wedge [2, \text{syntax}]$.

In principle, augmentation weights may be different for each index node. A good compromise between these specific weights and a single global weight may be the definition of type-specific weights, i.e., depending on the name of the index node root element. The optimum choice betweeen these possibilities will be subject to empirical investigations.

4.3.3 Data Types and Vague Predicates

Given the possibility of fine-grained markup in XML documents, we would like to exploit this information in order to perform more specific searches. For the content of certain elements, structural conditions are not sufficient, since the standard text search methods are inappropriate. For example, in an arts encyclopedia, it would be possible to mark artist's names, locations or dates. Given this markup, one could imagine a query like "Give me information about an artist whose name is similar to Ulbrich and who worked around 1900 near Frankfort, Germany", which should also retrieve an article mentioning Ernst Olbrich's work in Darmstadt, Germany, in 1899. Thus, we need *vague predicates* for different kinds of data types (person names, locations, dates, and so on). Besides similarity (vague equality), additional data type-specific comparison operators should be provided (e.g., 'near', $<$, $>$, or 'broader', 'narrower' and 'related' for terms from a classification or thesaurus). In order to deal with vagueness, these predicates should return a weight as a result of the comparison between the query value and the value found in the document.

The XML standard itself only distinguishes between three data types, namely text, integer and date. The XML Schema recommendation [111] extends these types towards atomic types and constructors (tuple, set) that are typical for database systems.

For the document-oriented view, this notion of data types is of limited use. This is due to the fact that most of the data types relevant for IR applications can hardly be specified at the syntactic level (consider for instance names of geographic locations, or English vs. French text). In the context of XIRQL, data types are characterized by their sets of vague predicates (such as phonetic similarity of names, English vs. French stemming). Thus, for supporting IR in XML documents, there should be a core set of appropriate data types, and the system should be designed in an extensible way so that application-specific data types can be added easily.

We do not discuss implementation issues here, but it is clear that the system needs to provide appropriate index structures, for structural conditions and also for the (possibly vague) search predicates — both for the core and the application-specific data types, of course. This problem is rather challenging, as we suspect that separate index structures for the tree structure and for the search predicates will not be sufficient; rather, they have to be combined in some way.

Candidates for the core set are texts in different languages, hierarchical classification schemes, thesauri and person names. In order to perform text searches, some knowledge about the kind of text is necessary. Truncation and adjacency operators available in many IR systems are suitable for western languages only (whereas XML in combination with unicode allows for coding of most written languages). Therefore, language-specific predicates, e.g., for dealing with stemming, noun phrases and composite words should be provided. Since documents may contain elements in multiple languages, the language problem should be handled at the data type level. Classification schemes and thesauri are very popular now in many digital library applications; thus, the relationships from these schemes should be supported, perhaps by including narrower or related terms in the search. Vague predicates for this data type should allow for automatic inclusion of terms that are similar according to the classification scheme. Person names often pose problems in document search, as the first and middle names may sometimes be initials only (therefore, searching for "Jack Smith" should also retrieve "J. Smith", with a reduced weight). A major problem is the correct spelling of names, especially when transliteration is involved (e.g., "Chebychef"); thus, phonetic similarity or spelling-tolerant search should be provided.

Application-specific data types should support vague versions of the predicates that are common in this area. For example, in technical texts, measurement values often play an important role; thus, dealing with the different units, the linear ordering involved ($<$) as well as similarity (vague equality) should be supported ("show me all measurements taken at room temperature"). For texts describing chemical elements and compounds, it should be possible to search for elements of compounds, or to search for common generalizations (search for "aluminum salts", without the need to enumerate them).

As a framework for dealing with these problems, we adopt the concept of data types in IR from [124], where a data type T is a pair consisting of a domain $|T|$ and a set of (vague comparison) predicates $P_T = \{c_1, \ldots, c_n\}$. Like in other type systems, IR data types should also be organized in a type hierarchy (e.g., Text – Western-Language – English), where the subtype restricts the domain and/or provides additional predicates. (In the example, it could be n-gram matching for general text, plus adjacency and truncation for western languages, plus stemming and noun phrase search for English.) Through this mechanism, additional data types can be defined easily by refining the appropriate data type (introducing French as refinement of Western-Language, say)[1].

In order to exploit these data types in retrieval, the data types of the XML elements have to be defined. Although the XML Schema recommendation [111] is targeted towards the data-centric view of XML, it can also be used for our purpose. Most of the data types discussed above are simple types in terms of XML Schema (that is, they have no internal structure), but do not belong to the builtin types of XML Schema. Thus, they have to be derived by means of restriction from the builtin types. However, in most cases, it is not possible to give necessary conditions for the restriction (consider English as a specialization of normalizedString). In addition, XML Schema does not deal with (vague) predicates of data types; they can be listed as application info only and are treated like comments by the schema processor.

In principle, XIRQL queries can also be processed for collections where no DTD or XML schema is given. However, in this case, XIRQL would assume that the content of all elements belongs to the same basic data type text, for which only basic predicates (like string equality and substring search) are provided. The more information about the data type of elements is provided, the more appropriate search predicates for the different elements can be provided by XIRQL. On the other hand, when no DTD is given, it will be very difficult for a user to formulate meaningful queries with structural conditions — most queries of this type would retrieve no documents at all.

4.3.4 Structural Vagueness

Since typical queries in IR are vague, the query language should also support vagueness in different forms. Besides relevance-based search as described above, relativism with respect to elements and attributes seems to be an important feature. The XPath distinction between attributes and elements may not be relevant for many users. In XIRQL, author searches an element,

---

[1] Please note that we make no additional assumptions about the internal structure of the text data type (and its subtypes), like representing text as set or list of words.

@author retrieves an attribute and =author is used for abstracting from this distinction.

Another possible form of relativism is induced by the introduction of data types. For example, we may want to search for persons in documents, without specifying their role (author, editor, referenced author, subject of a biography) in these documents. Thus, we provide a mechanism for searching for certain data types, regardless of their position in the XML document tree. For example, #persname searches for all elements and attributes of the data type persname.

Currently, we are working on further generalizations of structural conditions. One direction is based on ontologies over element names. For example, assuming that region is a subproperty of the more general element named geographic-area, which in turn has additional subproperties continent and country, we would expand the original element name region into the disjunction region | country | continent. The sequence of elements in a path can also be subject to vague interpretations (e.g., author = "Smith" should also match vaguely author/name and author/name/lastname).

4.4 Graphical User Interfaces for XML IR

A graphical user interface for retrieval should support two tasks, namely query formulation and result presentation. In the following, we first describe a mechanism for visually constructing XIRQL queries without having to know the syntax of the query language, and without being intimately acquainted with the document structure (DTD). Then we present two approaches for displaying the result list along with the size of answer elements and structural relationships between them.

4.4.1 Visual Query Formulation

With all the features of XIRQL described above, it is obvious that query formulation in XIRQL is a rather complex task. However, we assume that most end users will not have to formulate XIRQL queries, since there will be applications which generate XIRQL queries from user input to easy-to-use interfaces. For the remaining cases where XIRQL queries have to be formulated interactively, we want to provide an appropriate user interface. This interface should support the formulation of syntactically and semantically correct queries:

- With regard to query syntax, we take a menu-based approach, which covers only a subset of the full query syntax. In addition, the user can edit directly the generated XIRQL formulation.
- Semantically correct queries are supported by giving information about the structure of the XML documents to be queried, the data types of fields and the applicable predicates.

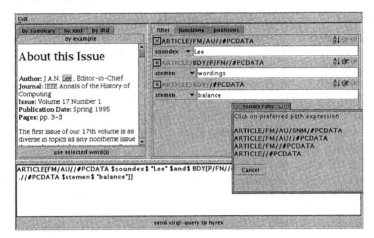

Fig. 4.2. Interface for formulating queries.

A screenshot of our interface can be seen in Figure 4.2. There are three areas: On the left, the *structure condition area* enables users to formulate single query conditions. On the right, the *condition list area* allows users to edit the query conditions and to specify how to combine them to form the whole query. At all times, a paraphrase of the current query in XIRQL syntax is kept up to date in the *paraphrase area* at the bottom.

For formulating a single query condition, the main mechanism is *Query by Example*. It comes in three variants. In the screenshot, the layout-oriented variant is shown. The user can click on a word in that document and the system derives from it a *structural condition* (candidate) and a *value condition* (candidate). The structural condition describes the list of element names on the path from the root node to the leaf node in the XML tree. From it, a number of generalizations (using the // operator and the * wild card) are produced and shown to the user (see the popup window in the lower right of the screenshot). After selecting the structural condition, the query condition is added to the condition list area, where additional changes can be made: The comparison value (defaulting to the word the user selected) can be edited, and a search predicate can be chosen for this condition.

In addition to the layout-oriented variant of Query by Example, we offer a structure-oriented variant where people see an expandable tree of the XML document, as well as a structure-oriented variant which shows a document surrogate only. Finally, as an alternative to Query by Example, we offer a *DTD oriented* method for specifying the structure condition which does not rely on an example document.

The next step is to specify how the query conditions thus collected should be combined to form the whole query. Here, we focus on the *structural dependence* between the conditions. This is achieved by specifying a common prefix for two query conditions. For example, in the third condition, /ARTICLE/BDY is grayed out. This means the match for the second and third conditions must be in the same BDY element (and hence within the same ARTICLE element). The graying-out connects two adjacent conditions; by making it possible to move conditions up and down in the list, structual dependence between any two conditions can be expressed. In addition to the structural dependence, the *Boolean connectors* between the conditions also need to be specified. We do this in a simple manner, allowing the user to choose between **and** and **or** between any two conditions, but we plan more elaborate support, possibly based on Venn diagrams.

To test the usefulness of this approach, we performed a small preliminary user study. Three retrieval tasks (against the INEX collection, [126]) were given in natural language. Five users performed the tasks with the graphical interface described here, two of them also used a command-line tool to directly enter XIRQL queries. The results indicate that even people with no knowledge of XIRQL are enabled to pose queries using this interface. For more complex queries, the interface might speed up users who know XIRQL. The layout-oriented variant of Query by Example was popular with all users, the DTD-based method was rarely used.

4.4.2 Result Presentation

The objective of traditional document retrieval systems is to select documents from a collection. For XML documents, the obvious extension is to select parts (elements) of documents, too. Whereas traditional result presentation uses a linear list in order to illustrate the ranking (or the corresponding retrieval status values) this approach does not cover the following two new aspects of XML retrieval:

- Structural relationships: Since different result elements may contain each other, the containment relationship must be visualized.
- Size of answer elements: In classical IR applications, it is assumed that all documents are approximately equal in size. Since XML elements may contain anything from a few words to a complete article, result element size should be illustrated.

As a typical result set contains elements from several documents, we need a compact representation so that more than one document can be displayed at the same time.

As a first step in this direction, we developed TextBars, which are based on *TileBars* as described by [158, 159]. Here, a document is presented as one long bar (where length indicates text size), which is segmented according to the XML structure. The start of an element is indicated with a red line. With this method, only elements present in the result set are shown. Since a retrieval result is always a weighted set, this visualization needs to be extended to deal with the weights, too. For the weights, a visual variable is needed that can be used together with TextBars. Since the weights impose a linear order on the

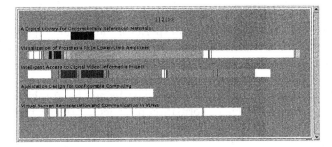

Fig. 4.3. Result presentation with TextBars.

results, the visual variable should be selective (allowing distinction between objects with and without a certain property) as well as ordered (allowing a less-than comparison between values). We choose brightness as the visual variable to use. This is implemented via shades of gray, where white means zero (the object is not relevant at all) and black means one (the object is highly relevant). An example of this visualization method is shown in Figure 4.3.

Whereas TextBars are (in principle) a one-dimensional representation of a document, Treemaps (see [181]) use two dimensions in order to illustrate the structure of an XML document (see Figure 4.4 for an example). Here a document is represented as a rectangular area, which is split horizontally for the first level nodes, vertically for the next level again horizontally for the third level, and so on.

However, for XML documents with a rich structure, this representation is too cluttered. Therefore, we augment the concept and introduce *Partial Treemaps*, where we omit nodes in case they are not a retrieved item or an ancestor of a retrieved item (see [194]).

Tool-tips provide additional information about each retrieved item. In addition to a list of Partial Treemaps, the document itself is shown (processed by an XSL style-sheet) together with a 'table of contents' view. The table of contents is a tree view of the document, but certain 'unimportant' XML elements are left out to constrict the size of the tree. The elements to retain are those that contribute to the overall logical structure of the document. (Typically, the section element would be included, but the bold element would not be included.) As with TextBars, retrieval weights are illustrated as shades of gray. The resulting interface is shown in Figure 4.5.

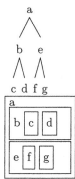

Fig. 4.4. A simple tree and its treemap.

We performed a small user study to test the effect of the visualization on the time the users needed, and on the quality of the relevance judgments. Five users were given nine queries each, together with a visualization of the query results. Each user chose three queries (query results) for judgment with a textual result representation, and three queries for each of our visualizations. The results indicated that TextBars outperform the textual representation in terms of precision, and partial treemaps improve precison even further. On the other hand, the time used for the judgements were about the same for all three methods; participants reported that they had a closer look at the retrieval results and their relationships when using the graphical methods. Thus, it seems that the added information provided by the graphical method improved the quality of the judgments.

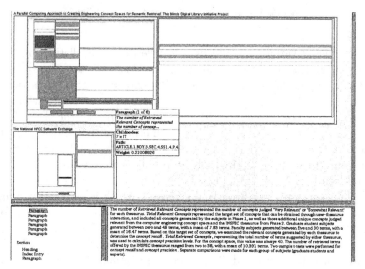

Fig. 4.5. Result presentation with Partial Treemaps. Each element in the treemap has a tool-tip with a summary about that element. In the bottom left, we show a 'table of contents' (tree showing certain elements) and in the bottom right, we show the document itself, at the spot corresponding to the element in the treemap that the user has clicked on.

4.5 Related Work

Our work presented here is based on the document-centric view of XML, which requires a query language that mainly supports selection based on conditions with respect to both structure and content, taking into account the intrinsic uncertainty and vagueness of content-based retrieval. In contrast, the W3C working group on XML query languages has focused on the data-centric view. Following earlier proposals for XML query languages like XML-QL ([96]) or Quilt ([66]), the proposed query language XQuery ([34]) draws heavily on concepts from query languages for object-oriented databases (e.g., OQL) or semistructured data (e.g., Lorel [4]). Due to this origin, XQuery has a much higher expressiveness than XPath and XIRQL. The latter two offer only selection operators, thus results are always complete elements of the original documents. In contrast, XQuery also provides operators for restructuring results as well as for computing aggregations (count, sum, avg, max, min).

A typical XQuery expression has the following structure:

```
FOR PathExpression
WHERE AdditionalSelectionCriteria
RETURN ResultConstruction
```

Here, `PathExpression` may contain one or more path expressions following the XPath standard, where each expression is bound to a variable. Thus, the FOR clause returns ordered lists of tuples of bound variables. The WHERE clause prunes these lists of tuples by testing additional criteria. Finally, the RETURN clause allows for the construction of arbitrary XML documents by combining constant text with the content of the variables.

Since XIRQL is based on XPath, it can be seen as an extension of a subset of XQuery (i.e., only a FOR clause, with a single `PathExpression`) in order to support IR.

The current version of XQuery supports querying for single words in texts only. Recently, discussions about text retrieval extensions for XQuery have started, which aim at providing restricted forms of weighting and ranking (see the requirements [58] and the use cases [10]). However, most of the use cases presented there do not take weighting into account and operate on the syntactical level. (For example, proximity search is required to handle phrases, rather than allowing for linguistic predicates.) Furthermore, ranking is only applicable to full-text search predicates whereas we consider weighting and ranking to be an important feature for other data types, as well, including numbers.

In information retrieval, previous work on structured documents has focused on two major issues:

- The *structural* approach enriches text search by conditions relating to the document structure, e.g., that words should occur in certain parts of a document, or that a condition should be fulfilled in a document part preceding the part satisfying another condition. [228] give a good survey on work in this direction. However, all these approaches are restricted to Boolean retrieval, so neither weighting of index terms nor ranking are considered.
- *Content-based* approaches aim at the retrieval of the most relevant part of a document with respect to a given query. In the absence of explicit structural information, passage retrieval has been investigated by several researches ([157]). Here the system determines a sequence of sentences from the original document that fit the query best.

Only a few researchers have dealt with the combination of explicit structural information and content-based retrieval. [223] use belief networks for determining the most relevant part of structural documents, but allows only for plain text queries, without structural conditions. The FERMI multimedia model ([70]) mentioned before is a general framework for relevance-based retrieval of documents. [196] and [127] describe refinements of this approach based on different logical models.

Comparing the different approaches described above, it turns out that they address different facets of the XML retrieval problem, but there is no approach that solves all the important issues: The data-centric view as well as the structural approach in IR only deal with the structural aspects, but do not support any kind of weighting or ranking. On the other hand, the content-based IR approaches address the weighting issue, but do not allow for structural conditions.

Only a few researchers have tried to combine structural conditions with weighting. [295] extend XML-QL by weighted document indexing; however, this approach is not based on a consistent probabilistic model. As another approach based on XML-QL, [71] introduce an operator for text similarity search on XML documents; so this extension supports only a very specific type of queries. A nice theoretical concept for vagueness with respect to both value conditions and structural conditions is proposed by [268]; however, the underlying query language is rather restricted.

Recently, several approaches have been suggested for integrating structural and content-oriented conditions in a single query, such as the approach by [238] (based on Bayesian Networks) and [233] (based on Language Models). However, there is no support for different data types and corresponding search predicates. [140] present an approach based on the vector space model which allows binary retrieval on non-text conditions and ranked retrieval on text conditions. This model takes into account contextual term weights. This way, terms that are common in the text of an article, say, but rare in the title, get proper treatment for queries regarding both types of context.

The path algebra approach for processing XIRQL is similar to the proximal nodes model described by [228]. (The close relationship between XQL and proximal nodes is discussed by [18].) However, we give a more formal specification of the semantics of the different operators and we also consider hyperlinks. Furthermore, we extend this model by dealing with data types and weighting.

4.6 Conclusions

In this chapter, we have described a query language for information retrieval in XML documents. Current proposals for XML query languages lack most IR-related features, which are weighting and ranking, relevance-oriented search, data types with vague predicates, and structural relativism. We have presented the new query language XIRQL which integrates all these features, and we have described the concepts that are necessary in order to arrive at a consistent model for XML retrieval.

In order to ease query formulation, we have developed a user interface supporting formulation of syntactically and semantically correct queries. For result presentation of XML retrieval, we have described a solution which visualizes also sizes of result elements and structural relationships between elements.

Based on the concepts described in this chapter, we have implemented a retrieval engine named HyREX (*Hy*permedia *R*etrieval *E*ngine for *X*ML). HyREX is designed as an extensible IR architecture. The whole system is open source and can be downloaded from `http://www.is.informatik.uni-duisburg.de/projects/hyrex`. For specific applications, new data types can be added to the system, possibly together with new index structures.

5

Tamino – A Database System Combining Text Retrieval and XML

Harald Schöning

5.1 Introduction

In 1999, Software AG released the first version of its native XML server *Tamino* [276, 274, 275], which includes a native XML database. The term *native* has become popular since then, being used with differing meanings. While some sources, e.g. [10], define a native XML database system only by its appearance to the user (*"Defines a (logical) model for an XML document ... and stores and retrieves documents according to that model. ... For example, it can be built on a relational, hierarchical, or object-oriented database ..."*), Software AG takes the definition further by requiring that a native XML database system has been built and designed for the handling of XML, and is not just a database system for an arbitrary data model with an XML layer on top.

XML by itself leaves many choices for the modeling of data. Two modeling approaches are contrasted by [42]: *Data-centric* documents have a regular structure, order typically does not matter, and mixed content does not occur. This is the type of information usually stored in a relational or object-oriented database. *Document-centric* documents are characterized by a less regular structure, often considerably large text fragments, the occurrence of mixed content, and the significance of the order of the elements in the document. Of course, all choices in between these two extremes are possible.

As a consequence, text retrieval functionality is essential for the efficient search in XML documents, in particular for the document-centric parts of documents. However, it is not sufficient to have this functionality only on the level of the whole document. The structure imposed to documents by XML is significant for the semantics and has to be considered in text retrieval. In addition, it is desirable to combine retrieval with conditions on the well-structured data-centric parts of an XML document. Consider a set of maintenance manuals in XML format. The query *"Find the manuals which were written earlier than 2003 and where in an element 'Caution' the word 'alcohol' is mentioned"*

H. Blanken et al. (Eds.): Intelligent Search on XML Data, LNCS 2818, pp. 77–89, 2003.

combines a numerical comparison on an attribute "CreationDate" with a text search on the element "Caution".

From the beginning, Tamino has provided (Boolean) retrieval functionality on XML documents, elements and attributes. By offering this functionality in an extension to *XPath* [176], Tamino enables the combination of text search with structure-based and value-based search. Since December 2002, Tamino supports the evolving new XML query language *XQuery* [34] in addition to its XPath-based query language. Here, Tamino has chosen to provide its text search functionality via a set of dedicated functions in a Tamino-specific name space, which fits well with the XQuery language.

The next section shortly introduces Tamino's data organization. Then, the text retrieval capabilities in Tamino's XPath-based query language are discussed. The following section shows how Tamino integrates even more text retrieval functionality into XQuery. Text retrieval is very sensitive to languages and scripts used. This aspect is discussed before some remarks on text indexing and a short sketch of related work conclude the chapter.

5.2 Organisation of Data in Tamino

A Tamino database consists of multiple so-called *collections* (Figure 5.1). These are just containers to group documents together. Each document stored in Tamino's data store resides in exactly one collection. A collection can have an associated set of W3C XML Schema descriptions. In each schema description, *doctypes* can be defined using a Tamino specific notation in the extensibility area of W3C XML Schema (*appinfo* element). A doctype identifies one of the global elements declared in a W3C XML Schema as root element. Within a collection, each document is stored as member of exactly one doctype. Tamino can also store document for which no schema description is known. In this case, the doctype name is derived from the root element name of the document. In addition to XML documents, Tamino can also store other objects. If these are text-based (e.g. HTML documents), the search functionality as described below is also available.

Queries operate on a single collection, which is specified in the context of a query, i.e., not in the query itself.

5.3 Text Retrieval Capabilities of Tamino

As pointed out in the introduction, for an XML database system, text retrieval capabilities are mandatory, because XML documents very likely contain considerable amounts of text. Text retrieval on XML must combine structural information with text analysis. A typical question is *"Which book contains the word XML in its abstract?"* rather than *"Which XML documents contain the word XML?"*. As a consequence, it must be possible to focus text retrieval

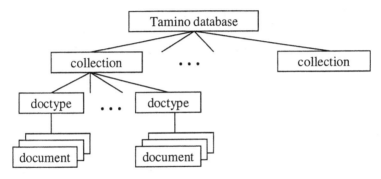

Fig. 5.1. Organization of Data in a Tamino Database

functions on a dedicated attribute value, element content, or maybe even on other nodes such as comments or processing instructions. The textual content of an attribute value does not need much discussions – it's the attribute value after the substitution of all character references and entities. From this textual content, a sequence of words can be derived by disregarding punctuation characters etc. For the moment, we will rely on the reader's intuitive understanding of the term *word*. We will elaborate on this in the section on internationalization issues. In the sequel, we will call this sequence of words the *token value* of a node. On this token value, text retrieval functionality can be applied. For element content, the token value is not always obvious. For element without sub-elements, the token value can be derived from the element's string value as defined be XPath. For elements with sub-elements, this might also be a valid choice. Consider the following XML fragment

```
<Text>XML is an acronym for e<b>x</b>tensible
<b>m</b>arkup <b>l</b>anguage</Text>
```

For the element "Text", the string value is "XML is an acronym for extensible markup language". It makes sense to derive the token value from this string value. In this example, the token value corresponds exactly to the string value, because there is no punctuation etc. to be ignored. Now consider this XML fragment

```
<Author>
<First>Harald</First><Last>Schöning</Last>
</Author>
```

The string value of the element "Author" is "HaraldSchöning" (i.e., a single token). If this string value is used to derive the token value, it will consist of a single word only, and text retrieval searching for "Harald" would fail. It might make more sense to define the token value as "Harald Schöning" in this case, i.e., consider element boundaries as token separators.

In Tamino, the administrator can give directions how to derive the token value of a non-leaf element. There are three available modes:

1. The token value is always derived from the string value of an element.
2. The token value is derived by replacing all sub-element tags by delimiters before computing the string value of an element, and computing the token value from this string value.
3. Flexible token value computation: if the element has mixed content, method 1 is used, otherwise method 2 is used.

The choice among these three methods is orthogonal to the text retrieval functions described in the following sections – these operate on token values, regardless how these have been computed. In the following we describe how structure-aware text retrieval has been embedded in Tamino's query languages.

5.4 First Approach: Extending XPath

As already mentioned, Tamino has chosen XPath [176] as the basis of its first query language. This choice was based on the fact that XPath is standardized and well understood. However, the XPath standard does not contain any text retrieval functionality. There are some functions on sub-string matching basis, which allow to find elements or attributes containing a certain string. For example, the function `contains` returns `true` if the first argument string contains the second argument string, and otherwise returns `false`. Exact matching is required for these functions, even concerning the case of the search strings. As a consequence, systems that want to provide even basic text retrieval functionality have to provide functionality that is not supported by XPath. This can be done by using a completely different query language or by extending XPath.

Tamino has chosen to extend XPath's *equality expression* by the retrieval operator $\sim=$. The left hand side of this operator can be a node (i.e. XML element, attribute, comment, etc.). In the simplest case, the right hand side is just a single token (a word). The result of an expression involving $\sim=$ is a Boolean value. In this simple scenario, the expression returns `true` if the token value of the node specified on the left hand side contains a word matching the token on the right hand side. By default, matching is case-insensitive and ignores accents and similar modifications of characters (see Section 5.6 for details). Consider the following sample XML instance:

```
<?xml version="1.0"?>
<DatabaseSystem company="Software AG" rating="5">
<!-- text generated on Feb. 28 -->
<name>Tamino XML Server</name>
<description>
Software AG's Tamino has been released in 1999. Currently, version
4.1 is available. Tamino is a native XML database system. It stores
XML documents without transforming them to another data model. Its
```

```
query capabilities include text retrieval functionality
</description>
</DatabaseSystem>
```

The query /DatabaseSystem[description ∼= "xml"] returns this instance, because the word XML is contained in the token value of the description element. However, the query /DatabaseSystem[description ∼= "function"] does not match this XML document, because the word function does not occur in this text. The ∼= operator does not operate on sub-string matching, but on word matching. For this reason, the word functionality, which is contained in the text, does not match the search term "function". The query //node()[. ∼= "text"] returns three nodes: the comment node, the description element and the text node which is a child of the description element.

The right hand side of the ∼= operator can also consist of a term specifying multiple search tokens and their interrelation. Two proximity operators can be used to specify the relationship of search tokens: adj requires the tokens to appear adjacent to each other, in the specified order, while near does not require a specific order (but the matches for the search terms have to be adjacent to each other). For example, the query /DatabaseSystem[name ∼= "server" near "xml"] matches the sample instance, while /DatabaseSystem[name ∼= "server" adj "xml"] does not. As a short hand notation for the adj operator, tokens can be separated by spaces, e.g. /DatabaseSystem[description ∼= "another data model"].

Wildcards can be used to search for parts of words. The asterisk matches zero or more characters within a word. For example, the term "*dat*" matches words such as "update", "date", "data", "database", etc. The query /DatabaseSystem[description ∼="a* data model"] matches the description element of the sample instance, while the query /DatabaseSystem [description ∼="a* model"] does not, because it is equivalent to the query /DatabaseSystem [description ∼="a*" adj "model"] and there is no occurrence of a word starting with "a" immediately preceding the word model. A single asterisk matches a single word. As a consequence, the query /DatabaseSystem [description∼="a* * model"] also matches our example.

Of course, conditions can be combined with other conditions on text and with conventional conditions, e.g. on numerical values. The query *Show me all database systems from Software AG with a rating higher than 3, which carry the word XML in their name and in their description* can be written as /DatabaseSystem[@company= "Software AG" and @rating>3 and name∼="XML" and description∼="XML"]. Note that the comparison with the company name is a usual XPath comparison, which means that it is case sensitive.

While this XPath extension gives a considerable amount of retrieval functionality, it has its drawbacks:

- The ∼= operator is a non-standard extension of XPath

- The right hand side uses a proprietary syntax to express proximity conditions. Adding further functionality means extending this syntax by further proprietary constructs.
- The approach cannot be easily extended to introduce advanced functionality such as ranking, highlighting etc.

For these reasons, Software AG has chosen a different approach when integrating text retrieval functionality into its XQuery implementation.

5.5 Adding Text Retrieval Functionality to XQuery

Starting with version 4.1, Tamino supports XQuery in addition to its "traditional" XPath-based query language. Of course, Tamino's retrieval functionality must be available via XQuery as well. While it would have been easy to adopt the XPath extension described above to XQuery (because XQuery includes XPath's path expressions), Software AG has chosen a different approach.

XQuery has the concept of functions. Built-in functions belong to a dedicated XQuery name space, and user defined functions can be assigned to any other name space. Software AG provides another package of built-in functions from a Software AG name space which include Tamino's text retrieval functionality.

5.5.1 Replacements for the ~= Operator

The function `containsText` accepts a node and a search string and returns a Boolean value which indicates whether there is a match between the node's content and the search string. This function implements the functionality of ~= except that the explicit `adj` and `near` operators are not supported. For example, the XPath-based query /DatabaseSystem[description ="a* * model"] can be written as[1]

```
declare namespace
tf="http://namespaces.softwareag.com/tamino/TaminoFunction"
for $d in input()/DatabaseSystem
where tf:containsText($d/description, "a* * model")
return $d
```

or, more compact, as

```
declare namespace
tf="http://namespaces.softwareag.com/tamino/TaminoFunction"
input()/DatabaseSystem[tf:containsText(
                       description, "a* * model")]
```

---

[1] The function `input()` returns all documents of the context collection.

The functionality of `adj` and `near` is provided in an extended form by the functions `containsAdjacentText` and `containsNearText`. In addition to a variable number of search strings consisting of single tokens these functions accept a parameter `distance`. If `distance` is 1, this corresponds to the semantics of `adj` or `near`, respectively, i.e., `containsText(.,"a b")` is equivalent to `containsAdjacentText(., 1, "a", "b")`. If distance is 2, a 1-word gap between the search tokens is accepted, i.e., `containsAdjacentText` `(input()/DatabaseSystem/description, 2, "another", "model")` applied to our sample instance yields `true`. This functionality is not available in the XPath-based query language. The functions can operate on an arbitrary number of search strings. The distance parameter is then used to compute the maximum overall distance between matching words. For example, for `containsAdjacentText(., 4, "a", "b", "c")` to return `true`, the context node must contain "a", "b", and "c" within 6 subsequent words, e.g. "a f g h b c"[2].

5.5.2 Extended Retrieval Functionality

Search strings as discussed above consist of words, or of word fragments combined with wildcards. Due to the matching rules, each such search string can match several words. This is obvious for wildcards (e.g., "dat*" matches "date", "data", etc.), but also holds for singe-word search terms as explained in Section 5.6 below. The concepts presented so far rely on syntactic similarity of words. In the current Tamino version 4.1.4, search can also be based on phonetic similarity (words that sound similar) and linguistic similarity (words that have the same stem). The function `phonetic` matches words that sound like the token passed to the function as argument. The function `stem` matches words that have the same stem(s) as the token passed as argument. For example, the expression `containsAdjacentText(., 1,` `tf:phonetic("Tamino"), "XML", tf:stem("server"))` returns `true` if the context node contains a word that sounds like Tamino immediately preceding the word "XML" immediately before a word that has the same stem as "server" (e.g. "servers").

5.5.3 Highlighting

A common requirement in text retrieval is to highlight the places where search terms match a document of the result set. For example, when searching a set of HTML documents for the word "XML", one could expect that in a browser-based display of the result, the word "XML" is highlighted in all matching documents. For HTML documents, it might be easy to define a method for highlighting parts of the document, e.g., using a differently colored

---

[2] The maximum matching sequence length is computed as distance + number of tokens in search string - 1.

background. For XML, the method is less obvious. There is no presentation-related standard markup in XML. Furthermore, matching documents might not be displayed, but be processed by some application, which then needs to identify the matches. As a consequence, the method of highlighting must be left to the application. However, to enable the application to do highlighting, references to the matching places must be passed. For such a reference, it is not sufficient to point to an entire element or attribute which contains a match, but the match reference must point into the content of a node. Tamino provides a set of functions to create such references: `createTextReference`, `createAdjacentTextReference`, and `createNearTextReference` work analogously to `containsText`, `containsAdjacentText`, and `containsNearText`. However, they do not return a Boolean result, but a sequence of references (one for each match). For example, this sequence can be used as input for the function `highlight`, which encloses each referenced match with a pair of processing instructions whose target name is passed as function argument. The body of the processing instruction consists of a + or − (begin or end highlighting) and a running number. For example, the query

```
declare namespace
tf="http://namespaces.softwareag.com/tamino/TaminoFunction"
for $x in input()//description
let $hi := tf:createTextReference($x,"XML")
where $hi
return tf:highlight($x, $hi, "HI")
```

when applied to our sample document, yields the result

```
<description> Software AG's Tamino has been released in 1999.
Currently, version 4.1 is available. Tamino is a native
<?HI + 1?>XML<?HI - 1?> database system. It stores
<?HI + 2?>XML<?HI - 2?> documents without transforming them to
another data model. Its query capabilities include text
retrieval functionality.
</description>
```

Processing instructions have been chosen for this purpose, because they do not change the well-formedness or schematic validity of a document, and can be applied even if the matching sequence in the document spans multiple elements.

The sequence of references can also be used to derive the number of matches found (`count(tf:createTextReference($x, "XML"))`), e.g., for returning the documents with the most matches first (ranking).

5.6 Internationalization Issues

Retrieval functionality highly depends on the language and script used, and sometimes also on the application area. In particular, in the context of Tamino, two issues deserve special attention: the identification of a token and the matching of tokens.

5.6.1 Token Identification

In Western languages and scripts, words are typically separated by spaces. In addition, punctuation characters such as question mark or comma might indicate word boundaries. Words become tokens; the punctuation characters themselves are not considered to contribute to tokens. While this seems to be an easy rule, a detailed investigation shows that it has to be refined, and has to be adapted to language or application rules. Which characters have to be considered as punctuation characters? The list might differ with the language used. Even within one language, some issues can be discussed. For example, the handling of the character "&" is not immediately clear: while it might make sense to handle "R&D" as a single token (i.e. consider "&" as a character), if might as well make sense to treat "research&development" as three tokens ("&" as token on its own) or as two tokens (ignoring "&").

Tamino has a pre-defined handling for all Unicode characters, e.g. defining a character class such as `character`. This classification has been derived from the Unicode database [300]. An administrator can tailor this pre-defined handling. This is done by storing an XML document, which describes the modifications to Tamino's default, into a dedicated doctype `ino:transliteration` (see below). The actual definition defines the rules to determine what is considered to be a token.

However, there are languages and scripts where these character-based token recognition methods fail, e.g. for Japanese, where words typically are not separated by spaces. For such languages, token identification methods must be more elaborated, e.g. dictionary-based. Tamino supports such methods for Japanese, Simplified and Traditional Chinese, and Korean.

5.6.2 Matching Words

When searching for a token, some character variations might be insignificant for some languages. For example, accents should be ignored when doing retrieval in a German text. When searching an English text it might be a good idea to ignore diereses, while in German e.g. "ä" is treated as a character on its own. On the other hand, in German it is common to replace "ä" by "ae", such that retrieval for the word "Bär" should also match "Baer". Again, `ino:transliteration` can be used to define matching rules on character basis.

As already mentioned, Tamino by default does case-insensitive search. Some applications might prefer case-sensitive handling. This also can be switched via `ino:transliteration`. When the following XML document is stored into `ino: transliteration`, it defines the following rules:

- case-insensitive matching (ino:translation="true");
- each character matches all other characters with the same base character defined in the Unicode database (ino:baseChar="true");
- the ampersand is treated as a character;
- the German character "ß" is handled equivalently to the character sequence "SS".

```
<?xml version="1.0"?>
<ino:transliteration
xmlns:ino="http://namespaces.softwareag.com/tamino/response2"
     ino:baseChar="true" ino:translation="true">
<ino:character  ino:value="&amp;"
                    ino:class="character"/>
<ino:character  ino:value="ß"
                    ino:class="character" ino:mapTo="SS" />
</ino:transliteration>
```

5.6.3 Other Internationalization Issues

Unfortunately, there are even more internationalization issues involved in text retrieval than described so far. A commonly recognized issue is that of collation sequences: when two strings are compared, are they equal, or which one is less than the other? While text retrieval functionality does not care if a string is less than another, the aspect of equality might matter. For example, in a German collation, the strings "Straße" and "Strasse" might be considered to be equal. Although Tamino supports collation sequences, we have decided not to use the equality definitions of these collations for word matching, but use the entirely independent mechanism of ino:transliteration as described above. The rationale behind this decision is that for text retrieval, typically a much more tolerant notion of equality (matching) is needed, e.g. concerning case sensitivity.

Tamino has functions that consider the stem of a word. These functions inherently are language dependent. The same holds for phonetic search. Support of languages not included in the Tamino delivery can be added by providing dedicated program libraries with appropriate support for stemming and derivation of phonetic patterns.

5.7 Index Support

Tamino's retrieval functionality is available on all XML documents (and other text documents) stored in Tamino, even without dedicated index definitions. However, performance is considerably increased by the definition of text indexes over data that is often searched by the retrieval functionality. Such indexes can be defined on any node in an XML schema, regardless of its content model. Indexing is done on the token value of the node as defined above.

A text index is defined in the XML schema for a doctype. Tamino uses the annotation mechanism of XML schema [297] to preserve standard conforming XML schema documents while adding Tamino-specific information. The following fragment of an XML schema illustrates the definition of a text index on the element description.

```
<?xml version = "1.0" encoding = "UTF-8"?>
<xs:schema
  xmlns:tsd = "http://namespaces.softwareag.com/tamino/
TaminoSchemaDefinition"
  xmlns:xs = "http://www.w3.org/2001/XMLSchema">
<!-- left out other definitions -->
<xs:element name = "description" type = "xs:string">
  <xs:annotation>
    <xs:appinfo>
      <tsd:elementInfo>
        <tsd:physical>
          <tsd:native>
            <tsd:index>
              <tsd:text/>
            </tsd:index>
          </tsd:native>
        </tsd:physical>
      </tsd:elementInfo>
    </xs:appinfo>
  </xs:annotation>
</xs:element>
```

5.8 Related Work

The XQuery Working Group and the XSL Working Group of W3C have created a draft of full-text requirements [58] that an XQuery extension for text retrieval should fulfill and corresponding full-text use cases [10]. The Tamino text-retrieval functionality matches all the requirements except that Tamino does not provide a wildcard for a single character and does not support stop words. The requirement to support stop words is questionable anyway as it adds no power to the text retrieval functionality.

Oracle 9iR2 also contains some text retrieval functionality on values of XMLType. The function CONTAINS accepts search strings that can refer to XPath expressions. The expression CONTAINS(DatabaseSystem, 'XML INPATH (//description)') returns a numerical value which is zero if the path //description does not point to a text containing the word "XML", and otherwise is a positive numeric value that increases with the number of matches found. However, the CONTAINS function can only be applied if an appropriate index has been defined on the referenced column. Furthermore, it is not possible to combine multiple predicates on the same sub-tree of an XML document. Oracle has also extended XPath by a function ora:contains which does not need and does not use a text index. The following Oracle query finds the name of all database systems whose description contains the word "XML" or the word "HTML".

```
SELECT D.DatabaseSystem.extractValue('//name')
    AS name
FROM DBMS D
WHERE D.DatabaseSystem.existsNode(
      '/DatabaseSystem[ora:contains(
                    description,"XML" OR "HTML")>0]');
```

In DB2 UDB, the *Text Extender* can be used for text search on XML. If a corresponding XML-aware index has been defined properly, the following expression returns true if the description of a database system contains the words "XML" or "HTML": CONTAINS(DatabaseSystem,'model DatabaseSystem sections (/DatabaseSystem/description) ("XML"|"HTML")'). This function does not search on sub-elements. Multiple predicates on a sub-tree cannot be combined.

Progress Software's (formerly eXcelon) eXtensible Information Server has integrated two dedicated text retrieval functions into its XPath and XQuery implementations: xln:contains-words and xln:icontains-words. The difference between these two is that xml:icontains-words is case insensitive, while xln:contains-words is not. These functions can search for a set of words. An option specifies whether this set is treated as a sequence of contiguous words, or a set of which any or all words have to be found in any order. Furthermore, search can be restricted to the first level of child nodes. Another option controls whether markup separates tokens or not. Wildcards are supported, but only at the end of words. Tokenization can be switched to Japanese. Text indexes are available, but optional.

In [46], XQuery is extended by a new keyword for text retrieval purposes. This is an extension that modifies the XQuery syntax, while Software AG's approach integrates well with XQuery as defined by W3C.

5.9 Conclusions

As its first query language, Tamino has extended XPath to include a text retrieval operator. With this approach, it has been possible to specifically query all levels of a document, and combine predicates on text with predicates on structure and other content of a document. For its second query language

XQuery, Tamino uses another approach to integrate text retrieval functionality. A dedicated set of functions provides the requested functionality while preserving XQuery standard conformity and even extending the functional power of the first query language. Text retrieval can be based on similarity of syntax, of sound, and of linguistic stem. For the next version of Tamino, a set of thesaurus-based functions is planned, which then enable searching by the similarity of meanings of words.

The process of XQuery standardization is not yet finished. It is unlikely that the first XQuery recommendation will contain text retrieval functionality. Rather, a separate recommendation for text retrieval in XQuery might be created. Such a recommendation might trigger further enhancements to Tamino's text retrieval functionality.

Part III

Retrieval Models

Introduction

XML will be the method of choice for representing all kinds of documents in product catalogs, digital libraries, scientific data repositories, and across the Web and the Grid. However, despite the additional structure and annotations in XML data, searching a specific piece of information or all parts of documents that are relevant for a specific topic often poses major challenges. Several technologies can serve as starting points for research towards intelligent searching of XML data, but each of them alone is inherently limited:

- From a *database system viewpoint*, the natural approach is to use XML query languages such as XQuery or XPath. These languages exploit the structure and labels of XML documents in a combination of pattern matching and traditional SQL-style logical conditions, but there is no notion of semantic similarity and thus no way of producing ranked retrieval results. Boolean retrieval, however, all too often either produces way too many matches or yields an (almost) empty result list.
- In the *information retrieval area*, most prior work, including the state-of-the-art Web search engines, do not consider the structure of XML-style data and latent ontological information that is implicit in the element and attribute labels of XML documents, DTDs, and XML schemas, thus missing a great opportunity for more effective search.
- In the *field of ontological and categorization frameworks*, with its roots in Artificial Intelligence, the construction of ontologies and classification of documents has been studied for a long time, but the interest in more complete ontologies and machine learning techniques for automatic assignment of documents to topics has been revived only recently.

Obviously, careful integration of several techniques from the above directions promises synergies. This part of the book presents various approaches for such methodological combinations. As XML retrieval is a new field, there is a natural diversity of different approaches, and this is reflected in the following chapters. The emphasis of this part is on the models for XML query semantics, in particular, how to define similarity between an XML document and a user query and how to compute scores and rankings. All of the presented methods have also been implemented in prototype systems or, in one case, even in a commercial product.

Chapter 6 by Grabs and Schek presents a flexible vector space model for representing XML data, where vector spaces and their corresponding tf*idf weights are generated "on the fly" based on the choice of significant tags. This also provides support for flexibly delivering subdocuments at different levels of XML hierarchies as query results, as opposed to fixed retrieval granularities that would always return entire documents or individual elements.

Chapter 7 by Hiemstra presents a statistical language modeling approach for XML retrieval. In this kind of model, the data is interpreted as being generated by a probabilistic distribution, for example, a Gaussian or Poisson mixture, whose parameters are fitted to the data. Then, Bayesian reasoning with appropriately chosen priors can be used to compute relevance scores for and rank query results. The chapter also presents experiments that demonstrate the effectiveness of this approach.

Chapter 8 by Schenkel, Theobald, and Weikum discusses how ontologies can be exploited for improved retrieval quality. Starting with ontological knowledge from external thesauri like WordNet, a graph-based ontology is constructed with edge weights reflecting the strength of relationships between concepts. These weights are factored into the evaluation of similarity predicates on XML element names and text content. This approach has been implemented in the XXL prototype system.

Chapter 9 by Weber describes relevance feedback methods in the context of XML retrieval. Motivated by cognitive models and empirical studies of user behavior, it decomposes the approach into five different dimensions of query refinement as a reaction to the user's relevance assessment of an initial query's top results.

Chapter 10 by Theobald, Schenkel, and Weikum presents an approach for automatic classification of XML documents. When dealing with non-schematic XML data or heterogeneous collections of schemas that can not be easily reconciled, machine learning techniques for classification can help to better organize the data into topic directories. The chapter shows how structural properties and the tag paths in XML documents can be exploited for improved accuracy of classifiers. It also discusses how mappings of tags and content words into ontological concepts can help in this context.

Chapter 11 by Abholhassani, Fuhr, and Gövert addresses the construction of XML documents with semantically meaningful tags. For plain text or documents with simple annotations only such as HTML data, information extraction techniques can be used to automatically generate markup for named entities such as persons, institutions, places, dates, etc. The chapter surveys the state of the art and presents an approach that combines several techniques such as regular expression matching into an extensible workbench.

6

Flexible Information Retrieval on XML Documents

Torsten Grabs and Hans-Jörg Schek

6.1 Introduction

XML – short for the eXtended Markup Language defined by the World Wide Web Consortium in 1998 – is very successful as a format for data interchange. The reason is the high flexibility of the semistructured data model underlying XML [3]. Therefore, XML documents are well suited for a broad range of applications covering both rigidly structured data such as relations as well as less rigorously structured data such as text documents. So far, research on database systems has spent much effort on *data-centric processing* of rigidly structured XML documents. However, the importance of *document-centric processing* increases the more XML extends to application domains requiring less rigorously structured data representation.

In the context of document-centric XML processing, this chapter focuses on the problem of *flexible ranked and weighted retrieval* on XML documents [139]. Like information retrieval on text, XML retrieval aims to effectively and efficiently cover the information needs of users searching for relevant content in a collection of XML documents. However, due to the flexibility inherent to XML, conventional text retrieval techniques are not directly applicable to ranked and weighted retrieval on XML documents.

First, the notion of a document collection must be refined in the context of XML. This is because often a single large XML document comprises all the content. Figure 6.1 illustrates such an XML document representing a collection of books. A document collection in the context of conventional information retrieval in contrast usually comprises many documents. For instance, global collection-wide IR statistics such as document frequencies, i.e., the number of documents a word occurs in, build on the conventional notion where a collection comprises many documents.

Second, different parts of a single XML document may have content from different domains. Figure 6.1 illustrates this with the different branches of the bookstore – one for medicine books and one for computer science books. Intuitively, the term 'computer' is more significant for books in the medicine

H. Blanken et al. (Eds.): Intelligent Search on XML Data, LNCS 2818, pp. 95–106, 2003.
© Springer-Verlag Berlin Heidelberg 2003

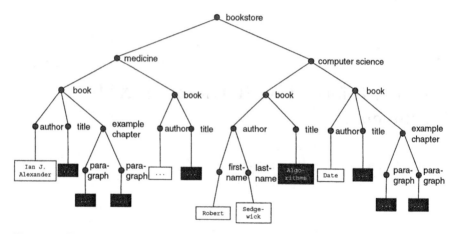

Fig. 6.1. Exemplary XML document with textual content represented as shaded boxes

branch than in the computer science branch. Conventional information retrieval however assumes that the documents of the collection are from the same domain. Again, global IR statistics such as document frequencies depend on this assumption that seems not longer appropriate in the context of XML. Note that this is indeed an issue when users refer to the different domains when posing their queries. We distinguish two different cases in this respect, namely *single-category retrieval* and *multi-category retrieval*.

Single-category retrieval stands for queries that refer to a single domain or *category* in isolation, i.e., only content from one category is subject to the query. The difficulty with this type of queries is that global IR statistics such as document frequencies may not be meaningful depending on the scope of the query. Think again of a collection with only a single large XML document: conventional document frequencies cannot be larger than 1 in this case. Document frequencies of terms occurring in the collection always equal 1 since there is only a single large document. Document frequencies of the other terms are 0, as usual. Hence, a more fine-grained resolution of global IR statistics is needed in the context of XML retrieval, as the following XML illustrates.

Example 1 (Single-Category Retrieval). Consider a user searching for relevant books in the computer science branch of the example document in Fig. 6.1. Obviously, he restricts his queries to books from this particular category. Thus, it is not appropriate to process this query with term weights derived from both the categories medicine and computer science in combination. This is because the document frequencies in medicine may skew the overall term weights such that a ranking with term weights for computer science in isolation would increase retrieval quality.

Now think of another user who wants to process a query on several categories, or he does not care at all to which category the retrieved content belongs. We call these queries *multi-category retrieval*. The difficulty with this type of queries is again that conventional IR statistics are not meaningful in the XML context, as already argued above. A more promising alternative in turn is to rely on IR statistics reflecting the scope, i.e., the granularity, of the query in the XML document. We denote this type of statistics as *query-specific statistics* in the following. We expect query-specific statistics to avoid inappropriate ranking and to increase retrieval quality. The need for query-specific statistics follows from the requirement that users want to dynamically, i.e., at query time, define the granularity of retrieval in the context of XML. Hence, retrieval processing must dynamically derive the query-specific statistics in order to appropriately reflect the different combinations of domains covered by the query.

Example 2 (Multi-Category Retrieval). Recall the XML document from the previous example (cf. Fig. 6.1). The document in the figure reflects the different categories of books such as medicine or computer science with separate elements for the respective categories. Think of a user who does not care to which category a book belongs, as long as it covers the information need expressed in his query. The granularity of his query are all categories. Hence, the query is an example of *multi-category retrieval* which requires query-specific statistics. Taking again the document in Fig. 6.1, this means statistics must be derived from both categories medicine and computer science in combination.

Third, XML allows to hierarchically structure information within a document such that each document has tree structure. Users want to refer to this structure when searching for relevant information. The intuition behind this is that an XML element is composed from different parts, i.e., its children elements. For instance, a chapter element may comprise a title and one or several paragraph elements. This is an issue since the children elements may contribute to the content of an XML element by different degrees. Fuhr at al. for instance reflect the importance of such composition relationships with so-called augmentation weights (cf. Chap. 4). This also affects relevance-ranking for XML retrieval, as the following example shows.

Example 3 (Nested Retrieval). Consider again the XML document shown in Fig. 6.1. Think of a query searching for relevant book elements in the medicine branch. Such a query has to process content that is hierarchically structured: the title elements as well as the paragraph elements describe a particular book element. Intuitively, content that occurs in the title element is deemed more important than that in the paragraphs of the example chapter, and relevance ranking for books should reflect this.

Our aim with information retrieval on XML documents is to provide for *effective retrieval over arbitrary combinations of element types* – or briefly *flexible retrieval* from XML documents. We start with a discussion of related work in Sect. 6.2. Section 6.3 then explains our document and query model in more detail. The main innovation presented in Sect. 6.3 is a retrieval model to dynamically derive the query-specific statistics from underlying basic statistics. We generalize previous work on indexing nodes for XML [128], augmentation [127], and multi-category retrieval from flat documents [137] to flexible information retrieval on XML documents. The section also discusses the semantics of different query types under the vector space retrieval model. Section 6.4 concludes the chapter and points to future work.

6.2 Related Work

Previous work on information retrieval from structured documents has already investigated different approaches to combine queries on document structure and document content. [17] gives an overview and taxonomy of these approaches, including PAT expressions [257], Tree Matching [187], Proximal Nodes [228], and Lists of References [206]. However, these approaches disregard advanced retrieval models providing for term weighting and ranking. But, weighting and ranking are indispensable for competitive retrieval quality, as already [119, 261] argue. Therefore, the mere capability to search for keywords in textual content of XML elements [118] or to match regular expressions over character strings does not suffice for retrieval on XML documents. Instead, support for state-of-the-art retrieval models with weighting and relevance ranking similar to conventional approaches such as vector space retrieval or probabilistic retrieval models is needed for effective retrieval from XML.

To tackle this issue, Theobald et al. propose the query language XXL and its implementation with the XXL Search Engine [296]. Regarding IR statistics their approach treats XML documents as flat structures. Fuhr et al. have already argued in [127, 128] that this comes too short for semi-structured data such as XML. Fuhr et al. tackle this issue by a technique denoted as *augmentation*. The idea is to introduce so-called *augmentation weights* that downweigh statistics such as term weights when the terms are propagated upwards in the document tree. To do so, Fuhr et al. [128] group XML elements to so-called *indexing nodes* that implement the inverted lists for efficient retrieval. They constitute the granularity of retrieval with their approach. Users can search at the granularity of the indexing nodes and hierarchical combinations of them. Term weights are properly augmented in this case. However, global IR statistics such as document frequencies are still derived for the document collection as a whole. Hence, consistent retrieval with this approach requires all document components to come from the same domain. In other words, retrieval from heterogeneous XML content is not supported. Another drawback of the approach is that the assignment of XML elements to indexing nodes is static. Hence, users cannot retrieve dynamically, i.e., at query time, from arbitrary combinations of element types. In other words, retrieval is only feasible at the granularity of indexing nodes and hierarchical combinations of them.

Our approach takes over some of these ideas and generalizes them such that consistent retrieval with arbitrary query granularities, i.e., arbitrary combinations of element types, is feasible. This makes the restriction of retrieval granularity to indexing nodes obsolete and allows for flexible retrieval from XML collections. Our approach to guarantee consistent ranking builds on our own previous work on conventional retrieval with flat (unstructured) documents from different domains [137]. We extend this previous work here to cover hierarchically structured documents such as XML documents as well.

6.3 Flexible Retrieval on XML Documents

6.3.1 Vector Space Retrieval on Flat Document Texts

As already argued in Sect. 6.2, weighted and ranked retrieval models provide superior retrieval quality as compared to Boolean retrieval models. With ranked retrieval, the top ranked and probably most relevant documents appear at the beginning of the lists of documents that are returned to the users as the results to their queries. One of the most popular ranked retrieval models is vector space retrieval. With the *vector space retrieval model* [263], queries are plain text or a sequence of keywords. There are no operators to combine query terms, as it is the case with Boolean retrieval. Vector space retrieval represents both document texts and query texts as vectors in an n-dimensional space. Each such dimension stands for a distinct term of the vocabulary (or a stem of a word in case of stemming). The model maps each document text d to a vector v in this space as follows: for each term t, map the number of occurrences of t in d, i.e., the *term frequency* of t, to position i in v, where i is the dimension assigned to t in the n-dimensional space. A query text is mapped analogously to a vector q. The intuition of vector space retrieval given some query vector q and a set of document vectors C is as follows: the document with $v \in C$ that has the smallest distance to q is deemed most relevant to the query. In practice however, computation of relevance or retrieval status value (*rsv* for short) is a function of the vectors q and d in the n-dimensional space. Different functions are conceivable such as the inner product of vectors or the cosine measure. The remainder of this chapter builds on the popular so-called *tf idf ranking function* [262]. *tf idf* ranking – compared to the other ranking measures – has the advantage that it approximates the importance of terms regarding a document collection. This importance is represented by the so-called *inverted document frequency* of terms, or *idf* for short. The *idf* of a term t is defined as $idf(t) = \log \frac{N}{df(t)}$, where N stands for the number of documents in the collection and $df(t)$ is the number of documents that contain the term (the so-called *document frequency* of t). Given a document vector d and a query vector q, the retrieval status value $rsv(d, q)$ is defined as follows:

$$rsv(d, q) = \sum_{t \in terms(q)} tf(t, d) \; idf(t)^2 \; tf(t, q) \qquad (6.1)$$

Going over the document collection C and sorting each document-query-pair by decreasing $rsv(d, q)$ $(d \in C)$ yields the ranking, i.e., the result for the query.

In contrast to Boolean retrieval, ranked retrieval models and in particular vector space retrieval assume that documents are flat, i.e., unstructured information. Therefore, a straight-forward extension to cover retrieval from semistructured data such as XML documents is not obvious. But, ranked retrieval models are known to yield better retrieval results as outline previously. In the following, we therefore refine conventional IR statistics to more fine-grained ones. In particular, the element frequency $ef(t)$ and the term frequency $tf(t, e)$ refine the resolution of the conventional document frequency and term frequency for flexible retrieval on XML documents. The following subsections investigate this problem in more detail and presents approaches to combine flexible retrieval granularity with query-specific statistics.

6.3.2 Document and Query Model for Flexible XML Retrieval

In the context of this chapter, XML documents are represented as trees. We rely on the tree structures defined by the W3C XPath Recommendation [176]. This yields tree representations of XML documents such as the one shown in Fig. 6.1. Obviously, all textual content of a document is located in the leaf nodes of the tree (shaded boxes in the figure). For ease of presentation, we further assume that the collection comprises only a single XML document – a situation one frequently encounters also in practical settings (cf. Chap. 18). Note that this is not a restriction: it is always possible to add a virtual root node to compose several XML documents into a single tree representation such that the subtrees of the virtual root are the original XML documents.

Flexible retrieval on XML now aims to identify those subtrees in the XML document that cover the user's information need. The granularity of retrieval in our model are the nodes of the tree representation, i.e., subtrees of the XML document. The result of a query is a ranked list of such subtrees. Users define their queries using so-called *structure constraints* and *content constraints*.

Structure constraints define the scope, i.e., the granularity, of the query. With our query model, the granularity of a query is defined by a label path. Taking the XML document in Fig. 6.1 for instance, the path /bookstore/medicine/book defines a query scope. The extension of the query scope comprises all nodes in the XML document tree that have the same path originating at the root node. The extension of /bookstore/medicine/book comprises two instances – the first and the second medicine book in the document. Users formulate their structure constraints using path expressions. With the XPath syntax [176] and the XML document in Figure 6.1, the XPath path expression //book for instance yields a query granularity comprising /bookstore/medicine/book and /bookstore/computer-science/book.

Content constraints in turn work on the actual XML elements in the query scope. We distinguish between so-called *vague content constraints* and *precise content constraints*. A vague content constraint defines a ranking over the

XML element instances in the query scope. A precise content constraint in turn defines an additional selection predicate over the result of the ranking. In the following, we exclude precise content constraints from our discussion and focus instead on vague content constraints for ranked text search. The following example illustrates the use of structure and content constraints in combination.

Example 4 (Content Constraints and Structure Contraints). Using the XIRQL syntax as outlined in Chap. 4, consider the query //book[. cw 'XML Introduction'] on the XML document in Fig. 6.1. The query searches for books relevant to 'XML Introduction'. The structure constraint is the path expression //book. Hence, the scope of the query are /bookstore/medicine/book and /bookstore/computer-science/book. The content constraint in turn is the vague predicate [. cw 'XML Introduction']. It specifies to rank the elements in the query scope in descending order according to their relevance to the query text 'XML Introduction'.

6.3.3 Basic Indexing Nodes: Fine-Granular Indexing for XML

To increase the flexibility of retrieval granularities for searching XML, Fuhr et al. group XML elements (at the instance level) to so-called *indexing nodes*, as outlined in Sect. 6.2 already. They constitute the granularity of ranking with their approach while IR statistics such as *idf* term weights are derived for the collection as a whole. The drawback of the approach is that the assignment of XML elements to indexing nodes is static. Users cannot retrieve dynamically, i.e., at query time, from arbitrary combinations of element types. Moreover, this can lead to inconsistent rankings when users restrict the scopes of their queries to element types that do not directly correspond to indexing nodes and whose IR statistics and especially term distributions differ from the collection-wide ones.

A naive solution to support flexible retrieval with consistent rankings would be to keep indexes and statistics for each combination of element types and element nestings that could possibly occur in a query. However, the amount of storage that this approach requires for indexes and statistics is prohibitively large and is therefore not a viable solution. We therefore refine the notion of indexing nodes to keep indexes and statistics only for basic element types. When it comes to single-category retrieval, multi-category retrieval or nested retrieval, the approach proposed here derives the required indexes and statistics from the underlying basic ones on-the-fly, i.e., at query runtime. This has the advantage that the amount of storage needed to process IR queries on XML content is small as compared to the naive approach.

The difficulty with multi-category queries and nested retrieval is to compute the query-specific statistics to reflect the scope, i.e., the granularity, of the query. Otherwise, query processing may lead to unexpected rankings. This is in contrast to conventional retrieval where the retrieval granularity is the complete document or a predefined field such as abstract or title.

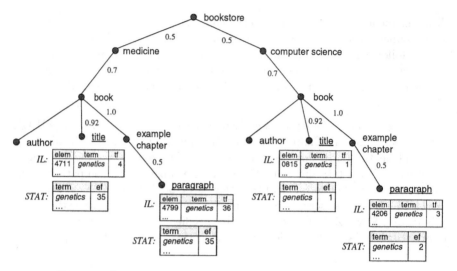

Fig. 6.2. Basic indexing nodes of the XML document in Fig. 6.1

To address this issue, flexible retrieval on XML documents first requires to identify the basic element types of an XML collection that contain textual content. These nodes are denoted as *basic indexing nodes*. There are several alternatives how to derive the basic indexing nodes from an XML collection:

- The decision can be taken completely automatically such that each distinct element type at the leaf level with textual content is treated as a separate indexing node.
- An alternative is that the user or an administrator decides how to assign element types to basic indexing nodes.

These approaches can further rely on an ontology that, for instance, suggests to group element types summary and abstract into the same basic indexing node. For ease of presentation, let us assume that the basic indexing nodes have already been determined, and the respective textual XML content already underwent IR pre-processing, including term extraction and stemming. Flexible retrieval then annotates the basic indexing nodes of the element type structure with the IR indexes and statistics derived from their textual content. Figure 6.2 illustrates this for the Data Guide [133, 132] of the example document in Figure 6.1. Element types with underlined names in the figure stand for basic indexing nodes and have been annotated with inverted lists (*IL*) and statistics (*STAT*) for vector space retrieval. The annotations of the edges in the figure represent augmentation weights. Their meaning is explained in more detail in the subsequent discussion of nested retrieval.

The concept of basic indexing nodes is in contrast to the notion of indexing nodes proposed by [128]. [128] derive IR statistics for the collection as a whole while the approach proposed here keeps different IR statistics for each basic indexing node. Building on the notion of basic indexing nodes, we explain in the following how flexible IR on XML content is feasible with single-category retrieval, multi-category retrieval and nested retrieval.

6.3.4 Flexible Retrieval Granularity for XML Retrieval

Single-Category Retrieval

Single-category retrieval with XML works on a basic indexing node. For example, the path /bookstore/medicine/book/title defines a single category in Fig. 6.2. The granularity of retrieval are the elements in the category.

The following discussion takes over the usual definition of retrieval status value with the vector space retrieval model (cf. Definition 6.1): As usual, t denotes a term, and $tf(t, e)$ is its term frequency in an element e. Let N_{cat} and $ef_{cat}(t)$ denote the number of elements at the single category cat and the element frequency of term t with cat, respectively. In analogy to the inverted document frequency for conventional vector space retrieval, we define *inverted element frequency (ief)* as

$$ief_{cat}(t) = \log \frac{N_{cat}}{ef_{cat}(t)} \qquad (6.2)$$

The retrieval status value of an element e for a single-category query q is then

$$rsv(e, q) = \sum_{t \in terms(q)} tf(t, e) \ ief_{cat}(t)^2 \ tf(t, q) \qquad (6.3)$$

Our motivation to rely on different element frequencies depending on the category queried is analogous to conventional vector space retrieval where collection-specific statistics such as document frequencies have been shown to increase retrieval quality [119, 261].

Multi-category Retrieval

In contrast to single-category retrieval, *multi-category retrieval* with XML works with *multi-categories*. Multi-categories are defined by path expressions: /bookstore/medicine/book/title|/bookstore/computerscience/book/title for example defines a multi-category query (cf. Fig. 6.2). As with single-category retrieval, the granularity of retrieval with a multi-category query are all elements that match this path expression. A multi-category query is given by a path expression that may contain choices. When it comes to multi-category retrieval, the query-specific statistics and the *rsv* must reflect this. The approach for flexible XML retrieval proposed in the following is similar to integrating statistics for queries over different document categories with conventional retrieval [137]. We extend this notion now such that statistics for multi-category retrieval integrate the statistics of each category that occurs in the query. As the subsequent definitions show, query processing first computes the statistics for each single-category as defined in Definition 6.3 and then integrates them to the multi-category ones as follows. Let $\mathcal{M}_q$ denote the set of basic indexing nodes that the multi-category query q covers. Thus, the integrated inverted element frequency for multi-category retrieval is

$$ief_{mcat}(t, \mathcal{M}_q) = \log \frac{\sum_{cat \in \mathcal{M}_q} N_{cat}}{\sum_{cat \in \mathcal{M}_q} ef_{cat}(t)} \tag{6.4}$$

where $ef_{cat}(t)$ denotes the single-category element frequency of term t with category cat. The retrieval status value of an element e for a multi-category query q is then using again $tfidf$ ranking:

$$rsv(e, q) = \sum_{t \in terms(q)} tf(t, e) \; ief_{mcat}(t, \mathcal{M}_q)^2 \; tf(t, q) \tag{6.5}$$

This definition integrates the frequencies of several single categories to the query-specific ones. It equals Definition 6.3 in the trivial case with only one category in the multi-category.

Nested Retrieval

Another type of requests are those that operate on complete subtrees of the XML documents. The path expression /bookstore/medicine/book/ for instance defines such a subtree for the XML document in Fig. 6.1. However, there are the three following difficulties with this retrieval type:

- A path expression such as the one given above comprises different categories in its XML subtree. With the element types from Fig. 6.2 for instance, these are the title and paragraph elements. Hence, retrieval over the complete subtree must consider these element types in combination to provide a consistent ranking.
- Terms that occur close to the root of the subtree are typically considered more significant for the root element than ones on deeper levels of the subtree. Intuitively: the larger the distance of a node from its ancestor is, the less it contributes to the relevance of its ancestor. Fuhr et al. [127, 128] tackle this issue by so-called *augmentation weights* which downweigh term weights when they are pushed upward in hierarchically structured documents such as XML documents.
- Element containment is at the instance level, and not at the type level. This is because some element may contain a particular sub-element while others do not. Take the XML document from Fig. 6.1 for instance: some book elements do not have an example chapter. Consequently, element containment relations cannot be derived completely from the element type nesting.

Let $e \in cat$ denote an element from category cat where cat qualifies for the path expression of the nested-retrieval query. Let $SE(e)$ denote the set of sub-elements of e including e, i.e., all elements in the sub-tree rooted at e. For each $se \in SE(e)$, $l \in path(e, se)$ stands for a label along the path from e to se, and $aw_l \in [0.0; 1.0]$ is its augmentation weight as defined by the annotations of the edges in the XML structure (cf. Fig. 6.2). $ief_{nest}(t)$ stands for the integrated inverted element frequency of term t with nested retrieval, and

$$ief_{nest}(t) = \log \frac{N_{cat}}{ef_{cat}(t)} = \log \frac{N_{cat}}{\sum_{e \in cat} \chi(t, e)} \tag{6.6}$$

where N_{cat} is again the number of elements in category cat and $ef_{cat}(t)$ is the number of occurrences of term t in cat. To determine $ef_{cat}(t)$, we define $\chi(t, e)$ as follows:

$$\chi(t, e) = \begin{cases} 1, \text{ if } \sum_{se \in SE(e)} tf(t, se) > 0 \\ \\ 0, \text{ otherwise} \end{cases} \tag{6.7}$$

Thus, $\chi(t, e)$ is 1 if at least e or one of its sub-elements contains t. The retrieval status value rsv of an element $e \in cat$ under a nested-retrieval query q using $tf idf$-ranking is then:

$$rsv(e, q) = \sum_{se \in SE(e)} \sum_{t \in terms(q)} (\prod_{l \in path(e, se)} aw_l) tf(t, se) \, ief_{nest}(t)^2 \, tf(t, q) \tag{6.8}$$

Definition 6.8 reverts to the common $tf idf$ ranking for conventional retrieval on flat documents when all augmentation weights are equal to 1.0 and when the elements queried are the root nodes of the XML documents. In the trivial case where a nested query only comprises one single-category, Definition 6.8 equals Definition 6.3.

6.4 Conclusions

Flexible retrieval is crucial for document centric processing of XML. Flexible retrieval means that users may dynamically, i.e., at query time, define the scopes of their queries. So far, consistent retrieval on XML collections has only been feasible at fixed granularities [128, 296]. The difficulty is to treat statistics such as document frequencies properly in the context of hierarchically structured data with possibly heterogeneous contents. Our approach allows for flexible retrieval over arbitrary combinations of element types. In this chapter, we propose *single-category retrieval*, *multi-category retrieval*, and *nested retrieval* for flexible retrieval from XML documents. To tackle the aforementioned difficulty, we rely on basic index and statistics data and integrate them on-the-fly, i.e., during query processing, to *query-specific statistics* that properly reflect the scope of the query. Taking the vector space retrieval model for instance, our approach dynamically generates the appropriate vector space for each query from the underlying basic ones. A nice characteristic of our approach is that it covers conventional retrieval on flat documents as a special case.

An extensive experimental evaluation has already investigated dynamically integrating statistics for different categories of flat documents [137]. Our findings from this previous work show that the overhead of dynamic statistics integration is less than 30% with up to 16 different categories, compared to a setting with pre-computed statistics. We are currently extending the implementation of our XML repository with the functionality for flexible retrieval on XML documents as outlined here. Our expectation is that the overhead for generating appropriate vector spaces on-the-fly is also reasonable for retrieval on XML documents such that we can guarantee interactive retrieval response times.

A further expectation is that flexible retrieval on XML documents with query-specific statistics yields better retrieval results as compared to retrieval with conventional information retrieval statistics. In the light of the recent development of INEX (cf. Chap. 19), we plan to tune and to evaluate our approach using this benchmark.

Statistical Language Models for Intelligent XML Retrieval

Djoerd Hiemstra

7.1 Introduction

The XML standards that are currently emerging have a number of character-istics that can also be found in database management systems, like schemas (DTDs and XML schema) and query languages (XPath and XQuery). Fol-lowing this line of reasoning, an XML database might resemble traditional database systems. However, XML is more than a language to mark up data; it is also a language to mark up textual documents. In this chapter we specif-ically address XML databases for the storage of 'document-centric' XML (as opposed to 'data-centric' XML [42]).

Document-centric XML is typically semi-structured, that is, it is charac-terised by less regular structure than data-centric XML. The documents might not strictly adhere to a DTD or schema, or possibly the DTD or schema might not have been specified at all. Furthermore, users will in general not be inter-ested in retrieving data from document-centric XML: They will be interested in retrieving *information* from the database. That is, when searching for doc-uments about "web information retrieval systems", it is not essential that the documents of interest actually contain the words "web", "information", "re-trieval" and "systems" (i.e., they might be called "internet search engines").

An intelligent XML retrieval system combines 'traditional' data retrieval (as defined by the XPath and XQuery standards) with information retrieval. Essential for information retrieval is ranking documents by their probability, or degree, of relevance to a query. On a sufficiently large data set, a query for "web information retrieval systems" will retrieve many thousands of doc-uments that contain any, or all, of the words in the query. As users are in general not willing to examine thousands of documents, it is important that the system ranks the retrieved set of documents in such a way that the most promising documents are ranked on top, i.e. are the first to be presented to the user.

Unlike the database and XML communities, which have developed some well-accepted standards, the information retrieval community does not have

H. Blanken et al. (Eds.): Intelligent Search on XML Data, LNCS 2818, pp. 107–118, 2003.

any comparable standard query language or retrieval model. If we look at some practical systems however, e.g. internet search engines like Google and AltaVista, or online search services as provided by e.g. Dialog and LexisNexis, it turns out that there is much overlap in the kind of functionality they provide.

```
1. IT magazines
2. +IT magazine* -MSDOS
3. "IT magazines"
4. IT NEAR magazines
5. (IT OR computer) (books OR magazines OR journals)
6. XML[0.9] IR[0.1] title:INEX site:utwente.nl
```

Fig. 7.1. Examples of complex information retrieval queries

Figure 7.1 gives some example queries from these systems. The first query is a simple "query by example": retrieve a ranked list of documents about IT magazines. The second query shows the use of a mandatory term operator '+', stating that the retrieved document *must* contain the word IT,[1] a wild card operator '*' stating that the document might match "magazine", but also "magazines" or "magazined" and the '−' operator stating that we do not prefer IT magazines about MSDOS. The third and fourth query searches for documents in which "IT" and "magazines" occur respectively adjacent or near to each other. The fifth query shows the use of the 'OR' operator, stating that the system might retrieve documents about "IT magazines", "computer magazines", "IT journals", "IT books", etc. The sixth and last query shows the use of structural information, very much like the kind of functionality that is provided by XPath; so "title:INEX" means that the title of the document should contain the word "INEX". The last query also shows additional term weighting, stating that the user finds "XML" much more important than "IR".

An intelligent XML retrieval system should support XPath and all of the examples above. For a more comprehensive overview of information retrieval requirements, we refer to Chap. 3.

This chapter shows that statistical language models provide some interesting alternative ways of thinking about intelligent XML search. The rest of the chapter is organised as follows: Section 7.2 introduces the language modelling approach to information retrieval, and shows how language modelling concepts like priors, mixtures and translation models, can be used to model intelligent retrieval from semi-structured data. Section 7.3 reports the exper-

---

[1] Note that most retrieval systems do not distinguish upper case from lower case, and confuse the acronym "IT" with the very common word "it".

imental results of a preliminary prototype system based on language models. Finally, Section 7.4 concludes this chapter.

7.2 Language Modelling Concepts

In this section, we introduce the language modelling approach to information retrieval. First we describe the language modelling approach that resembles traditional vector space information retrieval models that use so-called *tf.idf* weighting. In the sections that follow, we introduce a number of more advanced language modelling constructs like priors, mixtures and translation models, and show how these can be used to model intelligent retrieval from semi-structured data.

7.2.1 The Basic Model

The idea behind the language modelling approach to information retrieval [163, 215] is to assign to each XML element X the probability $P(X|q_1, \cdots, q_n)$, i.e., the probability that the element X is relevant, given the query $Q = q_1, \cdots, q_n$. The system uses the probabilities to rank the elements by the descending order of the probabilities. Using Bayes' rule we can rewrite this as follows.

$$P(X|q_1, q_2, \cdots, q_n) = \frac{P(q_1, q_2, \cdots, q_n|X)P(X)}{P(q_1, q_2, \cdots, q_n)} \tag{7.1}$$

Note that the denominator on the right hand side does not depend on the XML element X. It might therefore be ignored when a ranking is needed. The prior $P(X)$ however, should only be ignored if we assume a uniform prior, that is, if we assume that all elements are equally likely to be relevant in absence of a query. Some non-content information, e.g. the number of accesses by other users to an XML element, or e.g. the length of an XML element, might be used to determine $P(X)$.

Let's turn our attention to $P(q_1, q_2, \cdots, q_n|X)$. The use of probability theory might here be justified by modelling the process of generating a query Q given an XML element as a random process. If we assume that the current page in this book is an XML element in the data, we might imagine picking a word at random from the page by pointing at the page with closed eyes. Such a process would define a probability $P(q|X)$ for each term q, which would be defined by the number of times a word occurs on this page, divided by the total number of words on the page. Similar generative probabilistic models have been used successfully in speech recognition systems [243], for which they are called "language models".

The mechanism above suggests that terms that do not occur in an XML element are assigned zero probability. However the fact that a term is never observed does not mean that this term is never entered in a query for which the XML element is relevant. This problem – i.e., events which are not observed in the data might still be reasonable in a new setting – is called the *sparse data problem* in the world of language models [209]. In general, zero probabilities should be avoided. A standard solution to the sparse data problem is to interpolate the model $P(q|X)$ with a background model $P(q)$ which assigns a non-zero probability to each query term. If we additionally assume that query terms are independent given X, then:

$$P(q_1, q_2, \cdots, q_n|X) = \prod_{i=1}^{n} \Big((1-\lambda)P(q_i) + \lambda P(q_i|X) \Big) \qquad (7.2)$$

Equation 7.2 defines our basic language model if we assume that each term is generated independently from previous terms given relevant XML element. Here, λ is an unknown mixture parameter, which might be set using e.g. relevance feedback of the user. The probability $P(q_i)$ is the probability of the word q_i in 'general query English'. Ideally, we would like to train $P(q_i)$ on a large corpus of queries. In practice however, we will use the document collection to define these probabilities as the number of times the word occurs in the database, divided by the size of the database, measured in the total number of word occurrences. It can be shown by some simple rewriting that Equation 7.2 can be implemented as a vector space weighting algorithm, where $\lambda P(q_i|X)$ resides on the '*tf*-position' and $1 / (1-\lambda)P(q_i)$ resides on the '*idf*-position'. The following 'vector-space-like' formula assigns zero weight to words not occurring in a XML element, but ranks the elements in exactly the same order as the probability measure of Equation 7.2 [163]:

$$P(q_1, q_2, \cdots, q_n|X) \propto \sum_{i=1}^{n} \log\Big(1 + \frac{\lambda P(q_i|X)}{(1-\lambda)P(q_i)} \Big) \qquad (7.3)$$

Why would we prefer the use of language models over the use of e.g. a vector space model with some *tf.idf* weighting algorithm as e.g. described by [259]? The reason is the following: our generative query language model gives a nice intuitive explanation of *tf.idf* weighting algorithms by means of calculating the probability of picking at random, one at a time, the query terms from an XML element. We might extend this by any other generating process to model complex information retrieval queries in a theoretically sound way that is not provided by a vector space approach.

For instance, we might might calculate the probability of complex processes like the following: What is the probability of sampling eiter "Smith" or "Jones" from the `author` element, and sampling "software" and "engineering" from either the `body` element or from the `title` element? Probability theory will provide us with a sound way of coming up with these probabilities, whereas a vector space approach provides us with little clues on how to combine the scores of words on different XML elements, or how to distinguish between "Smith" or "Jones", and "Smit" *and* "Jones".

7.2.2 Mixture Models and Augmentation Weights

Equation 7.2 shows a model consisting of a *mixture* of two components: the element component $P(q_i|X)$ and a general component $P(q_i)$. In this formula, λ is an unknown mixture parameter. The two-component mixture effectively models the following generation process: What is the probability of sampling the words q_1, q_2, etc. at random from either the XML element X, or from the XML database in total? We might easily extent this to mixtures with an arbitrary number of components, for instance to model the fact that we would prefer XML elements X whose descendant title or abstract (or both) contain the query terms, over elements of which the descendant title or abstract do not contain the query terms. A three-component mixture like this might be described by the following generation process: What is the probability of sampling the words q_1, q_2, etc. from either the XML element X, or from the descendant title element, or from the descendant abstract element? The corresponding probability measure would be:

$$P(q_1, q_2, \cdots, q_n|X) = \prod_{i=1}^{n}\Big(\alpha P(q_i|X) + \beta P(q_i|X, \mathtt{title}) + \gamma P(q_i|X, \mathtt{abstract})\Big)$$

Instead of one unknown mixture parameter, we now have to set the value of two unknown mixture parameters: α and β (where $\gamma = 1 - \alpha - \beta$). $P(q_i|X, \mathtt{title})$ would simply be defined by the number of occurrences of q_i in the descendant title of X divided by the total number of words in the descendant title of X, and $P(q_i|X, \mathtt{abstract})$ would be defined similarly for the descendant abstract.

In other words, the mixture expresses something similar to the logical OR: if a word q should match either XML element X or a related XML element Y, then the probability is calculated by a mixture. Note that we cannot simply add the probabilities without the mixture parameters, because the two events are not disjoint, that is, a word might match both X and Y.

The unknown mixture parameters play a role that is similar to the augmentation weights described in Chap. 4 and 6 of this book. Both are essentially unknown parameters that determine the importance of XML elements relatively to some related XML elements. The main difference between the augmentation weights and the mixture parameters of the language models, is that the augmentation weights are propagated upwards from a leaf node to its parent, whereas the language models might combine XML elements in an ad-hoc way. Interestingly, as said above, a two-component mixture of an element and the document root, behaves like a vector space approach with *tf.idf* weights.

7.2.3 Statistical Translation and the Use of Ontologies

Another interesting advanced language modelling construct is the combination of a language model with a statistical translation model [28, 162, 323].

Such a combined model describes a two-stage sampling process: What is the probability of sampling at random a word q from the XML element X, from which we in turn – given that q defines an entry in a probabilistic translation dictionary – sample at random the possible translation c_i? Such a model might be applied to cross-language information retrieval. In cross-language retrieval, the user poses a query in one language, e.g. Dutch, to search for documents in another language, e.g. English documents. For instance, the user enters the Dutch word "college", which has as its possible translations "lecture", "course", "reading" or "class", each possibly with a different probability of the Dutch word given the English word. The system now ranks the elements using the following probability measure:

$$P(c_1, c_2, \cdots, c_n | X) = \prod_{i=1}^{n} \sum_{q} \Big(P(c_i|q) P(q|X) \Big) \qquad (7.4)$$

In this formula, q sums over all possible words, or alternatively over all words for which $P(c_i|q)$ is non-zero. Given the example above, the sum would include $P(c|\texttt{lecture})\,P(\texttt{lecture}|X)$, $P(c|\texttt{course})\,P(\texttt{course}|X)$, etc. Superficially, this looks very similar to the mixture model. Like the mixtures, the translation models also express something similar to the logical OR: if an element should match either the word "lecture", or the word "course", then we can add the probabilities weighted by the translation probabilities. Note however, that the translation probabilities do not necessarily sum up to one, because they are conditioned on different qs. Adding the probabilities is allowed because the qs are disjoint, i.e. the occurrence of one word can never be "lecture" *and* "course". This is like adding the probabilities of tossing a 5 or a 6 with a fair die, it is impossible to throw a 5 *and* a 6 with only one toss, so we can add the probabilities: $1/6 + 1/6 = 1/3$.

Translation models might play a role in using ontologies for 'semantic' search of XML data as described in Chap. 8 by Schenkel, Theobald and Weikum. They introduce a new operator to express semantic similarity search conditions. As in cross-language retrieval, ontology-based search will retrieve an element that matches words that are related, according to the ontology, to the word in the query. If we follow the approach by Schenkel et al., the ontology might define $P(c_i|q)$ in Equation 7.4 as the probability of a concept c_i, given a word q.

7.2.4 Element Priors

Maybe the easiest language modelling concept to experiment with is the XML element prior $P(X)$. The prior $P(X)$ defines the probability that the user likes the element X if we do not have any further information (i.e., no query). An example of the usefulness of prior knowledge is the PageRank [49] algorithm that analyses the hyperlink structure of the world wide web to come up with pages to which many documents link. Such pages might be highly recommended by the system: If we do not have a clue what the user is looking for, an educated guess would be to prefer a page with a high pagerank over e.g. the personal home page of the author of this chapter. Experiments show that document priors can provide over 100 % improvement in retrieval performance for a web entry page search task [192]. The usefulness of some simple priors for XML search are investigated in Section 7.3.

7.2.5 A Note on Global Word Statistics

As said above, ideally, the probability $P(q_i)$ is defined as the probability of the word q_i in 'general query English'. In practice it is estimated on any sufficiently large collection of documents, e.g. quite conveniently, the XML document collection we are currently searching.

Note that this viewpoint is quite different from most other approaches to XML retrieval. The approach presented in Chap. 6 by Grabs and Schek makes a successful effort in reconstructing the global frequencies of the part of the database that is the scope of the query, while still keeping the size of the database reasonably small. The language modelling approach suggests that it is not necessary to reconstruct the total number of times a word occurs in a certain XML element type (or to reconstruct the total number of XML elements of a certain type that contain the word, that is, the so-called 'document frequency' of the word). The model suggests that $P(q)$ is the probability of a word in "general query English": It is the same for all queries, whatever the scope of the query. Furthermore, to avoid the sparse data problem, it should be estimated on as much data as possible, and not – in case of a selective query – on a relatively small part of the database.

Van Zwol [304] compared the effect of fixed global frequencies vs. on-the-fly (fragmented) computation of global frequencies, and concluded that the exact definition of global word statistics has no measurable influence on the performance of an intelligent XML retrieval system. The advantage of fixed global frequencies over on-the-fly computation of global frequencies is that the former approach allows for simpler and more efficient query plans.

7.2.6 Discussion

This section presented some interesting new ways of thinking about intelligent XML retrieval. Whether these approaches perform well in practice, has to be determined by experiments on benchmark test collections as e.g. provided by INEX. Preliminary experiments are described in the next section.

However, experience with language models on other tasks look promising. Recent experiments that use translation models for cross-language retrieval [162], document priors for web search [192], and mixture models for video retrieval [315] have shown that language models provide top performance on these tasks. Other systems that use language models for intelligent XML retrieval are described by Ogilvie and Callan [233], and by List and De Vries [204].

7.3 Preliminary Evaluation on INEX

In this section we describe a preliminary prototype system for intelligent XML retrieval, based on the language modelling approach described above. The system is evaluated using the INEX testbed. We briefly describe the system, the tasks and evaluation procedure, the experimental setup and research questions, and finally the experimental results.

7.3.1 A First Prototype

The preliminary prototype should in principle support 'all of XPath and all of IR'. In order to support XPath, the system should contain a complete representation of the XML data. The system should be able to reproduce any part of the data as the result of the query. For XPath we refer to [29].

For our first prototype we implemented the XML relational storage scheme proposed in Chap. 16 by Grust and Van Keulen. They suggest to assign two identifiers (id) to each instance node: one id is assigned in pre-order, and the other in post-order. The pre and post order assignment of XML element ids provides elegant support for processing XPath queries, forming an alternative to explicit parent-child relations which are often used to store highly structured data in relational tables [116, 303, 271].[2]

Note that pre and post order assignment can be done almost trivially in XML by keeping track of the order of respectively the opening and closing tags. Since we are going to build a textual index for content-based retrieval, we assign an id (or position) to each word in the XML text content as well. The word positions are used in a term position index to evaluate phrasal queries and proximity queries. Interestingly, if we number the XML data as a linearised string of tokens (including the content words), we obey the pre/post order id assignment, but we also allow the use of theory and practice of region algebras (see Chap. 12). For a more detailed description of the storage scheme, we refer to [161].

7.3.2 The INEX Evaluation

INEX is the Initiative for the Evaluation of XML Retrieval. The initiative provides a large testbed, consisting of XML documents, retrieval tasks, and relevance judgements on the data. INEX identifies two tasks: the content-only task, and the content-and-structure task.

The content-only task provides 30 queries like the following example: `//*[. =~ "computational biology"]` ("XPath & IR" for: any element about "computational biology"). In this task, the system needs to identify the most

---

[2] Actually, Grust et al.store the id of the parent as well. Similarly, Schmidt et al. [271] add a field to keep track of the order of XML elements; here we emphasise different view points.

appropriate XML element for retrieval. The task resembles users that want to search XML data without knowing the schema or DTD.

The content-and-structure task provides 30 queries like the following: `//article[author =~ "Smith|Jones" and bdy =~ "software engineering"]` ("XPath & IR" for: retrieve articles written by either Smith or Jones about software engineering). This task resembles users or applications that *do* know the schema or DTD, and want to search some particular XML elements while formulating restrictions on some other elements.

For each query in both tasks, quality assessments are available. XML elements are assessed based on *relevance* and *coverage*. Relevance is judged on a four-point scale from 0 (irrelevant) to 3 (highly relevant). Coverage is judged by the following four categories: N (no coverage), E (exact coverage), L (the XML element is too large), and S (the XML element is too small).

In order to apply traditional evaluation metrics like precision and recall, the values for relevance and coverage must be quantised to a single quality value. INEX suggests the use of two quantisation functions: Strict and liberal quantisation. The strict quantisation function evaluates whether a given retrieval method is capable of retrieving highly relevant XML elements: it assigns 1 to elements that have a relevance value 3, and exact coverage. The liberal quantisation function assigns 1 to elements that have a relevance value of 2 and exact coverage, or, a relevance value of 3 and either exact, too small, or too big coverage. An extensive overview of INEX is given in Chap. 19 of this volume.

7.3.3 Experimental Setup and Research Questions

We evaluate a system that only has limited functionality. First of all, we assume that $\lambda = 1$ in Equation 7.2, so we do not have to store the global word statistics. The system supports queries with a content restriction on only one XML element, so the example content-and-structure query in the previous section is not supported: Either the restriction on the `author` tag, or the restriction on the `bdy` tag has to be dropped. The system supports conjunction and disjunction operators, which are evaluated as defined by Equation 7.4 where the translation probabilities were set to 1. All queries were manually formulated from the topic statements.

The experiments are designed to answer the following research question: Can we use the prior probability $P(X)$ (see Equation 7.1) to improve the retrieval quality of the system? We present three experiments using the system described in this chapter, for which only the prior probabilities $P(X)$ differ. The baseline experiment uses a uniform prior $P(X) = c$, where c is some constant value, so each XML element will have the same a priori probability of being retrieved. A second experiment uses a length prior $P(X) = number of tokens in the XML element$, where a token is either a word or a tag. This means that the system will prefer bigger elements, i.e. elements higher up the XML tree, over smaller elements. A third experiment uses a prior that is somewhere in between the two extremes. The prior is defined by $P(X) = 100 + number\ of$ *tokens in the XML element*. Of course, the priors should be properly scaled, but the exact scaling does not matter for the purpose of ranking. We hypothesise that the system using the length prior will outperform the baseline system.

7.3.4 Evaluation Results

This section presents the evaluation results of three retrieval approaches (no prior, 'half' prior, and length prior) on two query sets (content-only, and content-and-structure), following two evaluation methods (strict and liberal). We will report for each combination the precision at respectively 5, 10, 15, 20, 30 and 100 documents retrieved.

Strict Evaluation

Table 7.1 shows the results of the three experiments on the content-only queries following the strict evaluation. The precision values are averages over 22 queries. The results show an impressive improvement of the length prior on all cut-off values. Apparently, if the elements that need to be retrieved are not specified in the query, users prefer larger elements over smaller elements.

Table 7.1. Results of content-only (CO) runs with strict evaluation

precision	no prior	'half' prior	length prior
at 5	0.0455	0.0455	0.1909
at 10	0.0364	0.0455	0.1591
at 15	0.0303	0.0424	0.1394
at 20	0.0341	0.0364	0.1318
at 30	0.0364	0.0424	0.1318
at 100	0.0373	0.0559	0.1000

Table 7.2 shows the results of the three experiments on the content-and-structure queries following the strict evaluation. The precision values are averages over 28 queries. The baseline system performs much better on the content-and-structure queries than on the content-only queries. Surprisingly, the length prior again leads to substantial improvement on all cut-off values in the ranked list.

Liberal Evaluation

Table 7.3 shows the results of the three experiments on the content-only queries using the liberal quantisation function defined above for evaluation.

Table 7.2. Results of content-and-structure (CAS) runs with strict evaluation

precision	no prior	'half' prior	length prior
at 5	0.1929	0.2357	0.2857
at 10	0.1964	0.2321	0.2857
at 15	0.1976	0.2333	0.2714
at 20	0.1929	0.2232	0.2589
at 30	0.1786	0.2060	0.2607
at 100	0.0954	0.1107	0.1471

Table 7.3. Results of content-only (CO) runs with liberal evaluation

precision	no prior	'half' prior	length prior
at 5	0.1130	0.1391	0.4261
at 10	0.0957	0.1304	0.3609
at 15	0.0957	0.1333	0.3304
at 20	0.1000	0.1152	0.3000
at 30	0.1087	0.1232	0.2812
at 100	0.0896	0.1222	0.2065

Table 7.4. Results of content-and-structure (CAS) runs with liberal evaluation

precision	no prior	'half' prior	length prior
at 5	0.2429	0.2929	0.4000
at 10	0.2286	0.2823	0.3750
at 15	0.2262	0.2881	0.3738
at 20	0.2268	0.2821	0.3607
at 30	0.2179	0.2583	0.3595
at 100	0.1279	0.1571	0.2054

The precision values are averages over 23 queries. Again, the results show a significant improvement of the length prior on all cut-off values.

Table 7.4 shows the results of the three experiments on the content-and-structure queries following the liberal evaluation. The precision values are averages over 28 queries. The length prior again shows better performance on all cut-off values. Note that the content-only task and the content-and-structure task show practically equal performance if the liberal evaluation procedure is followed.

7.4 Conclusions

In this chapter we described in some detail the ideas behind the language modelling approach to information retrieval, and suggested several advanced language modelling concepts to model intelligent XML retrieval. We presented a preliminary implementation of a system that supports XPath and complex information retrieval queries based on language models. From the experiments we conclude that it is beneficial to assign a higher prior probability of relevance to bigger fragments of XML data than to smaller XML fragments, that is, to users, more information seems to be better information.

Whether the advanced modelling contructs presented in Section 7.2 will in fact result in good retrieval performance will be evaluated in the CIRQUID project (Complex Information Retrieval Queries in a Database). In this project, which is run in cooperation with CWI Amsterdam, we will develop a logical data model that allows us to define complex queries using advanced language modelling primitives.

8

Ontology-Enabled XML Search

Ralf Schenkel, Anja Theobald, and Gerhard Weikum

8.1 Introduction

8.1.1 Motivation

XML is rapidly evolving towards the standard for data integration and ex-change over the Internet and within intranets, covering the complete spec-trum from largely unstructured, ad hoc documents to highly structured, schematic data. However, established XML query languages like XML-QL [96] or XQuery [34] cannot cope with the rapid growth of information in open en-vironments such as the Web or intranets of large corporations, as they are bound to boolean retrieval and do not provide any relevance ranking for the (typically numerous) results. Recent approaches such as XIRQL [128] or our own system XXL [295, 296] that are driven by techniques from information retrieval overcome the latter problem by considering the relevance of each potential hit for the query and returning the results in a ranked order, using similarity measures like the cosine measure. But they are still tied to keyword queries, which is no longer appropriate for highly heterogeneous XML data from different sources, as it is the case in the Web or in large intranets.

In such large-scale settings, both the structure of documents and the ter-minology used in documents may vary. As an example, consider documents about courses in computer science, where some authors talk about "lectures" while others prefer to use "course", "reading", or "class". Boolean queries searching for lectures on computer science cannot find any courses or other synonyms. Additionally, courses on database systems will not qualify for the result set, even though database systems is a branch of computer science. So in order to find all relevant information to a query, additional knowledge about related terms is required that allows us to broaden the query, i.e., extend-ing the query with terms that are closely related to the original query terms. However, imprudent broadening of the query may be misleading in some cases, when the extended query yields unwanted, irrelevant results. Consider a user searching for lectures on stars and galaxies. When we extend the query using

H. Blanken et al. (Eds.): Intelligent Search on XML Data, LNCS 2818, pp. 119–131, 2003.

related terms to "star", we will add terms like "sun" and "milky way" that help in finding better results, but also terms like "movie star" or "hollywood" which are clearly misleading here. This can happen because words typically have more than one sense, and it is of great importance to choose the right sense for extending the query. Such information can be delivered by an ontology, which models terms with their meanings and relationships between terms and meanings.

8.1.2 Related Work

Researchers in artificial intelligence first developed logic-based ontologies to facilitate knowledge sharing and reuse. In the last decade ontologies have become a popular research topic and several AI research communities such as knowledge engineering, natural language processing and knowledge representation have investigated them. The interest in ontologies has been revived with the recent discussion about the "Semantic Web" [321, 220, 285]. In contrast to the extremely ambitious early AI approaches toward building universal ontologies (see, e.g., [198, 255]), more recent proposals are aiming at domain- or user-specific ontologies and are based on more tractable logics (see, e.g., [166, 285]).

Recent publications on formalization of ontologies cover a wide spectrum from algebraic approaches [27] and logic-based languages for modeling ontologies [92, 43] to ontologies for conceptual data modeling and data interpretation [148, 232, 287]. Similar work has been done in the context of multi-databases, for example, [48] proposes a summary schemas model where the semantic power comes from the linguistic knowledge representation in an online taxonomy, [236] presents a conceptual organization of the information space. These publications do not consider the quantification of relationships.

Adding similarity measures to ontologies or, more generally, similarity measures for words has been an active research topic in linguistics for several decades. Among the first results are Rubenstein and Goodenough's [252] judgements for semantic similarity of 65 pairs of nouns that were estimated by 51 experts. This experiment was repeated by Miller and Charles [217] with a reduced set of 30 pairs of nouns, which has served as a basis for comparison to automatically generated similatity measures since then. The first automatic approaches for term similarity concentrated on exploiting statistical correlations between terms [199], especially for the problem of query expansion [241, 242]. Early work on similarity measures for ontologies like WordNet [114] or other semantic nets concentrated on the graph structure of the ontology, computing similarity between two concepts by counting edges between them [244], considering the relative depth of the concepts in the graph [290, 197, 322] or the direction of the edges between them [164], or taking the density of the ontology graph into account [249, 6, 200]. Since the mid of the 90ies, researchers started connecting both worlds, yielding similarity measures that take into account both the graph structure as well as statistics on a large corpus [247, 179, 203, 248]. A detailed comparison of similarity measures for WordNet can be found in [52]; [211] and [175] compare measures based on WordNet with similar measures for Roget's Thesaurus [174].

Semi-automatic or automatic ontology construction is proposed in [207, 208, 186, 195, 188, 286, 50] and is mostly based on methods of text mining and information extraction based on natural language processing using an existing thesaurus or a text processor such as SMES [207] or GATE [87]. Merging ontologies across shared sub-ontologies is described in [27, 202]. Some comprehensive systems for developing or using ontologies are OntoBroker [92], Text-To-Onto [207, 208], GETESS [286, 50], Protégé 2000 [232], LGAccess [8], KAON [43], Ontolingua [113], and FrameNet [20].

To our knowledge, the role of ontologies in searching semistructured data has not yet been discussed in any depth. The unique characteristic of our approach lies in the combination of ontological knowledge and information retrieval techniques for semantic similarity search on XML data.

8.1.3 Outline of the Chapter

In this chapter, we show how ontologies can be applied to increase retrieval quality for XML data. In Section 8.2, we present formal underpinnings for ontologies by introducing important concepts of an ontology and a well-founded model for an ontology graph which is later on used to derive a similarity measure on the elements of the ontology and to disambiguate terms. In Section 8.3, we present key concepts of our XXL search engine that makes use of the ontology to support relevance ranking on XML data.

8.2 The XXL Ontology

8.2.1 Formal Underpinnings of the Ontology Graph

A widely accepted definition for an ontology is the one by Gruber and Guarino [145, 148]): *An ontology is a specification of representational vocabulary of words (or terms) including hierarchical relationships and associative relationships between these words. It is used for indexing and investigation as well as for support knowledge sharing and reuse.* However, this definition is not precise enough to be used for building search engines and information management applications; we need a formal apparatus to this end. In this section, we develop a model for an ontology that, while still capturing the ideas of the informal definition, is precise enough to be implemented in our XXL search engine for ranked retrieval on XML data.

As a building block and information pool for building our ontology, we make use of Wordnet [114], an extensive electronic lexical database. WordNet captures the different senses of words and semantic relationships between them, among them hypernomy, synonymy and holonymy. Given a word, Word-net returns the senses of this word (represented by a short phrase that explains the sense), optionally together with related words for each sense. For example, for the word "star" WordNet returns the following word senses, denoted by their textual descriptions and ordered by descending usage frequency:

1. (astronomy) a celestial body of hot gases that radiates energy derived from thermonuclear reactions in the interior
2. someone who is dazzlingly skilled in any field
3. a plane figure with 5 or more points; often used as an emblem
4. an actor who plays a principal role
5. a performer who receives prominent billing

and two further senses that are less commonly used. Another prominent example is "Java" with three completely different senses (the programming language, the island and the coffee).

In fact, most words are ambigous, i.e., they have more than one word sense. For example, WordNet currently covers about 75,000 different senses of nouns, but about 138,000 noun-sense pairs, so each word has about two different senses on average. The word alone is therefore not enough to uniquely represent one of its senses, so we are using pairs of the form (word,sense) to represent semantic concepts. More formally, we are considering words as terms over a fixed alphabet Σ. A word w together with its *word sense s* (or *sense* for short) forms a *concept* $c = (w, s)$, i.e., the precise meaning of the word when used in this sense. The set of all such concepts is called the *universe U*.

In order to determine which concepts are related, we introduce semantic relationships between concepts. Among the most common relationships in ontologies are hypernomy and hyponomy: we say that a concept c is a *hypernym* (*hyponym*) of another concept c' if the sense of c is more general (more specific) than the sense of c'. We are also considering holonyms and meronyms, i.e., c is a holonym (meronym) of c' if c' means something that is a part of something meant by c (vice versa for meronyms). Finally, two concepts are called synonyms when there senses are identical, i.e., their meaning is the same. Note that these are exactly the relationships supported by WordNet. There may be further semantic relationships between concepts that could be easily integrated into our framework, but we restrict ourselves to hypernomy and synonymy in this chapter.

Based on these definitions we now define the ontology graph which is a data structure to represent concepts and relationships between them. This graph has the concepts as nodes and an edge between two concepts whenever there is a semantic relationship between them. Additionally, we label each edge with the type of the underlying relationship of the edge. Figure 8.1 shows an example for an excerpt of the ontology graph around the first sense for the term "star", limited to hypernym, holonym and synonym edges for better readability, and already augmented with edge weights that will be explained in the next subsection. As each hypernym edge is accompanied by a hyponom edge in the opposite direction, an implementation may choose not to explicitly store hyponym (and, by an analogous argument, meronym edges). Alternatively, we could also shrink such a pair of edges into a single, undirected edge between the nodes, yielding an undirected graph structure. However, it will turn out that the actual direction of the relationships becomes important later on when we discuss quantification and disambiguation, so our graph structure is directed.

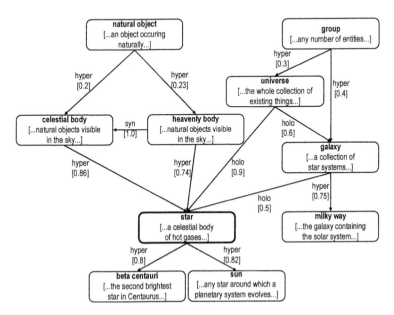

Fig. 8.1. Excerpt of an ontology around the first sense of the term "star", augmented with edge weights

8.2.2 Quantifying Relationships

Using the graph presented in the previous section, we can easily determine which concepts are semantically related. Unfortunately, the graph typically forms one big connected component, so that each concept is related to any other concept, so this does not help in finding similar concepts. What is still missing is a quantification of the relationships, i.e., a similarity measure for concepts that represents the semantic similarity of the concepts.

For a first approach to determine the similarity of two concepts, we ignore the graph structure for a moment and apply standard techniques from information retrieval. We treat the term of a concept together with the textual description of its sense as a document and, after elimination of stop words and applying some stemming algorithm, derive a feature vector from it. The similarity of two such feature vectors would then be computed using a standard metric on vector spaces, e.g. the cosine measure. However, as such feature vectors would typically be quite sparse, the distance of most concepts would be close to or equal to zero, which is too restrictive.

A more promising approach is to apply probabilistic models using the probability distribution of the concepts, i.e., the words in their selected sense, in documents. If we manage to capture this distribution, we obtain an approximation of the similarity by computing the correlation of the concepts. However, in our setting (with the Web as the source for documents), the concept distribution is unknown, so we have to use some pragmatic approach for collecting statistics. We could approximate the concept distribution using approximations of the frequency $f(c)$ of a concept c in a very large text corpus, e.g., the result of a topic-specific crawl or the entire Web. Here, $f(c)$ means how often the word of c and all the words from the textual represenation of its sense occur in pages in the corpus. In order to use the Web, we apply a Web search engine like Google or Altavista to get approximations for the frequencies. While the numbers that these engines return for the frequencies are not meant to be exact in any way, we believe that the relationship between the numbers is reasonable.

Based on the frequency values, we compute the correlation of the concepts using correlation coefficients. Among the candidates are the Dice coefficient, the Jaccard coefficient or the Overlap coefficient (see Table 8.1). We choose the Dice coefficient for our statistics. As an example, consider the semantic simi-

Table 8.1. candidates for correlation coefficients

correlation coeff.	formula
Dice coeff.	$2\frac{f(x\cap y)}{f(x)+f(y)}$
Jaccard coeff.	$\frac{f(x\cap y)}{f(x\cup y)}$
Overlap coeff.	$\frac{f(x\cap y)}{min\{f(x),f(y)\})}$

larity between the concepts "universe" and "galaxy" shown in Figure 8.1. To compute their Dice coefficient, we execute Web queries of the form "universe collection existing things", "galaxy collection star systems",and "universe collection existing things galaxy star systems" to obtain the counts for $f(x)$, $f(y)$, and $f(x \cap y)$, respectively. For synonyms, we always set the similarity to 1.

However, while this gives good results for most concept pairs, it can still be improved. The word itself and the textual representation may not always contain enough words to discriminate the different senses of the word. As an example, consider again the concepts "universe" and "galaxy". When we evaluate the query "universe collection existing things" to compute $f(x)$, this yields not only documents about astronomy, but many other, nonrelated documents, so the resulting frequency value will be too high. In order to make frequency values more precise, it may be helpful to consider not only the terms of the concept and its textual description, but also the terms of a local context of the concept, i.e., other concepts that are closely related, like synonyms, hypernyms, hyponyms, or siblings in the graph (i.e., successor of predecessor of a given node). When we apply such a context in the example, the resulting query for $f(x)$ could be "universe collection existing things star body hot gases", integrating terms from the holonym "star".

8.2.3 Similarity of Ontology Concepts

For very large ontologies like WordNet it is impossible to precompute this information for every pair of concepts in the ontology (which would require the computation of over 18 billion pairwise similarities), so we introduce an additional measure that is based on the ontology graph. We augment each edge of the graph with a weight to express the similarity of the two corresponding nodes. This similarity is computed using the statistical techniques presented above. As there are far fewer edges between concepts in the graph than pairs of concepts, the cost for the computation of all edge weights is several orders of magnitude lower than computing the similarity for all possible pairs. Figure 8.1 already shows the additional edge weights for the excerpt of the ontology graph. For two arbitrary nodes v and w in the graph that are connected by a path $p = (v = n_1, \ldots, n_l = w)$, we then define the similarity $sim_p(v, w)$ of the start node v and the end node w along this path to be the product of the weights of the edges on the path:

$$sim_p(v, w) = \prod_{j=1}^{l-1} weight(< n_j, n_{j+1} >) \tag{8.1}$$

The similarity $sim(v, w)$ of the two nodes is then defined as the maximal similarity over all paths between v and w:

$$sim(v, w) = \max\{sim_p(v, w)\} \tag{8.2}$$

The rationale for this formula is that the length of a path has direct influence on the similarity score. The similarity score for a short path will typically be better than the similarity score for a longer one, unless the path consists only of synonyms that have similarity 1 by definition. However, the shortest path does not need to be the path with the highest similarity, as the triangle inequality does not necessarily hold for the ontological graph structure. So in order to determine the similarity of two concepts, it is not sufficient to calculate the similarity score along the shortest path between the concepts. Instead, we need an appropriate algorithm that takes into account all possible paths between the concepts, calculates the similarity scores for all paths and chooses the maximum of the scores for the similarity of the concepts.

This algorithm is a variant of the single-source shortest-path problem in a directed graph with weighted edges, so a good algorithm to find the similarity of each concept is a variant of Dijkstra's algorithm [81] that takes into account that we multiply the edge weights on the path and search for the path with maximal rather than minimal weight. Using this algorithm, we can even compute the similarity of a given concept c to all other concepts in the ontology graph, with runtime complexity $O(\#concepts \cdot \log(\#concepts) + \#edges)$ if we implement the priority queue using a Fibonacci heap [81]. We can stop the algorithm once we arrive at our target concept. A particularily nice property of the algorithm is that it computes the similarities starting with the largest ones. As we are typically interested only in concepts whose similarity is beyond some threshold, we can stop the algorithm once the priority of the top element in the queue falls below this threshold, yielding a very fast algorithm. The algorithm sketched in Figure 8.2 maintains an array w that keeps the

```
RELAX(u,v,weight)
  If w[v]<w[u]*weight(u,v) Then
     w[v]:=w[u]*weight(u,y)

DIJKSTRA(s,V,E,weight)
  PriorityQueue Q=V; // priorities are in array w[]
  Set S:=empty;
  For Each vertex v In V Do
    w[v]=0;
  w[s]=1;

  While(Q Not empty) Do
    u=Q.extract_max();
    S.insert(u);
    For Each vertex v In AdjacentNodes[u] Do
      RELAX(u,v,weight)
```

Fig. 8.2. The Dijkstra algorithm

current estimation for the maximal distance of each node to the start node s, which is initialized with 0 for all nodes except the start node s (that represents the given concept c). All nodes are inserted into a priority queue Q with the priority being their value in the array w. Inside the main loop, the node with the highest similarity is extracted from the priority queue and inserted into the set S that keeps all nodes for which the computation is finished. All nodes that are direct neighbors of the current node are then considered for updating their similarity by the RELAX operation that assigns a new similarity to a node if its current similarity is smaller than the similarity over the path from the start node over the current node to the considered neighbor.

8.2.4 Disambiguation

We already discussed that words may have more than a single sense, so it is not immediately clear in which sense a word is used in a query or in a document. It is fundamental to disambiguate the word, i.e., determine its current sense, in order to make use of the ontology graph to find related concepts, e.g. to broaden or refine a query. In this subsection we show how this process of disambiguation works.

Starting with word w that may be a keyword of the query or a term in a document, we look up w in our ontology graph, i.e., we find one or more candidate concepts $c_1, \ldots, c_m$ in the graph that have w as their term, and identify possible word senses $s_1, \ldots, s_m$. As an example, consider again the word "star" for which we found seven different word senses before. Now the key question is: which of the possible senses of w is the right one? Our approach to answer this question is based on word statistics for local contexts of the candidate concepts on one hand and the word itself in either the query or the document on the other hand. As far as the word context $con(w)$ is concerned, we choose other words around the word in the document or the complete set of query terms if w is a keyword of a query, because we think that the keywords in the query give the best hints towards the actual topic of the query. Note, however, that disambiguizing query terms is typically harder than finding the right concept for a term of a document because there are far less keywords in queries than words in documents. For the context of a candidate concept c_i we consider not only the concept itself but also some context of c_i in the ontology graph. Candidates for such a context of c are its synonyms, all other immediate neighbors, and also the hyponyms of the hypernyms (i.e., the siblings of c in the ontology graph). For the concepts in the context of c_i, we form the union of their words and corresponding texts, eliminate stopwords, and construct thus the *local context $con(c_i)$ of candidate concept c_i*.

The final step towards disambiguizing the mapping of a keyword onto a word sense is to compare the query terms with the contexts of candidates $con(c_1)$ through $con(c_m)$ in terms of a similarity measure between bags of words. The standard IR measure for this purpose would be the cosine similarity between the set of keywords and $con(s_j)$, or alternatively the Kullback-Leibler divergence between the two word frequency distributions (note that the context construction may add the same word multiple times, and this information is kept in the word bag). Our implementation uses the cosine similarity for its simpler computation. Finally, we map the keyword w onto the candidate concept c_i whose context has the highest similarity to the set of keywords.

However, sometimes the information in the keywords of the query will not be sufficient for a disambiguation. For example, a user may only specify that she wants to find documents that have a title with the word "star". In such cases, it may be helpful to the user to broaden the query using all possible candidate concepts and present the result grouped by the word sense. In our example, we may present separate lists for all 7 senses of the term "star", provided we got results for all of the broadened queries. While this is not as good as an automatic disambiguation, it helps the user to get only the results that she intended, especially when we allow her to manually refine her query to search only in one of the seven senses of the word.

8.3 Ontology-Enabled Ranked Retrieval on XML Data with XXL

8.3.1 The Flexible XML Query Language XXL

The Flexible XML Search Language XXL has been designed to allow SQL-style queries on XML data. We have adopted several concepts from XML-QL, XQuery and similar languages as the core, with certain simplifications and resulting restrictions, and have added capabilities for ranked retrieval and ontological similarity. As an example for a query in XXL, consider one of our examples from the introduction where someone searches for lectures on stars and galaxies. This query could be expressed using XXL as shown in Figure 8.3. The SELECT clause of an XXL query specifies the output of the query, e.g., all

```
SELECT  T               // output of the XXL query
FROM INDEX              // search space of the XXL query
WHERE   #.~lecture AS L   // search condition
     AND L.title AS T
     AND L.description ~ "star"
     AND L.description ~ "galaxy"
```

Fig. 8.3. An example query in XXL

bindings of certain element variables. The FROM clause defines the search space, which can be a set of URLs or the index structure that is maintained by the XXL engine. The WHERE clause specifies the search condition; it consists of the logical conjunction of *path expressions*, where a path expression is a regular expression over *elementary conditions* and an elementary condition refers to the name or content of a single element or attribute. Regular expressions are formed using standard operators like '.' for concatenation, '|' for union, and '*' for the Kleene star. The operator '#' stands for an arbitrary path of elements. Each path expression can be followed by the keyword AS and a variable name that binds the end node of a qualifying path (i.e., the last element on the path and its attributes) to the variable, that can be used later on within path expressions, with the meaning that its bound value is substituted in the expression.

In contrast to other XML query languages we introduce a new operator '~' to express semantic similarity search conditions on XML element (or attribute) names as well as on XML element (or attribute) contents. The result of an XXL query is a subgraph of the XML data graph, where the nodes are annotated with local relevance probabilities called similarity scores for the elementary search conditions given by the query. These similarity scores are combined into a global similarity score for expressing the relevance of the entire result graph. Full details of the semantics of XXL and especially the probabilistic computation of similarity scores can be found in [295, 296].

8.3.2 Architecture of the XXL Search Engine

The XML search language is implemented within the XXL search engine (see Figure 8.4). The XXL search engine is a client-server system with a Java-based GUI. The server consists of the following core components:

- *service components*: the crawler and the query processor (QP), both Java servlets
- *algorithmic components*: parsing and indexing documents, parsing and checking XXL queries
- *data components*: data structures and their methods for storing various kinds of information like the element path index (EPI), the element content index (ECI), and the ontology index (OI).

The EPI contains the relevant information for evaluating simple path expressions that consist of the concatenation of one or more element names and path wildcards #. The ECI contains all terms that occur in the content of elements and attributes, together with their occurrences in documents; it corresponds to a standard text index with the units of indexing being elements rather than complete documents. The OI implements the ontology graph presented in Section 8.2.

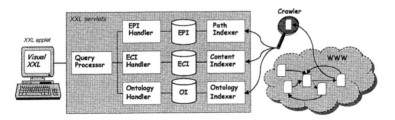

Fig. 8.4. Architecture of the XXL search engine

8.3.3 Query Processing in the XXL Search Engine

The evaluation of the search conditions in the WHERE clause consists of the following two main steps:

- The XXL query is decomposed into subqueries. A global evaluation order for evaluating the various subqueries and a local evaluation order in which the components of each subquery are evaluated are chosen.
- For each subquery, subgraphs of the data graph that match the query graph are computed, exploiting the various indexes to the best possible extent. The subresults are then combined into the result for the original query.

Query Decomposition

The WHERE clause of an XXL query is of the form "WHERE P1 AS V1 AND ... AND Pn AS Vn" where each P_i is a regular path expression over elementary conditions and the V_i are element variables to which the end node of a matching path is bound. Each regular path expression corresponds to a subquery and can be described by an equivalent non-deterministic finite state automaton (NFSA).

We restrict XXL queries so that the dependency graph between binding and usage of variables is acyclic. Furthermore, we estimate the selectivity of each subquery using simple statistics about the frequency of element names and search terms that appear as constants in the subquery. Then we choose to evaluate subqueries and bind the corresponding variables in ascending order of selectivity (i.e., estimated size of the intermediate result).

The local evaluation order for a subquery specifies the order in which it is attempted to match the states of the subquery's NFSA with elements in the data graph. The XXL prototype supports two alternative strategies: in top-down order the matching begins with the start state of the NFSA and then proceeds towards the final state(s); in bottom-up order the matching begins with the final state(s) and then proceeds towards the start state.

Query Evaluation Using Index Structures

For each subquery, simple path expressions with element names and the wildcard symbol # are looked up in the EPI. For example, all occurrences of a pattern #.lecture.description or lecture.#.description can be retrieved from the EPI. Content conditions are evaluated by the ECI, a text index on element and attribute contents. For semantic similarity conditions such as description ~ "star" the ECI yields approximate matches and a similarity score based on IR-style tf*idf measures [19, 209] and semantic distances between concepts in the ontology. Finally, for semantic similarity conditions on element names, for example, ~lecture, the OI is used to expand the query in order to capture semantically related element names such as course; again, a similarity score is computed for result ranking.

The ranked lists of relevant subgraphs from the index-based subquery evaluation are composed into a list of global graphs, each of which has assigned to it a global similarity score derived from the local scores by elementary probability computation. The QP finally extracts the result as specified by the SELECT clause and constructs an XML document that is returned to the XXL client.

More details about the query processor of the XXL search engine can be found in [296].

8.4 Conclusions

Ontologies are increasingly seen as a key asset to further automation of information processing. Although many approaches for representing and applying ontologies have already been devised, they have not found their way into search engines for querying XML data. In this chapter we have shown how ontologies with quantified semantic relationships can help to increase both the recall and precision for queries on semistructured data. This is achieved by broadening the query with closely related terms, thus yielding more results, but only after disambiguizing query terms, so only relevant results are included in the result of the query.

Using Relevance Feedback in XML Retrieval

Roger Weber

9.1 Introduction

Information retrieval has a long tradition: in the early days, the main focus was on the retrieval of plain text documents and on search systems for books and structured documents in (digital) libraries. Often, users were assisted by well-trained librarians or specialists to retrieve documents fitting their information need. With the proliferation of the internet, retrieval systems for further media types like images, video, audio and semi-structured documents have emerged. But more importantly, an ever increasing number of untrained users deploy retrieval systems to seek for information. Since most users lack a profound understanding of how retrieval engines work and of how to properly describe an information need, the retrieval quality is often not satisfactory due to bad query formulations. As an illustration of this, Jansen et al. [177] reported that 62% of queries submitted to the Excite web search engine consisted of less than three query terms. Obviously, this is by far insufficient to accurately describe an information need. But search systems often do not support users (or only rudimentary) to adjust their queries to improve retrieval effectiveness.

As a countermeasure for the query refinement problem, relevance feedback was introduced in the late 1960's [169, 251]. The basic idea is to model the search as an iterative and interactive process (cf. Figure 9.1) during which the system assists users with the task of query refinement. To this end, the user has to assign relevance values to the retrieved documents. This feedback together with the original query is processed according to a feedback model and yields a new query which, hopefully, returns new and more relevant documents. This iteration can continue until the user is satisfied or the retrieval process is aborted. The feedback process bears a number of design options: 1) capturing of feedback (implicit vs. explicit, granularity, feedback values), 2) reformulation of a query given the feedback (feedback model), and 3) provision of methods for users to accept/reject parts of the refined query.

In this chapter, we focus on relevance feedback techniques for XML-retrieval. In this context, we describe and deploy a retrieval model that

H. Blanken et al. (Eds.): Intelligent Search on XML Data, LNCS 2818, pp. 133–143, 2003.
© Springer-Verlag Berlin Heidelberg 2003

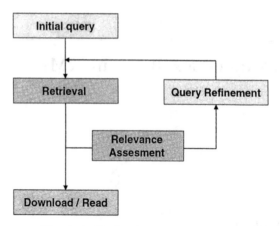

Fig. 9.1. Feedback interaction model.

comprises both structural as well as content related query parts following the principles of augmentation [127, 128] and query specific retrieval statistics (cf. Chapter 6 in this book). We describe how relevance feedback methods may refine such queries: for that purpose, we have identified five dimensions for query adaptation, namely: 1) query expansion, i.e., the addition and removal of query terms, 2) query term weighting, 3) recalculation of the discrimination power of terms, 4) structural weighting, and 5) selection of the retrieval model or parts of the model. Along each of these dimensions, we describe feedback methods adopted from approaches for text retrieval. We further summarize some of the cognitive results from earlier work [191] with respect to the design of feedback interaction. Finally, this chapter does not contain an evaluation of the different feedback techniques due to the lack of an appropriate benchmark with relevance assessments on the retrieved documents. However, in light of the recent development of INEX [125], we plan to implement, to tune, and to evaluate the different feedback models with this benchmark.

This chapter is organized as follows: Section 9.2 describes a generic retrieval model for XML documents. Section 9.3 adapts previous work on relevance feedback to the context of XML retrieval. Section 9.4 concludes this chapter.

9.2 XML Retrieval Model

Relevance feedback techniques are always tightly bound to the underlying retrieval model. In the following, we shortly summarize an XML retrieval model which provides flexible means to query XML documents by structure

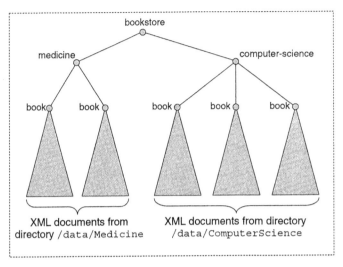

Fig. 9.2. Universal view of an XML collection.

and content. For more details, we refer to Chapter 6 which discusses the model in more details.

9.2.1 Document Model

In the context of XML, the traditional document granularity of text retrieval is no longer adequate. Mostly, this is because a single XML file can span an entire data collection and because queries can restrict the search to specific sub-trees (e.g., <book> or <chapter> elements). As a consequence, we first have to define the collection for XML retrieval and its content.

For that purpose, we assume that all data is contained by a single "universal" document. If this is not the case, i.e., several documents comprise the data collection, we may construct a virtual universal document as indicated by Figure 9.2: each XML file of the collection represents a distinct subtree of the universal document. The subtrees may further be connected by a number of hierarchical layers at the top of the universal document possibly reflecting the directory hierarchy of the original XML files. In the figure, for instance, we connected two XML files from the /data/Medicine folder with three XML files from the /data/ComputerScience folder. The notion of documents as in traditional text retrieval is replaced with the notion of elements (or nodes in the XML document). Each element is described by a unique XPath expression and a non-deterministic label path from the root of the document to the root of the element. Elements are the granularity of our retrieval model, i.e., a query selects a set of elements and the retrieval systems ranks them according to the content-based query part (see next subsection).

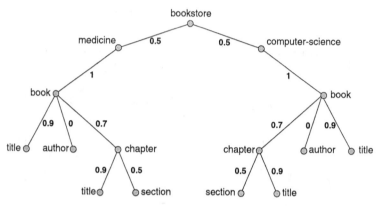

Fig. 9.3. DTD of the global XML document illustrating the principle of augmentation.

As in traditional retrieval models, elements are characterized by high-dimensional vectors with binary components (boolean retrieval, probabilistic retrieval) or with components denoting the term frequency of terms in the elements' content. For leaf elements or elements with mixed content, we obtain a first feature vector from the terms directly connected to these nodes. For the vector space model, for instance, we obtain the components of this vector by counting the number of term occurrences $tf(i, e)$ of terms i in an element e. For inner elements, we derive term frequencies by inheriting term frequencies from their child nodes following the approach of augmentation from Fuhr et al. [127, 128] (also see Chapter 6 for more details on how to obtain these vectors). The intuition behind this is as follows (see Figure 9.3): considering <chapter> elements in Figure 9.3, we may argue that terms in <title> elements are more important than terms in <section> elements. Hence, term appearances in the former element type should count more (have larger weights) than term appearances in <section> elements. With augmentation, we assign weights for each edge in the DTD of the universal document (or its DataGuide if no DTD exists) and determine the occurrence weight of a term in a sub-element s of an element e by multiplying the weights along the path from e to s.

9.2.2 Query Model

In this document model, a query consists of four parts: 1) a structural part defining the possible element types of the result, 2) predicates on the contents of the elements[1], 3) a set of keywords describing the desired content of selected element instances, and 4) weights and parameters for the ranking function to influence the order of retrieved elements. Query evaluation first determines

---

[1] 1) and 2) may be given with a single XPath-expression [176].

the set of elements fulfilling the type constraint (label path to elements) and the content constraint (predicates on the instance's data). This set is then ordered according to a retrieval function that takes query part 3 and 4 into account. For more details on query processing, we refer to Chapter 6.

9.2.3 Relevance Ranking

In the following, we describe two approaches for relevance ranking of text documents. We first describe the original proposals for flat text document and then extend the models for XML retrieval.

Vector Space Retrieval. With vector space retrieval, also known as TFIDF ranking, documents are represented by vectors containing the term frequencies of a controlled set of terms within the documents. Thereby, we assume that the more frequent a term appears within a document the better the document matches a query containing this term. For multi-term queries, we have to distinguish between important terms and unimportant terms. To this end, the inverse document frequency (idf) was introduced based on the Zipf distribution of terms over the document collection: let df_i denote the number of documents containing term i, and N be the total number of documents. Then, the idf-weight for term i is $idf_i = \log_2(N) - \log_2(df_i) + 1^2$. Given the term vector $\mathbf{d_j}$ of a document j, the term vector $\mathbf{q}$ of a query and the idf-weighting vector $\mathbf{idf}$, the rsv of that document for the query is determined, for example, by the cosine measure as:

$$rsv^{cos}(\mathbf{d_j}, \mathbf{q}, \mathbf{idf}) = \frac{(\mathbf{idf}.*\mathbf{d_j}) \cdot (\mathbf{idf}.*\mathbf{q})}{\|\mathbf{idf}.*\mathbf{d_j}\|_2 \cdot \|\mathbf{idf}.*\mathbf{q}\|_2} \tag{9.1}$$

with $.*$ denoting the element-wise multiplication of two vectors, and $\|\cdot\|_2$ denoting the length of a vector (L_2-norm). rsv^{cos} determines the cosine of the angle between the weighted document vector and the weighted term vector. Hence, a document receives a high rsv if it contains all the terms of the query, and if the ratios of frequencies of query terms are similar to the ones of the query. This definition bears some potential problems: for instance, a query "XML retrieval" ranks those documents at the top which contain the terms "XML" and "retrieval" equally often. However, the most relevant documents are likely to have different term frequencies for the two keywords. There also exists a number of further rsv-functions, each having its own advantages and disadvantages. The most common ones among them are the dot-product and the Euclidean distance to asses similarities between documents[3]:

$$rsv^{dot}(\mathbf{d_j}, \mathbf{q}, \mathbf{idf}) = (\mathbf{idf}.*\mathbf{d_j}) \cdot (\mathbf{idf}.*\mathbf{q}) \tag{9.2}$$

$$d^{sim}(\mathbf{d_j}, \mathbf{q}, \mathbf{idf}) = \|(\mathbf{idf}.*\mathbf{d_j}) - (\mathbf{idf}.*\mathbf{q})\|_2 \tag{9.3}$$

In the context of XML documents, we must slightly adapt the notions of traditional TFIDF ranking. Instead of statistics (term frequencies and inverse

---

[2] Sometimes, $\log_2(N+1)$ and $\log_2(df_i+1)$ are used to prevent numerical problems.
[3] Note that the definitions of rsv and distances are converse: while large rsv-values are better, small distances denote a better similarity match.

document frequencies) at the document level, we need statistics (element frequencies and inverse element frequencies) at all the element levels in the XML document. In terms of inverse element frequencies (ief), we follow a query specific approach instead of using global ief statistics, i.e., we always recompute the ief-values over the selected elements of query part 1) and 2). By this, we strictly follow the principle of conventional TFIDF ranking as these methods always recommend to compute idf-values based on the current collection. There exists no "universal" weights for terms in text retrieval as their characteristic power depends on the collection. Consider the example in Figure 9.3: obviously, a term like "computer" is more characteristic in the collection of medicine books than in the collection of computer science books. Hence, such terms should obtain different (ief-)weights depending on whether queries run over the "medicine" subtree or over the "computer-science" subtree.

Probabilistic Retrieval. Instead of the popular vector space model, we may also deploy probabilistic retrieval models to rank elements by their relevance. In the following, we apply the Binary Independence Retrieval (BIR) model [123, 250] for XML retrieval. For that purpose, we transform element and query vectors to binary vectors with component values of 0 and 1 denoting the absence and presence of a term i, respectively. Instead of idf/ief-weights, probabilistic models determine term weights based on the probabilities that a term appears in relevant and non-relevant documents. Initially, probabilities are roughly estimated based on document frequencies. Subsequently, relevance assessments of users for retrieved elements allow for more accurate estimates for these probabilities. I.e., probabilistic models like BIR already incorporate relevance feedback into the retrieval process.

The Binary Independence Retrieval (BIR) model [123, 250] is an early attempt for probabilistic retrieval. It assumes that probabilistic events of term appearances in relevant and non-relevant documents are independent from each other. Let r_i be the probability that term i appears in a relevant document, and n_i be the probability that it appears in a non-relevant document. Then, the weight for query term i is $c_i = log(r_i(1 - n_i)) - log(n_i(1 - r_i))$. Intuitively, c_i becomes large if term i appears only in relevant documents; it becomes small (negative) if the term appears often in non-relevant documents. The rsv for a document j is determined as sums over all terms i as follows:

$$rsv^{BIR}(\mathbf{d_j}, \mathbf{q}, \mathbf{c}) = \sum_{i,\ (d_j)_i=1,\ q_i=1} c_i = \sum_{i,\ (d_j)_i=1,\ q_i=1} log\frac{r_i(1 - n_i)}{n_i(1 - r_i)} \tag{9.4}$$

Finally, we need to compute the probabilities r_i and n_i. Initially, these values are estimated by $r_i = 0.5$ and $n_i = df_i/N$. After relevance assessments of users, the probabilities are refined: let k be the total number of retrieved documents and k_i the number of documents that contain the term i. Further, let l be the number of relevant documents and l_i the number of relevant documents that contain the term i. Then, r_i and n_i are intuitively given as (with some corrections to avoid numerical instabilities):

$$r_i = \frac{l_i + 0.5}{l + 1}, \qquad n_i = \frac{k_i - l_i + 0.5}{k - l + 1} \tag{9.5}$$

Again, in the context of XML retrieval we have to replace the notion of a document with the notion of an element.

9.3 Feedback Models

The idea of feedback interaction was implemented in many retrieval systems including search engines for web documents, images, and plain text documents [110, 253, 258]. In the following, we apply feedback techniques for TFIDF-based XML retrieval as described in the last section. However, the approaches are more general and may be adapted to other retrieval models as well. First, let us summarize the dimensions of the parameter space of query refinement:

- **Query terms.** Feedback models may add or remove terms to improve the description of users' information needs.
- **Weights on query terms.** Term frequencies in queries, i.e., weights on query terms, have a great influence on the ranking of retrieved nodes.
- **Discrimination power.** *idf* (*ief*) weights represent default settings for the discrimination power of terms appearing in the collection. It is unlikely, that these settings are appropriate for all query scenarios.
- **Structural weights.** Similarly, it is unlikely that the initial structural weights obtained by augmentation are suitable for all queries (cf. Figure 9.3).
- **Model selection.** TFIDF is one retrieval model among many others. Similarly, the cosine measure is one *rsv* function among many variants. So far, the observation is that no retrieval model is most appropriate for all query types. Hence, choosing a retrieval model for query evaluation has a great influence on the quality of its result.

9.3.1 Capturing Feedback Information

In its simplest form, feedback methods only require positive examples, i.e., they adjust queries only with the relevant documents. We may further take non-relevant documents into account. Ide [169] reported that this seems to raise the ranks of high-ranking relevant documents, and, however, to lower the ranks of some low-ranking relevant documents. As a consequence of this, Ide proposed a method that only considers the top-ranking non-relevant document (Ide dec-hi) apart of the relevant ones. Instead of relevance assessments, a system could query for preferences of the form *"document A fits better to my information need than document B"* [121].

Further, it is possible to capture feedback information at finer granularities, e.g., users have to explicitly mark relevant portions in retrieved documents. This would greatly help to reduce the noise introduced by the non-relevant areas of documents marked as relevant. Yet, this would also increase the burden on users which is likely to be not accepted. White et al. [316] have compared *explicit* capturing of feedback, i.e., users mark documents as relevant, with *implicit* capturing of feedback, i.e., users' behavior like mouse pointer navigation and the time spent to view a document were interpreted as relevance indications. Their empirical study revealed that users performed equally well on the implicit and explicit system. However, more empirical studies are needed to investigate how implicit evidence is best collected.

9.3.2 Query Expansion and Query Weighting

In the vector space model, sparse high-dimensional vectors represent queries and documents. Depending on the *rsv* function, the query vector denotes a direction (cosine measure), location (similarity measure) or preference of terms (dot-product) for supposedly relevant documents in a query-specific sub-space. In the late 1960's, Rocchio [251] suggested a weighted combination of the original query vector $\mathbf{q}$ with the vectors of the relevant documents ($\mathbf{r_j}$, $0 \leq j \leq m_r$) and the ones of the non-relevant documents ($\mathbf{s_j}$, $0 \leq j \leq m_n$):

$$\mathbf{q}^r = \alpha \mathbf{q} + \frac{\beta}{m_r} \sum_{j=0}^{m_r} \mathbf{r_j} - \frac{\gamma}{m_n} \sum_{j=0}^{m_n} \mathbf{s_j} \tag{9.6}$$

Intuitively, the relevant documents attract the query while the non-relevant ones repel it. The parameters α, β, and γ have to be determined with extensive experiments. [260, 267] reported that the settings $\alpha = 1$, $\beta = 0.75$ and $\gamma = 0.25$ lead to best results. Ide [169] simplified Rocchio's formula as follows:

$$\text{(Regular)} \;\; \mathbf{q}^r = \mathbf{q} + \sum_{j=0}^{m_r} \mathbf{r_j} - \sum_{j=0}^{m_n} \mathbf{s_j} \qquad \text{(dec} - \text{hi)} \;\; \mathbf{q}^r = \mathbf{q} + \sum_{j=0}^{m_r} \mathbf{r_j} - \mathbf{s_0} \tag{9.7}$$

In the second equation, it is assumed that $\mathbf{s_0}$ denotes the top-ranking non-relevant document. Several evaluations report that Ide dec-hi performs best since the influence of negative feedback is only minimal [152, 260].

Rocchio's and Ide's formulae automatically expand queries with terms from the retrieved documents, and assign positive and negative weights for term appearances in relevant and non-relevant documents, respectively. Obviously, the query vector becomes more dense and therefore negatively affects retrieval efficiency. Using inverted files, retrieval costs linearly depend on the number of query terms, i.e., the number of non-zero elements in the query vector. Further, if a query term has a small weight, its influence on the *rsv* is only marginal. Hence, [267] suggests to keep only the k elements of $\mathbf{q}^r$ having the largest absolute values. Again, obtaining good values for k is subject to extensive testing ([267] used $k = 30$).

The principles behind these approaches are *query expansion* and *query weighting*. In the case of query expansion and apart of Rocchio and Ide, numerous approaches were followed to determine a good set of terms for refined queries, e.g., in [152, 205]. Basically, the set of terms is sorted according to a relevance value which often takes document frequencies and appearances (postings) of terms in relevant and non-relevant documents into account.

However, it appears that fine tuning these relevance values heavily depends on the document collection and the query requirements. Further, [152, 205] report that best retrieval results were achieved if only 10 to 20 terms were added to the original query. Hence, keeping the number of query terms small is not only desirable from an efficiency point of view but also from an effectiveness perspective.

9.3.3 Discrimination Power of Terms

In the vector space model and also in probabilistic retrieval models, a lot of research addressed the core problem of how to determine the discrimination power of terms. The presented idf-formulae in this chapter are only some proposals among many others. Several evaluations, however, have shown that there is no "correct" or "optimal" formula to compute how characteristic a term is over a collection. Often, the discrimination power depends on the query context of the user. With relevance feedback, we have the opportunity to take this query context into account when selecting the idf-weighting scheme. Following the ideas of the next subsection, we can select out of the many proposals the one method that best separates relevant elements from non-relevant elements.

Another approach is to use the term weighting schemes of probabilistic models for vector space retrieval [152]. To this end, idf-weights are replaced by the c_i-weights of the BIR model after a feedback step. Terms that only appear in relevant documents obtain a higher weights than terms that appear in both groups or only in the non-relevant documents.

9.3.4 Structural Weights and Model Selection

Our approach for structural re-weighting works as follows: let $\mathcal{E}$ be one of the element types selected by the path expression of the query, and $\mathcal{S}$ be one of its sub-element types. The aim is to determine how characteristic the contents of $\mathcal{S}$ is to distinguish between relevant and non-relevant elements of type $\mathcal{E}$. To this end, we determine a ranking for the last query by only consulting the content of sub-elements of type $\mathcal{S}$. If this ranking contains many relevant documents at the top, we may say that $\mathcal{S}$ is important for the current query, and, if relevant documents obtain low ranks, the contents of $\mathcal{S}$-elements is not well-suited. A number of measures are available to asses result quality, e.g., R-precision, normalized sums over the ranks of relevant documents [313], or the usefulness measure if partial relevance ordering exists [121].

A similar idea was implemented in the MARS image retrieval engine to select and weight image features [253]. We may deploy their approach to select an "optimal" model from a set of different retrieval models. As with structural weights, we determine the effectiveness for each retrieval model given the relevance assessments of the user. Now, we have two options: either we select the most effective model and run the refined query for that model.

Or, we select a number of retrieval models and combine their scores to obtain an overall score for elements.

9.3.5 Cognitive Experiences

Although it was reported in several papers that relevance feedback significantly improves retrieval effectiveness, e.g., [152, 260], only little work exists on the impact of relevance feedback on the information seeking behavior and performance of users [25, 191]. Even more, if we consider current web search engines, almost none of them provides relevance feedback methods. If they exist, they are rather rudimentary: e.g., Teoma[4] provides a number of automatically refined queries based on frequent terms and phrases in the result set. Another type of query refinement is offered by Vivisimo[5] which hierarchically clusters retrieved documents. Users can select clusters to see only those results within the selected clusters, i.e., feedback interaction is provided only at the level of browsing but not at the level of query refinement.

Often, when asked, developers of search engines argue that users do not ask for relevance feedback or that users do not understand how to use feedback methods even if they exist. Koenemann et al. [191], however, have empirically shown that even untrained individuals easily capture the notion of relevance feedback and are able to increase their retrieval performance. Moreover, it seems that users should have some kind of control on the refinement process. In their study, a group of users were able to accept or reject query terms that the feedback method has chosen for refinement. The empirical evaluation revealed that this group of users performed significantly better than users with no control. Indeed, the later group of users were asking for explicit information about how the feedback influenced their initial query.

9.4 Conclusions

In this chapter, we have presented a number of relevance feedback techniques adapted from classical information retrieval scenarios to an XML retrieval scenario. Our retrieval model provides means to retrieve elements of arbitrary types from a global XML document, and orders them according to their similarity to the textual part of the query. In this model, we have identified five dimensions for query refinement: 1) query expansion, 2) query term weighting, 3) adjusting of the discrimination power of terms, 4) structural weighting, and 5) selection of the retrieval model. For each of these dimensions, we have described a number of feedback methods to refine the query according to the relevance assessments of users. Although the feedback models were described in isolation, we may apply a number (or all) of them at each stage of the

---

[4] http://www.teoma.com/
[5] http://www.vivisimo.com

refinement process. We further have summarized important cognitive experiences with relevance feedback: the burden to enter feedback should not be too large (ideally, feedback is implicitly captured), and, the user should obtain control over the query refinement process (e.g., by explaining how the query was changed and by allowing for further modifications). Most of the presented feedback models require carefully chosen parameters to obtain good results. However, these settings require extensive evaluations and fine tuning towards the intended document collection and query scenarios. In light of the recent development of the INEX [125] benchmark for XML retrieval, we plan to implement, to tune, and to evaluate the different feedback models, and to report about the usefulness of the proposed methods for XML retrieval.

10

Classification and Focused Crawling for Semistructured Data

Martin Theobald, Ralf Schenkel, and Gerhard Weikum

10.1 Introduction

Despite the great advances in XML data management and querying, the currently prevalent XPath- or XQuery-centric approaches face severe limitations when applied to XML documents in large intranets, digital libraries, federations of scientific data repositories, and ultimately the Web. In such environments, data has much more diverse structure and annotations than in a business-data setting and there is virtually no hope for a common schema or DTD that all the data complies with. Without a schema, however, database-style querying would often produce either empty result sets, namely, when queries are overly specific, or way too many results, namely, when search predicates are overly broad, the latter being the result of the user not knowing enough about the structure and annotations of the data.

An important IR technique is automatic classification for organizing documents into topic directories based on statistical learning techniques [218, 64, 219, 102]. Once data is labeled with topics, combinations of declarative search, browsing, and mining-style analysis is the most promising approach to find relevant information, for example, when a scientist searches for existing results on some rare and highly specific issue. The anticipated benefit is a more explicit, topic-based organization of the information which in turn can be leveraged for more effective searching. The main problem that we address towards this goal is to understand which kinds of features of XML data can be used for high-accuracy classification and how these feature spaces should be managed by an XML search tool with user-acceptable responsiveness.

This work explores the design space outlined above by investigating features for XML classification that capture annotations (i.e., tag-term pairs), structure (i.e., twigs and tag paths), and ontological background information (i.e., mapping words onto word senses). With respect to the tree structure of XML documents, we study XML twigs and tag paths as extended features that can be combined with text term occurrences in XML elements. XML twigs

H. Blanken et al. (Eds.): Intelligent Search on XML Data, LNCS 2818, pp. 145–157, 2003.
© Springer-Verlag Berlin Heidelberg 2003

are triples of the form *(ancestor element, left sibling element, right sibling element)* which allow a shallow structure-aware document representation, while tag paths merely describe linear ancester/descendant relationships with no regard for siblings. Moreover, we show how to leverage ontological background information, more specifically, the WordNet thesaurus, for the construction of more expressive feature spaces.

The various options for XML feature spaces are implemented within the BINGO! [281] focused crawler (also known as *thematic crawler* [63]) for expert Web search and automated portal generation. BINGO! has originally been designed for HTML pages (including various formats of unstructured text like PDF, Word, etc.), and is now extended not only to extract contents from XML documents but to exploit their structure for more precise document representation and classification.

10.2 Overview of the BINGO! System

The BINGO! [1] focused crawling toolkit consists of six main components that are depicted in Figure 10.1: the multi-threaded crawler itself, an HTML document analyzer that produces a feature vector for each document, the classifier with its training data, the feature selection as a "noise-reduction" filter for the classifier, the link analysis module as a distiller for topic-specific authorities and hubs, and the training module for the classifier that is invoked for periodic retraining.

Topic-specific bookmarks play a key role in the BINGO! system. The crawler starts from a user's bookmark file or some other form of personalized or community-specific topic directory [22]. These intellectually classified documents serve two purposes: 1) they provide the initial seeds for the crawl (i.e., documents whose outgoing hyperlinks are traversed by the crawler), and 2) they provide the initial contents for the user's topic tree and the initial training data for the classifier. The classifier, which is the crucial filter component of a focused crawler, detects relevant documents on the basis of these bookmark samples, while it discards off-the-topic documents and prevents their links from being pursued. The following subsections give a short overview of the main components of BINGO!. For more details see [282, 281].

10.2.1 Crawler

The crawler processes the links in the URL queue using multiple threads. For each retrieved document the crawler initiates some analysis steps that depend on the document's MIME type (e.g., HTML, XML, etc.) and then invokes the classifier on the resulting feature vector. Once a crawled document has been successfully classified, BINGO! extracts all links from the document and adds

---

[1] **Bookmark-Induced Gathering of !nformation**

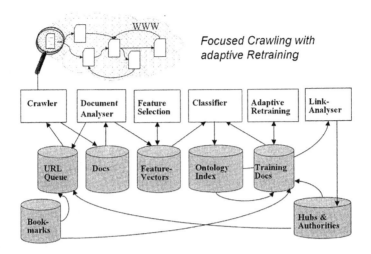

Fig. 10.1. The BINGO! architecture and its main components

them to the URL queue for further crawling. The ordering of links (priority) in the crawler queue is based on the classification confidence provided by the specific classification method that is used. This confidence measure is derived from either statistical learning approaches (e.g., Naive Bayes [19, 209]) or the result of regression techniques (e.g., Support Vector Machines [57, 306, 180]). All retrieved documents are stored in our database index including the features, links and available metadata like URL(s), title, authors, etc.

10.2.2 Document Analyzer

BINGO! computes feature vectors for documents according to the standard bag-of-words model, using stopword elimination, Porter stemming, and $tf*idf$ based term weighting [19, 209]. We consider our local document database as an approximation of the corpus for idf computation and recompute it lazily upon each retraining.

The standard document analyzer for unstructured data can address a wide range of content handlers for different document formats (in particular, PDF, MS Word, MS PowerPoint etc.) as well as common archive files (zip, gz) and converts the recognized contents into simple HTML. So these formats can be processed by BINGO! like usual web pages (except for the link extraction).

For semistructured data like XML, document analyzation offers challenging possibilities to generate more meaningful features under the consideration of annotation and structure which is a main issue of our recent work (see section 10.3). Because of the inherent differences between structured and unstructured feature sets, training documents of these two kinds cannot be merged under the same classification model. Hence, classification could only take place with two different classifiers for structured and unstructured data. Therefore, our recent efforts are directed towards a unified view for structured and unstructured data including the automatic transformation and annotation of HTML to embed XML-style document handling into crawling over the Web.

10.2.3 Classifier

Document classification consists of a training phase for building a mathematical decision model based on intellectually preclassified documents and a decision phase for classifying new, previously unseen documents fetched by the crawler. We chose *Support Vector Machines (SVM)* [57, 306, 180] as a leading-edge classification method. More specifically, we use Thorsten Joachim's SVM-light V5.00 software restricting ourselves to linear SVMs.

The SVM algorithm is a learning algorithm that consists of a supervised training phase for a *binary set of topics*. A separating hyperplane defined as $\mathbf{w} \cdot \mathbf{x} + b = 0$, where w denotes the normal vector of this hyperplane, and $|b|/\|w\|$ is the perpendicular distance from the hyperplane to the origin, is computed such that it maximizes the margin between a set of positive and negative feature vectors in the m-dimensional feature space. These feature vectors represent a user-specific document collection with positive samples for the user's topic of interest as well as explicit negative samples [281] in the vector space model.

The classification step for a test document $\mathbf{y}$ then simply consists of the computation of the algebraic sign of a decision function of the form $\mathbf{w} \cdot \mathbf{y} > 0$, the sign denotes on which side of the hyperplane the test vector is determined to be, and the value of the result yields the SVM classification confidence in form of the distance of the test vector to the separating hyperplane.

The *hierarchical multi-class* classification problem for a tree of topics is solved by training a number of binary SVMs, one for each topic in the tree. For each SVM the training documents for the given topic serve as positive samples, and we use the training data for the tree siblings as negative samples. The computed hyperplane that separates these samples then serves as the decision function for previously unseen test documents (by computing a simple scalar product). A test document is recursively tested against all siblings of a tree level starting by the root's children, and it is assigned to all topics for which the classifier yields a positive decision (or alternatively, only to the one with the highest positive classification confidence) [103, 68, 306].

10.2.4 Topic-Specific Feature Spaces

The feature selection algorithm provided by the BINGO! engine yields the most characteristic features for a given topic; these are the features that are used by the classifier for testing new documents. A good feature for this purpose discriminates competing topics from each other, i.e., those topics that are at the *same level of the topic tree*. Therefore, feature selection has to be topic-specific; it is invoked for every topic in the tree individually.

We use the *Mutual Information* (MI) measure to build topic-specific feature spaces. This technique, which is a specialized case of the notions of cross-entropy or Kullback-Leibler divergence [209], is known as one of the most effective methods [326, 325] that is slightly in favor of rare terms (i.e., the ones with a high *idf* value) which is an excellent property for classification.

Mutual information can be interpreted as a measure of how much the joint distribution of features and topics deviate from a hypothetical distribution in which features and topics are independent of each other (hence the remark about MI being a special case of the Kullback-Leibler divergence which measures the differences between multivariate probability distributions in general).

The root node of the taxonomy tree yields the unification of all topic-specific feature spaces and provides a simple dictionary data structure for one-to-one mapping of features (i.e., terms) to dimensions (i.e., integers) in the vector space which is used to generate the input vectors of the SVM.

10.2.5 Using the Link Structure for Topic Distillation

The link structure between documents in each topic is an additional source of information about how well they capture the topic. The BINGO! engine applies Kleinberg's link analysis method, coined HITS [189], iteratively to each topic in the taxonomy tree (i.e., HITS is invoked after a certain amount of new documents has been visited). Analogously to Google's Page Rank, the HITS algorithm uses the documents adjacency matrix A_c to exploit principle Eigenvectors of each topic-specific sub graph $G_c = (V_c, E_c)$ of the Web. While Page Rank uses A_c directly, HITS divides the task into the approximation of the principle Eigenvectors of the matrices $A_c^T A_c$, and $A_c A_c^T$ respectively, and thus produces a ranking for the best *hubs* (link collections) and the best *authorities* (most frequently referenced sources). Despite a numerical solution of this Eigenvalue problem, the HITS algorithm yields an approximation by iteratively summing up $x_p = \sum_{(q,p) \in E_c} y_q$ and $y_p = \sum_{(p,q) \in E_c} x_q$ and normalizing these values until they converge to $x^* = A_c^T y^*$ and $y^* = A_c x^*$ which provides an essential efficiency improvement with regard to the application of this method for Web crawling.

In a first approach, this method may be applied to XLinks [95] and XPointers [144] as well, however, without regarding the XPointer information and using XLinks as whole document pointers that aggregate the hub and authority weights for the root elements only. A more fine grained approach might overcome these limitations and exploit the tree sub-structure of XML documents by regarding the elements themselves as mini-documents, and thus, splitting documents into micro-hubs and micro-authorities to produce a more precise ranking for large, heterogeneous XML DOM [311] trees.

10.2.6 Retraining

Building a reasonably precise classifier from a very small set of training data is a challenging task. Effective learning algorithms for highly heterogeneous environments like the Web would require a much larger training basis, yet human users would rarely be willing to invest hours of intellectual work for putting together a rich document collection that is truly representative of their interest profiles. To address this problem we distinguish two basic crawl strategies:

- The *learning phase* serves to automatically identify the most characteristic documents of a topic, coined *archetypes*, and to expand the classifier's knowledge base among the bookmarks' neighbor documents with highest classification confidence and best authority score.
- The *harvesting phase* then serves to effectively process the user's information demands with improved crawling precision and recall.

BINGO! repeatedly initiates retraining of the classifier when a certain number of documents have been crawled and successfully classified with confidence above a certain threshold. At such points, a new set of training documents is determined for each node of the topic tree. For this purpose, the best archetypes are determined in two complementary ways. First, the link analysis is initiated with the current documents of a topic as its base set. The best authorities of a tree node are regarded as potential archetypes of the node. The second source of topic-specific archetypes builds on the confidence of the classifier's yes-or-no decision for a given node of the ontology tree. Among the automatically classified documents of a topic those documents whose yes decision had the highest confidence measure are selected as potential archetypes. The *intersection* of the top authorities and the documents with highest SVM confidence form a new set of candidates for the promotion to the training data.

After successfully extending the training basis with additional archetypes, BINGO! retrains all topic-specific classifiers and switches to the harvesting phase now putting emphasis on recall (i.e., collecting as many documents as possible) where the crawler is resumed with the best hubs from the link analysis.

10.3 Feature Spaces for XML Data

10.3.1 HTML to XML

The BINGO! engine can crawl both HTML and XML documents. However, there is surprisingly little Web data available in XML format, mostly because of the extra burden that XML (or some even more advanced Semantic-Web style representation such as RDF [320] or DAML+OIL [166]) would pose on non-trained users in terms of authoring and maintaining their Web pages. So, unless XML authoring is significantly improved [151], simply typing text and adding simple HTML-style markup is likely to remain the favorite format on the Web. Ironically, most of the dynamically generated information that can be obtained via Web portals (e.g., Amazon, eBay, CNN, etc.) is actually stored in backend databases with structured schemas but portal query results are still delivered in the form of almost unstructured HTML.

Following prior work on HTML wrapper generators and information extraction tools (see, e.g., [256, 82, 23, 265]), we have developed a toolkit for automatically transforming HTML documents into XML format. Our tool first constructs a valid XML document for input in plain text, HTML, PDF, etc., and then uses rules based on regular-expression matching to generate more meaningful tags. For example, keywords in table headings may become tags, with each row or cell of the table becoming an XML element. Our framework is currently being extended to use also machine-learning techniques such as Hidden Markov Models for more elaborated annotation. Since we are mostly interested in focused crawling and thematic portal generation, the tool has been designed for easy extensibility to quickly add domain specific rules.

10.3.2 Features from Tag Paths

Using only text terms (e.g., words, word stems, or even noun composites) and their frequencies (and other derived weighting schemes such as $tf * idf$ measures [209]) as features for automatic classification of text documents poses inherent difficulties and often leads to unsatisfactory results because of the noise that is introduced by the idiosyncratic vocabulary and style of document authors. For XML data we postulate that tags (i.e., element names) will be chosen much more consciously and carefully than the words in the element contents. We do not expect authors to be as careful as if they designed a database schema, but there should be high awareness of the need for meaningful and reasonably precise annotations and structuring. Furthermore, we expect good XML authoring tools to construct tags in a semi-automatic way, for example, by deriving them from an ontology or a "template" library (e.g., for typical homepages) and presenting them as suggestions to the user.

So we view tags as high-quality features of XML documents. When we combine tags with text terms that appear in the corresponding element contents, we can interpret the resulting (tag, term) pairs almost as if they were *(concept, value) pairs* in the spirit of a database schema with attribute names and attribute values. For example, pairs such as (programming_language, Java) or (lines_of_code, 15000) are much more informative than the mere co-occurrence of the corresponding words in a long text (e.g., describing a piece of software for an open source portal). Of course, we can go beyond simple tag-term pairs by considering entire *tag paths*, for example, a path "university/department/chair" in combination with a term "donation" in the corresponding XML element, or by considering *structural patterns* within some local context such as *twigs* of the form "homepage/teaching $\land$ homepage/research" (the latter could be very helpful in identifying homepages of university professors).

An even more far-reaching option is to map element names onto an ontological knowledge base and take advantage of the semantics of a term within its respective document context. This way, tags such as "university" and "school" or "car" and "automobile" could be mapped to the same semantic concept, thus augmenting mere words by their *word senses*. We can generalize this by mapping words to semantically related broader concepts (hypernyms) or more narrow concepts (hyponyms) if the synonymy relationship is not sufficient for constructing strong features. And of course, we could apply such mappings not just to the element names, but also to text terms that appear in element contents.

10.3.3 Combining Terms and Tags

When parsing and analyzing an XML document we extract relevant terms from element contents by means of simple stopword filtering or noun recognition, and we combine these text terms with the corresponding element name; these pairs are encoded into a single feature of the form *tag$term* (e.g., "car$Passat").

We include all tags in this combined feature space, but for tractability and also noise reduction only a subset of the terms. For each topic and its competing topics in the classification (i.e., the sibling nodes in the topic directory), we again compute from the training documents, the Kullback-Leibler divergence between the topic-specific distribution of the features and a distribution in which the features of documents are statistically independent of the topics. Note, that also for structure-aware feature sets the above argumentation for using cross-entropy remains valid.

Sorting the features in descending order of the MI measure gives us a ranking in terms of the discriminative power of the features, and we select the top n features for the classifier (with n being in the order of 500 up to 5000). We have two options for applying this selection procedure: 1) first ranking and selecting terms alone and then combining the selected ones with all tags, or 2) ranking the complete set of tag-term pairs that occur in the training data. We have chosen the second option, for different element types (i.e., with different tags) often seem to exhibit different sets of specifically characteristic terms. For example, in digital library documents terms such as "WWW" or "http" are more significant within elements tagged "content", "section", or "title" rather than elements tagged "address" where they may simply indicate the author's homepage URL. For efficiency, we introduce a pre-filtering step and eliminate all terms whose total frequency within the given topic is below some threshold; only the remaining terms, usually in the order of 10000, are considered for (tag, term) feature selection.

Term-based features are quantified in the form of $tf * idf$ weights that are proportional to the frequency of the term (tf) in a given document and to the (logarithm of the) inverse document frequency (idf) in the entire corpus (i.e., the training data for one topic in our case). So the highest weighted features are those that are frequent in one document but infrequent across the corpus. For XML data we could compute tf and idf statistics either for tags and terms separately or for tag-term pairs. Analogously to the arguments for feature selection, we have chosen the option with combined tag-term statistics. The weight $w_{ij}(f_i)$ of feature f_i in document j is computed as $w_{ij}(f_i) = tf_{ij} \, idf_i$ where idf_i is the logarithm of the *inverse element frequency* of term t_i. From the viewpoint of an individual term this approach is equivalent to interpreting every XML element as if it were a mini-document. This way, the idf part in the weight of a term is implicitly computed for each element type separately without extra effort.

For example, in a digital library with full-text publications the pair (journal_title, transaction) would have low idf value (because of ACM Transactions on Database Systems, etc.), whereas the more significant pair (content, transaction) would have high idf value (given that there have been relatively few papers on transaction management in the recent past). Achieving the same desired effect with separate statistics for tags and terms would be much less straightforward to implement.

10.3.4 Exploiting Structure

Using tag paths as features gives rise to some combinatorial explosion. However, we believe that this is a fairly modest growth, for the number of different tags used even in a large data collection should be much smaller than the number of text terms and we expect real-life XML data to exhibit typical context patterns along tag paths rather than combining tags in an arbitrarily free manner. These characteristic patterns should help us to classify data that comes from a large number of heterogeneous sources. Nevertheless, efficiency reasons may often dictate that we limit tag-path features to path length 2, just using (parent tag, tag) pairs or (parent tag, tag, term) triples.

Twigs are a specific way to split the graph structure of XML documents into a set of small characteristic units with respect to sibling elements. Twigs are encoded in the form "left child tag $ parent tag $ right child tag"; examples are "research$homepage$teaching", with "homepage" being the parent of the two siblings "research" and "teaching", or "author$journal_paper$author" for publications with two or more authors. The twig encoding suggests that our features are sensitive to the order of sibling elements, but we can optionally map twigs with different orders to the same dimension of the feature space, thus interpreting XML data as unordered trees if this is desired. For tag paths and twig patterns as features we apply feature selection to the complete structural unit.

10.4 Exploiting Ontological Knowledge

Rather than using tags and terms directly as features of an XML document, an intriguing idea is to map these into an ontological concept space. In this work we have used WordNet [114, 216] as underlying ontology, which is a fairly comprehensive common-sense thesaurus carefully handcrafted by cognitive scientists. WordNet distinguishes between *words* as literally appearing in texts and the actual *word senses*, the concepts behind words. Often one word has multiple word senses, each of which is briefly described in a sentence or two and also characterized by a set of synonyms, words with the same sense, called *synsets* in WordNet. In addition, WordNet has captured hypernym (i.e., broader sense), hyponym (i.e., more narrow sense), and holonym (i.e., part of) relationships between word senses.

In the following we describe how we map tags onto word senses of the ontology; the same procedure can be applied to map text terms, too. The resulting feature vectors only refer to word sense ids that replace the original tags or terms in the structural features. The original terms are no longer important while the structure of each feature remains unchanged. Obviously this has a potential for boosting classification if we manage to map tags with the same meaning onto the same word sense.

10.4.1 Mapping

A tag usually consists of a single word or a composite word with some special delimiters (e.g., underscore) or a Java-style use of upper and lower case to distinguish the individual words. Consider the tag word set $\{w_1, ..., w_k\}$. We look up each of the w_i in an ontology database and identify possible word sense $s_{i_1}, ..., s_{i_m}$. For example, for a tag "goal" we would find the word senses:

1. goal, end – (the state of affairs that a plan is intended to achieve and that (when achieved) terminates behavior to achieve it; "the ends justify the means")
2. goal – (a successful attempt at scoring; "the winning goal came with less than a minute left to play")

and two further senses. By looking up the synonyms of these word senses, we can construct the synsets {goal, end, content, cognitive content, mental object} and {goal, score} for the first and second meaning, respectively. For a composite tag such as "soccer_goal", we look up the senses for both "soccer" and "goal" and form the cross product of possible senses for the complete tag and represent each of these senses by the union of the corresponding two synsets. Obviously, this approach would quickly become intractable with growing number of words in a composite tag, but more than two words would seem to be extremely unusual.

The final step towards disambiguating the mapping of a tag onto a word sense is to compare the tag context $con(t)$ with the context of candidates $con(s_1)$ through $con(s_p)$ in terms of a similarity measure between bags of words. The standard IR measure for this purpose would be the cosine similarity between $con(t)$ and $con(s_j)$, or alternatively the Kullback-Leibler divergence between the two word frequency distributions (note that the context construction may add the same word multiple times, and this information is kept in the word bag). Our implementation uses the cosine similarity between the tf vectors of $con(t)$ and $con(s_j)$ for its simpler computation. Finally, we map tag t onto that sense s_j whose context has the highest similarity to $con(t)$ which is similar to the disambiguation strategy that the XXL [296] engine applies. Denote this word sense as $sense(t)$ and the set of all senses of tags that appear in the training data as $senses_{train} = \{sense(t_i)|t_i \ appears \ in \ training \ data\}$.

Putting everything together, a tag t in a test document d is first mapped to a word sense $s := map(t)$, then we find the closest word sense $s' := argmax_{s'}\{sim(s',s)|s' \in F\}$ that is included in the feature space F of the training data, and set the weight of s' in d to $sim(s', map(t))$.

10.4.2 Incremental Mapping

The feature space constituted by the mapping of tags onto word senses is appropriate when training documents and the test documents to be classified have a major overlap in their word senses (i.e., the images of their tag-to-word-sense mappings). In practice, this is not self-guaranteed even for test documents that would indeed fall into one of the trained topics. Suppose, for example, that we have used training documents with tags such as "goal", "soccer", and "shot", which are all mapped to corresponding word senses, and then a previously unseen test document contains tags such as "Champions_League", "football", and "dribbling", which correspond to a disjoint set of word senses. The classifier would have no chance to accept the test document for topic "sports"; nevertheless we would intellectually rate the test document as a good candidate for sports.

To rectify this situation, we define a similarity metric between word senses of the ontological feature space, and then map the tags of a previously unseen test document to the word senses that actually appeared in the training data and are closest to the word senses onto which the test document's tags would be mapped directly. For a detailed discussion how the semantic similarity $sim(s, s')$ of two concepts s and s' in the ontology graph can be estimated see Chapter 8.

If the training set itself yields rich feature spaces that already contain most of the classification-relevant terms we will ever encounter in our test documents, we cannot expect vast improvements by ontology lookups and thus leave out this step using only given tag-term pairs and twigs. With increasingly sparse training feature spaces (in comparison to the test set), we can stepwise add lookups for the strongest (most relevant) features (i.e. the tags) and/or terms, where infrequent nouns among the element contents would be the next source of potentially relevant features. Of course, full lookups for each term using the ontology service with its disambiguation function is best suited for very few training data but also has the highest costs and decreases performance.

10.4.3 Ontological Classification in the Vector Space

In the classification phase we aim to extend the test vector by finding approximate matches between the concepts in feature space and the formerly unknown concepts of the test document. Like the training phase, the classification identifies synonyms and replaces all tags/terms with their disambiguated synset ids. 1) If there is a direct match between a test synset s' and a synset in the training feature space (i.e., $s' \in senses_{train}$), we are finished and put the respective concept-term-pair in the feature vector that is generated for the test document. 2) If there is no direct match between the test synset s' and any synset derived from the training data (i.e., $s' \notin senses_{train}$), we replace the actual test synset with its most similar match. The weight $w_{ij}(f_i)$ of feature f_i in document j is now scaled by $sim(s, s')$, i.e., $w_{ij}(f_i) = sim(s, s') \, tf_{ij} \, idf_i$, to reflect the concept similarities of approximate matches in the feature weights.

In praxis, we limit the search for common hypernyms to a distance of 2 in the ontology graph. Concepts that are not connected within this threshold are considered as dissimilar for classification and obtain a similarity value of 0. To improve performance over frequently repeated queries, all mappings of similar synsets within the same document (i.e., the same context) and their retrieved similarities are cached.

Unlike related techniques using ontologies for query expansion, we do not change the length of the feature vectors (i.e., the amount of a document's features). Our approach is merely adjusting the weights of unknown test concepts according to their nearest match in the feature space with regard to correlations defined by the ontology; adding new features to the vector could produce more matches in the classification step and would distort the result. This ontology-based evaluation can be regarded as a "similarity kernel" for the SVM that goes beyond syntactic matching.

10.5 Conclusions

Preliminary experiments were run on XML representations of the IMDB (Internet Movie Database) collection and the Reuters-21578 data set taking into consideration the XML structure using simple tag-term pairs (only regarding a single ancestor tag) and twigs. These tests indicate a clear improvement of the classifiers' F-measure [19, 209] (the harmonic mean of precision and recall) for the structure aware feature sets over a purely text-based feature space. For the IMDB the structure-aware classifier improved the F-measure from approximately 0.7 that the text classifier achieved to about 0.8 when very few (5-20) documents were used for training. For the Reuters data mapping of text terms onto ontological concepts led to a similar improvement when few training documents were used. In both cases the text classifiers continuously converged to (but never ouperformed) the F-measure of the structural classifiers when we were feeding more training documents (up to 500 per topic) into the classifiers knowledge base which led to a saturation effect where ontology lookups could not replace any formerly unknown training concepts any more.

These tests show the potential of structural features like tag-term pairs and twigs towards a more precise document characterization and the computation of a structure-aware classifier. Ontology lookups are a promising way for disambiguating terms in a given document context and for eliminating polysemy of text terms.

Our approach is a first step towards understanding the potential of exploiting structure, annotation, and ontological features of XML documents for automatic classification. Our experiments are fairly preliminary, but the results indicate that the direction is worthwhile to be explored in more depth. Our current and near-future work includes more comprehensive experimental studies and making the ontological mapping more robust. In particular, we are working on incorporating other sources of ontological knowledge into our system, to go beyond the information provided by WordNet. This ongoing work is part of the BINGO! project in which we are building a next-generation focused crawler and comprehensive toolkit for automatically organizing and searching semistructured Web and intranet data.

11

Information Extraction and Automatic Markup for XML Documents

Mohammad Abolhassani, Norbert Fuhr, and Norbert Gövert

11.1 Introduction

As XML is going to become the standard document format, there is still the legacy problem of large amounts of text (written in the past as well as today) that are not available in this format. In order to exploit the benefits of XML, these legacy texts must be converted into XML. In this chapter, we discuss the issues of automatic XML markup of documents. We give a survey on existing approaches, and we describe a specific system in some detail.

When talking about XML markup, we can roughly distinguish between three types of markup:

- *Macro-level markup* deals with the global visual and logical structure of a document (e.g. part, chapter, section down to the paragraph level.)
- *Micro-level markup* is used for marking single words or word groups. For example, in news, person and company names, locations and dates may be marked up, possibly along with their roles in the event described (e.g. a company merger).
- *Symbol-level markup* uses symbolic names as content of specific elements in order to describe content that is not plain text (e.g. MathML for mathematical formulas and CML for chemical formulas). Since this type of content is usually represented in various formats in legacy documents, specific transformation routines should be applied in order to convert these into XML. We will not consider this type of markup in the remainder of this chapter.

Micro and macro-level markup require different methods for performing automatic markup: Whereas macro-level markup is mainly based on information about the layout of a document, micro-level markup typically requires basic linguistic procedures in combination with application-specific knowledge. We will describe the details of these two approaches in the following sections.

Adding markup to a document increases its value by making its information more accessible. Without markup, from a system's point of view, a

H. Blanken et al. (Eds.): Intelligent Search on XML Data, LNCS 2818, pp. 159–174, 2003.

document is just a long sequence of words, and thus the set of operations that can be performed on such a document is rather limited. Once we have markup, however, the system is able to exploit the implicit semantics of the markup tags, thus allowing for operations that are closer to the semantic level. Here we give a few examples:

- Markup at the macro level supports a user in navigating through the logical structure of a document.
- Content-oriented retrieval aims at retrieving meaningful units for a given query that refers only to the content, but not to the structure of the target elements. Whereas classical passage retrieval [183] can only select text passages of a fixed size, XML-based retrieval is able to select XML elements based on the explicit logical structure as represented in the macro-level markup.
- When micro-level markup is used for specifying the data type of element content (e.g. date, location, person name, company name), type-specific search predicates may be used in retrieval, thus supporting high-precision searches.
- Another dimension of micro-level markup is the role of element content (e.g. author vs. editor, departure location vs. arrival location, starting date vs. ending date). Here again, precision of retrieval can be increased by referring to these elements; also, browsing through the values occurring in certain roles may ease information access for a user.
- Text mining can extract the contents of specific elements and stores them in a separate database in order to perform data-mining-like analysis operations.

The remainder of this chapter is structured as follows: In Section 11.2, we briefly describe methods for macro-level markup. In Section 11.3, we give a survey over Information Extraction (IE) methods and discuss their application for micro-level markup. In Section 11.4, we present a case study where a toolkit for automatic markup, developed by our research group, is applied to articles from encyclopedias of art. Finally, we conclude this chapter with some remarks.

11.2 Markup of Macro Structures

In case the original document is available in the electronic format, markup of the macro structure of the document is a matter of conversion, translation or transformation from the original structure to the target (XML) elements. Otherwise, providing an electronic representation of the document is the prerequisite of any markup at both macro and micro level.

In order to get an electronic representation, the original document must be processed. *Optical Character Recognition (OCR)* is the process of converting text from paper into a form that computers can manipulate, by scanning the paper, producing image, analysing it and providing an electronic file.

In this way, the textual content of the document as well as its structure can be extracted. The document structure can be expressed in two ways:

- Presentation oriented: how the document looks.
- Logically: how the document parts are related to each other.

Markup of these (macro) structures have different applications. Presentation markup can mainly be used for enhancing the layout of the document. Southall mentions that presentation markup helps us to display a document's visual structure which contributes to the document's meaning [284]. Logical markup serves for a variety of purposes, as mentioned in the previous section.

Taghva et al. introduce a system that automatically markups technical documents, based on information provided by an (OCR) device, which, in addition to its main task, provides detailed information about page layout, word geometry and font usage [292]. An automatic markup program uses this information, combined with dictionary lookup and content analysis, to identify structural components of the text. These include the document title, author information, abstract, sections, section titles, paragraphs, sentences and de-hyphenated words.

Moreover, the logical structure of a document can be extracted from its layout. For this purpose, there are two approaches:

Top-down: starting with the presentation markup and joining segmented pages into sections, sections into paragraphs, paragraphs into sentences and sentences into words. This is the preferred approach in the literature.
Bottom-up: starting with words and grouping words into sentences, sentences to paragraphs and paragraphs into sections.

Having detailed information about presentation attributes of single words (its page, exact location on the page and font) one can use this data to form sentences, paragraphs and sections [292].

Furthermore, Hitz et al. advocate the use of synthetic document images as a basis for extracting the logical structure of a document, in order to deal with different formats and document models [165].

11.3 Survey on Information Extraction

The task of information extraction can be considered as a problem of template filling: For a given domain, users are interested in facts of a certain type (e.g. joint ventures, management changes), which are to be extracted from a collection of texts. For this purpose, a template form has to be defined, and the system is supposed to fill it. Accordingly, the system has to scan large volumes of text and instantiate the template for each event of the specified type, by filling it with the data extracted from the text. Thus, we can assert that

Information Extraction (IE) is more challenging than Information Retrieval (IR): whereas the latter only aims at locating the relevant documents for a given query, the former goes one step further, by extracting facts from the text of the relevant documents. Since in IE, as in IR, systems cannot yield perfect results for a given task, the quality of the result is a crucial issue. For this purpose, standard IR measures like recall, precision and the F-measure are applied for IE as well. Evaluation of IE systems have been the major objective of the Message Understanding Conferences (MUC) [231], where participating groups were competing in developing systems for a given task. The MUC proceedings also give a good overview of the range of approaches tried.

In the following, we give a brief survey of the state of the art in information extraction. For a broader and more detailed description, see e.g. [15, 142, 86].

11.3.1 Approaches for Building IE Systems

For building information extraction systems, there are two generic types of approaches:

Knowledge engineering approach: Here the rules to be applied by the system are constructed manually by a so-called knowledge engineer. This strategy may be applied to the construction of the grammar rules as well as to the discovery and formulation of the domain patterns. Of course, effective rule sets can be constructed only iteratively, by starting with simple rule sets, evaluating the results and refining them stepwise. Thus the knowledge engineering approach is rather laborious.

Machine learning approach: To apply this approach, also called automatic training, we need annotated corpora. For example, a name recogniser would be trained by annotating a corpus of texts with the domain-relevant proper names. Alternatively, training data can be obtained by close interaction with the user, where the system proposes new rules, which are either confirmed or rejected by the user. For learning the rules, statistical methods are used.

These two types of approaches can be applied at various stages of the IE process (see below). Also, it is possible to mix the strategies, e.g. one can use machine learning for named entity recognition and knowledge engineering for formulating the domain patterns. Generally speaking, knowledge engineering should be preferred in case appropriate knowledge (e.g. lexicons) and human resources (i.e. rule writers) are available, whereas the machine learning approach should be preferred when the required knowledge and resources are missing, but enough training data is available. In terms of achievable performance, although the former approach has advantages, usually the latter approach also leads to good results.

11.3.2 System Architecture

A typical IE system consists of the following four major blocks:

1. *Tokenisation* performs word segmentation, which is trivial for European languages (words are separated by blanks and / or punctuation symbols), whereas some Asian languages require sophisticated methods for mapping a text into a sequence of words.
2. *Morphological and lexical processing* deals with the recognition of inflected word forms.
3. *Syntactic analysis* is applied to the output of the previous stage, and can be shallow or aim at full parsing.
4. *Domain analysis* finally fills the specified template based on the input from the previous stages.

In the following, we describe the last three stages in more detail.

Morphological and Lexical Processing

Following tokenisation, the system first has to detect inflectional variants of word forms. For some languages, e.g. English and Japanese, this task can be accomplished by simple string processing rules, whereas languages with a complex morphology, e.g. German and Finnish, usually require a lexicon in order to map the inflected word forms to the non-inflected ones. Furthermore, during this step compound words should be segmented into their components, which, again, requires a lexicon.

Following the morphological analysis, a lexical lookup retrieves syntactical and / or semantical information for the given words. However, many application domains use a specific sub language which is hardly covered by a standard lexicon. Thus, most approaches use small, domain specific lexicons. In any case, lexical coverage will always be limited, thus the system design has to take lexical incompleteness into account.

In order to ease subsequent syntactic analysis, most systems perform part of speech tagging. Simple approaches just collect the unigram tag frequencies of a word and then apply a rareness threshold, whereas other methods also take into account bigram frequencies in order to reduce the ambiguity of word senses.

The most important task in the morphological and lexical component is the recognition of names (e.g. person, product or company names, locations) and structured entities (e.g. dates, times), which are typically too numerous to be included in a lexicon. Whereas elements of the latter group can often be recognised by means of simple regular expressions, the elements of the former group require the development of appropriate recognisers, using either the knowledge engineering or the machine learning approach. Most name recognition systems use the latter strategy in combination with Hidden Markov Models. However, large training corpora (> 100 K words) are needed in order to achieve a high performance, and increasing the training data size only leads to log-linear improvements.

Syntactic Analysis

The most natural approach to syntactic analysis would be the development of a full parser. However, experiments have shown that such an approach results in a very slow system, which is also error-prone. Thus, most approaches in this area aim at shallow parsing, using a finite-state grammar. The justification for this strategy lies in the fact that IE is directed toward extracting relatively simple relationships among singular objects. These finite-state grammars focus mainly on noun groups and verb groups, since they contain most of the relevant information. As attributes of these constituents, numbers and definiteness are extracted from the determiner of noun groups, and tense and voice from verb groups. In a second parsing phase, prepositional phrases are handled; here mainly the prepositions "of" and "for" are considered, whereas treatment of temporal and locative adjuncts is postponed to the domain analysis phase.

Domain Analysis

Before the extraction of facts can start, first the problem of coreference must be solved. Since text writers typically use varying notations for referring to the same entity, IE systems struggle with the problem of resolving these coreferences (e.g. "IBM", "International Business Machines", "Big Blue", "The Armonk-based company"). Even person names already pose severe problems (e.g. "William H. Gates", "Mr. Gates", "William Gates", "Bill Gates", "Mr. Bill H. Gates"). In addition, anaphoric references (pronouns or discourse definite references) must be resolved. Although there is rich literature on this specific problem, most approaches assume full parsing and thus are not applicable for IE.

In [15], a general knowledge engineering approach for coreference is described: In the first step, for a candidate referring expression (noun phrase), the following attributes are determined: sortal information (e.g. company vs. location), number (single vs. plural), gender and syntactic features (e.g. name, pronoun, definite vs. indefinite). Then, for each candidate referring expression, the accessible antecedents are determined (e.g. for names the entire preceding text, for pronouns only a small part of it), which are subsequently filtered with a semantic / sortal consistency check (based on the attributes determined in the first step), and the remaining candidates are filtered by dynamic syntactic preferences (considering the relative location in the text).

Once there are solutions for all the problems described above, the core task of IE can be addressed. As a prerequisite, an appropriate template form must be defined: Typically, users would give an informal specification of the information bits they are interested, for which then an adequate and useful representation format must be specified.

For filling this template, there are two knowledge engineering approaches:

- The *molecular* approach aims at filling the complete template in one step. For this purpose, the knowledge engineer reads some texts in order to identify the most common and most reliably indicative patterns in which relevant information is expressed. For these patterns appropriate rules are formulated, then one moves on to less common but still reliable patterns. Thus, this approach aims initially at high precision, and then improves recall incrementally.

- The *atomic* approach, in contrast, is based on the assumption that every noun phrase of the right sort and every verb of the right type (independently of the syntactic relations among them) indicates an event / relationship of interest. Thus, one starts with high recall and low precision, with incremental development of filters for false positives. This approach is only feasible if entities in the domain have easily determined types, and there is scarcely more than one template slot where an entity of a given type may fit - as a negative example, a template for management changes would contain at least two slots (predecessor / successor) where a person can be filled in.

In most cases both approaches produce only partial descriptions, which must be merged subsequently (e.g. in a template for management changes, one portion of the text may mention company, position and the new person filling it, whereas the predecessor is mentioned in a subsequent paragraph). This merging step is a specific type of unification. A knowledge engineering approach for this problem is described in [15]: Starting from typed slots, type-specific procedures are developed which compare two candidates for inconsistencies, coreference and subsumption; in addition, application-specific heuristics are necessary in most cases.

In general, major parts of an IE system are rather application-dependent, and there is little experience with the development of portable systems. On the other hand, experience from the MUC conference shows that approaches based on general-purpose language analysis systems yield lower performance than application-specific developments.

11.3.3 Types of IE Problems

Above, we have described the general structure of IE tasks and the architecture of IE systems. A more detailed analysis and categorisation of IE problems is described in [83]. In this chapter, the authors distinguish between source properties and extraction methods, and develop taxonomies for issues related to these two subjects.

With respect to the source properties, the following aspects are considered to be the more important ones:

- *Structure* can be free, tagged or even follow a specified schema.
- *Topology* distinguishes between single and multiple documents to be considered for filling a single template.
- *Correctness* refers to the amount and type (format, content) of errors that may occur in the input.

- *Regularity* specifies whether instances of source documents may be regular in format or vary widely.
- *Stability* characterises type and frequency of source documents with respect to content and structure.
- *Interaction* specifies the ways in which a source notifies an IE system about data changes – which may invalidate the current extraction description – possibly along with a description of the changes.

Extraction methods may be characterised by the following features:

- The degree of *automation*, ranging from manual (programming by hand or by demonstration) to (semi-)automatic, where the type of the learning approach and the seed structure are important characteristics.
- The *extraction engine* may be based on a finite state automaton or a context-free grammar. Alternatively, if the source data already conforms to a certain data model, a query engine based on that model can be applied. Finally, some systems follow none of these approaches and use procedural descriptions instead.
- *Change and error handling* describes the ways in which the extraction engine copes with these problems. Without additional provisions, the system might fail; it should at least detect changes and give an appropriate warning. Some systems are able to compensate for errors to a certain extent. A detect and learn strategy would even go one step further and try to adapt the system dynamically.
- *Use of source knowledge* simplifies the rule set for IE. This knowledge may be at the syntactical as well as semantic level.
- *Use of target knowledge* refers to the fact that both syntax (e.g. free text vs. record structure) and semantics (e.g. predefined list of terms) of the desired output may be restricted
- Finally, *transformation capabilities* describe the level of transformation, which may be at the structural or the semantic level.

11.3.4 Information Extraction for Automatic Markup

The discussion above has focused on IE methods, and little has been said about their relationship with the problem of *Automatic Markup (AM)*. Cunningham distinguishes five levels of IE tasks, which can also be used for characterising different levels of automatic markup [86]:

- *Named entity recognition* extracts entities of one or more given types. For automatic markup, this method can be used for assigning appropriate tags to these names as they occur in the text.
- *Coreference resolution* recognises different notations for the same entity. In XML, this fact could be marked by adding ID / IDREF attributes to the tags.

- *Template element reconstruction* deals with structured entities, where entity names and attributes are coordinated. In terms of XML, this would correspond to a structured element.
- *Template relation reconstruction* requires the identification of the relation between the template elements, e.g. an employee relationship between a company and a person. For automatic markup, this step would result in assigning additional tags characterising the roles of entities in such a (binary) relationship
- *Scenario template production* finally refers to the filling of the complete template (including the merger process). This corresponds to automatic markup for DTD describing the relevant aspects of the application.

Following the machine learning approach, a number of algorithms specifically designed for automatic markup have been described in the literature.

MarkitUp! [112] is an early predecessor of automatic markup systems. It uses regular expressions and uses a kind of inductive logic programming for abstracting from the given examples. In addition, rules may be specified explicitly by the user, and the system combines both types of rules in a single grammar.

RAPIER [59] is a system for semi-structured text that uses a form of inductive logic programming for inferring rules from a corpus tagged with target templates. Here each slot filler has three fields: the target field, the tokens preceding the target phrase, and those following it. Rapier considers lexical, semantic and morphological constraints.

WHISK [283] is a rather general rule extraction system using regular expressions as extraction patterns. When combined with a parser, the system can also perform free text analysis. For learning, WHISK uses a covering algorithm inducing rules top-down.

SRV [122] considers all possible phrases as potential slot fillers. A multistrategy approach combines evidence from three classifiers (rote learner, naive Bayes classifier, relational rule learner).

LearningPINOCCHIO [73] is based on a covering algorithm that learns rules by bottom-up generalisation of instances in a tagged corpus. Unlike other systems, LearningPINOCCHIO recognises starting tags and ending tags separately, which allows for easier generalisation in rule writing.

11.4 The Vasari Project

Vasari[1] aims at developing a Web portal providing comprehensive knowledge about art, artists and works of arts for scientists and experts as well as for other interested people.

The starting point for the project are different encyclopedias of art in German which have been scanned and processed with an OCR software. The result is a collection of fairly unstructured plain texts representing the contents of the encyclopedias. An example of such texts is given in Figure 11.1[2]

The task of the Vasari project is to develop means for doing automatic markup of the knowledge contained in these texts at the micro level, for providing search and navigational structures that allow for effective exploration of the knowledge.

Da Vinci, Leonardo, born in Anchiano, near Vinci, 15 April 1452, died in Amboise, near Tours, 2 May 1519. Italian painter, sculptor, architect, designer, theorist, engineer and scientist. He was the founding father of what is called the High Renaissance style and exercised an enormous influence on contemporary and later artists. His writings on art helped establish the ideals of representation and expression that were to dominate European academies for the next 400 years. The standards he set in figure draughtsmanship, handling of space, depiction of light and shade, representation of landscape, evocation of character and techniques of narrative radically transformed the range of art. A number of his inventions in architecture and in various fields of decoration entered the general currency of 16th-century design.

Fig. 11.1. Example text of source documents

To arrive at a micro-level markup from the OCRed texts, the Vasari project follows the knowledge engineering approach. The project presents a language and a number of tools for this purpose. Rules for markup can be expressed in the *Vasari Language (VaLa)*. The *Vasari tool* serves the knowledge engineer in the iterative process of developing the rules. Having defined the set of rules for a given encyclopedia, the extraction tool *VaLaEx (Vasari Language Extractor)* uses them in order to automatically markup the plain texts. Furthermore, a toolkit has been specified around VaLaEx which includes tools that can be used to pre-/post-process the input/output of the VaLaEx extractor.

In the following we describe the Vasari project in more detail. In Section 11.4.1 we give a survey on VaLa. The Vasari tool for developing VaLa

---

[1] Giorgio Vasari, who lived in the 16th century in Florence, Italy, was an Italian painter and architect. His most important work is an encyclopedia of artist biographies ("The biographies of the most famous architects, painters and sculptors", published in an extended edition in 1568), which still belongs to the foundations of art history.

[2] Although our work principally deals with German texts, here we give an English example from *The Grove Dictionary of Art Online* (http://www.groveart.com/).

descriptions and the VaLaEx markup tool are described in Section 11.4.2. In Section 11.4.3 we show how additional tools can be applied to enhance the result of the markup process. We end the description of the Vasari project in Section 11.4.4 with a brief discussion on how the results can be improved by fusing knowledge obtained from different sources.

11.4.1 VaLa: The Vasari Language

Given a set of rather unstructured plain text documents, an appropriate description language for automatic markup must fulfill two requirements:

1. The logical structure of the documents implicitly inherent in the source documents must be made explicit within a description for automatic markup. Such a structure description defines the template which is to be filled through the markup process.
2. Given a source document, it must be stated how its contents can be mapped onto the elements of the template.

XML Schema [111] served as a starting point for VaLa. In our application however, XML Schema does not serve its original purpose to validate the structure of a given XML document, but to create such XML documents. The first requirement mentioned above is met by XML Schema directly. Structure can be defined in an elaborated way [297]. Elements within the structure can be further constrained by means of already built-in and extensible data types [31].

The second requirement can be accomplished for by the application specific data, which can be specified within xsd:annotation elements within XML Schemas. The VaLa extension to XML Schema contains means to specify filler rules defined within XML Schema. The filler rules define how text from the source documents are to be mapped onto the elements of the structure defined within the XML Schema. A filler rule may consist of up to three parts:

- Within the <vala:match> element constraints for the part of the source document - which is to be mapped into a given element - can be specified.
- The content of the <vala:pre> element describes constraints for the left context of a match for a given element.
- The content of the <vala:post> element describes constraints for the right context of a match for a given element.

In order to formulate the constraints within the filler rules, the following types of linguistic knowledge can be exploited:

- Character strings within source documents can be matched by *regular expressions*. The construction of complex regular expressions is facilitated by the option of nesting arbitrary expressions.
- Linguistic constructs like words and word classes can be matched by *computer linguistic categories*. For extracting such categories from the source documents external tools e.g. SPPC [229] can be used.

- Special types of entities (e.g. place names) can be matched by means of *registries* or *dictionaries* (e.g. gazetteers).

Figure 11.2 displays an excerpt from a VaLa description. Here, regular expressions are used for automatic markup of the artists' names. A name consists of two parts, a surname, followed by a given name. Both parts of the name start with an upper case letter, followed by at least one lower case letter, and may consist of more than one word separated by blanks ([A-Za-z]+); they are followed by a comma. A birth place is constrained by its left context which must consist of "born" followed by "in", with possible blanks and line feeds between and after them.

```
<xs:simpleType name="tSurName">
  <xs:annotation>
    <xs:appinfo>
      <vala:match type="regexp">[A-Za-z ]+</vala:match>
      <vala:post  type="regexp">,</vala:post>
    </xs:appinfo>
  </xs:annotation>
</xs:simpleType>

<xs:simpleType name="tGivenName">
  <xs:annotation>
    <xs:appinfo>
      <vala:match type="regexp">[A-Za-z ]+</vala:match>
      <vala:post  type="regexp">,</vala:post>
    </xs:appinfo>
  </xs:annotation>
</xs:simpleType>

<xs:simpleType name="tBirthPlace">
  <xs:annotation>
    <xs:appinfo>
      <vala:pre type="regexp">born[ /n]*in[ /n]*</vala:pre>
      <vala:match type="regexp">[^,]+</vala:match>
    </xs:appinfo>
  </xs:annotation>
</xs:simpleType>
```

Fig. 11.2. An excerpt from a VaLa description for automatic markup of the artists' data

Given a VaLa description for documents of a special type (in our case articles from an encyclopedia) the *VaLaEx* tool for automatic markup applies that description onto a set of source documents. Since a VaLa description defines a tree structure, the approach taken by VaLaEx is based on the recursive definition of trees. The source document is passed to the root of the structure tree. By means of its filler rules the root node selects that part of the document text which matches its filler rules. The matching part then is passed to the root's first child node, which in turn selects its matching text part and provides the respective markup. The remaining text is passed to the next child node, and so on. In case the filler rules within a child node cannot be matched, alternative solutions are tried through backtracking. For each child which receives text from its parent node, the algorithm is applied recursively.

Figure 11.3 displays the result of a VaLa description (the one mentioned above).

```
<?xml version="1.0" encoding="ISO-8859-1"?>
<Artist>
  <Name>
    <SurName>Da Vinci</SurName>,<GivenName> Leonardo</GivenName>
  </Name>, born in <MasterData>
    <BirthPlace>Anchiano</BirthPlace>, near Vinci, <BirthDate>
      <BirthDay>15</BirthDay> <BirthMonth>April</BirthMonth>
  <BirthYear>1452
  </BirthYear></BirthDate>, died
  in <DeathPlace>Amboise</DeathPlace>, near Tours, <DeathDate>
      <DeathDay>2</DeathDay> <DeathMonth>May</DeathMonth>
  <DeathYear>1519
  </DeathYear></DeathDate>. <Nationality>Italian</Nationality>
    <Profession> painter, sculptor,
    architect, designer, theorist, engineer and scientist</Profession>
  </MasterData>.
  <Description>He was the founding father of what is called the High
  ...
  </Description>
</Artist>
```

Fig. 11.3. The result of a VaLa description

11.4.2 Iterative Development of VaLa Descriptions

The production of a VaLa description for automatic markup of documents, which exploit only marginal structure, is a difficult task. On the one hand, given large amounts of source documents, it is not possible to take into consideration every single document for production of the rules. On the other hand as many cases as possible should be covered by the rules of a VaLa description.

In order to achieve this goal we provide for the *Vasari* tool for interactive and iterative development of such descriptions. Similar as with MarkItUp! [112] VaLa descriptions are developed from example source documents. The knowledge engineer starts with the definition of the structure it is aimed at for the resulting XML documents. The filler rules can then be developed by means of the example documents. At any stage of the development process the knowledge engineer can check the result by means of the example documents.

A VaLa description obtained in this way now can be improved iteratively. In each iteration step the knowledge engineer gives feedback to the system with regard to the result obtained up to then: The markup can be assessed as being wrong or correct; missing markup can be introduced into the XML documents. According to this kind of feedback, the VaLa description can then be improved further. Whenever a new version of the description is finished, the example documents are marked up using that version. Since feedback is available from earlier versions already, part of the assessment of the new result can be done by the system automatically and visualised to the user.

Figure 11.4 shows the main window of the Vasari user interface. The bottom part of the window contains the VaLa description developed up to then (see also Figure 11.2). The remaining upper part of the window is split into three parts: The left-hand part contains an overview of the example source documents. One of the source documents is displayed in the middle part, while the result of the markup process (using the VaLa description shown in the bottom part of the window) is displayed on the right hand side. As can be seen the artist's name and birth place has been marked up correctly. The knowledge engineer therefore marked the tags accordingly. Whenever markup of this part of the document is changed by any later version of the VaLa description, it is marked as being wrong automatically.

11.4.3 A Toolkit for Automatic Markup of Plain Texts

When developing means for markup of rather unstructured plain text documents, obtained from OCRed texts, we realized that there are some problems which are not directly related to automatic markup. This includes the correction of systematic OCR errors, the detection of document boundaries and the elimination of hyphenation of words in the pre-processing phase for the source documents. Also, some features of the VaLa language required the use of external tools, like SPPC to detect linguistic categories or entities. In order not to burden Vasari and VaLaEx with these tasks we developed a toolkit framework, of which VaLaEx is the core. Other tools for specific tasks in the markup process can be added arbitrarily.

All tools in the toolkit comply with a simple standard interface: The input as well as the output always consist of (sets of) XML documents - on the input side additional parameters, e.g. a VaLa description for the VaLaEx tool, might be provided. Hence a high degree of modularisation is achieved, and tools can be combined in an almost arbitrary way. The interface standard allows for easy integration of external tools, e.g. SPPC, by means of wrappers.

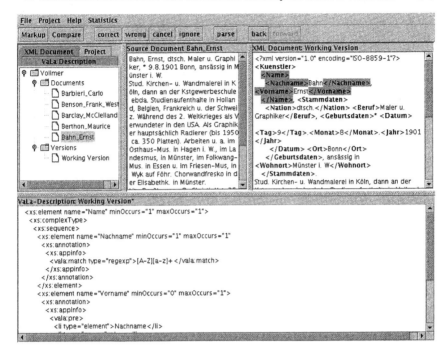

Fig. 11.4. Vasari user interface for interactive and iterative development of VaLa descriptions

11.4.4 Improving the Results

Characteristic for the Vasari application is that source documents from different encyclopedias are available, the contents of which intersect partly. This can be exploited to achieve an even better knowledge representation after the automatic markup process is completed. Knowledge from different sources can be fused, thus references implicitly available within the source documents can be made explicit. For example, given that an artist is described within different encyclopedias, the fused descriptions would lead to a more complete view on that artist. Even contradictions could be detected, triggering e.g. manual correction.

11.5 Conclusions

Automatic markup of (legacy) documents will remain a problem for a long time. Using XML as the target format for automatic markup leads to powerful search and navigational structures for effective knowledge exploration. In this chapter we summarised approaches for automatic markup of macro and micro structures within rather unstructured documents. In a case study we demonstrated how automatic markup is applied to build a Web portal for arts.

Future research in this area will focus on the development of markup and extraction methods which are less domain-specific.

Part IV

Implementing Intelligent XML Systems

Introduction

The previous parts of this book have investigated *effectiveness* of intelligent search on XML, i.e., how to formulate queries and which techniques yield – in terms of quality – the best answer to a given query. Practical settings, however, may be confronted with thousands or even millions of XML documents. Hence, intelligent XML search in practical settings requires efficient implementations of the concepts discussed in previous chapters of this book. Depending on the actual application, XML contents need to be stored persistently and must be available for later search. Important requirements regarding efficiency of systems for intelligent XML search are storage management and query processing on the tree structured original XML document data, as discussed in Part II of this book. Moreover, additional index structures are needed to make relevance-oriented search on textual content efficient using the different models discussed in Part III. This part of the book covers systems- and implementation-related questions of the previous parts of the book.

Similar to data centric XML processing, several alternative approaches to design and implement systems for intelligent XML search are conceivable. *Native XML approaches* aim at developing new systems specifically tailored for XML. The expectation is that XML-specific techniques are more efficient than other approaches which, for instance, rely on existing general-purpose storage managers. So-called *database mapping approaches* in turn follow the latter approach. They rely on storage managers such as relational database systems. XML content and XML processing are mapped to the interface and the storage structures of the underlying system. The motivation for this alternative is to leverage well-understood and efficient database functionality such as buffer management or indexing for XML processing. Combining the two aforementioned alternatives, *hybrid approaches* finally argue that existing general-purpose storage managers are well-suited as a basis for XML processing, but they should be extended with XML-specific functionality such as XML path indexes, for instance. The following chapters of this part reflect this spectrum of different approaches to systems for intelligent XML search.

Using a database mapping approach, Chapter 12 by de Vries, List and Blok discusses how to make relevance-oriented retrieval for intelligent search efficient. It proposes a multi-model database architecture and contributes XML and IR extensions at the logical level. The chapter presents in depth the implementation of Hiemstra's statistical language modeling approach for XML search from Chapter 7.

Chapter 13 presents the implementation of PowerDB-XML, an XML engine for combined data-centric and document-centric XML processing. PowerDB-XML builds on a cluster of relational database systems for efficient and scalable storage management. The chapter discusses how to map both XML content and IR index data for relevance-oriented search as presented in Chapter 6 to relational storage managers. It also reports on experimental results investigating PowerDB-XML's scalability with up to 128 cluster nodes.

Chapter 14 by Smiljanić and Feng investigates distributed XML query processing on the Internet. It first discusses important challenges of this distributed environment such as heterogeneous data sources or unreliability of data sources. Based on these challenges, it presents a classification of architecture and design choices for distributed query processing in general, and then relates it to prominent current approaches to internet-scale XML processing.

Chapter 15 by Windhouwer and van Zwol looks at multimedia retrieval from an XML perspective. It presents an approach for searching rich multimedia document collections based on concepts that are derived from features of the underlying image, video, or audio data.

Chapter 16 by Grust and van Keulen focuses on the important aspect of navigation in XML documents and evaluation of path expressions. This aspect is crucial for efficient implementations of the query languages discussed in Part II. This chapter is based in the XPath accelerator data structure. Storage management for XPath accelerator can be implemented solely by relational database systems. This chapter shows that further performance improvements are possible when making the database kernel aware of the tree-structured XML data model. Its main contribution is the *staircase join* – a new operator of the database kernel that completely encapsulates the tree-awareness.

In analogy to previous work on signature indexes, Chapter 17 by Zezula, Amato and Rabitti proposes to encode XML tree structures in so-called *tree signatures* based on the preorder and postorder traversal ranks of tree nodes. XML query processing can rely on tree signature as an additional index structure to speed up path expressions evaluation.

The Multi-model DBMS Architecture and XML Information Retrieval

Arjen P. de Vries, Johan A. List, and Henk Ernst Blok

12.1 Introduction

Since long, computer science has distinguished between information retrieval and data retrieval, where information retrieval entails the problem of ranking textual documents on their content (with the goal to identify documents relevant for satisfying a user's information need) while data retrieval involves exact match, that is, checking a data collection for presence or absence of (precisely specified) items. But, now that XML has become a standard document model that allows structure and text content to be represented in a combined way, new generations of information retrieval systems are expected to handle *semi-structured* documents instead of plain text, with usage scenarios that require the combination of 'conventional' ranking with other query constraints; based on the structure of text documents, on the information extracted from various media (or various media representations), or through additional information induced during the query process.

Consider for example an XML collection representing a newspaper archive, and the information need 'recent English newspaper articles about Willem-Alexander dating Maxima'.[1] This can be expressed as the following query (syntax in the spirit of the XQuery-Fulltext working draft [58]):[2]

```
FOR $article IN document("collection.xml")//article
WHERE $article/text() about 'Willem-Alexander dating Maxima'
  AND $article[@lang = 'English']
  AND $article[@pdate between '31-1-2003' and '1-3-2003']
RETURN <result>$article</result>
```

The terms 'recent' and 'English' refer to metadata about the newspaper articles, whereas the aboutness-clause refers to the news content. Because only

---

[1] Willem-Alexander is the Crown Prince of The Netherlands, who married Maxima Zorreguieta on 2-2-2002.

[2] Assume an interpretation in which 'recent' is equivalent to 'published during the last month', and *language* and *pdate* are attributes of the article tag. The *between ... and ...* construct does not exist in XQuery, but is used for simplicity.

H. Blanken et al. (Eds.): Intelligent Search on XML Data, LNCS 2818, pp. 179–191, 2003.
© Springer-Verlag Berlin Heidelberg 2003

recent English articles will be retrieved by this request, precision at low recall levels is likely to be improved. Note that this capability to process queries that combine content and structure is beneficial in ways beyond extending querying textual content with constraints on rich data types like numeric attributes (e.g., price), geographical information and temporal values. Egnor and Lord [105] suggest that new generations of information retrieval systems could exploit the potentially rich additional information in semi-structured document collections also for disambiguation of words through their tag context, and use structural proximity as part of the ranking model. Also, combined querying on content and structure is a necessary precondition for improving the IR process when taking into account Mizzaro's different notions of relevance (see [221]).

12.1.1 Dilemma

So, we observe a trend in software development where information retrieval and data retrieval techniques are combined; as a result of a desire to create applications that take advantage of the additional information made explicit in semi-structured document collections, and, as importantly, to provide a basis for improved information retrieval models, possibly achieving better recall and precision thanks to exploiting this additional information automatically.

Developments in hardware layout of computer systems pose another challenge – to be met in any resource-consuming application, not just IR. Due to the increasing importance of cache memory in modern CPUs, memory access cannot be thought of as random access any more: sequential access patterns can be many times faster than random accesses [39]. Since memory latency is *not* improving with Moore's law (unlike other properties of computer architecture), this problem will gain importance. At the same time, the price of (cheap) personal computers compared to (expensive) professional workstations stimulates distribution of work over 'workstation farms', taking advantage of shared-nothing parallelism. Similarly, server machines with two up to eight processors are not extremely expensive any more, making it more attractive to explore strategies that exploit shared-memory parallelism. The drawback of this increased complexity in computer architecture (hierarchical memory, parallelism, distribution) is that efficient usage of the available resources requires highly experienced programmers, who are fully aware of the low-level details of the machine architecture used.

As a result of these observed trends (software and hardware), a dilemma arises in the engineering of information retrieval systems: should their design be optimized for flexibility or for efficiency? Highly optimized stand-alone systems are, naturally, not very flexible. Experiments (e.g., with new models or adaptive learning strategies) require changes in complex low-level code, with the danger of affecting the correctness of the results. To circumvent such inflexibility, it is common practice to wrap the core IR system in a *black-box*, and implement additional features on top. Considering that we should optimize our systems for parallel and distributed computing and memory access patterns however, usage of black-box abstractions to obtain flexibility becomes ever less desirable: it leads easily to inefficient systems, as we do not *really* understand what happens inside the ranking process.

The essence of our problem is being trapped in an impasse solving the dilemma: gaining flexibility through abstraction causes an efficiency penalty which is felt most when we exploit this flexibility in new applications of IR or explore improvements upon existing models.

This problem is illustrated clearly in the processing of relevance feedback. Retrieval systems typically rank the documents with the initial query in a first pass and re-rank with an adapted query in a second pass. Jónsson et al. have shown in [182] that the resulting retrieval system is not optimal with respect to efficiency, unless we address buffer management while taking both passes into account. So, the inner workings of the original system must be changed for optimal performance of the full system. In other words, *we must break open the black-box*. This, obviously, conflicts with our previously stated desire for flexibility.

Another illustration of this dilemma appears when extending retrieval systems for multimedia data collections, strengthening our arguments against the pragmatic engineering practice of coupling otherwise stand-alone retrieval systems. In a multimedia retrieval system that ranks its objects using various representations of content (such as the system described in [302]), the number of independent black-box components that may contribute to the final ranking equals the number of feature spaces used in the system. It seems unlikely that computing these multiple rankings independently (i.e., without taking intermediate results into account) is the most efficient approach.

12.2 A Database Approach to IR

We seek a way out of this impasse between flexibility and efficiency by following 'the database approach'. Database technology provides flexibility by expressing requests in high-level, declarative query languages at the conceptual level, independent from implementation details such as file formats and access structures (thus emphasizing *data independence*). Efficiency is obtained in the mapping process from declarative specification (describing what should happen) into a query plan at the physical level (describing how it happens). The query optimizer generates a number of logically equivalent query plans, and selects a (hopefully) efficient plan using some heuristics.

There is not much consensus on how the integration of IR techniques in general-purpose database management systems (DBMSs) should take place. The typical system design couples two standalone black-box systems using a shallow layer on top: an IR system for the article text and a DBMS for the structured data. Their connection is established by using the same document identifiers in both component systems. State-of-the-art database solutions make available new functions in the query language of object-relational database management systems (OR-DBMSs); these functions interface to the otherwise still stand-alone software systems. Therefore, extending an OR-DBMS with an information retrieval module means no more than again 'wrapping' the IR system as a black-box inside the DBMS architecture (see also Figure 12.1). Apart from seriously handicapping the query optimizer, the IR module must handle parallelism and data distribution by itself. Therefore, adapting an OR-DBMS for the changing requirements identified in Section 12.1 may even be *more* complex than enhancing the stand-alone IR system.

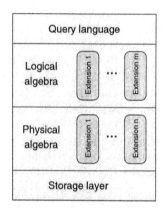 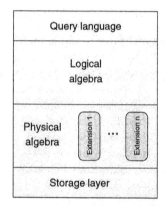

Fig. 12.1. Comparing a Multi-Model DBMS (left) to an Object-Relational DBMS (right).

We propose the *Multi-Model DBMS* architecture as a better alternative. It has been especially designed to enable the integration of databases and (multimedia) information retrieval [90]. As depicted graphically in Figure 12.1, this system can not only be extended at the physical level, but also at the logical level. Its extensibility at multiple layers in the architecture enables a strong notion of data independence between the logical and physical levels. We call this architecture the Multi-Model DBMS, since the data model used at the logical level can be different from that at the physical level.

In a prototype implementation, the Mirror DBMS, we have used the Moa (X)NF^2 algebra [303] at the logical level, and the binary relational algebra provided by MonetDB [37] at the physical level. Knowledge about IR is captured using Moa's extensibility with domain-specific structures. These extensions map high-level operations (such as probabilistic ranking of document content) to binary relational algebra expressions [90].

Creating a clear separation of concerns by introducing a logical and physical layer provides several advantages. First, operations defined at the physical level support facilities for features of the computer system architecture (e.g., shared-memory parallel processing) and can take full advantage of modern

CPU processing power. The mapping of operators by extensions at the logical level onto expressions at the (possibly extended) physical level is the appropriate place for encoding domain-specific knowledge, such as the Zipfian distribution of terms typical for IR (as demonstrated in [32]).

A good example is given by the tree-awareness for relational databases, introduced by Grust and Van Keulen (Chapter 16 of this book). The staircase join proposed is an example of an extension at the physical level, improving the efficiency of structural joins. A logical extension for handling trees based on their work encodes, e.g., the pruning predicates added to the WHERE clause of the SQL query, or the criteria for using the staircase join in the physical query plan.

Another advantage of the separation of concerns in the Multi-Model DBMS architecture is that it allows IR researchers to concentrate on retrieval models and reduce the effort of implementation involved with empirical studies. It separates representation from evidential reasoning and query formulation, which reduces the effort of changing the application logic significantly: the IR researcher makes necessary changes only to the IR processing extension, while the user applications do not require adaptation whenever the retrieval model is changed. This advantage has been called content independence [91], as a counterpart of data independence in database management systems. The notion of content independence helps to keep changes local (changes to the retrieval model) when experimenting with new theory.

12.3 Extensions for XML Information Retrieval

Our prototype system for information retrieval on XML collections exploits the separation of concerns discussed in Section 12.2, by introducing two separate extensions at the logical level: an XML extension for handling path expressions over XML documents and an IR extension for IR primitives. To illustrate a typical retrieval session (including the translation of a logical layer query to a possible physical query execution plan), consider again the example query of Section 12.1 (an example XML document is shown in Figure 12.2):

```
FOR $article IN document("collection.xml")//article
WHERE $article/text() about 'Willem Alexander dating Maxima'
  AND $article[@lang = 'English']
  AND $article[@pdate between '31-1-2003' and '1-3-2003']
RETURN <result>$article</result>
```

This query can be rewritten to include a ranking preference, typical for IR applications:

```
FOR $article IN document("collection.xml")//article
LET $rsv := about($article/text(), 'Willem-Alexander dating Maxima')
WHERE $article[@lang = 'English']
  AND $article[@pdate between '31-1-2003' and '1-3-2003']
ORDER BY $rsv DESCENDING
RETURN <result><rsv>$rsv</rsv>$article</result>
```

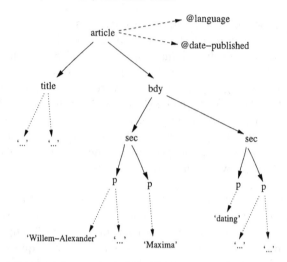

Fig. 12.2. Possible article excerpt of an XML newspaper archive; the leaf nodes contain index terms.

The *about* statement in the query above can be seen as an instantiation of the retrieval model used at the logical layer, taking as input the text of the articles in the collection (i.e., the article text regions) and the query text. An instantiation of the retrieval model requires the collection of component text and computation of term statistics, as well as calculating a score for the component under consideration.

The logical XML extension manages the document structure using a *storage scheme* at the physical level that is based on *text regions* [78, 173]. Text regions support dynamic computation of term statistics in any projection of the XML syntax tree, including transitive closures. They also offer flexibility for determining structural relationships between given sets of nodes, an important property for, e.g, efficient traversal along XPath axes.

We view an XML document instance as a linearized string or a set of *tokens* (including both entity tags and document text tokens), instead of as a syntax tree. Each component is then a *text region* or a contiguous subset of the entire linearized string. The linearized string of the example document in Figure 12.2 is shown below:

```
<article ... ><title>...</title><bdy><sec><p> ... </bdy></article>
```

A text region a can be identified by its starting point s_a and ending point e_a within the entire linearized string, where assignment of starting and ending points is simply done by maintaining a token counter. Figure 12.3 visualizes the start point and end point numbering for the example XML document and we can see, for example, that the *bdy*-region can be identified with the closed interval [5..24].

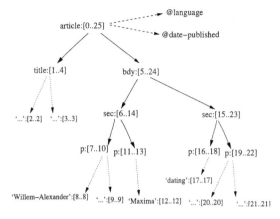

Fig. 12.3. Start point and endpoint assignment

At the physical level, our system stores these XML text regions as four-tuples $(region\_id, start, end, tag)$, where:

- $region\_id$ denotes a unique node identifier for each region;
- $start$ and end represent the start and end positions of each region;
- tag is the (XML) tag of each region.

The set of all XML region tuples is named the *node index* $\mathcal{N}$. Index terms present in the XML documents are stored in a separate relation called the *word index* $\mathcal{W}$. Index terms are considered text regions as well, but physically the term identifier is re-used as both start and end position to reduce memory usage. Node attributes are stored in the attribute index $\mathcal{A}$ as four-tuples $(attr\_id, region\_id, attr\_name, attr\_val)$. Furthermore, we extended the physical layer with the text region operators, summarized in Table 12.1. Note that we have put the text region operators in a relational context, delivering sets or bags of tuples.

Table 12.1. Region and region set operators, in comprehension syntax [56]; s_r and e_r denote the starting and ending positions of region r, o_r its *region_id*.

Operator	Definition
$a \supset b$	$true \iff s_b > s_a \wedge e_b < e_a$
$A \bowtie_\supset B$	$\{(o_a, o_b) \mid a \leftarrow A,\ b \leftarrow B,\ a \supset b\}$

12.4 Query Processing

To clarify the difference between a 'traditional', black-box system architecture and our proposed architecture, this section presents the query processing employed in the prototype system that takes place to evaluate the example query. To keep things simple, we present the physical layer as a familiar SQL database; in the prototype implementation however, we use the Monet Interface Language (MIL, [38]) gaining better control over the generated query plans.

Wordindex (W)

position	term
2	'...'
3	'...
8	'Will..'
9	'..'
12	'Maxi..'
17	'dating'
20	'..'
21	'..'
...	...

Nodeindex (N)

region_id	start	end	tag
0	0	25	article
1	1	4	title
2	5	24	bdy
3	6	14	sec
4	7	10	p
5	11	13	p
6	15	23	sec
7	16	18	p
8	19	22	p
...	...	...	...

Query (Q)

qterm
'Maxima'
'dating'

Attribute index (A)

region_id	attr_id	attr_name	attr_val
0	0	lang	...
0	1	pdate	...
...	...	...	...

Fig. 12.4. Database schema of our XML IR system.

12.4.1 XML Processing

The first part of the generated query plan focuses on the processing of structural constraints, and is handled in the logical XML extension. For the example query, it identifies the document components in the collection that are subsequently ranked by the IR extension, which implements the about function. The XML processing extension produces its query plans based upon the region indexing scheme outlined in Section 12.3, using the physical database schema shown in Figure 12.4. It selects the collection of article components specified by XPath expression //article/text() (a collection of bags of words), filtered by the specified constraints on publication date and language attributes:

```
articles :=
    SELECT n.region_id, start, end
    FROM nodeindex n,
         attributeindex al, attributeindex ap
    WHERE n.tag = 'article'
      AND al.region_id = n.region_id
```

```
AND al.name = 'lang'
AND al.value = 'English'
AND ap.region_id = n.region_id
AND ap.name = 'pdate'
AND ap.value BETWEEN '31-1-2003' AND '1-3-2003';

mat_articles :=
    SELECT a.region_id, w.position
    FROM articles a, wordindex w
    WHERE a.start < w.position AND w.position < a.end;
```

The resulting query plan is rather straightforward; it selects those article components satisfying the attribute constraints, and materializes the text occurring in these article components. Materialization of the text is handled by the containment-join $\bowtie_\supset$, specified in the second SQL query by the range predicates on the position attribute of word index $\mathcal{W}$.

Notice that the logical XML extension generates a query plan that is understood by the physical level of the system (and could be executed as is), but that this plan has not been executed yet, neither has the ordering in which the relational operators are to be evaluated been fixed at this point! A main advantage of deferring the query evaluation is that the physical layer can still use its statistics maintained about the data, for instance to decide upon the predicate that is most selective. This also improves the likelihood that intermediate query results can be reused, e.g., between sessions (when the same user always reads English articles only) or shared across different users (all selecting usually article nodes with recent publication date). A third advantage will be discussed after the logical extension for information retrieval processing has been introduced.

12.4.2 IR Processing

The next step in this discussion focuses on the logical extension for IR processing; in our example query, this extension handles the ranking of article components selected by the XML extension.

The prototype system uses Hiemstra's statistical language modeling approach for the retrieval model underlying the about function (Chapter 7 of this book). The selected XML sub-documents are thus ranked by a linear combination of term frequency (tf) and document frequency (df). The language model smoothes probability $P(T_i|D_j)$ (for which the tf statistic is a maximum likelihood estimator) with a background model $P(T_i)$ (for which the df statistic is a maximum likelihood estimator), computing the document component's retrieval status value by aggregating the independent scores of each query term.

The IR processing extension at the logical level manipulates collections of bag-of-words representations of the document components to be ranked. Let us first consider the calculation of the term probabilities. This requires the normalization of term frequency with document component length. Calculation of $P(T_i|D_j)$ is thus outlined in the following SQL fragment:

```
mat_art_len :=
    SELECT mat_articles.region_id, count(*) AS length
    FROM mat_articles GROUP BY mat_articles.region_id;

ntf_ij :=
    SELECT mat_articles.region_id, w.term,
       (count(*) / mat_art_len.length) AS prob
    FROM mat_articles, mat_art_len, wordindex w, query q
    WHERE w.term = q.qterm
      AND mat_articles.position = w.position
      AND mat_articles.region_id = mat_art_len.region_id
    GROUP BY mat_articles.region_id, w.term;
```

For generality, the computation of these probabilities has been assumed completely dynamic, for the IR extension cannot predict what node sets in the XML collection will be used for ranking. In practice however, when the collection is mostly static and the same node sets are used repeatedly for ranking (e.g., users ranking always subsets of //article/text()), the relations storing term counts and component lengths should obviously be maintained as materialized views.

Similar arguments hold for the estimation of $P(T_i)$, the term probability in the background model. As explained in [89] however, the collection from which the background statistics are to be estimated should be specified as a parameter of the about operator (alternatively, the right scope could be guessed by the system). Let the collection of all article nodes be appropriate in the example query (and not the subset resulting from the attribute selections), and the following queries compute the background statistics:

```
num_art :=
    SELECT COUNT(*) FROM nodeindex WHERE tag='article';

art_qterm :=
    SELECT DISTINCT n.region_id, w.term
    FROM nodeindex n, wordindex w, query q
    WHERE w.term = q.qterm
      AND n.tag = 'article'
      AND n.start < w.position AND w.position < n.end;

ndf_i :=
    SELECT term, (count(*) / num_art) AS prob
    FROM art_qterm GROUP BY term;
```

The final step computes the ranking function from the intermediate term probabilities in document and collection:

```
ranks :=
    SELECT ntf_ij.region_id,
       sum(log(1.0 + ((ntf_ij.prob / ndf_i.prob) *
```

```
           (0.15 / 0.85)))) AS rank
FROM ntf_ij, ndf_i
WHERE ntf_ij.term = ndf_i.term
GROUP BY ntf_ij.region_id
ORDER BY rank DESC LIMIT 100;
```

12.4.3 Inter-extension Optimization

We now present the third advantage of the Multi-Model DBMS architecture: optimization is not limited to *within* extensions themselves, but can also be performed *between* extensions. An example of such inter-extension optimization is the processing of the *text()*-function. Formally, this function materializes *all* text within an XML node and the generated plan for materialization of all article text has been presented. Assuming for example an object-relational approach with two blackbox extensions, one for XPath expressions and one for IR processing, the XPath blackbox extension would have had to materialize all text occurring in article nodes as result of `//articles/text()` that is the input for the about operator of the IR extension.

In our case however, the IR extension takes a query plan as input that it simply augments with its own operations. The physical layer of the architecture can easily detect that *only* the terms occurring in the query string have to be materialized to compute the correct results. The query term selection predicate (`wordindex.term = query.qterm`) is simply pushed up into the expression for `mat_articles`. The much smaller intermediate result to be materialized reduces significantly the bandwidth needed for evaluating the full XQuery expression - especially in cases when the query terms occur infrequently in the corpus.

Summarizing, the main benefit of the proposed Multi-Model DBMS architecture is the ability to make such optimization decisions (either within extensions or between extensions) at run-time. The logical extensions expose their domain knowledge in terms understood by the physical layer, still allowing it to intervene if necessary (instead of fixing the query execution order by themselves). Also, reuse of intermediate results is easier realized. The precise nature of the optimization process is a central focus in our current research.

12.5 Discussion

The information retrieval models discussed so far have been straightforward, ignoring semantic information from XML tags, as well as most of the logical and conceptual structure of the documents. In spite of the simplicity of the retrieval models discussed, these examples demonstrate the suitability of the 'database approach' for information retrieval applications. The next step in our research is to determine *what* extra knowledge we need to add to increase retrieval effectiveness. Development of new retrieval models (that exploit the full potential benefit of XML documents) can only be based on participation in evaluations (like INEX, see Chapter 19), and we expect the flexibility of the database approach to information retrieval to help invent these models more easily.

The integration of IR and database technology will offer more apparent advantages in future retrieval systems, supporting more complex search strategies and advanced query processing techniques. Consider for example a slightly modified scenario for our running example: we drop 'recent' from the information need, and assume automatic query expansion to be part of the IR process. It is quite likely that 'Willem-Alexander' is only referred to as 'the Dutch Crown Prince' in some of the English newspaper articles. Similarly, it is likely that some other articles mention both 'Willem-Alexander' and 'the Dutch Crown Prince'. Thus, we hypothesize that query expansion with terms from documents containing both 'Willem-Alexander' and 'Maxima' would improve recall with high likelihood.

Generalizing this scenario, we define a strategy for queries containing several (more than one) named entities. For these queries, we first retrieve a small number of documents that contain (most of) these named entities *and* rank high using the full query. Next, we perform query expansion with blind feedback using these documents. Finally, we rank the full collection using the expanded query.

In a retrieval system based on black-boxes, implementing a strategy like this can be rather tricky. Terms from the collection that are tagged as named entities would be stored outside the IR system, probably in a DBMS like structured data. The ranking system cannot usually be instructed to only retrieve documents that contain at least these terms. And, as argued before, the blind feedback process is often implemented on top of the core IR engine, which probably does not cache intermediate results. To process the full query, we travel between the boundaries of systems more than once, which will clearly reduce the efficiency of the system.

Advanced query processing techniques include optimization strategies adapted to an interactive environment, allowing search with precise queries, browsing based on online clustering of search results, and query refinement using relevance feedback. Horizontal fragmentation might be exploited for handling larger collections, like in [32]: distribute large sets of XML documents over a farm of servers and fragment the vocabulary based on term frequency, either globally or within documents (or document regions).

Using the quality assessments from the INEX evaluation, we can investigate trading quality for speed, as we did for full-text retrieval using TREC benchmark data [33]. Like in text retrieval, XQuery-Fulltext retrieval will result in many documents, and now also document regions, that match a query more or less. As mentioned before, this does require ranking and user feedback, resulting in an iterative process that should converge to a good final result set as quickly and effectively as possible. This means the user does not want the steps to get there to take very long. Also, in the first iterations explicitly presenting expectedly bad results to the user might very well speed up the entire process as the negative user feedback on those results will rule out significant parts of the search space for processing in further iterations. Trading quality for speed is an interesting option for the first steps of the user.

12.6 Conclusions

We have identified two types of challenges for IR systems, that are difficult to address with the current engineering practice of hard-coding the ranking process in highly optimized inverted file structures. We propose that the trade-off between flexibility and efficiency may be resolved by adopting a 'database approach' to IR. The main advantage of adhering to the database approach is that it provides a system architecture allowing to balance flexibility and efficiency. Flexibility is obtained by declarative specification of the retrieval model, and efficiency is addressed through algebraic optimization in the mapping process from specification to query plan.

Existing (relational) database system architectures are however inadequate for proper integration of querying on content and structure. The Multi-Model DBMS architecture is proposed as an alternative design for extending database technology for this type of retrieval applications. Discussing the query processing strategies for an example query combining content and structure, the main differences with existing blackbox approaches for extending database technology are explained.

The chapter has been concluded with a discussion of future directions in IR system implementation for which our proposed architecture is of even more importance. In particular, we claim that both fragmentation as well as the optimization though quality prediction would benefit greatly from an open, extensible, layered approach, i.e., the advantages of the Multi-Model DBMS architecture.

13

PowerDB-XML: Scalable XML Processing with a Database Cluster

Torsten Grabs and Hans-Jörg Schek

13.1 Introduction

The flexible data model underlying the W3C XML document format covers a broad range of application scenarios. These scenarios can be categorized into data-centric and document-centric ones. *Data-centric processing* stands for highly structured XML documents, queries with precise predicates, and workloads such as the ones with online transaction processing. *Document-centric processing* in turn denotes searching for relevant information in XML documents in the sense of information retrieval (IR for short). With document-centric scenarios, XML documents are typically less rigidly structured and queries have vague predicates. Today, different systems address these needs, namely database systems and information retrieval systems. XML however offers the perspective to cover them with a single integrated framework, and to make the above distinction obsolete at least in terms of the underlying system infrastructure. The aim of the PowerDB-XML engine being developed at ETH Zurich is to build an efficient and scalable platform for combined data-centric and document-centric XML processing. The following overview summarizes important requirements that a respective XML engine must cover efficiently:

- lossless storage of XML documents,
- reconstruction of the XML documents decomposed into storage structures,
- navigation and processing of path expressions on XML document structure,
- processing of precise and vague predicates on XML content, and
- scalability in the number and size of XML documents.

To cover these requirements efficiently and in combination is challenging since a semistructured data model underlies the XML format. Consequently, both the data and its structure are defined in the XML documents. This makes for instance optimization much more difficult than with rigidly structured data where a clear distinction into schema and data exists.

H. Blanken et al. (Eds.): Intelligent Search on XML Data, LNCS 2818, pp. 193–206, 2003.
© Springer-Verlag Berlin Heidelberg 2003

None of the storage schemes for XML documents available so far covers all the aforementioned requirements in combination. Native XML storage techniques lack standard database functionality such as transactions, buffer management, and indexing. This functionality however comes for free with approaches that map XML documents to databases. This makes relational database systems attractive as storage managers for XML documents. Nevertheless, relational databases currently fall short in supporting document-centric XML processing. The reason for this is that the database mapping techniques that have been proposed so far focus on data-centric processing only. Therefore, database mapping techniques in isolation are not a viable solution either in order to cover the requirements. Combinations of native XML storage with database mappings may appear as an attractive alternative. However, they are not available yet with commercial database systems or commercial XML engines.

In this chapter, we present the XML storage scheme of PowerDB-XML. It combines native XML storage management with database mappings and efficiently supports document-centric processing. Our approach builds on relational database systems as storage managers for XML documents. This covers efficient data-centric processing. Moreover, special interest is paid to efficient document-centric processing, in particular to flexible relevance-oriented search on XML, as explained in Chap. 6. Note that the full-text search functionality provided by database systems does not cover the requirements for flexible relevance-oriented search on XML documents. This is another argument why we must rule out commercial off-the-shelf approaches.

A further benefit of PowerDB-XML's storage management is that it nicely fits with a cluster of database systems as underlying infrastructure. A *cluster of databases* is a cluster of workstations or personal computers (PCs) interconnected by a standard network. With the PowerDB project at ETH Zurich, the idea is to use off-the-shelf components as much as possible regarding both hardware and software. Therefore, each *node* of the cluster runs a commercially available operating system. In addition, a relational database system is installed and running on each node. Such a cluster of databases is attractive as an infrastructure for information systems that require a high degree of scalability. This is because *scaling-out* the cluster is easy when higher performance is required: one adds further nodes to the cluster. This provides additional computational resources and storage capacities to the overall system, and ideally the envisioned system re-arranges data and workloads such that performance is optimal on the enlarged cluster. Figure 13.1 illustrates XML processing with PowerDB-XML and a cluster of databases.

13.2 Related Work

Two classification dimensions characterize the various approaches to XML storage management proposed in the literature. The first dimension is based

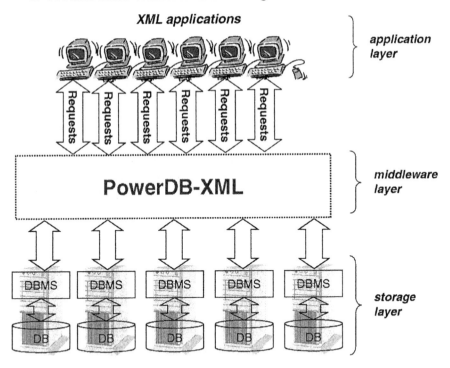

Fig. 13.1. XML processing with PowerDB-XML

on the physical storage design. The second one relies on the mapping function from XML documents to the actual storage structures.

Physical Storage Design

Regarding the first dimension, so-called native storage techniques for XML documents are distinguished from database storage for XML. *Native XML storage techniques* aim at developing new storage structures that reflect the semistructured data model of XML. Natix [160] and PDOM [167] are prominent examples of native XML storage managers. The expectation is that specific storage schemes for XML provide superior performance as compared to the following approach.

Database Storage for XML stores XML documents based on existing data structures of the underlying database systems. The XML structures are mapped onto the data model of the database system using mapping functions discussed subsequently. Here, the expectation is that leveraging existing and well-understood storage techniques such as today's database systems yields better performance for XML processing.

Mapping from XML to Storage Structures

The second classification dimension distinguishes the types of the mapping between XML documents and storage structures [328]. It differentiates between text-based mapping, model-mapping, and structure-mapping approaches.

Text-based mapping approaches simply store XML documents as character strings, for instance, in a VARCHAR or a CLOB table column, or as a flat file.

Model-mapping approaches create a generic database schema that reflects the data model of the XML format. The database schema is fixed and known in advance. Model-mapping approaches represent XML documents as graphs and store their nodes and edges. Prominent database model-mapping approaches are EDGE, BINARY and UNIVERSAL [117], XRel [328], and XPath accelerator [146]. A common drawback of model-mapping approaches is that they require extensive joins over the underlying database tables to reconstruct the original XML document.

Structure-mapping approaches infer the database mappings from the logical structure of the XML documents, i.e., the XML element structure or an XML Schema definition. The idea is to automatically derive a database schema that captures the semantics of the application. In contrast to model-mapping approaches, different XML applications with different XML document structures typically lead to different database schemas. Prominent structure-mapping approaches are STORED [97], LegoDB [35], or the mapping techniques for XML DTDs and XML Schema proposed by [190, 279].

13.3 SFRAG: Combining Data-Centric and Native XML Storage Management

The intuition behind the SFRAG storage scheme is to combine storage of XML document sub-trees – so-called *XML fragments* – with database mappings. Our motivation for this is to support both data-centric and document-centric processing efficiently: data-centric processing usually affects only small parts of XML documents. In particular, changes of XML document texts are costly since they usually require to load the document into the internal representation of an XML processor. In terms of update efficiency, it is promising to split the complete document text into smaller fractions, similar to native XML storage. Document-centric processing with document reconstruction in turn benefits from a coarse *storage granularity*. SFRAG reflects this trade-off, splits the XML documents into XML fragments and maintains them similar to native XML storage schemes.

SFRAG keeps the XML fragments in a so-called *document table* in order to efficiently reconstruct documents. So-called *side tables* defined by any of the relational database mappings discussed in Sect. 6.2 complement the document table to make data-centric processing more efficient. The core idea is to efficiently compute the *candidate set*, i.e., the set of documents that potentially qualify for a given request, using SQL statements over the side tables.

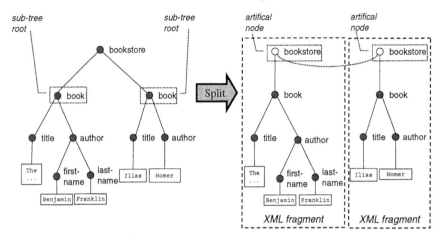

Fig. 13.2. XML document and its XML fragments

Document Storage Granularity

An XML fragment comprises sub-trees of the graph representation of an XML document. In addition, the paths in the fragment leading from the fragment root to a leaf node are the same as in the original XML document. Hence, splitting an XML document into fragments may require to introduce artificial (empty) nodes. Meta-data stored in XML attributes of the artificial nodes allows to reconstruct the original document if required. Figure 13.2 illustrates splitting an XML document into fragments.

The size of the fragments is an important optimization parameter. With SFRAG, a set of sub-tree root elements S and a threshold parameter k for the number of sub-trees per fragment determine the size of the fragment. Given an XML document, SFRAG iteratively adds sub-trees of the original document rooted at some $s \in S$ in document order to the fragment including any XML content between the sub-tree root nodes. SFRAG starts a new fragment when the number of sub-trees in the fragment exceeds k. From the original document, all nodes along the paths that lead to a fragment sub-tree are added as artificial nodes to the fragment. This has the advantage that the path leading to a node in the fragment is the same as in the original document. Thus, off-the-shelf XML processors can directly evaluate path expressions on the fragments if the path expressions are local to a fragment sub-tree. If an XML processor is already included in the database engine, additional implementation efforts are not needed for this class of requests.

Example 1 (XML fragments). With the fragmentation scheme illustrated by Fig. 13.2, the sub-tree root elements are defined by the set of location paths $S = \{/\text{bookstore/book}\}$ and the sub-tree number threshold k equals 1. The bookstore element nodes are artificial nodes of the fragments. The dashed lines connect the artificial nodes of the two fragments. Path expressions that are

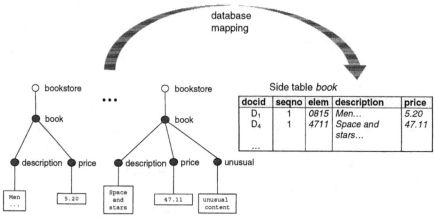

Fig. 13.3. XML fragments mapped with the SFRAG approach

local to /bookstore/book-sub-trees can be processed local to each fragment. That means integrating the fragments is not required. For instance, the path expression /bookstore/book/title does not require integration of fragments.

XML processing reverses the fragmentation process if it is necessary to reconstruct the logical document. Storing large portions of XML documents using SFRAG with a coarse storage granularity makes document reconstruction efficient with document-centric processing. Performing small updates on documents, however, is the more costly the larger the storage granularity. SFRAG reflects this tradeoff with the parameterized fragmentation of documents such that the administrator can define a fragmentation degree depending on the actual workload of the system.

Document Table

Table `xmldocument` stores the texts of the XML fragments. The columns of the table are the primary key columns `docid` and `seqno` and a column `doctext`. The column `docid` stores internal system generated document identifiers. Column `seqno` in turn stores the sequence number of the fragment. For lack of off-the-shelf native XML storage techniques with relational database systems, `doctext` currently stores the fragments as character-large-objects (CLOBs). However, as soon as more efficient extensions for XML become available with commercial database systems SFRAG can store them using native storage schemes instead of CLOBs which we expect to further improve performance.

This representation of documents is well-suited for fetching and updating complete document texts with document-centric XML processing. Both retrieval and update of the full document text map to the row-operations of the database system, which are efficient. In the following, we explain how to make data-centric processing efficient as well.

Side Tables

A side table materializes content of the XML documents in database tables. To do so, SFRAG deploys one or several of the database mapping schemes discussed in Sect. 6.2. In addition to the mapped XML content, each side table comprises the columns `docid` and `seqno`. They link the rows of a side table with the original document and its fragments in the document table. This makes database functionality available for XML contents. However, updates imply additional cost to keep documents and side tables mutually consistent.

An important further requirement of document-centric processing is efficient relevance-oriented search on XML content. SFRAG as discussed so far does not yet cover this aspect. The following section explains how PowerDB-XML addresses this issue.

13.4 XMLIR-to-SQL: Mapping Relevance-Oriented Search on XML Documents to Database Systems

Additional efforts are necessary to make IR-like relevance-oriented search on XML content efficient. An obvious alternative to cover these requirements are full-text indexing and ranked retrieval functionality of commercial database systems. However, these approaches rely on collection-wide IR statistics where the indexing granularity is the whole XML document. This is in contrast to flexible retrieval with fine-grained IR statistics, as discussed in Chap. 6. For similar reasons, loosely coupled approaches to combine database systems and IR systems as proposed by [308] are not viable. This chapter, therefore, proposes a different approach called *XMLIR-to-SQL*. It adapts ideas from own previous work [137, 135] and the one by Grossman et al. [143] to map IR processing to relational database technology.

In a nutshell, XMLIR-to-SQL works as follows: XMLIR-to-SQL takes the textual XML elements (or attributes) and obtains the descriptions of their content using common information retrieval functionality such as term extraction and stemming. The textual elements together with their index data serve as the basic indexing nodes (cf. Chap. 6). They allow to dynamically compute the IR descriptions needed for the different query types for flexible retrieval from XML content.

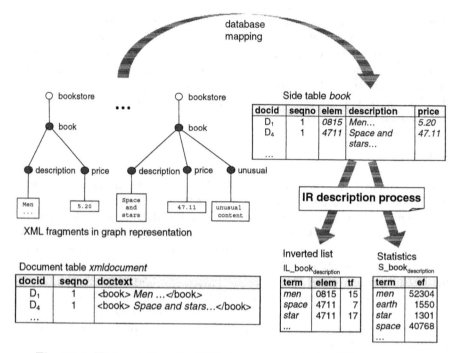

Fig. 13.4. IR-descriptions for XML documents with the SFRAG mapping

In more detail, XMLIR-to-SQL first identifies the basic searchable elements and then annotates them using database tables to store their IR descriptions. Fig. 13.4 illustrates XMLIR-to-SQL with an SFRAG storage scheme and textual XML content in the basic indexing node description.

Indexing of textual content with XMLIR-to-SQL works as follows: consider an element of element type t with textual content. XMLIR-to-SQL applies IR-specific functionality such as term extraction and stemming to obtain the descriptions of its content. As Fig. 13.4 shows, it generates an inverted list table IL_t that describes the content of the element, i.e., the inverted list stores terms and term frequencies. It comprises the columns term, elem, and tf. Column term holds a descriptor of the text of an element with the identifier elem. Column tf (term frequency) stores the number of occurrences of the descriptor in the text. Another table S_t keeps term statistics. With vector space retrieval and *tfidf* ranking, this table stores the element frequencies of terms, i.e., the *tfidf* of elements of type t that contain a given term. These extensions to store IR-descriptions are applicable to all database mapping techniques discussed in Sect. 13.2.

The following example illustrates how query processing with combined data-centric and document-centric requests works with PowerDB-XML.

Example 2 (Query processing). Consider the query //book[containsTFIDF(./description, 'space stars XML')][./price < 50] and the database schema shown

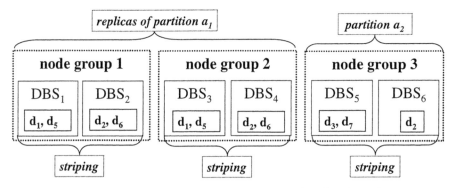

Fig. 13.5. Organization of XML documents with a database cluster

in Fig. 13.4. The query searches for books with a description relevant to the query 'space stars XML' under *tf idf* ranking and that cost less than 50 (\$). Processing this query with PowerDB-XML logically comprises three steps: the first step computes the ranking of book description elements using a SQL statement over the tables IL_book$_{description}$ and S_book$_{description}$. The second step then eliminates those books that do not fulfill the predicate over price using a SQL clause over the side table book. Finally, PowerDB-XML loads the XML fragments/documents identified by the previous steps from the xmldocument table. This is necessary when the XML documents comprise content not covered by database mappings and IR descriptions. Figure 13.4 illustrates this with the unusual elements which must be returned as part of the query result to guarantee lossless storage.

A detailed discussion of query processing with PowerDB-XML is beyond the scope of this chapter.

13.5 Mapping XML Processing to a Database Cluster

XML processing is resource intensive in terms of CPU and disk resources. CPU resources are required to generate appropriate representations of XML documents to process XML update and retrieval requests. Requirements regarding disk space are significant since efficient XML processing relies on materialized views over XML content as well as IR indexes and statistics. Therefore, a database cluster is well suited for XML processing since it typically comprises a high number of processors and disks. Consequently, PowerDB-XML builds on such an infrastructure. Using a cluster as the storage layer for XML processing, however, raises the question of how to physically organize document and index data and how to organize XML processing depending on the data organization chosen. The overall objective is to achieve good performance, i.e., low response times and high throughput, for XML processing.

Physical Data Organization with a Cluster of Databases

In the following, we discuss general techniques for physical data organization with a cluster of databases. The techniques that we discuss are independent of the choice of the actual local XML storage manager. All of the subsequent approaches work with any database mapping, native XML storage manager, or combination of them. Furthermore, improved XML storage techniques immediately yield performance improvements when deployed to the cluster-based infrastructure.

Irrespective of the underlying storage manager, a cluster-based infrastructure poses the question of physical data organization. Typically, the degree of redundancy is an important characteristic of physical data organization. The performance benefits of redundancy, however, depend on the workload of the system. Read-only queries obviously benefit from a high degree of redundancy as it allows to choose among a number of copies, for instance. With updates in turn, redundancy is disadvantageous because redundant data must be kept consistent. Consequently, the degree of redundancy must be carefully chosen depending on the actual or expected workload of the system.

A follow-up question is which actual data organization techniques to deploy. Several physical data organization techniques have been proposed already for distributed and parallel database systems, and they might be well suited for XML processing as well. The alternative is to develop a new data organization scheme that in particular fits XML processing on a cluster infrastructure. The main objective in either case is to avoid resource and data contention at the cluster nodes where a few nodes do all the work and all other other nodes remain idle.

Research on distributed and parallel databases has already proposed physical data organization schemes for distributed shared-nothing settings such as a cluster of databases, notably partitioning, replication and striping [235]. Usually, practical settings with both retrieval and updates require a combination of partitioning and replication, i.e., a hybrid approach. This is also the case for XML processing with a cluster of databases. But, before we can dwell more deeply upon such combinations of different data organization schemes, an appropriate granularity of distribution is needed. Without any further knowledge of the application scenario, replication and partitioning take place at the granularity of database rows (assuming relational storage managers at the cluster nodes). With XML processing, however, this may lead to a skewed distribution where IR index data and side table rows of the same document are stored on different nodes. This requires distributed query processing even for each single document. One could avoid this overhead when placing each document and its derived data at the same node. Therefore, PowerDB-XML keeps an XML document and its derived data, i.e., the document text, its side table entries, inverted list postings and statistics, at the same cluster node. Hence, the storage granularity of choice is the XML document respectively the XML fragment in combination with its derived data. Results from previous experiments have shown that this yields superior performance as compared to finer distribution granularities [136]. Using XML fragments as the granularity of distribution, the XML document collection is mapped to one or several cluster nodes using partitioning, striping, or replication. This means that we have to decide for each XML fragment which cluster nodes store the fragment. PowerDB-XML addresses this problem as follows.

PowerDB-XML logically divides the nodes of the database cluster in so-called *node groups*. For ease of presentation, let us pretend that node groups have the same size. Partitioning assigns the documents of a particular document type to a dedicated node group. Hence, the partitioning function takes the characteristics of XML into account, namely, that documents conform to the same DTD or XML Schema. An alternative to using the document type as partitioning criterion is to take the document content into account. For instance, content about 'medicine' could form a partition different from that on 'computer science'. In contrast to the previous partitioning function, this criterion does not require DTDs or XML Schema specifications. The advantage of partitioning is that requests regarding a particular document type or a certain domain are processed local to a node group.

Replication with PowerDB-XML in turn copies the data of some node group to another. Thus, any copy can evaluate a given query. The drawback is that each copy must process a given update. Transaction management functionality for XML processing guarantees that replica updates are atomic [138]. The *degree of replication* is the number of copies.

Striping randomly distributes the XML fragment data over several cluster nodes of the same node group. The number of these nodes is the *degree of striping*. A so-called *striping-replication ratio* $srr = degree\ of\ striping/degree$ *of replication* denotes the ratio between striping and replication when combining striping and replication. The idea is to adjust the srr to meet the performance requirements of the application. For instance, striping over two nodes with four replica of these nodes yields an srr of $2/4$. Figure 13.5 illustrates the data organization schemes introduced so far for $n = 6$ nodes and several XML fragments d_i.

XML Processing on a Database Cluster

Routing of XML requests depends on the data organization within the cluster. With partitioning, PowerDB-XML first determines which document types possibly qualify for the request. It then routes the request to the node groups of these document types and processes it there. With replication in turn, a retrieval request is processed at the node group with the smallest current workload. This leads to a good distribution of the workload among the cluster nodes. An update request, however, must run at all copies to keep replica consistent. This introduces additional overhead as compared to a single-copy setting. With striping, the request is routed to each node of the striped node group and processed there. Each node processes the request and contributes

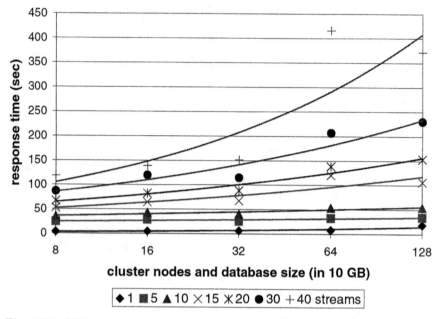

Fig. 13.6. XML retrieval request performance with PowerDB-XML, cluster sizes from 8 to 128 nodes, and database sizes from 80 GB to 1.3 TB

a partial result. Post-processing at the middleware layer combines and integrates the partial results to the overall result.

13.6 Experimental Evaluation

The following series of experiments investigates the scalability of XML processing when the size of the document collection grows. We restrict our discussion to the physical data organization scheme of striping. [134] provides for an extensive experimental evaluation and a respective discussion.

The experiments start with a collection of 8 GB of XML documents and an overall database size of 80 GB, distributed among 8 cluster nodes using striping at the XML fragment level as physical data organization scheme. The XML document collection has been generated using the XMark benchmark XML document generator (see Chap. 18). Starting with this setup, the experiments iteratively double collection size and cluster size at the same rate, up to 128 GB of XML documents, an overall database size of about 1.3 TB and 128 cluster nodes. With all these settings, the physical organization is striping over all cluster nodes. The experimental runs have tested the system with workloads of 1, 5, 10, 15, 20, 30, and 40 concurrent streams of XML requests. The streams emulate XML applications submitting one XML request

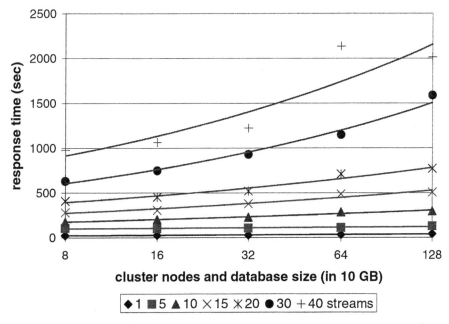

Fig. 13.7. XML update request performance with PowerDB-XML, cluster sizes from 8 to 128 nodes, and database sizes from 80 GB to 1.3 TB

after the other without any think time. Requests distribute equally over XML retrieval and XML updates. Each request loads about 0.1% of the XML documents of the collection. Note that our experimental evaluation reflects the worst case where loading of the XML fragment from the document table is necessary (third step in Example 2).

Figures 13.6 and 13.7 show the outcome of the experiments. As the curves for the different workloads in the figures show, increasing workloads lead to higher response times for both retrieval and updates with any cluster size and database size. So far, this is what one would expect when more parallel requests compete for shared resources. However, the figures illustrate an interesting observation: both retrieval and update requests scale less than linearly for high workloads when scaling out. For increasing collection sizes this means that there is an increase in response times when doubling both collection size and cluster size. For instance, average response times with a workload of 20 concurrent streams are about 50% higher with 128 cluster nodes and 1.3 TB overall database size than with 8 nodes and 80 GB. This is in contrast to the expectation of ideal scalability, i.e., that response times are constant when increasing cluster size and collection size at the same rate. Nevertheless, consider that the overall database size has grown by a factor of 16 while response times have only increased by a factor of 1.5. Hence, the overall result is still a positive one.

A further observation with these experiments is that request processing on XML fragments is still highly resource-intensive. Purely data-centric requests where access to the fragments is not necessary, i.e., SFRAG's database mappings already cover the query result and the third step of Example 2 is obsolete, reduces retrieval response times by up to 90%.

13.7 Conclusions

Database researchers have spent much effort on efficient storage management schemes for data-centric XML processing. In particular, efficient techniques are available to map XML documents with rigid structure to relational storage. However, the flexibility of the data model underlying the XML format supports a much broader range of applications including document-centric processing of less rigorously structured data. In this context, PowerDB-XML – the XML engine developed at ETH Zurich – aims at supporting XML applications that require both data-centric and document-centric processing in combination. As it has turned out, efficient storage management for these applications requires a combination of different storage schemes. Therefore, PowerDB-XML follows a hybrid approach called SFRAG. It implements native XML storage techniques on top of relational database systems and combines them with database mappings for XML documents. In addition, PowerDB-XML associates SFRAG with XMLIR-to-SQL, an efficient implementation of flexible XML retrieval in standard SQL. This allows to run PowerDB-XML on top of a cluster of database systems that serves as a scalable infrastructure for XML processing.

Due to the flexibility of the XML format, processing of XML documents is costly in terms of CPU and disk resources. The findings from our experimental evaluation of PowerDB-XML show that a database cluster is well-suited as a storage layer for XML applications with large or even growing XML collections. In the near future, we expect vendors of relational database systems to support XML data types with native XML storage management in the database engine. These approaches nicely complement the SFRAG storage management scheme of PowerDB-XML, and we expect further performance gains when integrating them into our infrastructure.

14

Web-Based Distributed XML Query Processing

Marko Smiljanić, Ling Feng, and Willem Jonker

14.1 Introduction

Web-based distributed XML query processing has gained in importance in recent years due to the widespread popularity of XML on the Web. Unlike centralized and tightly coupled distributed systems, Web-based distributed database systems are highly unpredictable and uncontrollable, with a rather unstable behavior in data availability, processing capability and data transfer speed. As a consequence, there exists a number of conspicuous problems that need to be addressed for Web-based distributed query processing in the novel context of XML. Some major ones are listed below.

- *High autonomy of participanting sites.* Data sources scattered on the Web may be equipped with either powerful query engines, say those which can support XPath, XQuery or some other XML query languages, or simple ones which offer limited processing capabilities, just like a plain Web server returning the whole XML files. In Web-based distributed database systems, both the data sources and their associated processing capabilities need to be modeled and used in query execution planning.
- *XML streaming data* is proliferating and flowing on the Web. As the size of the streaming data is usually enormous, it is not efficient to first wait for all data to arrive, store it locally and then query it. Instead, new techniques must be deployed for querying streaming XML data.
- *Unreliable response time* on the Web exists due to dozens of Internet routers that separate nodes participating in distributed processing. High delay and a total data jam must be taken into account. When congestions are detected by certain mechanisms like timers, querying should activate alternative execution plans to keep the system busy with performing some other relevant tasks.
- *Different expectations of query results.* The classical way of querying suggests the delivery of a complete and exact query result. In such systems, users prefer to have the "time to last" result as short as possible. However,

H. Blanken et al. (Eds.): Intelligent Search on XML Data, LNCS 2818, pp. 207–216, 2003.

in a dynamic environment like the Internet, more querying facilities must be introduced. For example, users may opt for getting the first element of the result quickly with others coming afterwords. The complete result is of no interest at the first instance. Such systems can thus be optimized to have "time to first" result shorter. Another approach is to have results available "on demand" at any stage of query processing. To this end, we can let the systems present the current state of the answer and then resume the processing.

The aim of this chapter is to survey recent research on Web-based distributed XML query processing, with the emphasis on technical innovations that have been devised in query planning, query execution and query optimization.

The reminder of the chapter is organized as follows. Section 2 describes several query processing schemas, including centralized vs. distributed schema, static vs. dynamic schema, and streaming data query processing schema. Section 3 presents several XML query optimization techniques. We review a few Web-based systems in Section 4. Section 5 gives the conclusion.

14.2 Web-Based Distributed XML Query Processing Schemas

Figure 14.1 shows a generic Web-based distributed XML query processing architecture, containing three nodes A, B and C. Each participant node accommodates some XML data and is equipped with a query processor. Users at the client site are unaware of such a distributed architecture. They pose queries via a single entry point, assigned to node A. Nodes in this system can be heterogeneous in terms of both data sources and query processors. Some systems also provide users with an integrated view, so that users can ask questions over the integrated view.

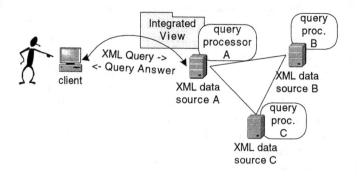

Fig. 14.1. A generic Web-based distributed query processing architecture

We now describe in detail various distributed query processing schemas. The taxonomies for classifying these schemas are based mainly on different approaches distributed query processors employ in query planning and execution in response to a user's query. Note that the following taxonomies are not orthogonal.

14.2.1 Centralized vs. Distributed Query Processing Schema

According to the location where queries are planned and executed, we categorize query processing into the following three groups.

Centralized Planning and Centralized Execution.

This is the simplest, and currently the most frequently used architecture in distributed Web systems. In such a system, one node carries all the responsibilities: it collects and warehouses XML data, plans and executes queries. Other nodes are accessed in the off-line mode and are asked only to provide the raw data. *Google*, a keyword-based search engine, falls in this group (though Google itself does not solely use XML data). Niagara system [227], a combination of a search engine and a query processing engine, allows users to raise arbitrary structured queries over the Internet. Niagara can perform "on-demand" retrievals on the distributed documents if they are not available in the local document repository, but are referenced by the full text search engine. Xyleme system [75] provides users with integrated views of XML data stored in its local warehouse.

Centralized Planning and Distributed Execution.

When a node receives a user's query over a virtual view of data sources, it produces a complete set of instructions that will evaluate the query in the distributed environment. These instructions will be sent to corresponding nodes which will optimize the execution of their local subqueries. In this case, we have a centralized distributed query processor, responsible for generating a complete query execution plan. However, the query execution that follows is delegated to respective local query processors.

Distributed Planning and Distributed Execution.

In contrast to centralized query planning carried out by one node, distributed query processors at multiple nodes can coordinate with each other to derive a global query plan. For example, node A, upon the receipt of a query, can plan initial stages of the query execution using its local data, and then send the "rest" of the query to some other nodes, say B and C, where involved data sources are located. Node B and C then plan further execution of the rest of the query. The query processors of participanting nodes can be either identical or different.

14.2.2 Static vs. Dynamic Query Processing Schema

Once a query plan is generated, it can either be altered or remain unchanged during the query execution phase.

The *static* query processing schema will execute the query plan until completion. The problem with the static query processing schema is that it is vulnerable to unexpected events, like long initial delay in data arrival or general traffic congestions. The need for dynamic query processing capability that can act upon the emergence of such events especially in the Web context is thus highly desirable.

In *dynamic* query processing schema, the query execution planner gets a feedback from the query execution engine on the status of the execution. If some delays are detected, the query planner produces alternative plans for finishing the query processing or just reorders the actions that were planned for later execution. [11] describes a dynamic query plan modification strategy for wide-area remote access, where a scrambling technique is used to generate the alternative execution plan when delays in arrival of data are experienced. As soon as the original data becomes available, the execution is continued at the point before the scrambled plan was used. Scrambling is based on the rescheduling of the operators in the execution plan. However, it must be taken into account that the scrambled processing increases the cost (CPU, I/O and memory usage) of the query execution.

14.2.3 Streaming Data Query Processing Schema

Significant amount of streaming data may be generated and transported from one site to another during the execution of a distributed query on the Web. As such streaming data can be of enormous size, it is not efficient to first wait for all data to arrive, store it locally and then to do the processing. Instead, techniques for processing of the streaming XML data are exploited. Such processing techniques are applicable to all the schemas discussed above.

In [172], it is shown that a group of regular XPath expressions can be simultaneously executed over streaming XML data. The proposed X-scan processor uses a state machine to detect the satisfaction of XPath expressions over incoming XML data. States of the state machine correspond to steps of the XPath queries and the input to the state machine is the data stream arriving from the input. The key challenges in this approach include dealing with cyclic data, preserving the order of elements and removing duplicate bindings that are generated when multiple paths lead to the same data elements. To cope with those problems, the X-scan engine parses the data, creates the structural index to enable fast IDREF to ID traversal and also maintains a "not-yet-seen" ID list.

Joining can be also done between two or more simultaneously incoming streams of XML data. Techniques for joining the streaming data are based on non-blocking pipelined hash join method. In this approach, data is arriving from two data sources from the network. Each data entity is first placed in the hash structure for that data source, and then the other hash is probed. As soon as a match is found, the result tuple is produced. In order to cope with the memory overflow due to the hash size, other techniques involving data storage on secondary storage medium are proposed. Some specifics of XML element joining are discussed in [299], demonstrating that Lattice-Join of XML documents can be implemented as merge operation.

If data streams are continuous like stock indexes, or simply too long, it is desirable for a system to be able to show the current status of results being generated. A query processor has been designed to support partial result generation for non-monotonic functions such as sort, average, and sum, etc. [278].

14.3 Web-Based Distributed XML Query Optimization

When comparing XML query processing with relational database query processing, one impression we have is that those two fields overlap on all the major problems. Indeed, techniques like selection pushdown or querying of materialized views are applicable to query optimization regardless of the data models used. What makes an essential distinction is the environment in which the two models are used and thus different requirements they shall satisfy in both performance and functional domains. In the following, we describe several techniques known from the "classical" query optimization approaches, and discuss how they fit the XML world.

14.3.1 Selectivity Estimation

Selectivity estimation is used by query optimizers to plan for the execution order of subexpressions. Expressions yielding smaller result sets are said to have higher selectivity and are scheduled for early execution. The more complex the operation used in an expression, the more difficult it is to have good selectivity estimation for it.

For XPath expressions containing no predicates on XML documents, selectivity estimation equals the number of elements selected by the XPath. This information can be provided by counting the markup particles in the documents. In the presence of predicates or joins in query expressions, such selectivity information must be extended with statistical data on the XML document content.

The selectivity information has to be stored and accessed with respect to performance requirements of the query planner. This inevitably puts limits on the selectivity estimation in both data size and complexity of selectivity calculation algorithms.

In [5], two methods for storing "basic" XPath selectivity information are used. First, the Path Trees come in the form of a schema tree for an XML document. Each node of such trees represents a path, leading from the root to that node. Each such node is assigned an accumulated number of element instances reached using the path described by the node. This number represents the selectivity for that path. It can be calculated in a single pass over the XML document. The second technique is named "Markov tables". A table is constructed with a distinct row for each path in the data up to the length of m. The calculation of the estimation for longer paths based on the data in the table is shown in [5]. Several summarizing techniques can be exploited to reduce the size and the complexity of the data structures used in both approaches.

14.3.2 Selection Pushdown

Selection pushdown is an optimization technique in which selection operators are scheduled early, e.g., before join operators. When executed, selection reduces the number of values that are to be fed to the expensive join operator, resulting in a low execution cost. This technique has a straightforward application in the XML field [172].

In [69], selection operator placement is analyzed in the context of query systems, which serve a large number of continuous queries (i.e. persistent queries, yielding results once available). Such simultaneous queries are analyzed for common subexpressions which are then grouped for joint execution. This provides resource and time savings. It is shown that in this setup, Push-Down (select first) technique is outperformed by the PullUp (join first) technique. The rational behind those results is that major improvement comes from the operator grouping (i.e. reuse) and not from the operator ordering. Executing the join first enables the wide reuse of the results of this expensive operation.

14.3.3 Integrated Views

In the presence of integrated views, query processors can start with query rewriting in such a way that a query over a global view is translated into a set of queries over local data sources. Such rewriting and creation of a distributed execution plan involves the techniques known as data-shipping and query-shipping. [210] describes an architecture for integrating heterogeneous data sources under an XML global schema, following the local-as-view approach, where local sources' schemas such as relational and tree-structured schemas are described as views over the global XML schema. Users express their queries against the XML global schema in XQuery, which is then translated into into one or several SQL queries over the local data sources. The advantage of using a relational query model lies in the benefit from the relational query capabilities that the relational or XML sources may have. The tuples resulting from the SQL query execution are then structured into the desired XML result.

In addition to facilitating query rewriting with views, using materialized views to answer a query can also greatly speed up query performance, especially when one is confronted with a large volume of data sources on the Web [67, 2, 212].

14.4 Web-Based Query Processing Systems

In this section, we overview a few Web-based database systems. The systems will be analyzed through the spectrum of architectural features covered in the previous sections.

14.4.1 Distributed Query Evaluation on Semistructured Data – Suciu

XML bears a close similarity to semi-structured data models [44, 54, 24]. One pioneering work on distributed querying over semistructured data was done by Dan Suciu [288], who proposed the efficiency definition for a distributed query from the following two aspects.

1) The total number of communication steps between the data sources is constant, i.e. independent on the data or on the query. A communication step can be a broadcast, or a gather, and can involve arbitrary large messages.

2) The total amount of data transferred during query evaluation should depend only on (a) the total number of links between data sources, and (b) the size of the total result.

Suciu investigates distributed queries in a context where data sources are distributed over a fixed number of nodes, and the edges linking the nodes are classified into local (with both ends in the same node) and cross edges (with ends in two distinct nodes). Efficient evaluation of regular path expression queries is reduced to efficient computation of transitive closure of a distributed graph. For more complex queries, where regular path expressions are intermixed freely with selections, joins, grouping, and data restructuring, a collection of recursive functions can be defined accordingly. Those iterate on the graph's structure. The queries in this formalism form an algebra $\mathcal{C}$, which is a fragment of UnQL [53, 55]. By following an algebraic rather than an operational approach, a query Q can be rewritten into Q', called a decomposed query, such that on a distributed database, Q can be evaluated by evaluating Q' independently at each node, computing the accessible part of all results fragments, then shipping and assembling the separate result fragments at the user site.

The proposed query evaluation algorithms provide minimal communication between data sources. Even if several logical 'jumps' (joins in queries) between data sources exist, execution is planned in such a way that those data sources exchange data between each other just once. This does not come without a price. The centralized query planner has to know all the metadata on the participating data sources to plan the query.

The algorithm and the systems described by Suciu fall in the category of centralized planning and distributed evaluation architectures.

Since the autonomy and the dynamics of the data sources are quite high on the Web, a high cost of maintaining a central metadata repository will be incurred. Some alternative approaches of query evaluation are thus raised in the sequel.

14.4.2 WEBDIS

WEBDIS system processes queries over Web documents by query shipping, where all the data sources are equipped with WEBDIS query servers running as daemon processes that can access the HTML, XML or other types of data [149]. An example query that WEBDIS can process is like *"Starting from COMPUTER SCIENCE HOMEPAGE find RESEARCH PROJECTS PAGES linked to it over maximum 5 links and return the available PhD PO-SITIONS."*

WEBDIS starts query execution at the user's site based on the initial execution plan. Parts of the query are processed locally, while the rest of the query is dispatched to other nodes. Those nodes then proceed in a similar fashion using their own plan generators. Hence we classify WEBDIS system in the group of systems where both query planing and query evaluation are performed in a distributed fashion. Some particular issues to be addressed by this distributed query processing system include:

1) *Query completion.* The query should migrate from one node to another without a control of the query issuer. To enable query completion monitoring, additional protocols are used.

2) *Query termination.* The cancellation request of an ongoing query should be dispatched to all active data sources. One simple solution is to close the communication sockets at the user site, which will eventually bring all participating data sources to cease the query processing.

3) *Avoiding query recomputation.* Some data sources may be faced with the same subquery during one query execution. Mechanisms to detect duplicated requests are introduced to prevent repeated computation of such queries.

4) *Result returning.* Results of the query can be directly sent to the user site from every participant node or collected by backtracking the path through which query was distributed.

14.4.3 Xyleme

Xyleme is designed to enable querying of large amounts of XML documents stored in its warehouse [75]. Documents are collected and refreshed by being (re)loaded from the Web. This activity involves crawling or subscription arrangements.

User can query the documents in the repository through a predefined integrated view. The integrated views for specific thematic domains are defined by domain experts but the mapping between each integrated view and the documents in the warehouse is established using the support of sophisticated mapping algorithms. Apart from that, the main strengths of Xyleme lie in the layered and clustered internal architecture. The architecture provides good scalability in terms of both the number of users and the number of XML documents stored in the system.

As illustrated, Xyleme falls in the group of Web-based databases with centralized planning and centralized evaluation approaches.

14.4.4 Niagara and Tukwila

Niagara [227] and Tukwila [171] are both data integration systems implementing XML query processing techniques .

Niagara system is built as a two-component system with the first component being a search engine and the second one being an XML query processing engine. Niagara allows users to ask arbitrary structured queries over the Web. Its search engine uses the full text index to select a set of the XML documents that match the structured content specified in the query, while its XML query engine is used to perform more complex actions on the selected documents and to present the requested results. Niagara can perform on-demand retrievals of XML documents if they are not available in the local document repository. Still, all the XML query processing is performed centrally.

In comparison, Tukwila provides a mediated schema over a set of heterogeneous distributed databases. The system can intelligently process the query over such mediate schema, reading data across the network and responding to data source sizes, network conditions, and other factors.

Both Tukwila and Niagara possess a dynamic feature. Their query processing is adaptable to changes in the unstable Web environment. Adaptability is thus defined as a special ability of the query processor, using which the execution plan of the query is changed during the course of its execution in response to unexpected environmental events. Both systems achieve adaptable query processing by implementing flexible operators within their query engines. In Niagara, operators are built in such a way that they provide non-blocking functioning. This means that they can process any data available at their input at any time. Faced with data delays, the operators can switch to process other arriving data, and resume the original task when data becomes available.

In Tukwila, a re-optimization is done on the level of query execution fragments - which are units of query execution. After each fragment is materialized, Tukwila compares the estimated and the achieved execution performance. If sufficiently divergent, the rest of the execution plan is re-optimized using the previous performance sub-results [227]. In addition, a collector operator is proposed for managing data sources with identical schemas. The collector operator can dynamically switch between alternative different data sources when getting the necessary data.

Table 14.1. A comparison of Web-based query processing systems

Feature	System				
	Suciu	WEBDIS	Xyleme	Niagara	Tukwila
Data Source	semistructured rooted labeled graphs	hyperlinked XML, HTML documents	XML data	XML data	XML data
Query Planning	static centralized	static distributed	static centralized	dynamic centralized	dynamic centralized
Query Execution	static distributed	static distributed	static centralized	dynamic centralized	static centralized
Querying of Streaming Data	-	-	-	yes	yes
Integrated View	-	-	yes	-	yes
Query Granularity	graph node	XML document	XML component	XML component	XML component
Query Language	UnQL	DISQL	XQL	XML-QL	XQuery

Table 14.1 summarizes different query processing schemas that the above systems utilize, together with their query facilities offered to users.

14.5 Conclusions

In this chapter, we address some major challenges facing Web-based distributed XML query processing. Recent work on distributed XML query processing and optimization were presented. We review and compare several existing systems according to their query planning and query execution strategies, as well as their query facilities offered to users.

With XML becoming the dominant standard for describing and interchanging data between various systems and databases on the Web, Web-based distributed XML query processing opens up a new research area, attracting lots of attention from both academic and practical activities nowadays. It is not possible and also not our intention to cover all the activities in this short chapter. Our purpose is to stimulate the interests among the data management community as we feel that there are still quite a number of issues to be addressed by both academic researchers and practitioners.

15

Combining Concept- with Content-Based Multimedia Retrieval

Menzo Windhouwer and Roelof van Zwol

15.1 Introduction

The Internet forms today's largest source of information, with public services like libraries and museums digitizing their collections and making (parts of) it available to the public. Likewise, the public digitizes private information, e.g., holiday pictures and movies, and shares it on the World Wide Web (WWW). This kind of document collections have often two aspects in common. They contain a high density of multimedia objects and its content is often semantically related. The identification of relevant media objects in such a vast collection poses a major problem that is studied in the area of *multimedia information retrieval*.

A generic multimedia information retrieval system is sketched in Fig. 15.1 (based on [93]). The left-hand side depicts the interactive process, where the user formulates her query, using relevance feedback. On the right-hand side of the figure a librarian is annotating the document collection. In the earlier stages of information retrieval, the annotation was done in a complete manual fashion. Today, this process is often supported by automatic annotation, which is also referred to as content-based retrieval.

The rise of XML as *the* information exchange format has also its impact on multimedia information retrieval systems. The semistructured nature of XML allows to integrate several more-or-less structured forms of multimedia annotations in the system, i.e., the database stores a collection of (integrated) XML documents. However, using the XML document structure directly for searching through the document collection is likely to lead to semantic misinterpretations. For example, an XML document contains the structure *company* → *director* → *name*. When searching for the name of the company, without any knowledge of the semantics of the implied structure the name of the director can, mistakenly, be found.

With the focus on document collections where the content is semantically related, it becomes feasible to use a conceptual schema that describes the content of the document collection at a semantical level of abstraction. This

H. Blanken et al. (Eds.): Intelligent Search on XML Data, LNCS 2818, pp. 217–230, 2003.
© Springer-Verlag Berlin Heidelberg 2003

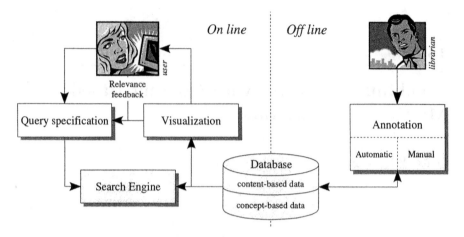

Fig. 15.1. Multimedia information retrieval system

approach, defined in the Webspace Method [305] allows the user to formulate complex conceptual queries that exceed the 'boundary' of a document. However, using a conceptual search alone is not satisfactory. The integration with a content-based technique, such as a feature grammar is essential.

A feature grammar is based on the formal model of a feature grammar system and supports the use of annotation extraction algorithms to automatically extract content-based information from multimedia objects [317].

This chapter describes the integration of the Webspace Method and feature grammars to realize a retrieval system for multimedia XML document collections. To illustrate the usability of the combined system fragments of the Australian Open case-study are used. This case study has been described in more detail in [319] and [318].

15.2 Automatic Annotation Extraction

The holy grail for *automatic annotation* is to extract all explicit and implicit semantic meanings of a multimedia object, i.e., take over a large part of the manual annotation burden. This ultimate goal may never be reached, but for limited domains knowledge can be captured well enough to automatically extract meaningful annotations. To realize this, the *semantic gap* between raw sensor data and "real world" concepts has to be bridged. The predominant approach to bridge this gap is the translation of the raw data into low-level features, which are subsequently mapped into high-level concepts.

These steps are illustrated in Fig. 15.2, which shows the annotation of an image of André Agassi. The image is classified by a boolean rule as a photo on basis of previously extracted feature values, e.g., the number and average

output/input dependencies

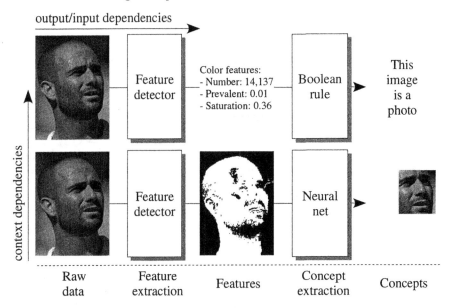

Fig. 15.2. Automatic information extraction steps.

saturation of the colors. Then a neural net, determines if the photo contains a human face, based on detected skin areas.

This example shows two kinds of dependencies: (1) *output/input dependencies*, e.g., the color features are input for the photo decision rule; and (2) *context dependencies*, e.g., the face classifier is only run when the image is a photo. Notice that context dependencies are inherently different from output/input dependencies. They are based on design decisions or domain restrictions and are not enforced by the extraction algorithm.

Feature grammars are based on a declarative language, which supports both output/input and context dependencies. Before introducing the language, the next section describes its solid and formal basis.

15.2.1 Feature Grammar Systems

As the name suggests *feature grammar systems* are related to grammars as known from natural languages, e.g., English or Dutch. Sentences in these languages are constructed from basic building blocks: words. Each language has a set of rules, which describe how words can be put in a valid order. These rules form the grammar of the language, and can be used to validate and build a parse tree of a specific sentence.

The fundamental idea behind feature grammar systems is that the same process of validation and derivation, and thus the underlying formal theories and practices, can be used as a driving force to produce the annotation of a

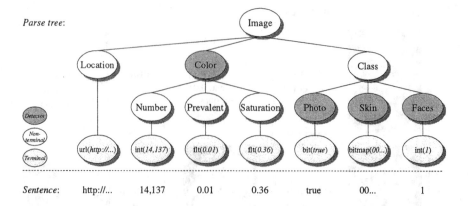

Fig. 15.3. Annotation sentence with parse tree.

multimedia object. In a feature grammar system individual information items in an annotation are seen as the words in an annotation sentence, on top of which a parse tree can be build (see Fig. 15.3).

The right-hand sides of grammar rules naturally capture contextual dependencies. However, they lack specification of output/input dependencies. The addition of feature grammar systems is the binding of extraction algorithms to specific grammar symbols, i.e., detectors. During derivation the output/input dependencies of these special symbols can be resolved within the parse tree. The following paragraphs will shortly introduce a formalization of this behaviour.

Grammars can cooperate in so-called *grammar systems* [85]. These systems where inspired by the will to model *multi-agent systems* according to the *blackboard architecture* [230]. In a *cooperating distributed (CD) grammar system* the common sentential form is on the blackboard and the *component grammars* are the knowledge sources, which take turn in rewriting this sentential form.

A feature grammar system is a specific instantiation of a CD grammar system, denoted as $(CD'_\infty CF, (lPC, C))$. In a feature grammar system there is a grammar component for each *detector*, or extraction algorithm. Such a grammar component describes, using a set of context-free (CF) production rules the output of the feature detector function. The output of the function is valid when it is a valid sentence in the language described by the grammar, which makes the grammar conditional (C). The input this function needs from the parse tree is specified by a regular path expression. To prevent deadlock situations only the left context of a detector is within its scope, allowing linear ordering of detectors. Hence the grammar is also a *left path-controlled (lPC) grammar*. The number of grammar components (and thus the detectors) is arbitrary, as indicated by the ∞ subscript. All components in a feature grammar system use the same alphabet (indicated by the prime (CD')).

15.2.2 Feature Grammar Language

The mathematical notation of a feature grammar system, although precise, is not very convenient in every day life. The *feature grammar language* allows to describe a feature grammar using just the normal ASCII set of characters. The basic version of the language allows the specification of exactly the core components of the underlying formal theory. The extended version allows the use of special shortcuts like modules, detector plug-ins and references. Due to space limitations the language is not described in detail but just an example is shown:

```
%module      Image;
%start       Image(Location);

%detector    Graphic(Number,Prevalent,Saturation);
%detector    Skin(Location);
%detector    matlab::Color(Location);

%classifier  bpnn::Faces(Skin);

%detector    Photo  [ Number     > 200
                      and Prevalent  <    0.26
                      and Saturation <    0.67 ];

%atom        www::url {^http://([^ :/]*)(:[0-9]*)?/?(.*)$};
%atom        image::bitmap {^[0|1]*$};

%atom url    Location;
%atom int    Number, Faces;
%atom flt    Prevalent, Saturation;
%atom bitmap Skin;

Image        : Location Color Class;
Color        : Number Prevalent Saturation;
Class        : Graphic | Photo Skin Faces;
```

This feature grammar describes declaratively the extraction process of Fig. 15.2. Notice that some detectors, i.e., whitebox detectors, and the detector parameters take the form of XPath expressions [29].

15.2.3 Feature Detector Engine

The *Feature Detector Engine (FDE)* uses a feature grammar and its associated detectors to steer an annotation extraction process. This process can now be implemented by a specific parsing algorithm. The control flow in a feature grammar system is top-down and favors leftmost derivations. The top-down algorithm used is based on an *exhaustive backtracking* algorithm. Backtracking indicates depth-first behavior: one alternative is chosen and followed until it either fails or succeeds. Upon failure the algorithm backtracks until an untried alternative is found and tries that one. The adjective exhaustive means that the algorithm also backtracks when the alternative is successful, thus handling ambiguity.

The FDE starts with validation of the start symbol, i.e., *Image*. The declaration of this start symbol specifies that at least the *Location* token should be available. In the example case the librarian provided the URL of the Australian Open picture of André Agassi. The FDE continues with building the parse tree until it encounters the first detector symbol: *Color*. The *Color* detector function needs the *Location* information, which is passed on as a parameter to the *matlab* plugin. This plugin connects to the matlab engine and requests execution of the *Color* function. The output of this function is a new sentence of three tokens: *Number*, *Prevalent* and *Saturation*. This sentence is subsequently validated using the rules for the *Color* detector. The FDE continues in this vain until the start symbol is proved valid.

The result of this proces is the following XML document:

```
<?xml version="1.0"?>
<fg:forest xmlns:fg="http://.../fg" xmlns:Image="http://.../Image">
 <fg:elementary idrefs="1@1" start="WWW:WebObject">
  <Image:Image id="5479@0">
   <Image:Location id="1@1">
    <Image:url id="2@1">http://...</Image:url>
   </Image:Location>
   <Image:Color idref="5480@0"/>
   <Image:Class id="9@1">
    <Image:Photo idref="5481@0"/>
    <Image:Skin idref="5482@0"/>
    <Image:Faces idref="5483@0"/>
   </Image:Class>
  </Image:Image>
 </fg:elementary>
 <fg:auxiliary>
  <Image:Color id="5480@0" idrefs="2@1">
   <Image:Number id="3@1">
    <fg:int id="4@1">14137</fg:int>
   </Image:Number>
   <Image:Prevalent id="5@1">
    <fg:flt id="6@1">0.01</fg:flt>
   </Image:Prevalent>
   <Image:Saturation id="7@1">
    <fg:flt id="8@1">0.36</fg:flt>
   </Image:Saturation>
  </Image:Color>
 </fg:auxiliary>
 <fg:auxiliary>
  <Image:Photo id="5481@0" idrefs="3@1 5@1 7@1"/>
 </fg:auxiliary>
```

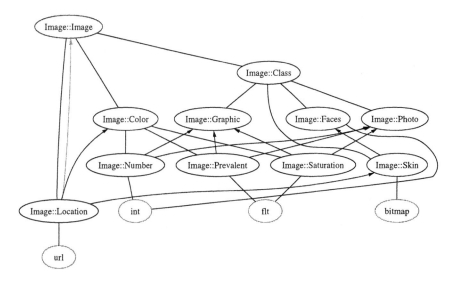

Fig. 15.4. Dependency graph.

```
<fg:auxiliary>
 <Image:Skin id="5482@0" idrefs="1@1">
  <Image:bitmap id="10@1"><![CDATA[00...]]></Image:bitmap>
 </Image:Skin>
</fg:auxiliary>
<fg:auxiliary>
 <Image:Faces id="5483@0" idrefs="10@1">
  <fg:int id="11@1">1</fg:int>
 </Image:Faces>
</fg:auxiliary>
</fg:forest>
```

This document contains the constructed parse tree (see Fig. 15.3), and hence the desired annotation information. The database contains a collection of these XML documents, thus storing the content-based data of the multimedia collection.

15.2.4 Feature Detector Schedular

Over time the source data on which the stored annotation information is based may change. Also new or newer extraction algorithms may come available. The declarative nature of a feature grammar gives the opportunity to incrementally maintain the stored information. Based on the output/input and context dependencies embedded in the feature grammar a dependency graph can be build (see Fig. 15.4). Using this graph the *Feature Detector Schedular (FDS)* can localize changes and trigger incremental parses of the

FDE. In an incremental parse the FDE only validates a single grammar component, thus only revalidating a partial parse tree. Following the links in the dependency graph the FDS can trigger other incremental parses based on the updated annotations.

The next section will describe the Webspace Method, which, combined with feature grammars, provides an advanced architecture for multimedia information retrieval.

15.3 Concept-Based Search

When shifting the focus from the WWW to certain sub-domains of the Internet, it becomes feasible to apply some of the ideas originally developed for databases to the Web. This leads to a significant improvement in retrieval performance, when using a combination of concept-based search and content-based retrieval, as discussed in [305, 304]. This kind of search engines should particularly focus on large collections of documents, such as intranet environments, digital libraries, or large websites, where the content is semantically related.

The central idea behind conceptual search is to formulate the user's information need in a conceptual query that is based on a schema containing the important concepts used in the document collection. The *Webspace Method* for modeling and searching web-based document collections [304] exploits this idea in three different stages. Ideally, during the first stage, the document collection is constructed in four steps as explained in Sect. 15.3.1. The second stage is responsible for building an index for the conceptual and multimedia information that can be derived from the document collection. Finally, in the third stage the document collection can be queried, using the conceptual (database) schema that is defined in the first stage.

By using a conceptual schema to describe the content of the document collection, a semantical level of abstraction is introduced that in the end allows a user to query the document collection as a whole. This means that queries can be formulated combining information that is physically stored in several documents, whereas traditionally search engines base their answers on information found in a single document. The Webspace search engine allows the user to formulate exactly what information he is interested in as the result of a query.

To achieve this two steps are crucial. First of all during the modeling stage of the Webspace Method the information stored in the documents should be semantically related to the concepts defined in the conceptual schema. Using XML, the structure of the documents can be made explicit. Each XML tag or attribute should then relate to a class, attribute, or association name in the conceptual schema.

Secondly, the integration of concept-based search with content-based retrieval also depends on the conceptual schema. For each of the different types

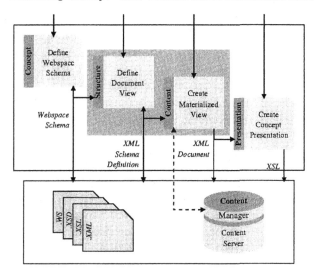

Fig. 15.5. Webspace Modeling Tool.

of media, that is going to be included in the search engine a conceptual class is included, and a link is made with the corresponding feature grammar. During the extraction stage all instances of multimedia classes are handed to the Feature Detector Engine for extracting the relevant meta-data.

The following subsections discuss the three stages of the Webspace Method in more detail, by the hand of an example based on the Australian Open case-study.

15.3.1 Modeling Stage

The modeling stage of the Webspace Method consists of four steps that are carried out to create a document collection. These four steps have been integrated in the Webspace modeling tool, which functions as an authoring tool for content management (see Fig. 15.5).

The first step is to identify concepts that adequately describe the content contained in the document collection. Once the *webspace schema* is (partially) defined, a view on the schema can be defined that describes the structure of the document that the author wants to create. This structure is then exported to an XML Schema Definition. Once the structure of the document is known, the content can be added. For maintenance reasons the content is ideally stored in a data management system, but the author can also choose to manually add the content to the document.

The result is an XML document that is seen as a materialized view on the webspace schema, since it contains both the data, and part of the conceptual schema. The XML document by itself is not suitable for presentation to the user. Therefore another XML-related technique is used for visualization purposes. During this last step, the author has to define a presentation for the document structure, using XSLT. Once this is done the document collection can be visualized and presented to the audience.

For standardization reasons it is desirable that the author starts with a default set of multimedia class definitions that enable the integration of concept-based search with content-based retrieval. Fig. 15.6 shows a fragment of the webspace schema that is used for the Australian Open webspace. It contains the class definition of a player with the attributes name, gender, country, picture, and history. The first three attribute are of type string, while the attribute picture and history are of class-type Image, and Hypertext, respectively. At this point the connection is made with the multimedia objects that are included in the document collection. Notice that Hypertext is used to refer to HTML-fragment that can be included in the XML document. This is motivated by the fact that there is always a trade-off between the concepts that are defined in the conceptual schema and conceptual information that is left out.

15.3.2 Extraction Stage

Before the Webspace search engine can be used, it is necessary to build an index that links the same instance of a class when it is defined in different documents. Furthermore, meta-data needs to be collected that realizes the integration of the conceptual framework used by the Webspace Method with the content-based retrieval component. In this case this is implemented by the FDE (see Sect. 15.2.3), which provides a highly advanced interface to indexing multimedia objects that are found on the Web.

Each (XML) document of the collection is parsed for instantiations of classes and associations defined in the webspace schema. Relevant information is extracted and if a multimedia object is found the pointer to this object is stored and handed to the FDE, where the object is further analyzed.

Fig. 15.6. Fragment from the Australian Open schema.

15.3.3 Query Stage

Since the webspace schema allows us to identify the same object when it occurs in different documents, inter-document relations can be determined and used to enhance the retrieval performance of the conceptual search engine. Furthermore, this allows us to find information across the 'boundary' of a document. It can be concluded that a user rather queries the document collection as a whole, rather than querying the content of a single document. The figures in the next section show the process that is followed when formulating a conceptual query over a webspace using the Webspace search engine.

15.4 Combined Search

The combined (conceptual and content-based) search engine uses a schema-based approach for querying a document collection. The formulation of a query over a document collection, can be divided into three steps. During the first step, the *query skeleton* is constructed, using the visualization of the conceptual schema. Secondly, the constraints of the query are formulated, using the attributes of classes used in the query skeleton. In the last step, the user has to define the structure of the result of the query, which is generated as a materialized view on the conceptual schema.

Before continuing with the individual steps of the query formulation process, the queries presented below are used to illustrate the power of the webspace search engine with respect to query formulation. The queries express the typical information need of an expert user querying the 'Australian Open' document collection. It also shows, how after each query, the information need of the user can be refined, resulting in a more complex query over a document collection.

Q1. *'Search for left-handed female players, who have played a match in one of the (quarter/semi) final rounds. For each of those players, show the player's name, picture, nationality, birth-date, and the document URLs containing information about this player. Also show category, round and court of the match'.*

Q2. *'Like query 1, with the extra constraint that the player has already won a previous Australian Open. Include that history in the result of the query'.*

Q3. *'Extend query 2 with the constraint that the result should also contain video-fragments, showing net-playing events'.*

The first example query shows how conceptual search is used to obtain specific information originally stored in three different documents. The second example query extends the first query and provides an example illustrating the integration of content-based text retrieval in the conceptual framework of the Webspace Method. The third example query extends the complexity of the query even more, by integrating content-based video retrieval in the Webspace Method.

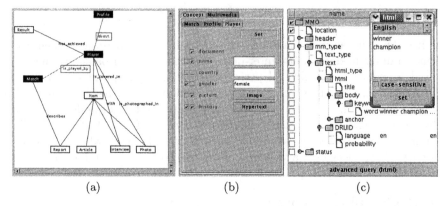

(a)   (b)   (c)

Fig. 15.7. Formulating a query.

1. **Constructing the query skeleton.** The first step of the query formulation process involves the construction of the query skeleton. This skeleton is created, using a visualization of the webspace schema. This visualization consists of a simplified class diagram, and only contains the classes and associations between the classes, as defined in the webspace schema. The user simply composes the query skeleton, based on his information need, by selecting classes and related associations from the visualization. The (single) graph that is created represents the query skeleton.

   In Fig. 15.7.a a fragment taken from the GUI of the webspace search engine is presented, which shows the query skeleton (depicted in black-filled text boxes), that is used for the query formulation of the three example queries.

2. **Formulating the constraints.** In the second step of the query formulation process, the constraints of the query are defined. In Fig. 15.7.b another fragment of the GUI of the webspace search engine is presented, showing the interface that is used for this purpose. For each class contained in the query skeleton a tab is activated, which allows a user to formulate the *conceptual constraints* of the query. As shown in the figure, a row is created for each attribute. Each row contains two check boxes, the name of the attribute, and either a text field or a button.

   The first checkbox is used to indicate whether the attribute is used as a constraint of the query. The second checkbox indicates whether the results of the query should show the corresponding attribute. If the type of the attribute is a BasicType, a textfield is available that allows the user to specify the value of the constraint, if the first checkbox is checked. If the attribute is of type WebClass, a button is available, which, if pressed, activates the interface that is used to query that particular multimedia object.

   Fig. 15.7.c shows the interface that is used to formulate queries over Hypertext-objects, i.e., define *content-based constraints*. The figure shows both a low-level and advanced interface to the underlying feature grammar system. In the low-level interface projection and selection criteria can be filled in. The advanced interface has an interface similar to the interfaces offered by the well-known search engines such as Google and Alta-Vista. The main part of the query-interface allows a user to formulate one or more terms, which are used to find relevant text-objects. The interface also allows the user to perform a case-sensitive search, and to select the language of the Hypertext-object in which the user is interested.

Fig. 15.7.b shows the attributes of class Player. The constraints with respect to the player, specified in the first two example queries, are transposed in the selections depicted in the figure. Two constraints are formulated. The constraint that the user is only interested in *female* players is defined by selecting the constraint checkbox in front of gender, and by specifying the conceptual term '*female*'. The second constraint refers to the second example query, where an extra condition with regard to the player's history is formulated. Again, the corresponding checkbox is activated, and the interface of Fig. 15.7.c is started, and completed. In this case, the query-terms '*winner*' and '*champion*' are used to find the relevant Hypertext-objects that are associated with the player's history.

3. **Defining the resulting view**. The second column of checkboxes is used to specify which attributes will be shown in the resulting views defined by the query. The XML document that is generated by the webspace search engine contains a (ranked) list of views on the webspace that is being queried. Besides selecting the attributes and the classes that will be shown as the result of the query, the user also has to determine which class is used as the *root* of the resulting view. In Fig. 15.8 a screenshot of the result for the third query is shown. It includes a link to a tennis scene of the match played by Monica Seles in the quarter final round. The tennis scene shows a video-fragment in which Monica Seles plays near the net.

15.5 Conclusions

This chapter introduced an approach for combining concept- and content-based search for multimedia objects. Both aspects are handled by seperate systems with very shallow connections, i.e., only a trigger. However, both approaches rely heavily on XML related technology and produce XML documents. Those documents can easily be stored in a shared XML database. A specific search engine can now easily combine content- and concept-based queries, as has been illustrated by the Australian Open case-study.

As stated the connection between the two systems is still shallow. Interaction between the two systems can be increased, e.g., by allowing the feature grammar system to access conceptual data and *vice versa*. This will make the annotation process semi-automatic, and increases the opportunities for using

1.83827948486295   ● **Player**
                    gender:female
                    name:monica seles
                    history

    Australian Opens Played: 5
    Best Singles Performance: Winner (1991, 1992, 1993, 1996)
    Best Doubles Performance: Semi Finalist (1991)

    Events Entered: Women s Singles Women s Doubles (with Martina Hingis)
                    documents
                    [0, 1, 2, 3, 4, 5, 6, 7, 8, 9, 10, 11, 12, 13, 14, 15, 16, 17, 18, 19, 20, 21, 22]
                    picture

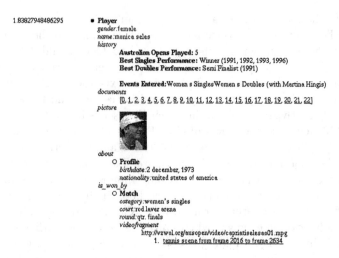

                    about
                        ○ **Profile**
                            birthdate:2 december, 1973
                            nationality:united states of america
                    is_won_by
                        ○ **Match**
                            category:women's singles
                            court:rod laver arena
                            round:qtr. finals
                            videofragment
                                http://vzwol.org/ausopen/video/capriatiselesao01.mpg
                                1. tennis scene from frame 2016 to frame 2634

Fig. 15.8. View on 'Australian Open' containing the result of example query 3.

knowledge in the automatic process and thus the quality of the extracted annotations.

16

Tree Awareness for Relational DBMS Kernels: Staircase Join

Torsten Grust and Maurice van Keulen

16.1 Introduction

Relational database management systems (RDBMSs) derive much of their efficiency from the versatility of their core data structure: *tables of tuples*. Such tables are simple enough to allow for an efficient representation on all levels of the memory hierarchy, yet sufficiently generic to host a wide range of data types. If one can devise mappings from a data type τ to tables and from operations on τ to relational queries, an RDBMS may be a premier implementation alternative. Temporal intervals, complex nested objects, and spatial data are sample instances for such types τ.

The key to efficiency of the relational approach is that the RDBMS is made *aware* of the specific properties of τ. Typically, such awareness can be implemented in the form of index structures (e.g., *R-trees* [150] efficiently encode the inclusion and overlap of spatial objects) or query operators (e.g., the *multi-predicate merge join* [331] exploits knowledge about containment of nested intervals).

This chapter applies this principle to the *tree* data type with the goal to turn RDBMSs into efficient XML and XPath processors [29]. The database system is supplied with a *relational* [193] XML document encoding, the *XPath accelerator* [146]. Encoded documents (1) are represented in relational tables, (2) can be efficiently indexed using index structures native to the RDBMS, namely B-trees, and (3) XPath queries may be mapped to SQL queries over these tables. The resulting purely relational XPath processor is efficient [146] and complete (supports all 13 XPath axes).

We will show that an enhanced level of *tree awareness*, however, can lead to a query speed-up by an order of magnitude. Tree awareness is injected into the database kernel in terms of the *staircase join* operator, which is tuned to exploit the knowledge that the RDBMS operates over tables encoding tree-shaped data. This is a local change to the database kernel: standard B-trees suffice to support the evaluation of staircase join and the query optimizer may treat staircase join much like other native join operators.

H. Blanken et al. (Eds.): Intelligent Search on XML Data, LNCS 2818, pp. 231–245, 2003.
© Springer-Verlag Berlin Heidelberg 2003

16.2 Purely Relational XPath Processing

We will work with a relational XML encoding that is *not* inspired by the document tree structure per se – like, e.g., the *edge mapping* [116] – but by our primary goal to support XPath efficiently. The encoding of document trees is faithful nevertheless: properties like *document order, tag names, node types, text contents*, etc., are fully preserved such that the original XML document may be serialized from the relational tables alone.

Observe that for any element node of a given XML instance, the four XPath axes preceding, descendant, ancestor, and following *partition* the document into four regions. In Fig. 16.1, these regions are depicted for *context node* f: the XPath expression $f/\text{following::node()}^1$ evaluates to the node sequence (i, j), for example. Note that all 10 document nodes are covered by the four disjoint axis regions (plus the context node):

$$\{a \dots j\} \quad = \quad \{f\} \cup \bigcup_{\substack{\alpha \in \{\text{preceding,descendant,} \\ \text{ancestor,following}\}}} f/\alpha \ . \tag{16.1}$$

The *XPath accelerator* document encoding [146] preserves this region notion. The key idea is to design the encoding such that the nodes contained in an axis region can be retrieved by a relational query simple enough to be efficiently supported by relational index technology (in our case *B-trees*). Equation (16.1) guarantees that all document nodes are indeed represented in such an encoding.

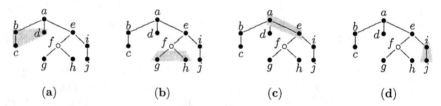

| (a) | (b) | (c) | (d) |

Fig. 16.1. XPath axes induce document regions: shaded nodes are reachable from context node f via a step along the (a) preceding, (b) descendant, (c) ancestor, (d) following axes. Leaf nodes denote either empty XML elements, attributes, text, comment, or processing instruction nodes; inner nodes represent non-empty elements

The actual encoding maps each node v to its *preorder* and *postorder* traversal ranks in the document tree: $v \mapsto \langle pre(v), post(v) \rangle$. In a preorder traversal, a node v is visited and assigned its preorder rank $pre(v)$ before its children are recursively traversed from left to right. Postorder traversal is defined dually: node v is assigned its postorder rank $post(v)$ after all its children have been

---

[1] In the sequel, we will abbreviate such XPath step expressions as $f/\text{following}$.

traversed. For the XML document tree of Fig. 16.1, a preorder traversal enumerates the nodes in *document order* $(a, \ldots, j)$ while a postorder traversal enumerates $(c, b, d, g, h, f, j, i, e, a)$, so that we get $\langle pre(e), post(e)\rangle = \langle 4, 8\rangle$, for instance.

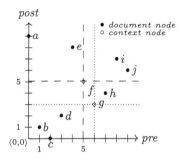

Fig. 16.2. *Pre/post* plane for the XML document of Fig. 16.1. Dashed and dotted lines indicate the document regions as seen from context nodes f $(- -)$ and g $(\cdots\cdots)$, respectively

Figure 16.2 depicts the two-dimensional *pre/post plane* that results from encoding the XML instance of Fig. 16.1. A given context node f, encoded as $\langle pre(f), post(f)\rangle = \langle 5, 5\rangle$, induces four *rectangular regions* in the *pre/post* plane, e.g., in the lower-left partition we find the nodes f/preceding $= (b, c, d)$. This characterization of the XPath axes is much more accessible for an RDBMS: an axis step can be evaluated in terms of a *rectangular region query* on the *pre/post* plane. Such queries are efficiently supported by concatenated $(pre, post)$ B-trees (or R-trees [146]).

The further XPath axes, like, e.g., following-sibling or ancestor-or--self, determine specific supersets or subsets of the node sets computed by the four partitioning axes. These are easily characterized if we additionally maintain *parent node* information for each node, i.e., use $v \mapsto \langle pre(v), post(v), pre(parent(v))\rangle$ as the encoding for node v. We will focus on the four partitioning axes in the following.

Note that all nodes are alike in the XPath accelerator encoding: given an arbitrary context node v, e.g., computed by a prior XPath axis step or XQuery expression, we retrieve $\langle pre(v), post(v)\rangle$ and then access the nodes in the corresponding axis region. Unlike related approaches [79], the XPath accelerator has no bias towards the document root element. Please refer to [146, 147] for an in-depth explanation of the XPath accelerator.

16.2.1 SQL-Based XPath Evaluation

Inside the relational database system, the encoded XML document tree, i.e., the *pre/post* plane, is represented as a table doc with schema *pre*|*post*|*type* .

Each tuple encodes a single node (with field *type* discriminating element, attribute, text, comment, processing instruction node types). Since *pre* is unique – and thus may serve as *node identity* as required by the W3C XQuery and XPath data model [115] – additional node information is assumed to be hosted in separate tables using *pre* as a foreign key.[2] A SAX-based document loader [266] can populate the doc table using a single sequential scan over the XML input [146].

The evaluation of an XPath path expression $p = s_1/s_2/\cdots/s_n$ leads to a series of n region queries where the node sequence output by step s_i is the context node sequence for the subsequent step s_{i+1}. The context node sequence for step s_1 is held in table context (if p is an *absolute* path, i.e., $p = /s_1/\cdots$, context holds a single tuple: the encoding of the document root node). XPath requires the resulting node sequence to be *duplicate free* as well as being sorted in *document order* [29]. These inherently set-oriented, or rather *sequence-oriented*, XPath semantics are implementable in plain SQL (Fig. 16.3).

```
1     SELECT DISTINCT v_n.*
2        FROM context c, doc v_1, ... , doc v_n
3        WHERE axis(s_1, c, v_1) AND axis(s_2, v_1, v_2) AND ··· AND axis(s_n, v_{n-1}, v_n)
4     ORDER BY v_n.pre ASC
```

$$
\begin{aligned}
axis(\texttt{preceding}, v, v') &\equiv v'.pre < v.pre \text{ AND } v'.post < v.post \\
axis(\texttt{descendant}, v, v') &\equiv v'.pre > v.pre \text{ AND } v'.post < v.post \\
axis(\texttt{ancestor}, v, v') &\equiv v'.pre < v.pre \text{ AND } v'.post > v.post \\
axis(\texttt{following}, v, v') &\equiv v'.pre > v.pre \text{ AND } v'.post > v.post
\end{aligned}
$$

Fig. 16.3. Translating the XPath path expression $s_1/s_2/\cdots/s_n$ (with context context) into an SQL query over the document encoding table doc

Note that we focus on the XPath core, namely location steps, here. Function $axis(\cdot)$, however, is easily adapted to implement further XPath concepts, like node tests, e.g., with XPath axis α and node kind $\kappa \in \{\texttt{text()},$ $\texttt{comment()}, \dots\}$:

$$
axis(\alpha::\kappa, v, v') \equiv axis(\alpha, v, v') \text{ AND } v'.type = \kappa \ .
$$

Finally, the existential semantics of XPath predicates are naturally expressed by a simple exchange of correlation variables in the translation scheme of Fig. 16.3. The XPath expression $s_1[s_2]/s_3$ is evaluated by the RDBMS via the SQL query shown in Fig. 16.4.

---

[2] In this chapter, we will not discuss the many possible table layout variations (in-line tag names or CDATA contents, partition by tag name, etc.) for doc.

```
1    SELECT DISTINCT v₃.*
2      FROM context c,doc v₁,doc v₂,doc v₃
3      WHERE axis(s₁,c,v₁) AND axis(s₂,v₁,v₂) AND axis(s₃,v₁,v₃)
4    ORDER BY v₃.pre ASC .
```

Fig. 16.4. SQL equivalent for the XPath expression $s_1[s_2]/s_3$ (note the exchange of v_1 for v_2 in $axis(s_3, v_1, v_3)$, line 3).

16.2.2 Lack of Tree Awareness in Relational DBMS

The structure of the generated SQL queries – a flat self-join of the doc table using a conjunctive join predicate – is simple. An analysis of the actual query plans chosen by the optimizer of IBM DB2 V7.1 shows that the system can cope quite well with this type of query. Figure 16.5 depicts the situation for a two-step query s_1/s_2 originating in context sequence context.

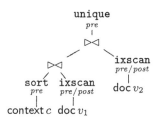

Fig. 16.5. Query plan

The RDBMS maintains a B-tree over concatenated ($pre, post$) keys. The index is used to scan the inner (right) doc table join inputs in pre-sorted order. The context is, if necessary, sorted by the preorder rank pre as well. Both joins may thus be implemented by *merge joins*. The actual region query evaluation happens in the two inner join inputs: the predicates on pre act as index range scan delimiters while the conditions on $post$ are fully sargable [277] and thus evaluated during the B-tree index scan as well. The joins are actually right semijoins, producing their output in pre-sorted order (which matches the request for a result sequence sorted in document order in line 4 of the SQL query).

As reasonable as this query plan might appear, the RDBMS treats table doc (and context) like any other relational table and remains ignorant of tree-specific relationships between $pre(v)$ and $post(v)$ other than that both ranks are paired in a tuple in table doc. The system thus gives away significant optimization opportunities.

To some extent, however, we are able to make up for this lack of tree awareness at the SQL level. As an example, assume that we are to take a **descendant** step from context node v (Fig. 16.6). It is sufficient to scan the ($pre, post$) B-tree in the range from $pre(v)$ to $pre(v')$ since v' is the rightmost

Fig. 16.6. Nodes with minimum *post* (v'') and maximum *pre* (v') ranks in the subtree below v

leaf in the subtree below v and thus has maximum preorder rank. Since the *pre*-range $pre(v)$–$pre(v')$ contains exactly the nodes in the **descendant** axis of v, we have[3]

$$pre(v') = pre(v) + |v/\texttt{descendant}| \; . \tag{16.2}$$

Additionally, for any node v in a tree t we have that

$$|v/\texttt{descendant}| = post(v) - pre(v) + \underbrace{level(v)}_{\leqslant h} \tag{16.3}$$

where $level(v)$ denotes the length of the path from t's root to v which is obviously bound by h, the overall *height* of t.[4] Equations (16.2) and (16.3) provide us with a characterization of $pre(v')$ expressed exclusively in terms of the current context node v:

$$pre(v') \leqslant post(v) + h \; . \tag{16.4}$$

A dual argument applies to leaf v'', the node with minimum postorder rank below context node v (Fig. 16.6). Taken together, we can use these observations to further delimit the B-tree index range scans to evaluate **descendant** axis steps:

$$axis(\texttt{descendant}, v, v') \;\equiv\; v'.pre > v.pre \text{ AND } v'.pre \leq v.post + h \text{ AND}$$
$$v'.post \geq v.pre + h \text{ AND } v'.post < v.post \; .$$

Note that the index range scan is now delimited by the actual size of the context nodes' subtrees – modulo a small misestimation of maximally h which is insignificant in multi-million node documents – and independent of the document size. The benefit of using these shrunk **descendant** axis regions is substantial, as Fig. 16.7 illustrates for a small XML instance. In [146], a speed-up of up to three orders of magnitude has been observed for 100 MB XML document trees.

Nevertheless, as we will see in the upcoming section, the index scans and joins in the query plan of Fig. 16.5 still perform a significant amount of wasted work,

---

[3] We use $|s|$ to denote the cardinality of set s.

[4] The system can compute h at document loading time. For typical real-world XML instances, we have $h \leqslant 10$.

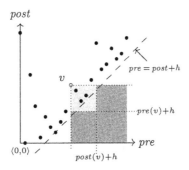

Fig. 16.7. Original (dark) and shrunk (light) *pre* and *post* scan ranges for a **descendant** step to be taken from v

especially for large context sequences. Being uninformed about the fact that the **doc** tables encodes tree-shaped data, the index scans repeatedly re-read regions of the *pre/post* plane only to generate duplicate nodes. This, in turn, violates XPath semantics such that a rather costly duplicate elimination phase (the **unique** operator in Fig. 16.5) at the top of the plan is required.

Real tree awareness, however, would enable the RDBMS to improve XPath processing in important ways: (1) since the node distribution in the *pre/post* plane is not arbitrary, the **ixscans** could actually *skip* large portions of the B-tree scans, and (2) the context sequence induces a partitioning of the plane that the system can use to fully avoid duplicates.

The necessary tree knowledge *is* present in the *pre/post* plane – and actually available at the cost of simple integer operations like $+, <$ as we will now see – but remains inaccessible for the RDBMS unless it can be made explicit at the SQL level (like the **descendant** window optimization above).

16.3 Encapsulating Tree Awareness in the Staircase Join

To make the notion of *tree awareness* more explicit, we first analyze some properties of trees and how these are reflected in the *pre/post*-plane encoding. We introduce three techniques, *pruning*, *partitioning*, and *skipping*, that exploit these properties. The section concludes with the algorithm for the *staircase join*, a new join operator that incorporates the three techniques.

16.3.1 Pruning

In XPath, an axis step is generally evaluated on an *entire sequence* of context nodes [29]. This leads to duplication of work if the *pre/post* plane regions associated with the step are independently evaluated for each context node.

Figure 16.8 (a) depicts the situation if we are about to evaluate an **ancestor-or-self** step for context sequence (d, e, f, h, i, j). The darker the

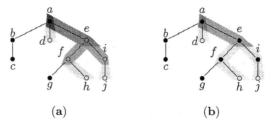

(a)   (b)

Fig. 16.8. (a) Intersection and inclusion of the `ancestor-or-self` paths of a context node sequence. (b) The pruned context node sequence covers the same `ancestor-or-self` region and produces less duplicates (3 rather than 11)

path's shade, the more often are its nodes produced in the resulting node sequence – which ultimately leads to the need for a costly duplicate elimination phase. Obviously, we could remove nodes e, f, i – which are located along a path from some other context node up to the root – from the context node sequence without any effect on the final result (a, d, e, f, h, i, j) (Fig. 16.8 (b)). Such opportunities for the simplification of the context node sequence arise for all axes.

Figure 16.9 depicts the scenario in the *pre/post* plane as this is the RDBMS's view of the problem (these planes show the encoding of a slightly larger XML document instance). For each axis, the context nodes establish a different boundary enclosing a different area. Result nodes can be found in the shaded areas. In general, regions determined by context nodes can *include* one another or *partially overlap* (dark areas). Nodes in these areas generate duplicates.

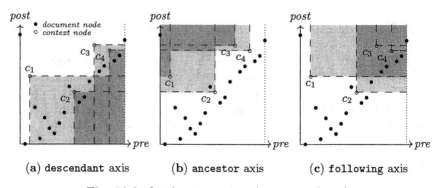

(a) descendant axis   (b) ancestor axis   (c) following axis

Fig. 16.9. Overlapping regions (context nodes c_i)

The removal of nodes e, f, i earlier is a case of *inclusion*. Inclusion can be dealt with by removing the covered nodes from the context: for example,

c_2, c_4 for (a) descendant and c_3, c_4 for (c) following axis. The process of identifying the context nodes at the cover's boundary is referred to as *pruning* and is easily implemented involving a simple postorder rank comparison (Fig. 16.14).

After pruning for the descendant or ancestor axis, all remaining context nodes relate to each other on the preceding/following axis as illustrated for descendant in Fig. 16.10. The context establishes a boundary in the *pre/post* plane that resembles a *staircase*.

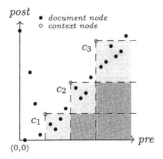

Fig. 16.10. Context pruning produces proper staircases

Observe in Fig. 16.10 that the three darker subregions do not contain any nodes. This is no coincidence. Any two nodes a, b partition the *pre/post* plane into nine regions R through Z (see Fig. 16.11). There are two cases to be distinguished regarding how both nodes relate to each other: (a) on ancestor/descendant axis or (b) on preceding/following axis. In (a), regions S, U are necessarily empty because an ancestor of b cannot precede (region U) or follow a (region S) if b is a descendant of a. Similarly, region Z in (b) is empty, because a, b cannot have common descendants if b follows a. The empty regions in Fig. 16.10 correspond to such Z regions.

A similar *empty region analysis* can be done for all XPath axes. The consequences for the preceding and following axes are more profound. After pruning for, e.g., the following axis, the remaining context nodes relate to each other on the ancestor/descendant axis. In Fig. 16.11 (a), we see that for any two remaining context nodes a and b, (a, b)/following $= S \cup T \cup W$. Since region S is empty, (a, b)/following $= T \cup W = (b)$/following. Consequently, we can prune a from the context (a, b) without affecting the result. If this reasoning is followed through, it turns out that all context nodes can be pruned except the one with the maximum preorder rank in case of preceding and the minimum postorder rank in case of following. For these two axes, the context is reduced to a singleton sequence such that the axis step evaluation degenerates to a single region query. We will therefore focus on the ancestor and descendant axes in the following.

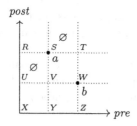

(a) Nodes a and b relate to each other on the ancestor/descendant axis

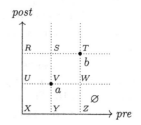

(b) Nodes a and b relate to each other on the preceding/following axis

Fig. 16.11. Empty regions in the *pre/post* plane

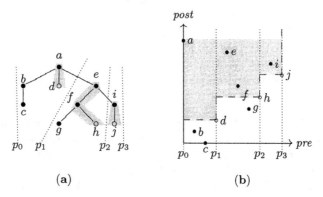

(a)   (b)

Fig. 16.12. The partitions p_0–p_1, p_1–p_2, p_2–p_3 of the ancestor staircase separate the ancestor-or-self paths in the document tree

16.3.2 Partitioning

While pruning leads to a significant reduction of duplicate work, Fig. 16.8 (b) exemplifies that duplicates still remain due to intersecting ancestor-or-self paths originating in different context nodes. A much better approach results if we *separate* the paths in the document tree and evaluate the axis step for each context node in its own partition (Fig. 16.12 (a)).

Such a separation of the document tree is easily derived from the staircase induced by the context node sequence in the *pre/post* plane (Fig. 16.12 (b)): each of the partitions p_0–p_1, p_1–p_2, and p_2–p_3 define a region of the plane containing all nodes needed to compute the axis step result for context nodes d, h, and j, respectively. Note that pruning reduces the number of these partitions. (Although a review of the details is outside the scope of this text, it should be obvious that the partitioned *pre/post* plane naturally leads to a parallel XPath execution strategy.)

16.3.3 Skipping

The empty region analysis explained in Sect. 16.3.1 offers another kind of optimization, which we refer to as *skipping*. Figure 16.13 illustrates this for the XPath axis step (c_1, c_2)/descendant. An axis step can be evaluated by scanning the *pre/post* plane from left to right and partition by partition starting from context node c_1. During the scan of c_1's partition, v is the first node encountered outside the descendant boundary and thus not part of the result.

Note that no node beyond v in the current partition contributes to the result (the light grey area is empty). This is, again, a consequence of the fact that we scan the encoding of a tree data structure: node v is following c_1 in document order so that both cannot have common descendants, i.e., the empty region in Fig. 16.13 is a region of type Z in Fig. 16.11 (b).

This observation can be used to terminate the scan early which effectively means that the portion of the scan between $pre(v)$ and the successive context node $pre(c_2)$ is *skipped*.

The effectiveness of skipping is high. For each node in the context, we either (1) hit a node to be copied into the result, or (2) encounter a node of type v which leads to a skip. To produce the result, we thus never touch more than |result| + |context| nodes in the *pre/post* plane, a number independent of the document size.

A similar, although slightly less effective skipping technique can be applied to the ancestor axis: if, inside the partition of context node c, we encounter a node v outside the ancestor boundary, we know that v as well as all descendants of v are in the preceding axis of c and thus can be skipped. In such a

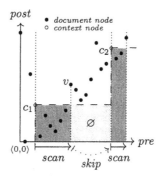

Fig. 16.13. Skipping technique for descendant axis

case, Equation (16.3) provides us with a good estimate – which is maximally off by the document height h – of how many nodes we may skip during the sequential scan, namely $post(v) - pre(v)$.

16.3.4 Staircase Join Algorithm

The techniques of pruning, partitioning, and skipping are unavailable to an RDBMS that is not "tree aware". Making the query optimizer of an RDBMS more tree aware would allow it to improve its query plans concerning XPath evaluation. However, incorporating knowledge of the *pre/post* plane should, ideally, not clutter the entire query optimizer with XML-specific adaptations. As explained in the introduction, we propose a special join operator, the *staircase join*, that exploits and encapsulates all "tree knowledge" of pruning, partitioning, and skipping present in the *pre/post* plane. On the outside, it behaves to the query optimizer in many ways as an ordinary join, for example, by admitting selection pushdown.

The approach to evaluating a staircase join between a document and a context node sequence is to sequentially scan the *pre/post* plane once from left to right selecting those nodes in the current partition that lie within the boundary established by the context node sequence (see Fig. 16.14). Along the way, encountered context nodes are pruned when possible. Furthermore, portions of a partition that are guaranteed not to contain any result nodes are skipped. Since the XPath accelerator maintains the nodes of the *pre/post* plane in the *pre*-sorted table doc, staircase join effectively visits the tree in document order. The nodes of the final result are, consequently, encountered and written in document order, too.

This algorithm has several important characteristics:

(1) it scans the doc and context tables sequentially,
(2) it scans both tables only once for an entire context sequence,
(3) it scans a fraction of table doc with a size smaller than $|result| + |context|$,
(4) it never delivers duplicate nodes, and
(5) result nodes are produced in document order, so no post-processing is needed to comply with the XPath semantics.

16.4 Query Planning with Staircase Join

The evaluation of an XPath path expression $p = s_1/s_2/\cdots/s_n$ leads to a series of n region queries where the node sequence output by step s_i is the context node sequence for the subsequent step s_{i+1} (see Sect. 16.2.1). One axis step s_i encompasses a location step and possibly a node test. The corresponding query plan, hence, consists of a staircase join for the location step and a subsequent selection for the node test. Figure 16.15 shows a possible query plan for the example query context/descendant::text()/ancestor::n ($\underset{\text{desc}}{\sqsupset}$

staircasejoin_desc (doc : TABLE $(pre,post)$, context : TABLE $(pre,post)$) $\equiv$
result Γ NEW TABLE $(pre, post)$;
/* partition $c_{from} \ldots c_{to}$ */
c_{from} Γ FIRST NODE IN context;
WHILE $(c_{to}$ Γ NEXT NODE IN context) DO
   IF $c_{to}.post < c_{from}.post$ THEN
      /* prune */
   ELSE
      scanpartition_desc $(c_{from}.pre + 1, c_{to}.pre - 1, c_{from}.post)$;
      c_{from} Γ c_{to};

n Γ LAST NODE IN doc;
scanpartition_desc $(c_{from}.pre + 1, n.pre, c_{from}.post)$;
RETURN result;

scanpartition_desc $(pre_{from}, pre_{to}, post)$ $\equiv$
FOR i FROM pre_{from} TO pre_{to} DO
   IF doc$[i].post < post$ THEN
      APPEND doc$[i]$ TO result;
   ELSE
      BREAK;   /* skip */

Fig. 16.14. Staircase join algorithm (**descendant** axis, **ancestor** analogous)

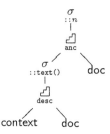

Fig. 16.15. Plan for two-step path query

and $\overset{\text{anc}}{\unicode{x2A0C}}$ depict the **descendant** and **ancestor** variants of the staircase join, respectively).

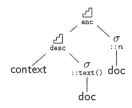

Fig. 16.16. Query plan with node test pushed down

There are, however, alternative query plans. Staircase join, like ordinary joins, allows for *selection pushdown*, or rather node test pushdown: for any location step α and node test κ

$$\sigma_{::\kappa}(\text{context} \underset{\alpha}{\sqcap} \text{doc}) = \text{context} \underset{\alpha}{\sqcap} (\sigma_{::\kappa}(\text{doc})) \ .$$

Figure 16.16 shows a query plan for the example query where both node tests have been pushed down.

Observe that in the second query plan, the node test is performed on the *entire* document instead of just the result of the location step. An RDBMS already keeps *statistics* about table sizes, selectivity, and so on. These can be used by the query optimizer in the ordinary way to decide whether or not the node test pushdown makes sense. *Physical database design* does not require exceptional treatment either. For example, in a setting where applications mainly perform qualified name tests (i.e., few ':: *' name tests), it is beneficial to fragment table doc by tag name. A pushed down name test $\sigma_{::n}(\text{doc})$ can then be evaluated by taking the appropriate fragment without the need for any data processing.

The addition of staircase join to an existing RDBMS kernel and its query optimizer is, by design, a local change to the database system. A standard B-tree index suffices to realize the "tree knowledge" encapsulated in staircase join. Skipping, as introduced in Sect. 16.3.3, is efficiently implemented by following the *pre*-ordered chain of linked B-tree leaves, for example.

We have found staircase join to also operate efficiently on higher levels of the memory hierarchy, i.e., in a main-memory database system. For queries like the above example, the staircase join enhanced system processed 1 GB XML documents in less than $1/2$ second on a standard single processor host [147].

16.5 Conclusions

The approach toward efficient XPath evaluation described in this chapter is based on a *relational* document encoding, the *XPath accelerator*. A preorder plus postorder node ranking scheme is used to encode the tree structure of an XML document. In this scheme, XPath axis steps are evaluated via joins over simple integer range predicates expressible in SQL. In this way, the XPath accelerator naturally exploits standard RDBMS query processing and indexing technology.

We have shown that an enhanced level of *tree awareness* can lead to a significant speed-up. This can be obtained with only a local change to the RDBMS kernel: the addition of the *staircase join* operator. This operator encapsulates XML document tree knowledge by means of incorporating the described techniques of *pruning*, *partitioning*, and *skipping* in its underlying algorithm. The new join operator requires no exceptional treatment: staircase join affects physical database design and query optimization much like traditional relational join operators.

Processing XML Queries with Tree Signatures

Pavel Zezula, Giuseppe Amato, and Fausto Rabitti

17.1 Introduction

With the rapidly increasing popularity of XML for data representation, there is a lot of interest in query processing over data that conforms to a labeled-tree data model. A variety of languages have been proposed for this purpose, all of which can be viewed as consisting of a pattern language and construction expressions. Since the data objects are typically trees, tree pattern matching is the central issue. The idea behind evaluating tree pattern queries, sometimes called *twig queries*, is to find all the ways of embedding the pattern in the data. Because this lies at the core of most languages for processing XML data, efficient evaluation techniques for these languages require appropriate indexing structures.

In query processing, signatures are compact (small) representations of important features extracted from actual documents in such a way that query execution can be performed on the signatures instead of the documents. In the past, see e.g. [298] for a survey, such a principle has been suggested as an alternative to the *inverted file* indexes. Recently, it has been successfully applied to indexing multi-dimensional vectors for similarity-based searching [314], image retrieval [225], and data mining [224].

We define the *tree signature* as a sequence of tree-node entries, containing node names and their structural relationships. Though other possibilities exist, here we show how these signatures can be used for efficient tree navigation and twig pattern matching.

17.2 Execution Strategies for XML Query Processing

Existing approaches to XML query processing are either based on mapping pathnames to their occurrences or on mapping element names to their occurrences. In the first case, entire pathnames, occurring in XML documents, are associated with sets of elements that can be reached through these paths. In

H. Blanken et al. (Eds.): Intelligent Search on XML Data, LNCS 2818, pp. 247–258, 2003.

the second case, element names are associated with references to the names' occurrences in XML documents. In the following, we briefly discuss the most important representatives.

17.2.1 Mapping Pathnames to Their Occurrences

DataGuides

DataGuides [133] were initially intended as a concise and accurate summary of the structure of any graph-structured data model: each occurring path is represented exactly once and nonexisting paths are not represented. However it has been shown that it can be used as a path index to speed-up query processing. A DataGuide of an XML document s is a graph d, such that every label path of s has exactly one data path instance in d, and every label path of d is a label path of s. Each node o, reached by a label path l in the DataGuide, is associated with the list of nodes reached by l in s. A DataGuide can be obtained by using an algorithm that was proven to be equivalent to the conversion of a non-deterministic finite automaton to a deterministic finite automaton. DataGuide can efficiently process, without the need of hierarchical relationship verification, path expressions composed of simple sequences of element names. It fails for more complex path expressions, such as those containing wildcards in arbitrary positions.

APEX

Based on the idea of DataGuide, APEX (Adaptive Path indEx for XML data) was defined in [72] . APEX does not keep all paths starting from the root, but only utilizes frequently accessed paths determined in the query workload by means of specialized *mining* algorithms. In addition to a *graph structure*, similar to a DataGuide, APEX also applies a *hash tree*. The graph structure represents a structural summary of XML data. The hash tree contains incoming label paths to nodes of the structure graph. Nodes of the hash tree are hash tables where entries may point to another hash table or to a node of the structure graph. The key of an entry in a hash table is an element name. Following a label path in the hash tree, the corresponding node in the structure graph is reached. The hash tree represents the frequently accessed paths and all paths of length two, so any path expression can be evaluated by using joins, without accessing the original data. A represented path need not start from the root. By using the hash tree, path expressions containing wildcards can also be processed efficiently, provided the corresponding label paths are included in the hash tree.

Index Fabric

An Index Fabric [79] is a disk based extension of the Patricia trie. It has the same scaling property, but it is balanced and optimized for disk based access.

In order to index XML documents by an Index Fabric, paths are encoded using *designators*, which are special characters or character strings. Each element name is associated with a unique designator. Text content of an element is not modified. For instance the XML fragment

```
<invoice>
  <buyer><name>ABC Corp</name></buyer>
<invoice>
```

can be encoded with the string "**IBN**ABC Corp", where bold letters **I**, **B**, and **N** represent, respectively, the element names `invoice`, `buyer`, and `name`. Each designator encoded path is inserted in the Index Fabric, and designators are treated as normal characters. A separate designator dictionary is used to maintain the mapping between the designators and the element names. Attributes are considered as children of the corresponding element. In addition to *raw paths*, i.e. paths from the root to the leaves occurring in XML documents, *refined paths*, i.e. specialized paths that optimize frequently occurring access patterns, are also inserted in the Index Fabric. Refined paths can be used to efficiently process specific queries with wildcards and alternates.

17.2.2 Mapping Elements to Their Occurrences

XXL

The *path index* from [296] associates each element name appearing in the indexed XML documents with a list of its occurrences. Each element name is stored exactly once in the index. An occurrence consists of the URL of the XML document, the unique identifier of the element name occurrence, a pointer to the parent element, pointers to the children elements, along with optional XLink and XPointer links. Attributes are uniformly treated as if they were special children of the corresponding element. All path expressions can be efficiently processed by using the explicitly maintained references to parents and children. However, this path index was implemented as a red-black tree, built on element names and maintained in the main memory. For query processing, the index must be first loaded from the disk.

Join Techniques

Instead of explicitly maintaining the hierarchical relationships, another possibility is to maintain information on the *position* of XML elements. This approach is discussed in [331]. An element name occurrence is encoded as $(docId, begin:end, level)$, where *docId* is the identifier of an XML document containing the occurrence; *level* is the nesting level of the occurrence in the XML structure; *begin* and *end* represent the *interval* covered by the occurrence, i.e the position of the start and end tags of the element in the XML text.

Given two sets of occurrences of elements E_1 and E_2, the *containment joins* represent a strategy to determine pairs of elements, one from E_1 and one from E_2, which are mutually contained inside each other. In [331], two implementations of this idea are compared. In the first case, the mapping between element names and occurrences is maintained in an inverted file. A variation of the merge join algorithm, the *Multi Predicate MerGe JoiN* (MPMGJN), for containment joins on inverted lists was also designed for efficient path expression processing. In the second case, the mapping between element names and occurrences is maintained in a relational database as a table $ELEMENTS(elementName, docId, begin, end, level)$. The actual processing of joins is then left on the SQL engine. It was shown in [331] that the first approach performs better, mainly due to the specialized containment join algorithm used.

The *holistic path joins* from [51] also rely on the *begin:end* encoding of the tree occurrences to efficiently process root-to-leaf path expressions. Specifically, two families of holistic path join algorithms are defined: *PathStack* and *PathMPMJ* (a generalization of the previously mentioned MPMGJN). In addition, a *holistic twig join* algorithm, *TwigStack*, is also proposed. In principle, it refines the *PathStack* to optimize the processing of entire twig queries.

Preorder/Postorder Numbering Schema

An alternative to previous tree encoding is proposed in [146], where Dietz's [98] numbering schema is used to represent positions of elements . Each element is assigned two ranks obtained through the *preorder* and the *postorder* traversal of the XML tree structure . The ancestor-descendant relationships can be verified as follows: given two elements e_1 and e_2, e_1 is an ancestor of e_2 if and only if e_1 occurs before e_2 in the preorder traversal and after e_2 in the postorder traversal. It was observed in [146] that all XPath axes can also be easily processed by this numbering schema. Since each element can be represented as a point in a two dimensional vector space, the ancestor-descendant relationships can be interpreted as spatial relationships. By exploiting this property, containment joins for path expressions can be executed on relational databases using a spatial access method like the R-Trees [150]. An extension of this work to the *Staircase Join* algorithm is in Chap. 16.

XISS

A limitation of the previous tree encodings is that positions must be recomputed when a new node is inserted. An equivalent encoding that takes this problem into account is proposed in XISS [201] . The position of an element is represented using an *extended preorder* and a *range of descendants* . Specifically, the position is represented by a pair *order:size* such that, given an element e_2 and its parent e_1, $order(e_1) < order(e_2)$ and $order(e_2) + size(e_2) \leq order(e_1) + size(e_1)$. That is, the interval $[order(e_2), order(e_2) + size(e_2)]$ is contained in the interval $[order(e_1), order(e_1) + size(e_1)]$. In addition, given two siblings e_1 and e_2 such that e_1 precedes e_2, $order(e_1) + size(e_2) <$ $order(e2)$. In fact, the *order* and *size* do not need to be exactly the preorder and the number of descendants of an element. They need to be numbers, which are larger than the preorder and the number of descendants, such that previous relationships are satisfied. This allows us to accommodate future insertions.

17.3 Tree Signatures

The idea of *tree signatures* [330] is to maintain a compressed representation of the tree structures, which is able to solve the tree inclusion problem as needed for XML data processing. Intuitively, we use the *preorder* and *postorder* ranks to linearize the tree structures and apply the sequence inclusion algorithms for strings.

An ordered tree T is a rooted tree in which the children of each node are ordered. If a node $i \in T$ has k children then the children are uniquely identified, left to right, as $i_1, i_2, \ldots, i_k$. A labelled tree T associates a label $t[i]$ with each node $i \in T$. If the path from the root to i has length n, we say that the node i is on the level n, i.e. $level(i) = n$. Finally, $size(i)$ denotes the number of descendants in a subtree rooted at i – the size of any leave node is zero. In the following, we consider ordered labelled trees.

The preorder and postorder sequences are ranked lists of all nodes of a given tree T. In a preorder sequence, a tree node v is traversed and assigned its (increasing) preorder rank, $pre(v)$, before its children have been recursively traversed from left to right. In the postorder sequence, a tree node v is traversed and assigned its (increasing) postorder rank, $post(v)$, after its children have been recursively traversed from left to right. As an illustration, see the preorder and postorder sequences of our sample tree in Figure 17.1 – the node's position in the sequence is its preorder/postorder rank.

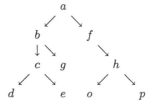

$$pre: a\ b\ c\ d\ e\ g\ f\ h\ o\ p$$
$$post: d\ e\ c\ g\ b\ o\ p\ h\ f\ a$$
$$rank: 1\ 2\ 3\ 4\ 5\ 6\ 7\ 8\ 9\ 10$$

Fig. 17.1. Preorder and postorder sequences of a tree with element ranks

As proposed in [146], such properties can be summarized in a two dimensional diagram, as illustrated in Figure 17.2, where the *ancestors* (A), *descendants* (D), *preceding* (P), and *following* (F) nodes of v can easily be found in the appropriate regions. Furthermore, for any $v \in T$, we have $pre(v) - post(v) + size(v) = level(v)$.

17.3.1 The Signature

The tree signature is a list of all the tree nodes obtained with a preorder traversal of the tree. Apart from the node name, each entry also contains the node's position in the postorder rank.

Definition 1. *Let T be an ordered labelled tree. The signature of T is a sequence, $sig(T) = \langle t_1, post(t_1); t_2, post(t_2); \ldots t_n, post(t_n) \rangle$, of $n = |T|$ entries, where t_i is a name of the node with $pre(t_i) = i$. The $post(t_i)$ value is the postorder value of the node named t_i and the preorder value i.*

For example, $\langle a, 10; b, 5; c, 3; d, 1; e, 2; g, 4; f, 9; h, 8; o, 6; p, 7 \rangle$ is the signature of the tree from Figure 17.1.

Tree Inclusion Evaluation

Suppose the data tree T and the query tree Q are specified by signatures

$$sig(T) = \langle t_1, post(t_1); t_2, post(t_2); \ldots t_m, post(t_m) \rangle,$$

$$sig(Q) = \langle q_1, post(q_1); q_2, post(q_2); \ldots q_n, post(q_n) \rangle.$$

Let $sub\_sig_Q(T)$ be the *sub-signature* (i.e. a subsequence) of $sig(T)$ determined by a name sequence-inclusion of $sig(Q)$ in $sig(T)$. A specific query signature can determine zero or more data sub-signatures. Regarding the node names,

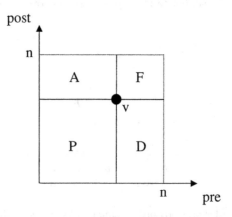

Fig. 17.2. Properties of the preorder and postorder ranks.

any $sub\_sig_Q(T) \equiv sig(Q)$, because $q_i = t_i$ for all i, but the corresponding entries may have different postorder values. It is important to understand that in general, the sequence positions of entries in sub-signatures do not correspond to the preorder values of the entries in T.

Lemma 1. *The query tree Q is included in the data tree T if the following two conditions are satisfied: (1) on the level of node names, $sig(Q)$ is sequence-included in $sig(T)$ determining $sub\_sig_Q(T)$, (2) for all pairs of entries i and j in $sig(Q)$ and $sub\_sig_Q(T)$, $i, j = 1, 2, \ldots |Q| - 1$ and $i + j \leq |Q|$, whenever $post(q_{i+j}) > post(q_i)$ it is also true that $post(t_{i+j}) > post(t_i)$.*

Proof. Because the index i increases according to the preorder sequence, node $i + j$ must be either the descendant or the following node of i. If $post(q_{i+j}) < post(q_i)$, the node $i + j$ in the query is a descendant of the node i, thus also $post(t_{i+j}) < post(t_i)$ is required. By analogy, if $post(q_{i+j}) > post(q_i)$, the node $i + j$ in the query is a following node of i, thus also $post(t_{i+j}) > post(t_i)$ must hold.

For example, consider the data tree T in Figure 17.1 and suppose the query tree Q consists of nodes $h, o,$ and p structured as in Figure 17.3. Such a query

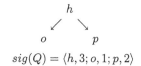

$$sig(Q) = \langle h, 3; o, 1; p, 2 \rangle$$

Fig. 17.3. Sample query tree Q

qualifies in T, because $sig(Q) = \langle h, 3; o, 1; p, 2 \rangle$ determines $sub\_sig_Q(T) = \langle h, 8; o, 6; p, 7 \rangle$, which is not only sequence-included on the level of names, but also has identical trends in postorder directions between neighboring entries of the query and the data sub-signature sequences. If we change h for f in our query, we get $sig(Q) = \langle f, 3; o, 1; p, 2 \rangle$. Such a modified query tree is also included in T, because Lemma 1 does not insist on the strict parent-child relationships, and implicitly considers all such relationships as ancestor-descendant. However, the query tree with the root g, resulting in $sig(Q) = \langle g, 3; o, 1; p, 2 \rangle$, does not qualify, even though it is also sequence-included (on the level of names) as sub-signature $sub\_sig_Q(T) = \langle g, 4; o, 6; p, 7 \rangle$. The reason is that the query requires the postorder to go down from g to o (from 3 to 1), while in the sub-signature it actually goes up (from 4 to 6). This means that o is not a descendant node of g, as required by the query, but a node that follows g, which can be verified in Figure 17.1.

Multiple nodes with common names may result in multiple tree inclusions. As demonstrated in [330], the tree signatures can easily deal with such situations by simply distinguishing between node names and their unique occurrences. Leaf nodes in signatures are all nodes with a postorder smaller than the postorder of the following node in the signature sequence – the last node is always a leaf. We can also determine the level of leaf nodes, because the level of a leaf node t_i with index i, $level(t_i) = i - post(i)$.

Extended Signatures

By extending entries of tree signatures with two preorder numbers representing pointers to the *first following*, ff, and the *first ancestor*, fa, nodes, the *extended signatures* are defined in [330]. The generic entry of the i-th extended signature entry is $\langle t_i, post(t_i), ff_i, fa_i \rangle$. This version of the tree signatures allows us to compute levels for any node $t - i$ as $level(t_i) = ff_i - post(i) - 1$. The cardinality of the descendant node set can also be computed: $size(t_i) = ff_i - i - 1$. Though the extended signatures are two times larger than the small signatures, they allow a more efficient implementation of navigation operations, as illustrated in [330], on the XPath axes. For the tree from Figure 17.1, the extended signature is

$$sig(T) = \langle a, 10, 11, 0; b, 5, 7, 1; c, 3, 6, 2; d, 1, 5, 3; e, 2, 6, 3;$$

$$g, 4, 7, 2; f, 9, 11, 1; h, 8, 11, 7; o, 6, 10, 8; p, 7, 11, 8 \rangle$$

17.3.2 XPath Navigation

XPath [176] is a language for specifying navigation in XML documents. Within an XPath Step, an Axis specifies the *direction* in which the document should be navigated. Given a context node v, XPath supports 12 axes for navigation. Assuming the context node is at position i in the signature, we describe how the most significant axes can be evaluated in the extended signatures, using the tree from Figure 17.1 as a reference:

Child. The first child is the first descendant, that is the node with index $i + 1$. The second child is indicated by pointer ff_{i+1}, provided the value is smaller than ff_i, otherwise the child node does not exist. All the other child nodes are determined recursively until the bound ff_i is reached. For example, consider node b with index $i = 2$. Since $ff_2 = 7$, there are 4 descending nodes, so the node with index $i + 1 = 3$ (i.e. node c) must be the first child. The first following pointer of c, $ff_{i+1} = 6$, determines the second child b (i.e. node g), because $6 < 7$. Due to the fact that $ff_6 = ff_i = 7$, there are no other child nodes.

Descendant. The descendant nodes (if any) start immediately after the reference object, that is in position $i + 1$, and the last descendant object is in position $ff_i - 1$. If we consider node c (with $i = 3$), we immediately infer that the descendants are in positions starting from $i + 1 = 4$ to $ff_3 - 1 = 5$, i.e. nodes d and e.

Parent. The parent node is directly given by the pointer fa. The **Ancestor** axis is just recursive closure of **Parent**.

Following. The following nodes of the reference in position i (when they exist) start in position ff_i and include all nodes up to the end of the signature sequence. All nodes following c (with $i = 3$) are in the suffix of the signature starting in position $ff_3 = 6$.

Preceding. All preceding nodes are on the left of the reference node as a set of intervals separated by the ancestors. Given a node with index i, fa_i points to the first ancestor (i.e. the parent) of i, and the nodes (when they exist) between i and fa_i precede i in the tree. If we recursively continue from fa_i, we find all the preceding nodes of i. For example, consider node g with $i = 6$: following the ancestor pointer, we get $fa_6 = 2, fa_2 = 1, fa_1 = 0$, so the ancestor nodes are b and a, because $fa_1 = 0$ indicates the root. The preceding nodes of g are only in the interval from $i - 1 = 5$ to $fa_6 + 1 = 3$ (i.e. nodes c, d, and e), because the second interval, from $fa_2 - 1 = 0$ to $fa_1 + 1 = 1$, is empty.

Following-sibling. In order to get the following siblings, we just follow the ff pointers while the following objects exist and the fa pointers are the same as fa_i. For example, given node c with $i = 3$ and $fa_3 = 2$, the ff_3 pointer moves us to the node with index 6, that is node g. Node g is the sibling following c, because $fa_6 = fa_3 = 2$. But this is also the last following sibling, because $ff_6 = 7$ and $fa_7 \neq fa_3$.

Preceding-sibling. All preceding siblings must be between the context node with index i and its parent with index $fa_i < i$. The first node after the i-th parent, which has the index $fa_i + 1$, is the first sibling. Then we use the **Following-sibling** strategy up to the sibling with index i. Consider the node f ($i = 7$) as the context node. The first sibling of the i-th parent is b, determined by pointer $fa_7 + 1 = 2$. Then the pointer $ff_2 = 7$ leads us back to the context node f, so b is the only preceding sibling node of f.

The experimental evaluation in [330] confirms that implementations of the axes on extended signatures are faster than on short signatures, and the larger the signature, the better. The actual improvements depend on the axes – the biggest advantage, counted in hundreds, was observed for the ancestor axis, above all when processing large low trees. In general, the execution costs of the axes depend on the shape of the tree and the position of the reference node in it. But in no circumstances, do the implementations on the short signatures ever outperform the implementations on the extended signatures.

17.4 Query Processing

Processing a query Q on a collection of XML documents represents a process of finding sub-trees for which content predicates and structural relationships, defined by the query, are satisfied. Query execution strategies determine the ways the query's predicates are evaluated. In principle, a predicate can be decided either by accessing a specific part of the document or by means of an index. So a specific strategy depends on the availability of indexes. We assume that tree signatures are used to support the verification of required structural relationships.

A query processor can also exploit tree signatures to evaluate *set-oriented* primitives similar to the XPath axes. For instance, given a set of elements R, the evaluation of $Parent(R, \texttt{article})$ returns the set of elements named `article`, which are parents of elements contained in R. We suppose that elements are identified by their preorder values, so sets of elements are in fact sets of element identifiers.

Verifying structural relationships can easily be integrated with evaluating content predicates. If indexes are available, a good strategy is to use these indexes to obtain sets of elements which satisfy the predicates, and then verify the structural relationships using signatures. Consider the following XQuery [176] query:

```
for $a in //people
where
        $a/name/first="John" and
        $a/name/last="Smith"
return
        $a/address
```

Suppose that content indexes are available on the `first` and `last` elements. A possible efficient execution plan for this query is:

1. let $R_1 = ContentIndexSearch(last\text{-}idx, \texttt{Smith})$;
2. let $R_2 = ContentIndexSearch(first\text{-}idx, \texttt{John})$;
3. let $R_3 = Parent(R_1, \texttt{name})$;
4. let $R_4 = Parent(R_2, \texttt{name})$;
5. let $R_5 = Intersect(R_3, R_4)$;
6. let $R_6 = Parent(R_5, \texttt{people})$;
7. let $R_7 = Child(R_6, \texttt{address})$;

First, the content indexes are used to obtain R_1 and R_2, i.e. the sets of elements that satisfy the content predicates. Then, tree signatures are used to navigate through the structure and verify structural relationships.

Now suppose that a content index is only available on the `last` element, the predicate on the `first` element has to be processed by accessing the content of XML documents. Though the specific technique for efficiently accessing the content depends on the storage format of the XML documents (plain text files, relational transformation, etc.), a viable query execution plan is as follows:

1. let $R_1 = ContentIndexSearch(last\text{-}idx,$ Smith$)$;
2. let $R_2 = Parent(R_1,$name$)$;
3. let $R_3 = Child(R_2,$first$)$;
4. let $R_4 = FilterContent(R_3,$John$)$;
5. let $R_5 = Parent(R_4,$name$)$;
6. let $R_6 = Parent(R_5,$people$)$;
7. let $R_7 = Child(R_6,$address$)$.

Here, the content index is first used to find R_1, i.e. the set of elements containing Smith. The tree signature is used to produce R_3, that is the set of the corresponding first elements. Then, these elements are accessed to verify that their content is John. Finally, tree signatures are used again to verify the remaining structural relationships.

17.5 Experimental Evaluation

In [330], we evaluated the performance of extended signatures for query processing, and we compared the results with the MPMGJN approach. We used the XML DBLP data set containing 3,181,399 elements and occupying 120 Mb of memory. We generated queries that had different *element name selectivity* (i.e. the number of elements having a given element name), *element content selectivity* (i.e. the number of elements having a given content), and the number of navigation steps to follow in the query pattern tree.

As would be expected, queries are executed faster when the selectivity is high. This is much more evident for the performance of the extended tree signatures, which, in such cases, are nearly one order of magnitude faster than the joins. The containment join strategy seems to be affected by the selectivity of the element name more than the tree signature approach. In fact, when using high content selective predicates, performance of signature files is always high, irrespectively of the element name selectivity. This can be explained by the fact that, using the signature technique, only those signature entries corresponding to elements that have parent relationships with the few elements satisfying the predicate are accessed. On the other hand, the containment join strategy has to process a large list of elements associated with low selective element names.

If there is low selectivity of the content predicate, the tree signature approach has a better response than the containment join except where low selectivity of both the content and the names of elements are tested. In this case, structural relationships are verified for a large number of elements that satisfy the low selective predicate. We believe that in practice such queries are not frequent.

The difference in performance of the signature and the containment join approaches is even more evident for queries with two navigation steps. While the signature strategy has to follow only one additional step for each qualifying element, that is to access one more entry in the signature, containment joins have to merge potentially large lists of references.

17.6 Conclusions

Inspired by the success of signature files in several application areas, we propose tree signatures as an auxiliary data structure for XML databases. The proposed signatures are based on preorder and postorder ranks and support tree inclusion evaluation, respecting sibling and ancestor-descendant relationships. Navigation operations, such as those required by the XPath axes, are computed very efficiently. Query processing can also benefit from the application of tree signature indexes. For highly selective queries, i.e. typical user queries, query processing with the tree signature is about 10 times more efficient, compared to the strategy with containment joins.

The proposed signature file approach also creates good basis for dealing with dynamic XML collections. Even though the preorder and postorder numbering scheme is affected by document updates – node ranks change when inserting or deleting a node – the effects are always *local* within specific signatures. So it is up to the database designer to choose a suitable signature granularity, which should be quite small for very dynamic collections, while relatively stable or static collections can use much larger signatures. This locality property cannot be easily exploited with approaches based on containment joins or approaches like [146], where updates (as well as insertions and deletions) usually require an extensive reorganization of the index.

Part V

Evaluation

Introduction

An evaluation methodology is needed to assess how well today's XML retrieval methods perform and to compare the quality of different approaches. Given the novelty of the field and the inherent difficulties of factoring the properties of the underlying data into the analysis, the evaluation is naturally *experimental* (as opposed to analytic and solely based on mathematical models). For systematic evaluation this calls for *benchmarks* that define what is measured on which data under which conditions. The evaluation criteria are twofold: on one hand, the *effectiveness* of an approach for providing search results that are considered satisfactory by the human user is a key goal; on the other hand, *efficiency* is crucial, too, so as not to exceed the user's tolerance regarding responsiveness.

Traditionally, benchmarks in the area data management and information systems have focused on one of the two criteria only. In the database area, the TPC-C and TPC-H benchmarks have played an important role for assessing the performance of transaction processing and query engines and have been driving improvements of research approaches and commercial systems in terms of throughput and response time. However, all operations in these benchmarks are geared for schematic and structured data with Boolean search predicates only (as opposed similarity predicates that require ranking). In the information retrieval area, on the other hand, the series of TREC benchmarks has been studying the effectiveness of a wide variety of techniques for ranking the results of keyword queries, text document filtering and classification, and question answering, with little regard to efficiency issues.

Although the ideal benchmark for XML retrieval would cover both effectiveness and efficiency, defining an appropriate benchmark for each aspect alone is already a challenge in a completely new field like searching semistructured data. This part of the book offers two chapters each of which focuses on one of the two evaluation criteria.

Chapter 18 by Schmidt, Waas, Manegold, and Kersten reviews the work on the XMark benchmark. This performance benchmark aims to stress the query engine of XML database systems and reports different measures of efficiency and scalability. XMark was developed at an early stage in the evolution of XML and the discussion also reflects how the perception of XML data management and querying has changed over the last three years. The chapter's emphasis is on lessons learned from defining the benchmark and running it on various platforms.

Chapter 19 by Kazai, Gövert, Lalmas, and Fuhr presents the first results of the recent INEX initiative for the evaluation of XML retrieval. Here the emphasis is on search effectiveness in the TREC style, and the chapter provides insights into all evaluation stages: from the preparation of the underlying test data collection and the definition of typical user queries to the assessment of benchmark runs and the reporting of aggregate evaluation criteria.

A Look Back on the XML Benchmark Project

Albrecht Schmidt, Florian Waas, Stefan Manegold, and Martin Kersten

18.1 Introduction

Database vendors and researchers have been responding to the establishing of XML [45] as the premier data interchange language for Internet applications with the integration of XML processing capabilities into Database Management Systems. The new features fall into two categories: *XML-enabled interfaces* allow the DBMS to speak and understand XML formats, whereas *XML extensions* add novel primitives to the engine core. Both kinds of innovations have the potential to impact the architecture of software systems, namely by bringing about a complexity reduction in multi-tier systems. However, it is often difficult to estimate the effect of these innovations. This is where the XML Benchmark Project tries to help with XMark. By providing an application scenario and a query workload, the benchmark suite can be used to identify strengths and weaknesses of XML-enabled software systems.

The queries of the benchmark suite target different aspects of querying of XML documents, both in isolation and in combination. We identify the following areas of potential performance impacts:

- The topology of XML structures as found in the original document is a potential candidate for queries; especially systems that implement document order on top of an unordered data model may not be properly prepared for this kind of challenge and have to turn rather simple queries into complex operations. This is also tested in several benchmark queries.
- The document-oriented nature of XML makes strings the basic data type applications have to deal with. Typing XML documents is therefore as important a challenge to make data processing more robust as enforcing other semantics constraints. Problems can also arise as the typing rules of query languages may clash with the more complex type systems of host programming languages. In addition, strings are often not efficient in database systems since their length can vary greatly, putting additional stress on the storage engine.

H. Blanken et al. (Eds.): Intelligent Search on XML Data, LNCS 2818, pp. 263–278, 2003.
© Springer-Verlag Berlin Heidelberg 2003

- The hierarchical structure of XML documents impacts queries in the form of path expressions. The hierarchical structure of documents in conjunction with complicated path expressions does not only result in potentially expensive join and aggregation operations but also in a search space that makes it hard for query optimizers to find good execution plans.
- The loose schema of XML data may not only make it hard for users to get an overview of the structure, which is a prerequisite for being able to user query languages sensibly and a notoriously error-prone activity when a user tries to specify long and complicated path expressions. It also poses optimization challenges to the database engine. Sparsely populated parts of the database do not only aggravate maintenance problems with respect to data statistics, they also inflate the size of the database with maintenance information and NULL values.
- Besides the tree structure, XML provides a number of additional features that influence a query processor. For example, the XML standard lists constraints on special attributes to ensure that references only connect existing elements. To cope with references efficiently, techniques like join indexes or logical OIDs might be of use. The resolution of namespaces is another topic that requires careful handling; XMark does not feature queries that challenge namespaces since its authors believe that the mechanism to handle them do not differ greatly from queries involving different parts of subtrees.

Due to complex interdependencies between these points and the different components of a system, implementation efforts tend to be hard to assess in a general fashion without putting them to a standardized test, which is most conveniently done in the form of a benchmark. The need for new benchmarks has been a recurring momentum in database research; consequently, over the past years the database community developed a rich tradition in performance assessment of systems ranging from research developments like the Hypermodel [13], OO1-Benchmark [62], OO7-Benchmark [60] or the BUCKY benchmark [61] to industrial standards like the family of TPC benchmarks [141] just to mention a few examples. However, none of the available benchmarks offers the coverage needed for XML processing. All of them are geared towards a certain data model but fail to take into account the flexibility and expressiveness of semi-structured data with their implicit schemas [1] and flexible data structures which exceed the capabilities of existing query languages.

The XMark Benchmark takes on the challenge and features a tool kit for evaluating the retrieval performance of XML stores and query processors: a workload specification, a scalable benchmark document and a comprehensive set of queries, which were designed to feature natural and intuitive semantics. To facilitate analysis and interpretation, each of the queries is intended to challenge the query processor with an important primitive of the underlying algebra. XML processing systems usually consist of various logical layers and can be physically distributed over a network. To make the benchmark results interpretable we abstract from the systems engineering issues and concentrate only on the core ingredients: the query processor and its interaction with the data store. We do not consider network overhead, communication costs or transformations to the output. As for the choice of language, we use XQuery [34] which is the result of incorporating experiences from various research languages [40] for semi-structured data and XML into a standard.

The target audience of the benchmark could comprise three groups. First, the framework presented here can help database vendors to verify and refine their query processors by comparing them to other implementations. Second, customers can be assisted in choosing between products by using our setting as a simple case study or pilot project that yet provides essential ingredients of the targeted system. For researchers, lastly, we provide example data and a framework for helping to tailor existing technology for use in XML settings and for refinement or design of algorithms.

18.2 Evolution of XML Technology and Benchmarks

Database benchmarks found in the literature cover a plethora of technologies and aspects of traditional data management ranging from query optimization to transaction processing. But even if we make use of established techniques to store and process XML, it is not clear if and in what way the semi-structured nature of the data impacts on performance and engineering issues. Therefore, to motivate the need for XML benchmarks we take a look at the evolution of XML standards and how it differs from that of established technologies.

The evolution of XML differs significantly from the evolution of relational databases in that for XML there was an early standard which was accepted and supported by a large community. It was then that implementations had to live up to the standards that were already present and in place. There was no organic and interactive development between standards and research as there was, for example, in the case of the SQL standards. Therefore it is sensible to design the benchmark with a top-down perspective in mind, i.e., to come up with challenges for query primitives anticipated as typical and thus provide a kind of thematic benchmark. In the case of XML, the W3C Use Cases [65] contained the research necessary to justify the relevance of the challenges. In this sense, the combination of traditional and new features present in XML processing systems in conjunction with the new approach to standards results in the need for a new quality of system development. The XMark benchmark tries to be a part of this endeavor.

Traditionally, database management systems have been deployed in settings where very regular, table-structured data format prevail. While it has been shown that these data-centric documents, i.e., documents which logically represent data structures [41], map effectively to relational databases (*e.g.*, see [117, 271, 279]) or object-relational databases [190], it is less clear how

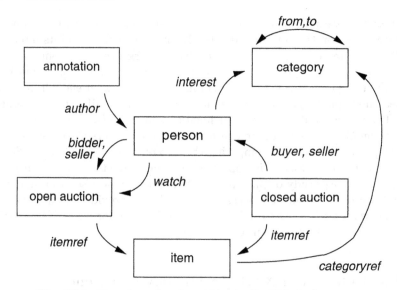

Fig. 18.1. Overview of main entities in the XMark document

the same systems can handle efficiently documents that are more document-centric [41], i.e., consisting mostly of natural language with mark-up only interspersed with the result of irregular path structures. Converted to relational tables in a naive way, the data and query profile often do not match the kind of pattern traditional database engines are optimized for.

18.3 The XMark Database

In this section, we give an overview of XMark's document database. One of the major design goals were good performance during generation, opportunities for formulating predictable and interesting queries, and that the database 'feels natural'. We first summarize the semantics of the document and then cover some of the more technical issues of generating such documents.

18.3.1 Main Entities and Their Relationships

The main syntactic constituent of XML documents is the recursive application of elements that contain other elements; it renders the typical tree structure of XML. Accordingly, element relationships play a crucial role in document design. The other important tool that designers have at hand are references which connect elements in a way that is orthogonal to the tree structure. In XMark, we decided to model the database after a schema that is typical for Internet auction sites. The main entities come in two groups: *person, open*

auction, *closed auction*, *item*, and *category* on the one side and entities akin
to *annotation* on the other side. The relationships between the entities in the
first group are expressed through references, as depicted with arrows in Figure 18.1. The relationships between the entities of the second group, which
take after natural language text and are document-centric element structures,
are embedded into the sub-trees to which they semantically belong. An ER diagram can be found in [47]. The entities we just mentioned carry the following
semantics:

- *Items* are the objects that are on sale in an auction or that already have
  been sold. Each *item* carries a unique identifier and bears properties like
  payment (credit card, money order, ...), a reference to the seller, a description *etc.*, all encoded as elements. Each item is assigned a world region
  represented by the item's parent element.
- *Open auctions* are auctions in progress. Their properties are the privacy
  status, the bid history (i.e., increases or decreases over time) with references to the bidders and the seller, the current bid, the time interval within
  which bids are accepted, the status of the transaction and a reference to
  the item being sold, among others.
- *Closed auctions* are auctions that are finished. Their properties are the
  seller (a reference to a person), the buyer (a reference to a person), a
  reference to the respective item, the price, the number of items sold, the
  date when the transaction was closed, the type of transaction, and the
  annotations that were made before, during and after the bidding process.
- *Persons* are characterized by name, email address, phone number, mail
  address, homepage URL, credit card number, profile of their interests, and
  the (possibly empty) set of open auctions they are interested in and get
  notifications about.
- *Categories* feature a name and a description; they are used to implement
  a classification scheme of *items*. A *category_graph* links categories into a
  network.

We emphasize that these entities constitute the relatively structured,
i.e., data-oriented part of the document. Their sub-element structure is fairly
regular on a per entity basis but there are predictable exceptions such as that
not every person has a homepage; in a relational DBMS, these exceptions
would typically be taken care of by NULL values. Another characteristic of
these entities is that, apart from occasional list types such as bidding histories, the order of the input is not particularly relevant. On the other hand, the
sub-elements of the document-centric part of the database, namely those of *annotation* and similar elements, do not accentuate the above aspects. Here the
length of strings and the internal structure of sub-elements varies greatly. The
markup now comprises itemized lists, keywords, and even visual formatting
instructions and character data, doing its best to imitate the characteristics
of natural language texts. This warrants that the benchmark database covers

the full range of XML instance incarnations, from marked-up data structures to traditional prose.

The arrows in Figure 18.1 are mainly implemented as IDREFs that connects elements with IDs. Care has been taken that the references feature diverse distributions, derived from uniformly, normally and exponentially distributed random variables. Also note that all references are typed, i.e., all instances of an XML element point to the same type of XML element; for example, references that model interests always refer to categories although this constraint does not materialize in the DTD that accompanies XMark.

The XML Standard [45] defines constructs that are useful for producing flexible markup but do not justify the definition of queries to challenge them directly. Therefore, we only made use of a restricted set of XML features in the data generator which we consider performance critical in the context of XML processing in databases. We do not generate documents with Entities or Notations. Neither do we distinguish between Parsed Character Data and Character Data assuming that both are string types from the viewpoint of the storage engine. Furthermore, we don't include namespaces into the queries. We also restrict ourselves to the seven bit ASCII character set. A DTD and schema information are provided to allow for more efficient mappings. However, we stress that this is additional information that *may* be exploited.

18.3.2 The Document Generator

We designed and implemented a document generator, called `xmlgen`, to provide for a scalable XML document database. Besides the obvious requirement to be capable of producing the XML document specified above we were eager to meet the following additional demands. The generation of the XML document should be:

- *platform independent* so that any user interested in running the benchmark is able to download the binary and generate the same document no matter what hardware or operating system is used; to achieve this plain ANSI C was used to implement `xmlgen`;
- *accurately scalable* ranging from a minimal document to any arbitrary size limited only by the capacity of the system;
- both *time and resource efficient*, i.e., elapsed time ideally scales linearly whereas the resource allocation is constant – independent of the size of the generated document;
- *deterministic*, that is, the output should only depend on the input parameters.

First, in order to be able to reproduce the document independently of the platform, we incorporated a random number generator rather then relying on the operating system's built-in random number generators. Together with basic algorithms which can be found in statistics textbooks the data generator `xmlgen` implements uniform, exponential, and normal distributions of fairly high quality. We assigned to each of the elements in the DTD a plausible distribution of its children and its references, observing consistency among referencing elements, that is, the number of items organized by continents equals the sum of open and closed auctions, *etc.* Second, to provide for accurate scaling we scale selected sets like the number of items and persons with the user-defined factor. Moreover, we calibrated the numbers to match a total document size of slightly more than 100 MB at scaling factor 1.0. Finally, it is a challenge to implement the data generator efficiently because references are created at various places throughout the document; since we have to abide by the integrity constraint that every reference points to a valid identifier, we could go for the straight-forward solution of keeping some sort of log and record which identifier has already been referenced; unfortunately this seems infeasible for large documents. We solved the problem by modifying the random number generation to produce several identical streams of random numbers. That way, we are able to implement a partitioning of sets like the item IDs that are referenced from both open and closed auctions. In its current version, `xmlgen` requires less than 2 MB of main-memory, and produces documents of sizes of 100 MB and 1 GB in 33.4 and 335.5 seconds, respectively (450MHz Pentium III). A more detailed description of the tool and downloads can be found on the project Web page [269].

18.4 The XMark Queries

In total, XMark contains 20 queries testing various concepts such as exact match, ordered access, casting, regular path expressions, chasing references, construction of complex results, joins on values, reconstruction, full text search, path traversals, missing elements, function application, sorting, and aggregation. Due to lack of space, we present only a representative selection of the queries, here. A complete description of all queries is available in [272] and the respective XQuery-code can be downloaded from the project Web site at [270].

Exact Match This simple query is mainly used to establish a performance baseline, which should help to interpret subsequent queries. It tests the database ability to handle simple string lookups with a fully specified path.

Q1: *Return the name of the person with ID 'person0'.*

Ordered Access These queries should help users to gain insight how the DBMS copes with the intrinsic order of XML documents and how efficiently they can expect the DBMS to handle queries with order constraints.

Q2: *Return the initial increases of all open auctions.*

This query evaluates the cost of array lookups. Note that it may actually be harder to evaluate than it looks; especially relational back-ends may have to struggle with rather complex aggregations to select the bidder element with index 1.

Q3: *Return the first and current increases of all open auctions whose current increase is at least twice as high as the initial increase.*

This is a more complex application of array lookups. In the case of a relational DBMS, the query can take advantage of set-valued aggregates on the index attribute to accelerate the execution. Queries Q2 and Q3 are akin to aggregations in the TPCD [141] benchmark.

Casting Strings are the generic data type in XML documents. Queries that interpret strings will often need to cast strings to another data type that carries more semantics. This query challenges the DBMS in terms of the casting primitives it provides. Especially, if there is no additional schema information or just a DTD at hand, casts are likely to occur frequently. Although other queries include casts, too, this query is meant to challenge casting in isolation.

Q5: *How many sold items cost more than 40?*

Regular Path Expressions Regular path expressions are a fundamental building block of virtually every query language for XML or semi-structured data. These queries investigate how well the query processor can optimize path expressions and prune traversals of irrelevant parts of the tree.

Q6: *How many items are listed on all continents?*

A good evaluation engine or path encoding scheme should help realize that there is no need to traverse the complete document tree to evaluate such expressions.

Q7: *How many pieces of prose are in our database?*

Also note that COUNT aggregations do not require a complete traversal of the document tree. Just the cardinality of the respective parts is queried.

Chasing References References are an integral part of XML as they allow richer relationships than just hierarchical element structures. These queries define horizontal traversals with increasing complexity. A good query optimizer should take advantage of the cardinalities of the operands to be joined.

Q8: *List the names of persons and the number of items they bought. (joins person, closed_auction)*

Q9: *List the names of persons and the names of the items they bought in Europe. (joins person, closed_auction, item)*

Construction of Complex Results Constructing new elements may put the storage engine under stress especially when the newly constructed elements are to be queried again. The following query reverses the structure of person records by grouping them according to the interest profile of a person. Large parts of the person records are repeatedly reconstructed. To avoid simple copying of the original database we translate the mark-up into French.

Q10: *List all persons according to their interest; use French markup in the result.*

Joins on Values This query tests the database's ability to handle large (intermediate) results. This time, joins are on the basis of values. The difference between these queries and the reference chasing queries Q8 and Q9 is that references are specified in the DTD and may be optimized with logical OIDs for example. The two queries Q11 and Q12 differ mainly in the size of the result set and hence provide various optimization opportunities.

Q11: *For each person, list the number of items currently on sale whose price does not exceed 0.02% of the person's income.*

Q12: *For each person with an income of more than 50000, list the number of items currently on sale whose price does not exceed 0.02% of the person's income.*

Missing Elements This is to test how well the query processors know to deal with the semi-structured aspect of XML data, especially elements that are declared optional in the DTD.

Q17: *Which persons don't have a homepage?*

The fraction of people without a homepage is rather high so that this query also presents a challenging path traversal to non-clustering systems.

Aggregation The following query computes a simple aggregation by assigning each person to a category. Note that the aggregation is truly semi-structured as it also includes those persons for whom the relevant data is not available.

Q20: *Group customers by their income and output the cardinality of each group.*

18.5 Experiences and Lessons Learned

In this section, we summarize some of the experiences we gathered during the design of the benchmark and when we ran the setup on a number of platforms.

18.5.1 Benchmark Document

In past database benchmarks, there have been two main routes to designing a database. On the one hand, designers may lean towards databases that exhibit properties close to what is found in real-world applications. This has the advantage that queries feel natural and that it is hard to question the usefulness of the scenario. On the other hand, it is often desirable to have another property which often is hard to combine with naturalness, namely predictable query behavior. If designers pursue predictability, they often go for very regular designs so that they can exactly and reliably predict what queries return. These designs are frequently based on mathematical models which allow precise predictions – at times at the trade-off however that the resulting databases 'feel' only little natural.

It is hard to position XML between the two extremes. For one, XML is not a pure machine format and therefore not exclusively consumed and produced by applications but also absorbed by humans – at least occasionally. Therefore, not only the semantics but also the documents themselves should still make sense to humans while it is primarily machines that produce and consume them. In XMark, we thus tried to reconcile the two competing goals as much as possible but, in case of conflicts, our policy was to favor predictability of queries and performance in the generation process.

We should mention that designers of other XML benchmarks had different policies in mind. For example, the Michigan Benchmark [254] features a very structured approach to database generation and want to maximize predictability on all levels and queries, much in the spirit of the Wisconsin Benchmark described in [141]. A hybrid approach is taken by XBench [327] who classify their documents according to a requirements matrix: their axes are Single-Document vs. Multi-Document Databases and Text-Centric vs. Data-Centric Databases, respectively. Other XML benchmarks like X007 [47] and XMach-1 [36] are also based on certain considerations with respect to document design.

While most people agree that performance is an important goal in query execution, it is equally important in data generation especially when it comes to large databases, which bring about significant generation overhead. In XMark, we pursued performance in that it was a design goal that the data generator should be able to output several megabytes of XML text per second, which we considered a necessary requirement should it be suitable for deployment in large-scale scenarios. After we finished a first prototype of the generator, we found out that a major performance bottleneck was random number generation. At first, we had chosen a high quality random number generator which turned out to be inadequate. In the sequel, we had to deal with the trade-off between the quality of random variables in general and their correlations in particular at one end of the scale and generation time at the other end. What turned out to be a problem was that when weak correlations were to be generated the quality of the random number generator may not be sufficient to make a correlation actually materialize in the generated database instance. On the other hand, using high-quality random number generators may be too costly in terms of resource consumption. We tackled the issue by fine-tuning the parameters that define the available scaling factors. As a final remark on correlations, we mention that it is quite easy to specify correlations between different entities that are logically sound but nearly impossible to materialize in the generated database due to the above-mentioned constraints. Hence, it is important to find a logic to describe or model the benchmark database that at the same time is non-contradictory and feasible. In the design of `xmlgen`, XMark's data generator, we put considerable effort into finding both economical and reliable ways of generating random numbers. Especially, `xmlgen` makes use of reproducible streams of random numbers to ensure that important correlations are preserved, most notably the well-formedness constraints imposed by the XML standard; technically,, we use deterministic number generation. When a fully customizable document generator is used, the language describing the document may contain contradictions; in this case, an important design rationale is to eliminate or minimize the contradictions, for example, by reporting them to the user through warning and error messages. We believe that there are still many open research issues with respect to data generation. Promising subjects include how to generate interesting chain correlations in large data sets and statistical guarantees for their materialization in the data sets, amongst others.

18.5.2 Running the Benchmark

Since XML was still at an early stage in its development, the actual implementation of the benchmark on a number of systems was a non-trivial task. The architectures and capabilities of query processors very much varied from system to system. Some systems could only bulkload small documents at a time; hence, we sometimes had to use the split feature of the data generator and feed the benchmark document in small pieces; at other times we were given the opportunity to specify (parts of) the XML-to-Database mapping by hand. The benchmark queries (see [273] for a complete list) often had to be translated to standard (SQL and XQuery) or proprietary query languages and possibly annotated with execution plan hints. All in all, there were many opportunities for hand-optimization which sometimes had to be taken advantage of to make the benchmark work on a system. However, we think that the technology has matured since we did the experiments and expect it to become more robust so that a detailed report of these experience would probably be already outdated. We therefore just mention some findings and refer to [272] and [273] which contain more detailed material.

The benchmark has been a group-design activity of academic and industry researchers and is known to be used with success to evaluate progress in both commercial and research settings. The evaluation in this section here is meant to present the highlights we encountered when running the benchmark

on a broad range of the systems; an in-depth analysis of the behavior of all
individual systems would be beyond the scope of this chapter. We anonymized
the systems due to well-known license restrictions and we simply speak of
systems A through F. These systems are designed as *large scale repositories*
and therefore can be expected to perform well at handling large amounts of
data. In the sequel, we will refer to these systems also as *mass storage systems*.
Some of the systems, namely A to C, are based on relational technology, come
with a cost-based query optimizer and allow the kind of hand-optimization
and hints as the relational product. While A and B do not require the user to
provide a mapping for physical data breakdown, System C reads in a DTD
and lets the user generate an optimized database schema. Systems D to F are
main-memory based and only come with heuristic optimizers; however, they
also allow rewriting the queries by hand if necessary.

A note on the analysis. Some systems provided us with the opportunity
to look at query execution in detail, i.e., find out how much time is spent for
query optimization, metadata access or during I/O wait; others only allowed a
black-box analysis augmented with the usual monitoring tools that operating
systems provide. The tools to run the benchmark document have been made
available on the project Web site [269]. They include the data generator and
the query set along with a mapping tool to convert the benchmark document
into a flat file that may be bulk-loaded into a (relational) DBMS; a variety of
formats are available.

All queries were run on machines equipped with 550 MHz Pentium III processors, SCSI Ultra2 harddisks and 1 GB of main memory; operating systems
were Windows 2000 Advanced Server and Linux 2.4 respectively depending
on what the packages required. Although the systems were all equipped with
at least two processors, only one processor was used during bulk load and
query execution.

Table 18.1. Database sizes

System	Size	Bulkload time
A	241 MB	414 s
B	280 MB	781 s
C	238 MB	548 s
D	142 MB	50 s
E	302 MB	96 s
F	345 MB	215 s

Concerning the scaling factor, all mass storage systems were able to process
the queries at scaling factor 1.0. Note that it took the XML parser expat [108]
4.9 seconds (user time on the above Linux machine including system time
and disk I/O) to scan the benchmark document (this time only includes the
tokenization of the input stream and normalizations and substitutions as required by the XML standard and no user-specified semantic actions). The

bulkload times are summarized in Table 18.1: they range from 50 seconds to 781 seconds. They are completed transactions and include the conversion effort needed to map the XML document to a database instance. Note that System C requires a DTD to derive a database schema; the time for this derivation is not included in the figure, but is negligible anyway. The resulting database sizes are also listed in Table 18.1; we remark that some systems which are not included in this comparison require far larger database sizes.

Table 18.2. Performance in ms of some queries

	System A	System B	System C	System D	System E	System F
Q 1	689	784	257	120	1597	2814
Q 2	3171	1971	707	2900	4659	7481
Q 3	41030	6389	1942	3900	4630	8074
Q 5	259	221	237	160	246	204
Q 6	293	331	509	10	336	508
Q 7	719	741	1520	10	287	2845
Q 8	1684	1466	667	470	3849	9143
Q 9	3530	10189	92534	980	5994	13698
Q 10	3414285	86886	1568	22000	54721	69422
Q 11	205675	2551760	2533738	8700	602223	741730
Q 12	126127	965118	976026	7500	268644	270577
Q 17	1008	1117	240	250	2103	3598
Q 20	821	939	1254	620	1065	1759

We now turn our attention to the running times and statistics as displayed in Table 18.2 and present some insights. Since we do not have the space to discuss all timings and experiments in detail, we only present a selection. In most physical XML mappings found in the literature, Query Q1 [269] consists of a table scan or index lookup and a small number of additional table lookups. It is mainly supposed to establish a performance baseline: At scaling factor 1.0, the scan goes over 10000 tuples and is followed by two table lookups if a mapping like [271] is used.

Table 18.3. Detailed timings of Q1 and Q2 for Systems A, B, C

Query	System	Compilation CPU	Compilation total	Execution CPU	Execution total
Q 1	A	16%	25%	31%	75%
	B	13%	51%	30%	49%
	C	0%	29%	20%	71%
Q 2	A	9%	13%	41%	87%
	B	12%	20%	65%	80%
	C	3%	16%	77%	84%

Queries Q2 and Q3 are the first ones to provide surprises. It turns out that the parts of the query plans that compute the indices are quite complex TPC/H-like aggregations: they require the computation of set-valued attributes to determine the bidder element with the least index with respect to the open auction ancestor. Therefore the complexity of the query plan is higher than the rather innocent looking XQuery representation [269] of the queries might suggest. Consequently, running times are quite high. Although System A was able to find an execution plan for Q3 which was as good as that of the other systems, it spent too much of its time on optimization. Table 18.3 displays some interesting characteristics of Q1 and Q2 that can be traced back to the physical mappings the systems use. System A basically stores all XML data on one big heap, i.e., only a single relation. System B on the other hand uses a highly fragmenting mapping. Consequently, System A has to access fewer metadata to compile a query than System B, thus spending only half as much time on query compilation (including optimization) as System B. However, this comes at a cost. Because the data mapping deployed in System A has less explicit semantics, the actual cost of accessing the real data is higher than in System B (75% vs 49%). System C as mentioned needs a DTD to derive a storage schema; this additional information helps to get favorable performance. Still in Table 18.3, we also find the detailed execution times for Q2. They show that mappings that structure the data according to their semantics can achieve significantly higher CPU usage (compare 77% of System C and 65% of System B vs System A's 41%). We remark that System C also uses a data mapping in the spirit of [279] that results in comparatively simple and efficient execution plans and thus outperforms all other systems for Q2 and Q3.

Query Q5 tries to quantify the cost of casting or type-coercion operations such as those necessary for the comparisons in Q3. For all mass-storage systems, the cost of this coercion is rather low with respect to the relative complexity of Q3's query execution plan and given the execution times of Q5. In any case, Q5 does not exhibit great differences in execution times. We note that all character data in the original document, including references, were stored as strings and cast at runtime to richer data types whenever necessary as in Queries 3, 5, 11, 12, 18, 20. We did not apply any domain-specific knowledge; neither did the systems use schema information nor pre-calculation or caching of casting results.

Regular path expressions are the challenge presented by queries Q6 and Q7. System D keeps a detailed structural summary of the database and can exploit it to optimize traversal-intensive queries; this actually makes Q6 and Q7 surprisingly fast. However, on systems without access to structural summaries, which effectively play the role of an index or schema, these queries often are significantly more expensive to execute. The problem that Q7 actually looks for non-existing paths is efficiently solved by exploiting the structural summary in the case of System D. For some systems, the cost of accessing schema information was very high and dominated query performance.

Queries Q8 and Q9 are usually implemented as joins. In the systems that we could analyze in detail, chasing the references basically amounted to executing equi-joins on strings. We were surprised that Q8 and Q9 were relatively cheap in comparison to Q2 and Q3 since we would have deemed the individual elements similarly expensive. For Q9, System C was not able to find a good execution plan in acceptable time. Apart from that anomaly, the implementation of the executed join algorithms seemed to determine the performance.

The construction of complex query results is addressed in Q10. The path expressions and join expression used in the query are kept simple so that the bulk of the work lies in the construction of the answer set which amount to more than 10 MB of (unindented) XML text. Whereas Q10 produced massive amounts of output data, Q11 and Q12 test the ability to cope with large intermediate results by theta-joining potential buyers and items that might be of interest to them. The theta-join produces more than 12 million tuples. Q12 especially is also a challenge to the query optimizer to pick a good execution plan and allows insights into how the data volume influences query and output performance. For Systems B and C, the optimizer chose a sub-optimal execution plan. For Systems D through F we had to experiment with several hand-optimized execution plans.

Q17 again stresses the loose schema of many XML documents by querying for non-existing data. The query execution plan computes the intersection of two sets. The timings in Table 18.2 show a typical situation: although all systems are able to process the query in less than four seconds, there is still an order of magnitude of difference in the performance. The aggregations of Q20 conclude the query set with a combination of three table scans and a set difference. All systems show similar performance.

In some of the performance figures certain systems (particularly Systems A to C) show pathological running times (c.f., Table 18.2). This does not necessarily mean that the relevant systems are inferior to the others; we rather relied on the built-in query optimizers and did not at all change or reformulate queries by hand. This was to show that the benchmark queries indeed present reasonable challenges that *can* be solved even if not optimally. The analysis of the query translation and optimization process showed that search spaces for XML queries are often larger than necessary since, during the translation from XQuery to a lower-level algebra, information especially about path expressions is often lost. To improve on this, experimenting with new pruning strategies and extended low-level algebras to better capture query semantics might be a good starting point.

18.6 Conclusions

In this chapter we outlined the design of XMark, a benchmark to assess the performance of query processors for XML documents. Based on an internet auction site as an application scenario, XMark provides a suite of queries that have been carefully crafted to highlight individual performance critical aspects inherent to the querying of XML. As work on the benchmark started at an early stage in the development of XML query processors, the philosophy behind it evolved to keep up with its targets. Since its release XMark has been widely adopted by both research communities and industry.

19

The INEX Evaluation Initiative

Gabriella Kazai, Norbert Gövert, Mounia Lalmas, and Norbert Fuhr

19.1 Introduction

The widespread use of the extensible Markup Language (XML) on the Web and in Digital Libraries brought about an explosion in the development of XML tools, including systems to store and access XML content. As the number of these systems increases, so is the need to assess their benefit to users. The benefit to a given user depends largely on which aspects of the user's interaction with the system are being considered. These aspects, among others, include response time, required user effort, usability, and the system's ability to present the user with the desired information. Users then base their decision whether they are more satisfied with one system or another on a prioritised combination of these factors.

The Initiative for the Evaluation of XML Retrieval (INEX) was set up at the beginning of 2002 with the aim to establish an infrastructure and provide means, in the form of a large XML test collection and appropriate scoring methods, for the evaluation of content-oriented retrieval of XML documents. As a result of a collaborative effort, with contributions from 36 participating groups, INEX created an XML test collection consisting of publications of the IEEE Computer Society, 60 topics and graded relevance assessments. Using the constructed test collection and the developed set of evaluation metrics and procedures, the retrieval effectiveness of the participating organisations' XML retrieval approaches were evaluated and their results compared [126].

In this chapter we provide an overview of the INEX evaluation initiative. Before we talk about INEX, we first take a brief look, in Section 19.2, at the evaluation practices of information retrieval (IR) as these formed the basis of our work in INEX. In our discussion of INEX we follow the requirements that evaluations in IR are founded upon [264]. These include the specification of the evaluation objective (e.g. what to evaluate) in Section 19.3, and the selection of suitable evaluation criteria in Section 19.4. This is followed by an overview of the methodology for constructing the test collection in Section 19.5. We

H. Blanken et al. (Eds.): Intelligent Search on XML Data, LNCS 2818, pp. 279–293, 2003.

describe the evaluation metrics in Section 19.6. Finally we close with thoughts for future work in Section 19.8.

19.2 Approaches to Evaluation

Evaluation means assessing the value of a system or product. It plays an important part in the development of retrieval systems as it stimulates their improvement. We can distinguish between comparative or goal-based evaluation approaches depending on whether a system is compared against others or is evaluated with respect to a given objective. Furthermore, evaluations may consider the individual components of a system or assess the system as a whole.

The evaluation of IR systems usually follows the comparative approach and considers a system in its entirety. A wealth of evaluation studies and initiatives to IR exist today. They can be classified into system- and user-centred evaluations, and these are further divided into engineering (e.g. efficiency), input (e.g. coverage), processing (e.g. effectiveness), output (e.g. presentation), user (e.g. user effort) and social (e.g. impact) levels [264, 74]. Most work in IR evaluation has been on system-centred evaluations and, in particular, at the processing level. At this level, the aspects most commonly under investigation are retrieval efficiency (e.g. speed, required storage) and retrieval effectiveness, i.e. the system's ability to satisfy a user's information need. For document retrieval systems, this is usually translated to the more specific criterion of a system's ability to retrieve in response to a user request as many relevant documents and as few non-relevant documents as possible.

The predominant approach to evaluate a system's retrieval effectiveness is with the use of test collections constructed specifically for that purpose. A test collection usually consists of a set of documents, user requests (topics), and relevance assessments (i.e. the set of "right answers" for the user requests). There have been several large-scale evaluation projects, which resulted in established IR test collections [74, 258, 280]. One of the largest evaluation initiatives is the Text REtrieval Conference (TREC)[1], which every year since 1992, runs numerous tracks based on an increasingly diverse set of tasks that are to be performed on continually growing test collections [153, 309].

Besides a test collection, the evaluation of retrieval effectiveness also requires appropriate measures and metrics. A number of measures have been proposed over the years. The most commonly used are recall and precision. Recall corresponds to, in the above specification of effectiveness, to "a system's ability to retrieve as many relevant documents as possible", whereas precision pertains to "a system's ability to retrieve as few non-relevant documents as possible". Given *Retr* as the set of retrieved documents and *Rel* as the set of relevant documents in the collection, recall and precision are defined as follows:

---

[1] http://trec.nist.gov/

$$\text{recall} = \frac{|Rel \cap Retr|}{|Rel|} \qquad \text{precision} = \frac{|Rel \cap Retr|}{|Retr|} \qquad (19.1)$$

Several metrics have been developed in order to apply these set-based measures to (possibly weakly ordered) rankings of documents. A recall/precision graph is typically used as a combined evaluation measure for retrieval systems. Such a graph, given an arbitrary recall value, plots the corresponding precision value. Raghavan et al.'s method [245] is based on the interpretation of precision as the probability $P(Rel|Retr)$ that a document viewed by a user is relevant. Assuming that the user stops viewing the ranking after a given number of relevant documents NR, precision is given as:

$$P(Rel|Retr)(NR) := \frac{NR}{NR + esl_{NR}} = \frac{NR}{NR + j + s \cdot i/(r+1)} \qquad (19.2)$$

The expected search length, esl_{NR}, denotes the total number of non-relevant documents that are estimated to be retrieved until the NRth relevant document is retrieved [80]. Let l denote the rank from which the NRth relevant document is drawn. Then j is the number of non-relevant documents within the ranks before rank l, s is the number of relevant documents to be taken from rank l, and r and i are the number of relevant and non-relevant documents in rank l, respectively.

Raghavan et al. also gave theoretical justification, that intermediary real numbers can be used instead of simple recall points only (here, n is the total number of relevant documents with regard to the user request in the collection; $x \in [0,1]$ denotes an arbitrary recall value):

$$P(Rel|Retr)(x) := \frac{x \cdot n}{x \cdot n + esl_{x \cdot n}} = \frac{x \cdot n}{x \cdot n + j + s \cdot i/(r+1)} \qquad (19.3)$$

Based on this probabilistic interpretation of precision, recall/precision graphs can be established. Moreover, given that a system is to be evaluated with regard to multiple user requests, average precision can be calculated for a set of arbitrary recall points. Thus, a recall/precision graph defined for a set of multiple user requests can be defined.

Although IR research offers a wealth of evaluation measures, metrics and test collections, their application to the evaluation of content-oriented XML retrieval is limited due to the additional requirements introduced when the structure of XML documents is taken into account. This is illustrated by the retrieval paradigm implemented by XML retrieval systems, which, given a typical IR style information need, allows document components of varying granularity – instead of whole documents – to be returned to the user. Furthermore, users of XML retrieval systems are also able to issue queries that exploit the structure of the data and restrict the search to specific structural elements within an XML collection. Traditional IR test collections are therefore not suitable for evaluating the retrieval effectiveness of content-oriented XML retrieval as they base their evaluation on the following implicit assumptions about the documents and the behaviour of users:

1. The relevance of one document is assumed to be independent of the relevance of any other documents in the collection.
2. A document is regarded as a well-distinguishable (separate) unit representing a retrievable entity.
3. Documents are considered as units of (approximately) equal size.
4. Given a ranked output list, the supposed user behaviour is that users look at one document after another and then stop at an arbitrary point. Thus, non-linear forms of output (e.g. sub-lists in Google) are not considered.

For content-oriented XML document retrieval, most of these assumptions do not hold and have to be revised:

1. Since arbitrary components of a document can be retrieved, multiple components from the same document can hardly be viewed as independent units.
2. XML documents consist of nested structures where document components of varying granularity may be retrieved, which cannot always be regarded as separate units.
3. The size of the retrieved components cannot be considered even approximately equal, but may vary from elements such as author names or paragraphs to complete documents or books.
4. When multiple components from the same document are retrieved, a linear ordering of the result items may confuse the user as these components may be interspersed with components from other documents. To address this issue some systems cluster components from the same document together, resulting in non-linear outputs.

The above assumptions also bear influence on the applied measures and metrics. For example, when computing precision at certain ranks, it is implicitly assumed that a user spends a constant time per document. Based on the implicit definition of effectiveness as the ratio of output quality vs. user effort, quality is measured for a fixed amount of effort in this case. However, the appropriateness of such a measure becomes questionable when the retrieved components significantly vary in size. It is therefore necessary to develop new measures and procedures for the evaluation of content-oriented XML retrieval. These and related issues are addressed in INEX and are further examined in the next sections.

19.3 Evaluation Objective

We set the evaluation objective to be the assessment of a system's retrieval effectiveness, where we defined effectiveness as a measure of a system's ability to satisfy both content and structural requirements of a user's information need. Based on a document-centric view of XML, the above definition corresponds to the task of retrieving the most specific relevant document components, which are exhaustive to the topic of request [70].

The combination of content and structural aspects were also reflected in the task that was set to be performed by the participating groups: the ad-hoc retrieval of XML documents. In IR, ad-hoc retrieval is described as a simulation of how a library might be used, and it involves the searching of a static set of documents using a new set of topics [153]. While the principle is the same, for the evaluation of the ad-hoc retrieval of XML documents, we consider additional requirements brought upon by the extensive development and use of XML query languages. These query languages allow users to issue (directly or indirectly) complex queries that contain structural conditions. Consequently, the ability to service such queries must also be assessed by the evaluation process. On the other hand, content-oriented XML retrieval systems should also support queries that do not specify structural conditions as users are often not familiar with the exact structure of the XML documents. Taking this into account, we identified the following two types of user requests:

Content-and-structure (CAS) queries are requests that contain explicit references to the XML structure, either by restricting the context of interest or the context of certain search concepts.

Content-only (CO) queries ignore the document structure and are, in a sense, the traditional topics used in IR test collections. Their resemblance to traditional IR queries is, however, only in their appearance. They pose a challenge to XML retrieval in that the retrieval results to such queries can be elements of various complexity, e.g. at different levels of the XML documents' hierarchy.

Based on these two types of queries, we essentially defined two sub-tasks within the ad-hoc retrieval of XML documents. According to the latter sub-task (using CO queries), effectiveness is measured as a system's ability to retrieve the most specific relevant document components, which are exhaustive to the topic of request. However, according to the sub-task based on CAS queries, a system's effectiveness is measured by its ability to retrieve the most specific relevant document components, which are exhaustive to the topic of request and also match the structural constraints specified in the query.

19.4 Evaluation Criteria

Traditional IR experiments designate relevance as a criterion for evaluating retrieval effectiveness. In INEX, retrieval effectiveness measures a combination of content and structural requirements. Relevance therefore is no longer sufficient as a single evaluation criterion, but has to be complemented with another dimension in order to allow reasoning about the structure. We chose the following two criteria:

Topical relevance, which is primarily a content related criterion. It reflects the extent to which the information contained in a document component satisfies the user's information need, e.g. measures the exhaustivity of the topic within a component.

Component coverage, which is a criterion that considers the structural aspects and reflects the extent to which a document component is focused on the information need, e.g. measures the specificity of a component with regards to the topic.

The basic threshold for relevance was defined as a piece of text that mentions the topic of request [153]. A consequence of this definition is that container components of relevant document components in a nested XML structure, albeit too large components, are also regarded as relevant. This clearly shows that relevance as a single criterion is not sufficient for the evaluation of content-oriented XML retrieval. Hence, the second dimension, component coverage, is used to provide a measure with respect to the size of a component by reflecting the ratio of relevant and irrelevant content within a document component. In actual fact, both dimensions are related to component size. For example, the more exhaustively a topic is discussed the more likely that the component is longer in length, and the more focused a component the more likely that it is smaller in size.

When considering the use of the above two criteria for the evaluation of XML retrieval systems, we must also decide about the scales of measurements to be used. For relevance, binary or multiple degree scales are known. In INEX, we chose a multiple degree relevance scale as it allows the explicit representation of how exhaustively a topic is discussed within a component with respect to its sub-components. For example, a section containing two paragraphs may be regarded more relevant than either of its paragraphs by themselves. Binary values of relevance cannot reflect this difference. We adopted the following four-point relevance scale [185]:

Irrelevant (0): The document component does not contain any information about the topic of request.

Marginally relevant (1): The document component mentions the topic of request, but only in passing.

Fairly relevant (2): The document component contains more information than the topic description, but this information is not exhaustive. In the case of multi-faceted topics, only some of the sub-themes or viewpoints are discussed.

Highly relevant (3): The document component discusses the topic of request exhaustively. In the case of multi-faceted topics, all or most sub-themes or viewpoints are discussed.

For component coverage we used the following four-category nominal scale:

No coverage (N): The topic or an aspect of the topic is not a theme of the document component.

Too large (L): The topic or an aspect of the topic is only a minor theme of the document component.

Too small (S): The topic or an aspect of the topic is the main or only theme of the document component, but the component is too small to act as a meaningful unit of information when retrieved by itself.

Exact coverage (E): The topic or an aspect of the topic is the main or only theme of the document component, and the component acts as a meaningful unit of information when retrieved by itself.

According to the above definition of coverage it becomes possible to reward XML search engines that are able to retrieve the appropriate ("exact") sized document components. For example, a retrieval system that is able to locate the only relevant section in an encyclopaedia is likely to trigger higher user satisfaction than one that returns a too large component, such as the whole encyclopaedia. On the other hand, the above definition also allows the classification of components as too small if they do not bear self-explaining information for the user and thus cannot serve as informative units [70]. Take as an example, a small text fragment, such as the sentence "These results clearly show the advantages of content-oriented XML retrieval systems.", which, although part of a relevant section in a scientific report, is of no use to a user when retrieved without its context.

Only the combination of these two criteria allows the evaluation of systems that are able to retrieve components with high relevance and exact coverage, e.g. components that are exhaustive to and highly focused on the topic of request and hence represent the most appropriate components to be returned to the user.

19.5 Methodology for Constructing the Test Collection

The aim of a test collection construction methodology is to derive a set of queries and relevance assessments for a given document collection. The methodology for constructing a test collection for XML retrieval, although similar to that used for building traditional IR test collections, has additional requirements [184]. The following sections detail the processes involved and describe the resulting test collection.

19.5.1 Documents

The document collection consists of the fulltexts of 12 107 articles from 12 magazines and 6 transactions of the IEEE Computer Society's publications, covering the period of 1995–2002, and totalling 494 megabytes in size. Although the collection is relatively small compared with TREC, it has a suitably complex XML structure (192 different content models in DTD) and contains scientific articles of varying length. On average, an article contains 1 532 XML nodes, where the average depth of a node is 6.9.

All documents of the collection are tagged using XML conforming to one common DTD. The overall structure of a typical article, shown in Figure 19.1, consists of a *front matter* (`<fm>`), a *body* (`<bdy>`), and a *back matter* (`<bm>`). The front matter contains the article's metadata, such as title, author, publication information, and abstract. Following it is the article's body, which contains the content. The body is structured into sections (`<sec>`), sub-sections (`<ss1>`), and sub-sub-sections (`<ss2>`). These logical units start with a title, followed by a number of paragraphs. In addition, the content has markup for references (citations, tables, figures), item lists, and layout (such as emphasised and bold faced text), etc. The back matter contains a bibliography and further information about the article's authors.

```
<article>                           <sec>
  <fm>                                <st>...</st>
                                      ...
    ...                               <ss1>...</ss1>
    <ti>IEEE Transactions on ...</ti> <ss1>...</ss1>
    <atl>Construction of ...</atl>    ...
    <au>                            </sec>
      <fnm>John</fnm>                ...
      <snm>Smith</snm>            </bdy>
      <aff>University of ...</aff> <bm>
    </au>                           <bib>
    <au>...</au>                      <bb>
    ...                                 <au>...</au>
  </fm>                                 <ti>...</ti>
  <bdy>                                 ...
    <sec>                             </bb>
      <st>Introduction</st>           ...
      <p>...</p>                     </bib>
      ...                           </bm>
    </sec>                        </article>
```

Fig. 19.1. Sketch of the structure of the typical INEX articles

19.5.2 Topics

The topics of the test collection were created by the participating groups. We asked each organisation to create sets of content-only (CO), and content-and-structure (CAS) candidate topics that were representative of what real users might ask and the type of the service that operational systems may provide. Participants were provided with guidelines to assist them in this four-stage task [126].

During the first stage participants created an initial description of their information need without regard to system capabilities or collection peculiarities. During the collection exploration stage, using their own XML retrieval engines, participants evaluated their candidate topics against the document collection. Based on the retrieval results they then estimated the number of relevant components to the candidate topics. Finally, in the topic refinement stage the components of a topic were finalised ensuring coherency and that each component could be used in the experiments in a stand-alone fashion (e.g. retrieval using only the topic title or description).

After completion of the first three stages, the candidate topics were submitted to INEX. A total of 143 candidate topics were received, of which 60 (30 CAS and 30 CO) topics were selected into the final set. The selection was based on the combination of different criteria, such as including equal number of CO and CAS topics, having topics that are representative of IR, database (DB) and XML-specific search situations, balancing the load across participants for relevance assessments, eliminating topics that were considered too ambiguous or too difficult to judge, and selecting topics with at least 2, but no more than 20 relevant items in the top 25 retrieved components.

Figures 19.2 and 19.3 show examples for both types of topics. As it can be seen, the four main parts of an INEX topic are the topic title, topic description, narrative and keywords. The topic title serves as a summary of both content and structure related requirements of a user's information need. It usually consists of a number of keywords that best describe what the user is looking for. It also allows, for CAS topics, the definition of containment conditions and target elements. Using containment conditions users can query with respect to the subject areas of specific components, for example, they can request that the abstract section of an article should highlight the "advantages of content-oriented XML retrieval". Target elements allow the specification of components that should be returned to the user. For example, the CAS topic shown in Figure 19.2 defines article titles as the target elements: <te>article//tig</te>. The containment condition, <cw>QBIC</cw><ce>bibl</ce>, specifies that the article's bibliogaphy component should cite the QBIC system. The single content condition of <cw>image retrieval</cw> expresses the user's interest in the area of image retrieval where no restrictions are placed upon the XML element that this concept should be a subject of. The topic title of the CO topic in Figure 19.3, on the other hand, consists only of <cw> components as, by definition, CO topics do not specify constraints over the structure of the result elements.

The topic description is a one- or two-sentence natural language definition of the information need. The narrative is a detailed explanation of the topic statement and a description of what makes a document/component relevant or not. The keywords component of a topic was added as a means to keep a record of the list of search terms used for retrieval during topic development.

Table 19.1 shows some statistics on the final set of INEX topics. We classified the target and context elements of the final 30 CAS topics based on their content type, e.g. components that contain facts, such as author or title information, or content, such as the text of an article or of a part of an article. Looking at the 25 CAS topics that specified target elements, we can see

```
<INEX-Topic topic-id="05" query-type="CAS">
  <Title>
    <te>article//tig</te>
    <cw>QBIC</cw>  <ce>bibl</ce>
    <cw>image retrieval</cw>
  </Title>
  <Description>
    Retrieve the title from all articles which deal with image
    retrieval and cite the image retrieval system QBIC.
  </Description>
  <Narrative>
    To be relevant a document should deal with image retrieval and also
    should contain (at least) one bibliographic reference to the
    retrieval system QBIC.
  </Narrative>
  <Keywords>
    QBIC, IBM, image, video, content query, retrieval system
  </Keywords>
</INEX-Topic>
```

Fig. 19.2. A CAS topic from the INEX test collection

```
<INEX-Topic topic-id="45" query-type="CO">
  <Title>
    <cw>augmented reality and medicine</cw>
  </Title>
  <Description>
    How virtual (or augmented) reality can contribute to improve the
    medical and surgical practice.
  </Description>
  <Narrative>
    In order to be considered relevant, a document/component must
    include considerations about applications of computer graphics and
    especially augmented (or virtual) reality to medicine (including
    surgery).
  </Narrative>
  <Keywords>
    augmented virtual reality medicine surgery improve computer
    assisted aided image
  </Keywords>
</INEX-Topic>
```

Fig. 19.3. A CO topic from the INEX test collection

that more than half requested facts to be returned to the user. Furthermore,
the majority of the CAS topics contained either only fact, or a mixture of

fact and content containment conditions, e.g. specifying the publication year and/or the author, or specifying the author and the subject of some document components.

Table 19.1. Statistics on CAS and CO topics in the INEX test collection

	CAS	CO
no of topics	30	30
avg no of `<cw>`/topic title	2.06	1.0
avg no of unique words/cw	2.5	4.3
avg no of unique words/topic title	5.1	4.3
avg no of `<ce>`/topic title	1.63	–
avg no of XML elements/`<ce>`	1.53	–
avg no of XML elements/topic title	2.5	–
no of topics with `<ce>` representing a fact	12	–
no of topics with `<ce>` representing content	6	–
no of topics with mixed fact and content `<ce>`	12	–
no of topics with `<te>` components	25	0
avg no of XML elements/`<te>`	1.68	–
no of topics with `<te>` representing a fact	13	–
no of topics with `<te>` representing content	12	–
no of topics with `<te>` representing articles	6	–
avg no of words in topic description	18.8	16.1
avg no of words in keywords component	7.06	8.7

19.5.3 Assessments

The final set of topics were distributed back to the participating groups, who then used these topics to search the document collection. The actual queries put to the search engines had to be automatically generated from any part of the topics except the narrative. As a result of the retrieval sessions, the participating organisations produced ranked lists of XML elements in answer to each query. The top 100 result elements from all sixty sets of ranked lists (one per topic) consisted the results of one retrieval run. Each group was allowed to submit up to three runs. A result element in a retrieval run was identified using a combination of file names and XPaths. The file name (and file path) uniquely identified an article within the document collection, and XPath allowed the location of a given node within the XML tree of the article. Associated with a result element were its retrieval rank and/or its relevance status value [126].

A total of 51 runs were submitted from 25 groups. For each topic, the results from the submissions were merged to form the pool for assessment [309]. The assessment pools contained between one to two thousand document components from 300–900 articles, depending on the topic. The result elements varied from author, title and paragraph elements through sub-section and section elements to complete articles and even journals. The assessment pools were then assigned to groups for assessment; either to the original topic authors or when this was not possible, on a voluntary basis, to groups with expertise in the topic's subject area.

The assessments were done along the two dimensions of topical relevance and component coverage. Assessments were recorded using an on-line assessment system, which allowed users to view the pooled result set of a given topic listed in alphabetical order, to browse the document collection and view articles and result elements both in XML (i.e. showing the tags) and document view (i.e. formatted for ease of reading). Other features included facilities such as keyword highlighting, and consistency checking of the assessments [126].

Table 19.2 shows a summary of the collected assessments for CAS and CO topics[2]. The table shows a relatively large proportion of sub-components with exact coverage compared with article elements, which indicates that for most topics sub-components of articles were considered as the preferred units to be returned to the user.

Table 19.2. Assessments at article and component levels

Rel+	CAS topics		CO topics	
Cov	article level	sub-components	article level	sub-components
3E	187	2 304	309	1 087
2E	59	1 128	165	1 107
1E	82	1 770	114	827
3L	173	424	394	1 145
2L	137	507	599	2 295
1L	236	719	854	2 708
2S	21	846	118	3 825
1S	54	1 119	116	3 156
All	949	8 817	2 669	16 150

---

[2] The figures are based on the assessments of 54 of the 60 topics; for the remaining six topics no assessments are available.

19.6 Evaluation Metrics

Due to the nature of XML retrieval, it was necessary to develop new evaluation procedures. These were based on the traditional recall/precision and, in particular, the metrics described in Section 19.2. However, before we could apply these measures, we first had to derive a single relevance value based on the two dimensions of topical relevance and component coverage. For this purpose we defined a number of quantisation functions, $\mathbf{f}_{quant}$:

$$\begin{aligned} \mathbf{f}_{quant} : Relevance \times Coverage &\rightarrow [0, 1] \\ (rel, cov) &\mapsto \mathbf{f}_{quant}(rel, cov) \end{aligned} \tag{19.4}$$

Here, the set of relevance assessments is $Relevance := \{0, 1, 2, 3\}$, and the set of coverage assessments is $Coverage := \{N, S, L, E\}$.

The rational behind such a quantisation function is that overall relevance of a document component can only be determined using the combination of relevance and coverage assessments. Quantisation functions can be selected according to the desired user standpoint. For INEX 2002, two different functions have been selected: $\mathbf{f}_{strict}$ and $\mathbf{f}_{generalised}$. The quantisation function $\mathbf{f}_{strict}$ is used to evaluate whether a given retrieval method is capable of retrieving highly relevant and highly focused document components:

$$\mathbf{f}_{strict}(rel, cov) := \begin{cases} 1 & \text{if } rel = 3 \text{ and } cov = \text{E}, \\ 0 & \text{else} \end{cases} \tag{19.5}$$

Other functions can be based on the different possible combinations of relevance degrees and coverage categories, such as $\mathbf{f}_{quant}(rel, cov) = 1$ if $rel > 1$ and $cov = \text{E}$. In order to credit document components according to their *degree of* relevance (generalised recall/precision), the quantisation function $\mathbf{f}_{generalised}$ is used:

$$\mathbf{f}_{generalised}(rel, cov) := \begin{cases} 1.00 & \text{if } (rel, cov) = 3\text{E}, \\ 0.75 & \text{if } (rel, cov) \in \{2\text{E}, 3\text{L}\}, \\ 0.50 & \text{if } (rel, cov) \in \{1\text{E}, 2\text{L}, 2\text{S}\}, \\ 0.25 & \text{if } (rel, cov) \in \{1\text{S}, 1\text{L}\}, \\ 0.00 & \text{if } (rel, cov) = 0\text{N} \end{cases} \tag{19.6}$$

Given this type of quantisation, each document component in a result ranking is assigned a single relevance value. In INEX 2002, overlaps of document components in rankings were ignored, thus Raghavan et al.'s evaluation procedure could be applied directly to the results of the quantisation function. To apply Equation 19.3 for $\mathbf{f}_{generalised}$ the variables n, j, i, r, and s are interpreted as expectations. For example, given a function assessment(c), which yields the relevance/coverage assessment for a given document component c, the number n of relevant components with respect to a given topic is computed as:

$$n = \sum_{c \in components} \mathbf{f}_{generalised}(\text{assessment}(c)) \tag{19.7}$$

Expectations for the other variables are computed respectively.

19.7 Participating Organisations

25 organisations from 12 countries on four continents submitted retrieval runs in INEX 2002[3]. Due to the diversity in the background of the participating groups a wide range of different approaches to XML retrieval were represented. We tried to classify these using the following three categories:

IR-oriented: Research groups that focus on the extension of a specific type of IR model (e.g. vector space, rule-based, logistic regression), which they have applied to standard IR test collections in the past, to deal with XML documents. 15 groups belonged to this category.

DB-oriented: Groups that are working on extending database management systems to deal with semistructured data; most of these groups also incorporate uncertainty weights, thus producing ranked results. 2 groups followed this approach.

XML-specific: Groups that, instead of aiming to extend existing approaches towards XML, developed models and systems specifically for XML. Although these groups have very different backgrounds they usually base their work on XML standards (like XSL, XPath or XQuery). 3 groups were classified under this category.

Table 19.3 lists the participants and the categories of retrieval approaches taken. Some of the approaches are described in detail within other chapters of this volume, i.e. Chapter 4 (Universität Dortmund / Universität Duisburg-Essen), Chapter 6 (ETH Zurich), Chapter 7 (University of Twente).

19.8 Conclusions

As a collaborative effort of research groups from 36 organisations worldwide, the INEX evaluation initiative in 2002 created an infrastructure for evaluating the effectiveness of content-oriented retrieval of XML documents. A document collection with real life XML documents from the IEEE Computer Society's digital library has been set up, 60 topics created and assessments provided for 54 of these topics. Based on the notion of recall and precision, metrics for evaluating the effectiveness of XML retrieval have also been developed. These were applied to evaluate the submitted retrieval runs of the participating groups.

---

[3] Another 11 organisations (not listed here) participated actively in the relevance assessment phase

Table 19.3. List of INEX 2002 participants

Organisation	Retrieval approach
Centrum voor Wiskunde en Informatica (CWI)	DB+IR
CSIRO Mathematical and Information Sciences	IR
doctronic GmbH	IR+XML
Electronics and Telecommunications Research Institute (ETRI)	DB+XML
ETH Zurich	DB+IR
IBM Haifa Labs	IR
Institut de Recherche en Informatique de Toulouse (IRIT)	IR
Nara Institute of Science and Technology	IR
Queen Mary University of London	IR
Queensland University of Technology	IR+XML
Royal School of Library and Information Science	other
Salzburg Research Forschungsgesellschaft	IR
Sejong Cyber University	XML
Tarragon Consulting Corporation	IR
Universitt Bayreuth	DB
Universitt Dortmund / Universitt Duisburg-Essen	IR
Universit Pierre et Marie Curie	IR+XML
University of Amsterdam	IR
University of California, Berkeley	IR
University of California, Los Angeles	
University of Melbourne	IR
University of Michigan	DB+XML
University of Minnesota Duluth	IR
University of North Carolina at Chapel Hill	IR
University of Twente	DB

In the second round of INEX, commencing from April 2003, we aim to extend the test collection and develop alternative evaluation measures and metrics addressing the issue of overlapping result elements. We are also working on a new topic format, which will allow the representation of vague structural conditions. In the long term future of INEX we aim to extend the range of tasks under investigation to include, in particular, interactive retrieval, which will be based on new evaluation criteria reflecting typical user interaction with structured documents.

References

1. S. Abiteboul. Querying Semi-Structured Data. In *Proceedings of the International Conference on Database Theory (ICDT)*, pages 1–18, 1997.
2. S. Abiteboul. On views and XML. In *Proceedings of the Eighteenth ACM SIGACT-SIGMOD-SIGART Symposium on Principles of Database Systems, May 31 - June 2, 1999, Philadelphia, Pennsylvania*, pages 1–9. ACM Press, 1999.
3. S. Abiteboul, P. Buneman, and D. Suciu. *Data on the Web – From Relations to Semistructured Data and XML*. Morgan Kaufmann Publishers, 2000.
4. S. Abiteboul, D. Quass, J. McHugh, J. Widom, and J. Wiener. The Lorel query language for semistructured data. *International Journal on Digital Libraries*, 1(1):68–88, May 1997.
5. A. Aboulnaga, A. Alameldeen, and J. Naughton. Estimating the selectivity of XML path expressions for Internet scale applications. In Apers et al. [14], pages 591–600.
6. E. Agirre and G. Rigau. Word sense disambiguation using conceptual density. In *Proceedings of the 16th International Conference on Computational Linguistics, Copenhagen, Denmark*, pages 16–22, 1996.
7. R. Agrawal, K. Dittrich, and A. H. Ngu, editors. *Proceedings of the 18th International Conference on Data Engineering (ICDE), February 26-March 1, 2002, San Jose, California*. IEEE Computer Society, 2002.
8. L. Ahmedi and G. Lausen. Ontology-based querying of linked XML documents. In *Proceedings of the Semantic Web Workshop (SemWeb) at the 11th International World Wide Web Conference (WWW), May 7-11, 2002, Honolulu, Hawaii, USA*, 2002.
9. G. Amato, D. Castelli, and S. Pisani. A metadata model for historical documentary films. In J. L. Borbinha and T. Baker, editors, *Proc. of the 4th European Conference ECDL*, pages 328–331. Springer, 2000.
10. S. Amer-Yahia and P. Case. XQuery and XPath full-text use cases. W3C working draft 14 february 2003, World Wide Web Consortium, Feb. 2003. http://www.w3.org/TR/xmlquery-full-text-use-cases.
11. L. Amsaleg, M. J. Franklin, and A. Tomasic. Dynamic query operator scheduling for wide-area remote access. *Distributed and Parallel Databases*, 6(3):217–246, 1998.

12. Anders Berlund, Scott Boag, Don Chamberlin, Mary F. Fernandez, Michael Kay, Jonathan Robie and Jrme Simon (Eds.). W3c working draft XML path language (XPath) 2.0. W3C Recommendation, http://www.w3.org/TR/xpath20, 2003.

13. T. Anderson, A. Berre, M. Mallison, H. Porter, and B. Schneider. The Hyper-Model Benchmark. In *Proc. of the Int. Conf. on Extending Database Technology*, volume 416 of *Lecture Notes in Computer Science*, pages 317–331, 1990.

14. P. M. G. Apers, P. Atzeni, S. Ceri, S. Paraboschi, K. Ramamohanarao, and R. T. Snodgrass, editors. *VLDB 2001, Proceedings of 27th International Conference on Very Large Data Bases, September 11-14, 2001, Roma, Italy*. Morgan Kaufmann, 2001.

15. E. Appelt and D. Israel. Introduction to Information Extraction Technology. A Tutorial Prepared for IJCAI 1999, 1999. http://www.ai.mit.edu/people/jimmylin/papers/intro-to-ie.pdf.

16. M. P. Atkinson, M. E. Orlowska, P. Valduriez, S. B. Zdonik, and M. L. Brodie, editors. *VLDB'99, Proceedings of 25th International Conference on Very Large Data Bases, September 7-10, 1999, Edinburgh, Scotland, UK*. Morgan Kaufmann, 1999.

17. R. A. Baeza-Yates and G. Navarro. Integrating contents and structure in text retrieval. *SIGMOD Record*, 25(1):67–79, 1996.

18. R. A. Baeza Yates and G. Navarro. XQL and Proximal Nodes. *Journal of the American Society of Information Systems and Technology*, 53(6):504–514, 2002.

19. R. A. Baeza-Yates and B. Riberto-Neto, editors. *Modern Information Retrieval*. Addison Wesley, 1999.

20. C. F. Baker, C. J. Fillmore, and J. B. Lowe. The Berkeley FrameNet project. In *Proceedings of the 36th Annual Meeting of the Association for Computational Linguistics and the 17th International Conference on Computational Linguistics (COLIN-ACL), August 10-14, 1998, Montreal, Quebec, Canada*, pages 86–90. ACL / Morgan Kaufmann Publishers, 1998.

21. Z. Bar-Yossef, Y. Kanza, Y. Kogan, W. Nutt, and Y. Sagiv. Querying semantically tagged documents on the WWW. In R. Y. Pinter and S. Tsur, editors, *Next Generation Information Technologies and Systems, 4th International Workshop, NGITS'99, Zikhron-Yaakov, Israel, July 5-7, 1999 Proceedings*, volume 1649 of *Lecture Notes in Computer Science*, pages 2–19. Springer, 1999.

22. Y. Batterywala and S. Chakrabarti. Mining themes from bookmarks. In *ACM SIGKDD Workshop on Text Mining*, 2000.

23. R. Baumgartner, S. Flesca, and G. Gottlob. Supervised wrapper generation with lixto. In Apers et al. [14], pages 715–716.

24. C. Beeri and Y. Tzaban. Sal: An algebra for semistructured data and xml. In Cluet and Milo [76], pages 37–42.

25. N. J. Belkin, C. Cool, J. Koenemann, K. B. Ng, and S. Park. Using relevance feedback and ranking in interactive searching. In *Proceeding of the 4th Text Retrieval Conference (TREC-4)*, pages 181–210, Gaithersburg, Maryland, USA, Nov. 1995. National Institute of Standards and Technology (NIST).

26. N. J. Belkin, A. D. Narasimhalu, and P. Willet, editors. *Proceedings of the 20th Annual International ACM SIGIR Conference on Research and Development in Information Retrieval*, New York, 1997. ACM.

27. T. J. M. Bench-Capon and G. Malcolm. Formalising ontologies and their relations. In *Proceedings of the 10th International Conference on Database and Expert Systems Applications (DEXA)*, pages 250–259, 1999.

28. A. Berger and J. Lafferty. Information Retrieval as Statistical Translation. In Gey et al. [131].

29. A. Berglund, S. Boag, D. Chamberlin, M. F. Fernandez, M. Kay, J. Robie, and J. Siméon. XML Path Language (XPath) 2.0, Nov. 2002. http://www.w3.org/TR/xpath20/.

30. T. Berners-Lee, J. Hendler, and O. Lassila. The Semantic Web. *Scientific American*, May 2001.

31. P. V. Biron and A. Malhotra. XML Schema Part 2: Datatypes. W3C recommendation, World Wide Web Consortium, May 2001. http://www.w3.org/TR/xmlschema-2/.

32. H. E. Blok. *Database Optimization Aspects for Information Retrieval*. PhD thesis, University of Twente, Enschede, The Netherlands, Apr. 2002.

33. H. E. Blok, D. Hiemstra, R. S. Choenni, F. M. G. de Jong, H. M. Blanken, and P. M. G. Apers. Predicting the Cost-Quality Trade-off for Information Retrieval Queries: Facilitating Database Design and Query Optimization. In Paques et al. [237].

34. S. Boag, D. Chamberlin, M. F. Fernandez, D. Florescu, J. Robie, and J. Siméon. XQuery 1.0: An XML Query Language. W3c recommendation, World Wide Web Consortium, 2002. http://www.w3.org/TR/xquery.

35. P. Bohannon, J. Freire, P. Roy, and J. Siméon. From XML Schema to relations: A cost-based approach to XML storage. In Agrawal et al. [7], pages 64–75.

36. T. Böhme and E. Rahm. XMach-1: A Benchmark for XML Data Management. In A. Heuer, F. Leymann, and D. Priebe, editors, *Proceedings of BTW2001, March 7-9, Oldenburg, Germany*, pages 264–273, 2001.

37. P. Boncz. *Monet: a Next Generation Database Kernel for Query Intensive Applications*. PhD thesis, CWI, 2002.

38. P. A. Boncz and M. L. Kersten. MIL Primitives for Querying a Fragmented World. *The VLDB Journal*, 8(2):101–119, 1999.

39. P. A. Boncz, S. Manegold, and M. L. Kersten. Database Architecture Optimized for the New Bottleneck: Memory Access. In Atkinson et al. [16].

40. A. Bonifati and S. Ceri. Comparative Analysis of Five XML Query Languages. *ACM SIGMOD Record*, 29(1):68–79, 2000.

41. R. Bourett. XML Database Products. available at http://www.rpbourret.com/xml/XMLDatabaseProds.htm, 2000.

42. R. Bourret. XML and databases. http://www.rpbourret.com/xml/XMLAndDatabases.htm.

43. E. Bozsak et al. KAON: Towards a large scale Semantic Web. In K. Bauknecht, A. M. Tjoa, and G. Quirchmayr, editors, *E-Commerce and Web Technologies, Third International Conference, EC-Web 2002, Aix-en-Provence, France, September 2-6, 2002, Proceedings*, volume 2455 of *Lecture Notes in Computer Science*, pages 304–313. Springer, 2002.

44. N. Bradley. *The XML Companion*. Addison Wesley, 1998.

45. T. Bray, J. Paoli, C. M. Sperberg-McQueen, and E. Maler. Extensible Markup Language (XML) 1.0 (Second Edition). available at http://www.w3.org/TR/REC-xml, 2000.

46. J.-M. Bremer and M. Gertz. XQuery/IR: Integrating XML document and data retrieval. In M. F. Fernandez and Y. Papakonstantinou, editors, *Proceedings of the 5th International Workshop on the Web and Databases (WebDB)*, pages 1–6, June 2002.

47. S. Bressan, G. Dobbie, Z. Lacroix, M. Lee, Y. Li, and U. Nambiar. X007: Applying 007 Benchmark to XML Query Processing Tools. In Paques et al. [237], pages 167–174.

48. M. W. Bright, A. R. Hurson, and S. H. Pakzad. Automated resolution of semantic heterogeneity in multidatabases. *ACM Transactions on Database Systems*, 19(2):212–253, 1994.

49. S. Brin and L. Page. The anatomy of a large-scale hypertextual search engine. *Computer Networks and ISDN Systems*, 30(1–7):107–117, Apr. 1998.

50. I. Bruder, A. Düsterhöft, M. Becker, J. Bedersdorfer, and G. Neumann. GET-ESS: Constructing a linguistic search index for an Internet search engine. In *Proceedings of the 5th Conference of Applications of Natural Language to Data Bases (NLDB)*, pages 227–238, 2000.

51. N. Bruno, N. Koudas, and D. Srivastava. Holistic twig joins: Optimal XML pattern matching. In Franklin et al. [120], pages 310–321.

52. A. Budanitsky and G. Hirst. Semantic distance in WordNet: An experimental, application-oriented evaluation of five measures. In *Proceedings of the Workshop on WordNet and Other Lexical Resources, Second meeting of the North American Chapter of the Association for Computational Linguistics*, 2001.

53. P. Buneman, S. Davidson, G. Hillebrand, and D. Suciu. A Query Language and Optimization Techniques for Unstructured Data. In H. V. Jagadish and I. S. Mumick, editors, *Proceedings of the 1996 ACM SIGMOD International Conference on Management of Data, Montreal, Quebec, Canada, June 4-6, 1996*, pages 505–516. ACM Press, 1996.

54. P. Buneman, W. Fan, J. Siméon, and S. Weinstein. Constraints for semistructured data and XML. *SIGMOD Record*, 30(1):47–54, Mar. 2001.

55. P. Buneman, M. F. Fernandez, and D. Suciu. UnQL: A query language and algebra for semistructured data based on structural recursion. *VLDB Journal*, 9(1):76–110, 2000.

56. P. Buneman, L. Libkin, D. Suciu, V. Tannen, and L. Wong. Comprehension Syntax. In *SIGMOD Record*, 1994.

57. C. Burges. A tutorial on Support Vector Machines for pattern recognition. *Data Mining and Knowledge Discovery*, 2(2), 1998.

58. S. Buxton and M. Rys. XQuery and XPath Full-Text Requirements. W3C working draft 14 february 2003, World Wide Web Consortium, Feb. 2003. http://www.w3.org/TR/xmlquery-full-text-requirements/.

59. M. E. Califf. *Relational Learning Techniques for Natural Language Extraction*. PhD thesis, University of Texas at Austin, Aug. 1998.

60. M. Carey, D. DeWitt, and J. Naughton. The OO7 Benchmark. In P. Buneman and S. Jajodia, editors, *Proceedings of the 1993 ACM SIGMOD International Conference on Management of Data, Washington, D.C., May 26-28, 1993*, pages 12–21. ACM Press, 1993.

61. M. Carey, D. DeWitt, J. Naughton, M. Asgarian, P. Brown, J. Gehrke, and D. Shah. The BUCKY Object-Relational Benchmark. In J. Peckham, editor, *SIGMOD 1997, Proceedings ACM SIGMOD International Conference on Management of Data, May 13-15, 1997, Tucson, Arizona, USA*, pages 135–146. ACM Press, 1997.

62. R. Cattell and J. Skeen. Object Operations Benchmark. *ACM Transactions on Database Systems*, 17(1):1–31, 1992.
63. S. Chakrabarti. *Mining the Web*. Morgan Kaufmann Publishers, 2002.
64. S. Chakrabarti, M. v. d. Berg, and B. Dom. Focused crawling: A new approach to topic-specific Web resource discovery. In *8th WWW Conference*, 1999.
65. D. Chamberlin, P. Fankhauser, D. Florescu, M. Marchiori, and J. Robie. XML Query use cases. W3c working draft 15 november 2002, W3C, November 2002. available at `http://www.w3.org/TR/xmlquery-use-cases/`.
66. D. Chamberlin, J. Robie, and D. Florescu. Quilt: An XML query language for heterogeneous data sources. In Suciu and Vossen [289], pages 53–62.
67. S. Chaudhuri, R. Krishnamurthy, S. Potamianos, and K. Shim. Optimizing queries with materialized views. In P. S. Yu and A. L. P. Chen, editors, *Proceedings of the Eleventh International Conference on Data Engineering, March 6-10, 1995, Taipei, Taiwan*, pages 190–200. IEEE Computer Society, 1995.
68. H. Chen and S. Dumais. Bringing order to the Web: Automatically categorizing search results. *ACM CHI Conference on Human Factors in Computing Systems*, 2000.
69. J. Chen, D. J. DeWitt, and J. Naughton. Design and evaluation of alternative selection placement strategies in optimizing continuous queries. In Agrawal et al. [7], pages 345–356.
70. Y. Chiaramella, P. Mulhem, and F. Fourel. A model for multimedia information retrieval. Technical report, FERMI ESPRIT BRA 8134, University of Glasgow, Apr. 1996.
71. T. Chinenyanga and N. Kushmerik. Expressive Retrieval from XML documents. In W. Croft, D. Harper, D. Kraft, and J. Zobel, editors, *Proceedings of the 24th Annual International Conference on Research and development in Information Retrieval*, pages 163–171, New York, 2001. ACM.
72. C.-W. Chung, J.-K. Min, and K. Shim. APEX: An adaptive path index for XML data. In Franklin et al. [120], pages 121–132.
73. F. Ciravegna. Learning to tag information extraction from text. In R. G. Fabio Ciravegna, Roberto Basili, editor, *ECAI Workshop on Machine Learning for Information Extraction*, 2000.
74. C. Cleverdon, J. Mills, and E. Keen. Factors determining the performance of indexing systems, vol. 2: Test results. Technical report, Aslib Cranfield Research Project, Cranfield, England, 1966.
75. S. Cluet et al. Views in a large scale XML repository. In Apers et al. [14], pages 271–280.
76. S. Cluet and T. Milo, editors. *ACM SIGMOD Workshop on The Web and Databases (WebDB'99), June 3-4, 1999, Philadelphia, Pennsylvania, USA*. informal proceedings, 1999.
77. Cochrane database of systematic reviews. `http://www.update-software.com/cochrane`.
78. M. Consens and T. Milo. Algebras for Querying Text Regions. In *Proceedings of the ACM Conference on Principles of Distributed Systems*, pages 11–22, 1995.
79. B. Cooper, N. Sample, M. J. Franklin, G. R. Hjaltason, and M. Shadmon. A fast index for semistructured data. In Apers et al. [14], pages 341–350.
80. W. S. Cooper. Expected search length: A single measure of retrieval effectiveness based on weak ordering action of retrieval systems. *Journal of the American Society for Information Science*, 19:30–41, 1968.

81. T. H. Cormen, C. E. Leiserson, and R. L. Rivest. *Introduction to Algorithms.* MIT Press, 2nd edition, 2001.

82. V. Crescenzi, G. Mecca, and P. Merialdo. RoadRunner: Towards automatic data extraction from large web sites. In Apers et al. [14], pages 109–118.

83. A. Crespo, J. Jannink, E. Neuhold, M. Rys, and R. Studer. A survey of semi-automatic extraction and transformation. Technical report, Stanford University, 1994.

84. W. Croft, D. Harper, D. Kraft, and J. Zobel, editors. *Proceedings of the 24th Annual International Conference on Research and development in Information Retrieval,* New York, 2001. ACM.

85. E. Csuhaj-Varhú, J. Dassow, J. Kelemen, and G. Păun. *Grammar Systems: A Grammatical Approach to Distribution and Cooperation,* volume 5 of *Topics in computer mathematics.* Gordon and Breach Science Publishers, 1994.

86. H. Cunningham. Information extraction: a user guide (revised version). Technical report, University of Sheffield, 1999.

87. H. Cunningham, D. Maynard, K. Bontcheva, and V. Tablan. GATE: A framework and graphical development environment for robust NLP tools and applications. In *Proceedings of the 40th Anniversary Meeting of the Association for Computational Linguistics (ACL'02),* 2002.

88. Database of abstracts of reviews of effects. `http://nhscrd.york.ac.uk/darehp.htm`.

89. A. de Vries and A. Wilschut. On the Integration of IR and Databases. In *Database Issues in Multimedia; short paper proceedings, International Conference on Database Semantics (DS-8),* pages 16–31, Rotorua, New Zealand, January 1999.

90. A. P. de Vries. *Content and Multimedia Database Management Systems.* PhD thesis, University of Twente, Enschede, The Netherlands, Dec. 1999.

91. A. P. de Vries. Content Independence in Multimedia Databases. *Journal of the American Society for Information Science and Technology,* 52(11):954–960, September 2001.

92. S. Decker, M. Erdmann, D. Fensel, and R. Studer. Ontobroker: Ontology based access to distributed and semi-structured information. In *Database Semantics - Semantic Issues in Multimedia Systems, IFIP TC2/WG2.6 Eighth Working Conference on Database Semantics (DS-8), Rotorua, New Zealand, January 4-8, 1999,* volume 138 of *IFIP Conference Proceedings,* pages 351–369. Kluwer, 1998.

93. A. Del Bimbo. *Visual Information Retrieval.* Morgan Kaufmann Publishers, Inc., 1999.

94. A. Delis, C. Faloutsos, and S. Ghandeharizadeh, editors. *SIGMOD 1999, Proceedings ACM SIGMOD International Conference on Management of Data, June 1-3, 1999, Philadelphia, Pennsylvania, USA.* ACM Press, 1999.

95. S. DeRose, E. Maler, and D. Orchard. XML linking language (XLink), version 1.0. W3C recommendation, 2001. `http://www.w3.org/TR/xlink/`.

96. A. Deutsch, M. Fernández, D. Florescu, A. Levy, and D. Suciu. XML-QL: A Query Language for XML. In M. Marchiori, editor, *QL'98 – The Query Languages Workshop,* Dec. 1998.

97. A. Deutsch, M. F. Fernandez, and D. Suciu. Storing semistructured data with STORED. In Delis et al. [94], pages 431–442.

98. P. F. Dietz. Maintaining order in a linked list. In *Proceedings of STOC, 14th Annual ACM Symposium on Theory of Computing, May 1982, San Francisco, CA*, pages 122–127. ACM, 1982.

99. Digital imaging and communication in medicine. http://medical.nema.org.

100. Y. Ding. Seminar semantic web technologies. Innsbruck University, 2003.

101. Dublin Core Metadata Initiative. Available at http://dublincore.org/.

102. R. Duda, P. Hart, and D. Stork. *Pattern Classification*. Wiley, 2000.

103. S. Dumais and H. Chen. Hierarchical classification of Web content. In N. J. Belkin, P. Ingwersen, and M.-K. Leong, editors, *SIGIR 2000: Proceedings of the 23rd Annual International ACM SIGIR Conference on Research and Development in Information Retrieval, July 24-28, 2000, Athens, Greece*, pages 256–263. ACM, 2000.

104. DVB Consortium. Multimedia home platform 1.1, 2001. http://www.mhp.org.

105. D. Egnor and R. Lord. Structured Information Retrieval using XML. In *ACM SIGIR 2000 Workshop On XML and Information Retrieval*, Athens, Greece, July 2000.

106. Embase. http://www.embase.com.

107. Env 1828. medical informatics – structure for classification and coding of surgical procedures. Brussels: CEN 251, 1995.

108. J. C. et al. Expat XML Parser. available at http://sourceforge.net/projects/expat/, 2001.

109. European CHronicles On-line. Available at http://pc-erato2.iei.pi.cnr.it/echo//.

110. EuroSpider. The eurospider retrieval engine. http://www.eurospider.ch/.

111. D. C. Fallside. XML Schema Part 0: Primer. W3C recommendation, World Wide Web Consortium, May 2001. http://www.w3.org/TR/xmlschema-0/.

112. P. Fankhauser and Y. Xu. Markitup! An incremental approach to document structure recognition. *Electronic Publishing*, 6(4):447–456, 1993.

113. A. Farquhar, R. Fikes, and J. Rice. The Ontolingua server: a tool for collaborative ontology construction. Technical Report KSL-96-26, http://www-ksl-svc.stanford.edu:5915/project-papers.html, 1996.

114. C. Fellbaum, editor. *WordNet: An Electronic Lexical Database*. MIT Press, 1998.

115. M. Fernandez, A. Malhotra, J. Marsh, M. Nagy, and N. Walsh. XML Query Data Model. Technical Report W3C Working Draft, World Wide Web Consortium, Nov. 2002. http://www.w3.org/TR/query-datamodel.

116. D. Florescu and D. Kossmann. A Performance Evaluation of Alternative Mapping Schemes for Storing XML Data in a Relational Database. Technical Report 3680, INRIA, Rocquencourt, France, May 1999.

117. D. Florescu and D. Kossmann. Storing and Querying XML Data using an RDMBS. *IEEE Data Engineering Bulletin*, 22(3):27–34, 1999.

118. D. Florescu, D. Kossmann, and I. Manolescu. Integrating Keyword Search into XML Query Processing. In *Proceedings of the International WWW Conference, Amsterdam, May 2000*. Elsevier, 2000.

119. E. Fox and M. Koll. Practical Enhanced Boolean Retrieval: Experiments with the SMART and SIRE Systems. *Information Processing and Management*, 24(3):257–267, 1988.

120. M. J. Franklin, B. Moon, and A. Ailamaki, editors. *Proceedings of the 2002 ACM SIGMOD International Conference on Management of Data, Madison, Wisconsin, June 3-6, 2002*. ACM, 2002.

121. H.-P. Frei, S. Meienberg, and P. Schäuble:. The perils of interpreting recall and precision values. In N. Fuhr, editor, *Proceedings of the GI/GMD-Workshop on Information Retrieval*, volume 289 of *Informatik-Fachberichte*, pages 1–10, Darmstadt, Germany, June 1991. Springer.

122. D. Freitag. *Machine Learning for Information Extraction in Informal Domains*. PhD thesis, Carnegie Mellon University, 1998.

123. N. Fuhr. Probabilistic models in information retrieval. *The Computer Journal*, 35(3):243–255, 1992.

124. N. Fuhr. Towards Data Abstraction in Networked Information Retrieval Systems. *Information Processing and Management*, 35(2):101–119, 1999.

125. N. Fuhr, N. Gövert, G. Kazai, and M. Lalmas. INEX: Initiative for the evaluation of XML retrieval. In *Proceedings ACM SIGIR 2002 Workshop on XML and Information Retrieval*, Tampere, Finland, Aug. 2002. ACM.

126. N. Fuhr, N. Gövert, G. Kazai, and M. Lalmas, editors. *INitiative for the Evaluation of XML Retrieval (INEX). Proceedings of the First INEX Workshop. Dagstuhl, Germany, December 8–11, 2002*, ERCIM Workshop Proceedings, Sophia Antipolis, France, Mar. 2003. ERCIM.

127. N. Fuhr, N. Gövert, and T. Rölleke. DOLORES: A system for logic-based retrieval of multimedia objects. In *Proceedings of the 21st Annual International ACM SIGIR Conference on Research and Development in Information Retrieval, Melbourne, Australia*, pages 257–265. ACM Press, Aug. 1998.

128. N. Fuhr and K. Großjohann. XIRQL: A query language for information retrieval in XML documents. In Croft et al. [84], pages 172–180.

129. N. Fuhr and T. Rölleke. A Probabilistic Relational Algebra for the Integration of Information Retrieval and Database Systems. *Transactions on Information Systems*, 14(1):32–66, 1997.

130. Generalised architecture for languages, encyclopaedias and nomenclatures in medicine. http://www.opengalen.org/about.html.

131. F. Gey, M. Hearst, and R. Tong, editors. *SIGIR '99: Proceedings of the 22nd Annual International ACM SIGIR Conference on Research and Development in Information Retrieval, August 15-19, 1999, Berkeley, CA, USA*. ACM, 1999.

132. R. Goldman, J. McHugh, and J. Widom. From Semistructured Data to XML: Migrating the Lore Data Model and Query Language. In Cluet and Milo [76], pages 25–30.

133. R. Goldman and J. Widom. DataGuides: Enabling query formulation and optimization in semistructured databases. In M. Jarke, M. J. Carey, K. R. Dittrich, F. H. Lochovsky, P. Loucopoulos, and M. A. Jeusfeld, editors, *VLDB'97, Proceedings of 23rd International Conference on Very Large Data Bases, August 25-29, 1997, Athens, Greece*, pages 436–445. Morgan Kaufmann, 1997.

134. T. Grabs. *Storage and Retrieval of XML Documents with a Cluster of Database Systems*. PhD thesis, Swiss Federal Institute of Technology (ETH) Zurich, 2003. Diss. ETH No. 15076.

135. T. Grabs, K. Böhm, and H.-J. Schek. PowerDB-IR - Scalable Information Retrieval and Storage with a Cluster of Databases. *Knowledge and Information Systems*. (to appear).

136. T. Grabs, K. Böhm, and H.-J. Schek. A parallel document engine built on top of a cluster of databases – design, implementation, and experiences –. Technical Report 340, Department of Computer Science, ETH Zurich, Apr. 2000.

137. T. Grabs, K. Böhm, and H.-J. Schek. PowerDB-IR – Information Retrieval on Top of a Database Cluster. In Paques et al. [237], pages 411–418.

138. T. Grabs, K. Böhm, and H.-J. Schek. XMLTM: Efficient transaction management for XML documents. In C. Nicholas, D. Grossman, K. Kalpakis, S. Qureshi, H. van Dissel, and L. Seligman, editors, *Proceedings of the 11th International Conference on Information and Knowledge Management (CIKM2002), November 4-9, 2002, McLean, VA, USA*, pages 142–152. ACM Press, 2002.

139. T. Grabs and H.-J. Schek. Generating vector spaces on-the-fly for flexible XML retrieval. In *XML and Information Retrieval Workshop - 25th Annual International ACM SIGIR Conference on Research and Development in Information Retrieval*, 2002.

140. T. Grabs and H.-J. Schek. Flexible Information Retrieval from XML with PowerDB-XML. In Fuhr et al. [126], pages 35–40.

141. J. Gray. Database and Transaction Processing Performance Handbook. available at http://www.benchmarkresources.com/handbook/contents.asp, 1993.

142. R. Grishman. Information Extraction: Techniques and Challenges. In *Information Extraction: A Multidisciplinary Approach to an Emerging Information Technology - International Summer School*, volume 1299 of *Lecture Notes in Computer Science*, pages 10–27. Springer, 1997.

143. D. A. Grossman, O. Frieder, D. O. Holmes, and D. C. Roberts. Integrating structured data and text: A relational approach. *Journal of the American Society for Information Science (JASIS)*, 48(2):122–132, Feb. 1997.

144. P. Grosso, E. Maler, J. Marsh, and N. Walsh. XPointer framework. W3C recommendation, 2003. http://www.w3.org/TR/xptr-framework/.

145. T. R. Gruber. Towards Principles for the Design of Ontologies Used for Knowledge Sharing. In N. Guarino and R. Poli, editors, *Formal Ontology in Conceptual Analysis and Knowledge Representation*, pages 89–95, Deventer, The Netherlands, 1993. Kluwer Academic Publishers.

146. T. Grust. Accelerating XPath location steps. In Franklin et al. [120], pages 109–120.

147. T. Grust, M. van Keulen, and J. Teubner. Staircase Join: Teach a Relational DBMS to Watch its (Axis) Steps. In *Proc. of the 29th Int'l Conference on Very Large Data Bases (VLDB)*, Berlin, Germany, Sept. 2003.

148. N. Guarino. Formal ontology and information systems. In N. Guarino, editor, *Proceedings of the 1st International Conference on Formal Ontologies in Information Systems, FOIS'98, Trento, Italy, 6-8 June 1998*, pages 3–15. IOS Press, 1998.

149. N. Gupta, J. Haritsa, and M. Ramanath. Distributed query processing on the Web. In *Proceedings of the 16th International Conference on Data Engineering, 28 February - 3 March, 2000, San Diego, California, USA*, page 84. IEEE Computer Society, 2000.

150. A. Guttman. R-trees: A dynamic index structure for spatial searching. In B. Yormark, editor, *Proceedings of the 1984 ACM SIGMOD International Conference on Management of Data, Boston, MA*, pages 47–57. ACM Press, 1984.

151. A. Halevy et al. Crossing the structure chasm. In *Proceedings of the First Semiannual Conference on Innovative Data Systems Research (CIDR)*, 2003.

152. D. Harman. Relevance feedback revisited. In N. J. Belkin, P. Ingwersen, and A. M. Pejtersen, editors, *Proc. of the Int. ACM SIGIR Conf. on Research and Development in Information Retrieval*, pages 1–10, Copenhagen, Denmark, June 1992. ACM.

153. D. Harman. The TREC conferences. In R. Kuhlen and M. Rittberger, editors, *Hypertext - Information Retrieval - Multimedia, Synergieeffekte elektronischer Informationssysteme, Proceedings HIM '95*, volume 20 of *Schriften zur Informationswissenschaft*, pages 9–28, Konstanz, Apr. 1995. Universitätsverlag Konstanz.

154. HaVi, Inc. HAVi (home audio/video interoperability architecture) user interface level 2, version 1.0, 2000. Available at http://www.havi.org.

155. Health level 7. http://www.hl7.org.

156. Health on the net foundation. http://www.hon.ch.

157. M. Hearst and C. Plaunt. Subtopic Structuring for Full-Length Document Access. In *Proceedings of the Sixteenth Annual International ACM SIGIR Conference on Research and Development in Information Retrieval*, pages 59–68, New York, 1993. ACM.

158. M. A. Hearst. Tilebars: Visualization of Term Distribution Information in Full Text Information Access. In *Proceedings of the Conference on Human Factors in Computer Systems, CHI'95*, pages 59–66, May 1995.

159. M. A. Hearst. User Interfaces and Visualization. In Baeza-Yates and Riberto-Neto [19].

160. S. Helmer, C.-C. Kanne, and G. Moerkotte. Isolation in XML bases. Technical Report MA-01-15, University of Mannheim, Germany, 2001.

161. D. Hiemstra. A database approach to content-based XML retrieval. In Fuhr et al. [126].

162. D. Hiemstra and F. de Jong. Disambiguation strategies for cross-language information retrieval. In S. Abiteboul and A.-M. Vercoustre, editors, *European Conference on Digital Libraries*, volume 1696 of *Lecture Notes in Computer Science*, pages 274–293. Springer, 1999.

163. D. Hiemstra and W. Kraaij. Twenty-One at TREC-7: Ad-hoc and cross-language track. In *Proceedings of the seventh Text Retrieval Conference TREC-7, NIST Special Publication 500-242*, pages 227–238, 1999.

164. G. Hirst and D. St-Onge. Lexical chains as representations of context for the detection and correction of malapropisms. In Fellbaum [114], pages 305–332.

165. O. Hitz, L. Robadey, and R. Ingold. Analysis of Synthetic Document Images. In *Fifth International Conference on Document Analysis and Recognition*, pages 374–377, 1999.

166. I. Horrocks. DAML+OIL: A reason-able web ontology language. In Jensen et al. [178], pages 2–13.

167. G. Huck, I. Macherius, and P. Fankhauser. PDOM: Lightweight persistency support for the document object model. In *Proceedings of the OOPSLA Workshop on Java and Databases: Persistence Options*, 1999.

168. B. L. Humphreys, D. A. B. Lindberg, H. M. Schoolman, and G. O. Barnett. The unified medical language system: An informatics research collaboration. *Journal of the American Medical Informatics Association*, 5(1):1–11, 1998.

169. E. Ide. New experiments in relevance feedback. In G. Salton, editor, *The Smart System - Experiments in Automatic Document Processing*, pages 337–354. Prentice-Hall Inc., Englewood Cliffs, N J, 1971.

170. ISO/IEC – International Organization For Standardization. 13249-2:2000: Information technology – Database languages – SQL Multimedia and Application Packages - Part 2: Full-Text, referenced in e.g. "SQL Multimedia and Application Packages (SQL/MM)". See http://www.acm.org/sigmod/record/issues/0112/standards.pdf, 2000.

171. Z. G. Ives, D. Florescu, M. Friedman, A. Y. Levy, and D. S. Weld. An adaptive query execution system for data integration. In Delis et al. [94], pages 299–310.

172. Z. G. Ives, A. Levy, and D. Weld. Efficient evaluation of reular path expressions on streaming XML data. Technical Report UW-CSE-2000-05-02, University of Washington, 2000.

173. J. Jaakkola and P. Kilpelainen. Nested Text-Region Algebra. Technical Report C-1999-2, Department of Computer Science, University of Helsinki, 1999.

174. M. Jamasz and S. Szpankowicz. Roget's thesaurus: A lexical resource to treasure. In *Proceedings of the NAACL Workshop "WordNet and Other Lexical Resources", Pittsburg*, pages 186–188, 2001.

175. M. Jamasz and S. Szpankowicz. Roget's thesaurus and semantic similarity. Technical Report TR-2003-01, University of Ottawa, Canada, 2003.

176. James Clark and Steve deRose. XML path language (XPath) 1.0. W3C Recommendation 16 November 1999, http://www.w3.org/TR/xpath, 1999.

177. B. J. Jansen, A. Spink, and T. Saracevic. Real life, real users, and real needs: a study and analysis of user queries on the web. *Information Processing and Management*, 36(2):207–227, 2000.

178. C. S. Jensen, K. G. Jeffery, J. Pokorný, S. Saltenis, E. Bertino, K. Böhm, and M. Jarke, editors. *Advances in Database Technology - EDBT 2002, 8th International Conference on Extending Database Technology, Prague, Czech Republic, March 25-27, Proceedings*, volume 2287 of *Lecture Notes in Computer Science*. Springer, 2002.

179. J. J. Jiang and D. W. Conrath. Semantic similarity based on corpus statistics and lexical taxonomy. In *Proceedings of the 10th International Conference on Research on Computational Linguistics (ROCLING), Taipeh, Taiwan*, pages 19–33, 1997.

180. T. Joachims. *The Maximum-Margin Approach to Learning Text Classifiers*. PhD thesis, 2002.

181. B. Johnson and B. Shneiderman. Tree-Maps: A Space Filling Approach to the Visualization of Hierarchical Information Structures. Technical Report CS-TR-2657, University of Maryland, Computer Science Department, Apr. 1991.

182. B. Jónsson, M. J. Franklin, and D. Srivastava. Interaction of Query Evaluation and Buffer Management for Information Retrieval. In L. M. Haas and A. Tiwary, editors, *SIGMOD 1998, Proceedings ACM SIGMOD International Conference on Management of Data, June 2-4, 1998, Seattle, Washington, USA*, pages 118–129. ACM Press, 1998.

183. M. Kaszkiel and J. Zobel. Passage Retrieval Revisited. In Belkin et al. [26], pages 178–185.

184. G. Kazai, M. Lalmas, and J. Reid. Construction of a test collection for the focussed retrieval of structured documents. In F. Sebastiani, editor, *25th European Conferenve on Information Retrieval Research (ECIR 2003)*, pages 88–103. Springer, 2003.

185. J. Kekäläinen and K. Järvelin. Using graded relevance assessments in IR evaluation. *Journal of the American Society for Information Science and Technology*, 53(13), Sept. 2002.

186. L. Kerschberg, W. Kim, and A. Scime. A semantic taxonomy-based personalizable meta-search agent. In M. T. Özsu, H.-J. Schek, K. Tanaka, Y. Zhang, and Y. Kambayashi, editors, *Proceedings of the 2nd International Conference on*

Web Information Systems Engineering (WISE'01), Organized by WISE Society and Kyoto University, Kyoto, Japan, 3-6 December 2001, Volume 1 (Main program), pages 41–52. IEEE Computer Society, 2001.

187. P. Kilpeläinen and H. Mannila. Retrieval from hierarchical texts by partial patterns. In R. Korfhage, E. M. Rasmussen, and P. Willett, editors, *Proceedings of the 16th Annual International ACM-SIGIR Conference on Research and Development in Information Retrieval. Pittsburgh, PA, USA*, pages 214–222. ACM, 1993.

188. H. Kimoto and T. Iwadera. Construction of a dynamic thesaurus and its use for associated information retrieval. In *Proceedings of the 13th annual international ACM SIGIR conference on Research and development in information retrieval*, pages 227–240. ACM Press, 1990.

189. J. Kleinberg. Authoritative sources in a hyperlinked environment. *Journal of the ACM*, 46(5), 1999.

190. M. Klettke and H. Meyer. XML and Object-Relational Database Systems - Enhancing Structural Mappings Based on Statistics. In Suciu and Vossen [289], pages 63–68.

191. J. Koenemann and N. J. Belkin. A case for interaction: a study of interactive information retrieval behavior and effectiveness. In *Proceedings of the SIGCHI conference on Human factors in computing systems*, pages 205–212, Vancouver, British Columbia, Canada, 1996. ACM Press.

192. W. Kraaij, T. Westerveld, and D. Hiemstra. The importance of prior probabilities for entry page search. In *Proceedings of the 25th annual international ACM SIGIR conference on Research and development in information retrieval*, pages 27–34. ACM Press, 2002.

193. H.-P. Kriegel, M. Pötke, and T. Seidl. Managing Intervals Efficiently in Object-Relational Databases. In A. E. Abbadi, M. L. Brodie, S. Chakravarthy, U. Dayal, N. Kamel, G. Schlageter, and K.-Y. Whang, editors, *Proc. of the 26th Int'l Conference on Very Large Databases (VLDB)*, pages 407–418, Cairo, Egypt, Sept. 2000. Morgan Kaufmann.

194. S. Kriewel. Visualisierung für Retrieval von XML-Dokumenten. Master's thesis, University of Dortmund, CS Dept., Dec. 2001.

195. O.-W. Kwon, M.-C. Kim, and K.-S. Choi. Query expansion using domain adapted, weighted thesaurus in an extended boolean model. In *Proceedings of the Third International Conference on Information and Knowledge Management (CIKM'94), Gaithersburg, Maryland, November 29 - December 2, 1994*, pages 140–146. ACM, 1994.

196. M. Lalmas. Dempster-Shafer's Theory of Evidence Applied to Structured Documents: Modelling Uncertainty. In Belkin et al. [26], pages 110–118.

197. C. Leacock and M. Chodrow. Combining local context and WordNet similarity for word sense disambiguation. In Fellbaum [114], pages 265–283.

198. D. B. Lenat and R. V. Guha. *Building Large Knowledge Based Systems*. Addison Wesley, 1990.

199. M. Lesk. Word-word association in document retrieval systems. *American Documentation*, 20(1):27–38, 1969.

200. W. D. Lewis. Measuring conceptual distance using WordNet: The design of a metric for measuring semantic similarity. *The University of Arizona Working Papers in Linguistics*, 12, 2002.

201. Q. Li and B. Moon. Indexing and querying XML data for regular path expressions. In Apers et al. [14], pages 361–370.

202. Q. Li, P. Shilane, N. Noy, and M. Musen. Ontology acquisition from on-line knowledge sources. In *AMIA Annual Symposium, Los Angeles, CA, 2000.*, 2000.

203. D. Lin. An information-theoretic definition of similarity. In J. W. Shavlik, editor, *Proceedings of the Fifteenth International Conference on Machine Learning (ICML 1998), Madison, Wisconson, USA, July 24-27, 1998*, pages 296–304. Morgan Kaufmann, San Francisco, CA, 1998.

204. J. A. List and A. P. de Vries. CWI at INEX 2002. In Fuhr et al. [126].

205. C. Lundquist, D. A. Grossman, and O. Frieder. Improving relevance feedback in the vector space model. In F. Golshani and K. Makki, editors, *Proc. of the Int. Conf. on Knowledge and Data Management*, pages 16–23, Las Vegas, Nevada, USA, Nov. 1997. ACM.

206. I. A. Macleod. A Query Language for Retrieving Information from Hierarchic Text Structures. *The Computer Journal*, 34(3):254–264, 1991.

207. A. Maedche and S. Staab. Semi-automatic engineering of ontologies from text. In *Proceedings of the 12th Internal Conference on Software and Knowledge Engineering, Chicago, USA*. KSI, 2000.

208. A. Maedche and S. Staab. Learning ontologies for the semantic web. In S. Decker, D. Fensel, A. P. Sheth, and S. Staab, editors, *Proceedings of the Second International Workshop on the Semantic Web - SemWeb'2001, Hongkong, China, May 1, 2001*, volume 40 of *CEUR workshop proceedings*, 2001. http://CEUR-WS.org/Vol-40/.

209. C. D. Manning and H. Schuetze. *Foundations of Statistical Natural Language Processing*. The MIT Press, 1999.

210. I. Manolescu, D. Florescu, and D. Kossmann. Answering xml queries on heterogeneous data sources. In *VLDB 2001, Proceedings of 27th International Conference on Very Large Data Bases, September 11-14, 2001, Roma, Italy*, pages 241–250. Morgan Kaufmann, Sept. 2001.

211. M. L. McHale. A comparison of WordNet and Roget's taxonomy for measuring semantic similarity. In *Proceedings of the Workshop on Content Visualization and Intermedia Representations (CVIR'98)*, 1998.

212. J. McHugh and J. Widom. Query optimization for XML. In Atkinson et al. [16], pages 315–326.

213. Medical subject headings. http://www.nlm.nih.gov/mesh/meshhome.html.

214. MedPICS certification and rating of trustful and assessed health information on the Net. http://www.medcertain.org.

215. D. R. H. Miller, T. Leek, and R. M. Schwartz. A hidden markov model information retrieval system. In Gey et al. [131], pages 214–221.

216. G. A. Miller. Wordnet: A lexical database for english. *Communications of the ACM*, 38(11):39–41, Nov. 1995.

217. G. A. Miller and W. G. Charles. Contextual correlates of semantic similarity. *Language and Cognitive Processes*, 6(1):1–28, 1991.

218. T. Milo and D. Suciu. Index structures for path expressions. In C. Beeri and P. Buneman, editors, *Database Theory - ICDT '99, 7th International Conference, Jerusalem, Israel, January 10-12, 1999, Proceedings*, volume 1540 of *Lecture Notes in Computer Science*, pages 277–295. Springer, 1999.

219. T. Mitchell. *Machine Learning*. McGraw Hill, 1996.

220. P. Mitra, G. Wiederhold, and M. L. Kersten. A graph-oriented model for articulation of ontology interdependencies. In Zaniolo et al. [329], pages 86–100.

221. S. Mizzaro. How Many Relevances in Information Retrieval? *Interacting With Computers*, 10(3):305–322, 1998.
222. Motion Picture Experts Group. Available at `http://mpeg.cselt.it`.
223. S. Myaeng, D.-H. Jang, M.-S. Kim, and Z.-C. Zhoo. A Flexible Model for Retrieval of SGML Documents. In W. B. Croft, A. Moffat, C. J. van Rijsbergen, R. Wilkinson, and J. Zobel, editors, *Proceedings of the 21st Annual International ACM SIGIR Conference on Research and Development in Information Retrieval*, pages 138–145, New York, 1998. ACM.
224. A. Nanopoulos and Y. Manolopoulos. Efficient similarity search for market basket data. *VLDB Journal*, 11(2):138—152, 2002.
225. M. Nascimento, E. Tousidou, V. Chitkara, and Y. Manolopoulos. Image indexing and retrieval using signature trees. *Data and Knowledge Engineering*, 43(1):57–77, 2002.
226. B. Nash, C. Hicks, and L. Dillner. Connecting doctors, patients, and the evidence. *British Medical Journal*, 326:674, 2003.
227. J. Naughton et al. The Niagara internet query system. *IEEE Data Engineering Bulletin*, 24(2):27–33, June 2001.
228. G. Navarro and R. A. Baeza-Yates. Proximal Nodes: A Model to Query Document Databases by Content and Structure. *ACM Transactions on Information Systems (TOIS)*, 15(4):400–435, 1997.
229. G. Neumann and J. Piskorski. A Shallow Text Processing Core Engine. *Journal of Computational Intelligence*, 18(3):451–476, 2002.
230. N. J. Nilsson. *Artificial Intelligence – A New Synthesis*. Morgan Kaufmann, 1998.
231. NIST. *Proceedings of the 7th Message Understanding Conference (MUC)*, 1998.
232. N. F. Noy, R. W. Fergerson, and M. A. Musen. The knowledge model of Protégé-2000: Combining interoperability and flexibility. In R. Dieng and O. Corby, editors, *Knowledge Acquisition, Modeling and Management, 12th International Conference, EKAW 2000, Juan-les-Pins, France, October 2-6, 2000, Proceedings*, volume 1937 of *Lecture Notes in Computer Science*, pages 17–32. Springer, 2000.
233. P. Ogilvie and J. Callan. Language Models and Structure Document Retrieval. In Fuhr et al. [126], pages 18–23.
234. D. O'Leary. Reengineering and knowledge management. In D. Fensel and R. Studer, editors, *Knowledge Acquisition, Modeling and Management, 11th European Workshop, EKAW '99, Dagstuhl Castle, Germany, May 26-29, 1999, Proceedings*, volume 1621 of *Lecture Notes in Computer Science*, pages 1–12. Springer, 1999.
235. M. T. Özsu and P. Valduriez. *Principles of Distributed Database Systems*. Prentice Hall, second edition, 1999.
236. M. P. Papazoglou and S. Milliner. Content-based organization of the information space in multi-database networks. In B. Pernici and C. Thanos, editors, *Advanced Information Systems Engineering, 10th International Conference CAiSE'98, Pisa, Italy, June 8-12, 1998, Proceedings*, volume 1413 of *Lecture Notes in Computer Science*, pages 251–272. Springer, 1998.
237. H. Paques, L. Liu, and D. Grossman, editors. *Proceedings of the 2001 ACM CIKM International Conference on Information and Knowledge Management, Atlanta, Georgia, USA, November 5-10, 2001*. ACM, 2001.
238. B. Piwowarski, G.-E. Faure, and P. Gallinari. Bayesian Networks and INEX. In Fuhr et al. [126], pages 7–12.

239. M.-F. Plassard, editor. *Functional Requirements for Bibliographic Records - Final Report*, volume 19 of *UBCIM Publications New Series*. K.G. Saur München, 1998. Available at http://www.ifla.org/VII/s13/frbr/frbr.htm.

240. Public medline. http://www.pubmed.org.

241. Y. Qiu and H.-P. Frei. Concept-based query expansion. In *Proceedings of SIGIR-93, 16th ACM International Conference on Research and Development in Information Retrieval*, pages 160–169, Pittsburgh, US, 1993.

242. Y. Qiu and H.-P. Frei. Improving the retrieval effectiveness by a similarity thesaurus. Technical Report 225, Swiss Federate Institute of Technology, Zürich, Switzerland, 1995.

243. L. Rabiner. A tutorial on hidden markov models and selected applications in speech recognition. In A. Waibel and K. Lee, editors, *Readings in speech recognition*, pages 267–296. Morgan Kaufmann, 1990.

244. R. Rada, H. Mili, E. Bicknell, and M. Blettner. Development and application of a metric on semantic nets. *IEEE Transactions on Systems, Man, and Cybernetics*, 19(1):17–30, 1989.

245. V. V. Raghavan, P. Bollmann, and G. S. Jung. A critical investigation of recall and precision as measures of retrieval system performance. *ACM Transactions on Office Information Systems*, 7(3):205–229, 1989.

246. A. Rector. Conceptual knowledge: the core of medical information systems. In *Proceedings of Medical Informatics*, pages 1420–1426, 1992.

247. P. Resnik. Using information content to evaluate semantic similarity in a taxonomy. In *Proceedings of the Fourteenth International Joint Conference on Artificial Intelligence, IJCAI 95, Montréal, Québec, Canada, August 20-25 1995*, volume 1, pages 448–453, 1995.

248. P. Resnik. Semantic similarity in a taxonomy: An information-based measure and its application to problems of ambiguity in natural language. *Journal of Artificial Intelligence Research*, 11:95–130, 1999.

249. R. Richardson, A. Smeaton, and J. Murphy. Using WordNet as a knowledge base for measuring semantic similarity between words. In *Proceedings of the AICS Conference*, 1994.

250. S. Robertson and K. Sparck-Jones. Relevance weighting of search terms. *Journal of the American Society for Information Science*, 27(3):129–146, 1976.

251. J. Rocchio Jr. *Relevance Feedback in Information Retrieval, The SMART Retrieval System: Experiments in Automatic Document Processing*, chapter 14, pages 313–323. Prentice Hall, Englewood Cliffs, New Jersey, USA, 1971.

252. H. Rubenstein and J. B. Goodenough. Contextual correlates of synonymy. *Communications of the ACM*, 8(10):627–633, 1965.

253. Y. Rui, T. Huang, and S. Mehrotra. Relevance feedback techniques in interactive content-based image retrieval. In *Proceedings of IS&T and SPIE Storage and Retrieval of Image and Video Databases VI*, pages 25–36, San Jose, California, USA, Jan. 1998.

254. K. Runapongsa, J. M. Patel, H. V. Jagadish, and S. Al-Khalifa. The michigan benchmark: A micro-benchmark for xml query processing system. Informal Proceedings of EEXTT02, electronic version available at http://www.eecs.umich.edu/db/mbench/, 2002.

255. S. Russel and P. Norvig. *Artificial Intelligence - A Modern Approach*. Prentice Hall, 1995.

256. A. Sahuguet and F. Azavant. Web ecology: Recycling HTML pages as XML documents using W4F. In Cluet and Milo [76].

257. A. Salminen and F. W. Tompa. PAT Expressions: an Algebra for Text Search. *Acta Linguistica Hungarica*, 41(1-4):277–306, 1993.

258. G. Salton, editor. *The SMART Retrieval System - Experiments in Automatic Document Processing*. Prentice Hall, Englewood, Cliffs, New Jersey, 1971.

259. G. Salton and C. Buckley. Term-weighting approaches in automatic text retrieval. *Information Processing & Management*, 24(5):513–523, 1988.

260. G. Salton and C. Buckley. Improving retrieval performance by relevance feedback. *Journal of the American Society for Information Science*, 41(4):288–297, 1990.

261. G. Salton, E. A. Fox, and H. Wu. Extended Boolean Information Retrieval. *Communications of the ACM*, 26(12):1022–1036, 1983.

262. G. Salton and M. J. McGill. *Introduction to Modern Information Retrieval*. McGraw-Hill, first edition, 1983.

263. G. Salton, A. Wong, and C. S. Yang. A Vector Space Model for Automatic Indexing. *CACM*, 18(11):613–620, 1975.

264. T. Saracevic. Evaluation of evaluation in information retrieval. In E. Fox, P. Ingwersen, and R. Fidel, editors, *Proceedings of the 18th Annual International ACM SIGIR Conference on Research and Development in Information Retrieval*, pages 138–146, New York, 1995. ACM. ISBN 0-89791-714-6.

265. S. Sarawagi. Automation in information extraction and data integration. In S. Christodoulakis, D. L. Lee, and A. O. Mendelzon, editors, *VLDB 2002, Tutorial notes of the 28th International Conference on Very Large Data Bases, August 20-23, Hong Kong, China*, pages 1–28, 2002.

266. SAX (Simple API for XML). http://sax.sourceforge.net/.

267. P. Schäuble. *Multimedia Information Retrieval, Content-based Information Retrieval from Large Text and Audio Databases*. Kluwer Academic Publishers, Zurich, Switzerland, 1997.

268. T. Schlieder and M. Meuss. Result Ranking for Structured Queries against XML Documents. In *DELOS Workshop: Information Seeking, Searching and Querying in Digital Libraries*, Zurich, Switzerland, Dec. 2000. http://page.inf.fu-berlin.de/~schlied/publications/delos2000.pdf.

269. A. Schmidt, M. Kersten, D. Florescu, M. Carey, I. Manolescu, and F. Waas. The XML Store Benchmark Project, 2000. http://www.xml-benchmark.org.

270. A. Schmidt, M. Kersten, D. Florescu, M. Carey, I. Manolescu, and F. Waas. XMark Queries, 2002. available at http://www.xml-benchmark.org/Assets/queries.txt.

271. A. Schmidt, M. Kersten, M. Windhouwer, and F. Waas. Efficient Relational Storage and Retrieval of XML Documents. In Suciu and Vossen [289], pages 47–52.

272. A. Schmidt, F. Waas, M. Kersten, M. Carey, I. Manolescu, and R. Busse. XMark: A Benchmark for XML Data Management. In P. A. bernstein, Y. E. Ioannidis, R. Ramakrishnan, and D. Papadias, editors, *VLDB 2002, Proceedings of 28th International Conference on Very Large Data Bases, August 20-23, Hong Kong, China*, pages 974–985. Morgan Kaufmann, 2002.

273. A. Schmidt, F. Waas, M. Kersten, D. Florescu, I. Manolescu, M. Carey, and R. Busse. The XML Benchmark Project. Technical Report INS-R0103, CWI, Amsterdam, The Netherlands, April 2001.

274. H. Schöning. Tamino – a DBMS designed for XML. In *Proceedings of the 17th International Conference on Data Engineering, April 2-6, 2001, Heidelberg, Germany*, pages 149–154. IEEE Computer Society, 2001.

275. H. Schöning. Tamino – Software AG's native XML server. In A. B. Chaudhri, A. Rashid, and R. Zicari, editors, *XML Data Management: Native XML and XML-Enabled Database Systems*. Addison Wesley, 2003.

276. H. Schöning and J. Wäsch. Tamino - an internet database system. In Zaniolo et al. [329], pages 383–387.

277. P. G. Selinger, M. M. Astrahan, D. M. Chamberlin, R. A. Lorie, and T. G. Price. Access Path Selection in a Relational Database Management System. In P. A. Bernstein, editor, *Proceedings of the 1979 ACM SIGMOD International Conference on Management of Data, Boston, Massachusetts, May 30 - June 1*, pages 23–34, Boston, Massachusetts, USA, 1979. ACM Press.

278. J. Shanmugasundaram et al. Architecting a network query engine for producing partial results. In Suciu and Vossen [289], pages 17–22.

279. J. Shanmugasundaram, K. Tufte, C. Zhang, G. He, D. J. DeWitt, and J. F. Naughton. Relational Databases for Querying XML Documents: Limitations and Opportunities. In Atkinson et al. [16], pages 302–314.

280. W. M. Shaw, J. B. Wood, R. E. Wood, and H. R. Tibbo. The cystic fibrosis database: Content and research opportunities. *Library and Information Science Research*, 13:347–366, 1991.

281. S. Sizov et al. The BINGO! system for information portal generation and expert web search. In *Proceedings of the First Semiannual Conference on Innovative Data Systems Research (CIDR)*, 2003.

282. S. Sizov, M. Theobald, S. Siersdorfer, and G. Weikum. BINGO!: Bookmark-induced gathering of information. In *Proceedings of the 3rd International Conference on Web Information Systems Engineering (WISE 2002), 12-14 December 2002, Singapore*, pages 323–332. IEEE Computer Society, 2002.

283. S. Soderland. Learning Information Extraction Rules for Semi-Structured and Free Text. *Machine Learning*, 1999.

284. R. Southall. Visual structure and transmission of meaning. In *International Conference on Electronic Publishing, Document Manipulation and Typography*, pages 35–45. Cambridge University Press, 1988.

285. S. Staab, J. Angele, S. Decker, M. Erdmann, A. Hotho, A. Maedche, H.-P. Schnurr, R. Studer, and Y. Sure. Semantic community web portals. *Computer Networks*, 33(1–6):473–491, 2000.

286. S. Staab et al. GETESS - searching the web exploiting german texts. In *Proceedings of the 3rd Conference on Cooperative Information Agents (CIA)*, pages 113–124, 1999.

287. S. Staab and A. Maedche. Ontology engineering beyond the modeling of concepts and relations. In *Proceedings of the 14th European Conference on Artificial Intelligence (ECAI), Workshop on Applications of Ontologies and Problem-Solving Methods*, 2000.

288. D. Suciu. Distributed query evaluation on semistructured data. *ACM Transactions on Database Systems (TODS)*, 27(1):1–62, 2002.

289. D. Suciu and G. Vossen, editors. *The World Wide Web and Databases: Third International Workshop WebDB 2000, Dallas, Texas, USA, May 18-19, 2000*, volume 1997 of *Lecture Notes in Computer Science*, Berlin, Heidelberg, 2001. Springer.

290. M. Sussna. Word sense disambiguation for free-text indexing using a massive semantic network. In B. K. Bhargava, T. W. Finin, and Y. Yesha, editors, *CIKM 93, Proceedings of the Second International Conference on Information*

and Knowledge Management, Washington, DC, USA, November 1-5, 1993, pages 67–74. ACM, 1993.

291. Systematized nomenclature of medicine. http://www.snomed.org.

292. K. Taghva, A. Condit, and J. Borsack. An evaluation of an automatic markup system. In *Proceedings of the IS&T/SPIE 1995 International Symposium on Electronic Imaging Science and Technology*, pages 317–327, 1995.

293. J. Tan. *Health Management Solutions*. Aspen, 1995.

294. The international statistical classification of diseases and related health problems, 10th edition. http://www.who.int/whosis/icd10.

295. A. Theobald and G. Weikum. Adding Relevance to XML. In Suciu and Vossen [289], pages 105–124.

296. A. Theobald and G. Weikum. The index-based XXL search engine for querying XML data with relevance ranking. In Jensen et al. [178], pages 477–495.

297. H. S. Thompson, D. Beech, M. Maloney, and N. Mendelsohn. XML Schema Part 1: Structures. W3C recommendation, World Wide Web Consortium, May 2001. http://www.w3.org/TR/xmlschema-1/.

298. P. Tiberio and P. Zezula. Storage and retrieval: Signature file access. In A. Kent and J. Williams, editors, *Encyclopedia of Microcomputers*, volume 16, pages 377–403. Marcel Dekker Inc., New York, 1995.

299. K. Tufte and D. Maier. Merge as lattice-join of XML documents. available at http://www.cs.wisc.edu/niagara/Publications.html, 2002.

300. Unicode Consortium. The Unicode standard, version 3.2.0.

301. J. van Bemmel. *Handbook of Medical Informatics*. Springer, 1997.

302. M. G. M. van Doorn and A. P. de Vries. The Psychology of Multimedia Databases. In *Proceedings of the 5th ACM Digital Libraries Conference (DL'00)*, pages 1–9, San Antonio, Texas, USA, June 2000.

303. M. van Keulen, J. Vonk, A. P. de Vries, J. Flokstra, and H. E. Blok. Moa: Extensibility and Efficiency in Querying Nested Data. Technical Report TR-CTIT-02-19, Centre for Telematics and Information Technology, University of Twente, Enschede, The Netherlands, July 2002.

304. R. van Zwol. *Modelling and searching web-based document collections*. PhD thesis, Centre for Telematics and Information Technology (CTIT), Enschede, the Netherlands, April 2002. ISBN: 90-365-1721-4; ISSN: 1381-3616 No. 02-40 (CTIT Ph.D. thesis series).

305. R. van Zwol and P. M. Apers. Retrieval performance experiment with the webspace method. In B. Eaglestone, S. North, and A. Poulovassilis, editors, *Proceedings of the 19th British National Conference on Databases*, pages 150–165, Sheffield, U.K., July 2002.

306. V. Vapnik. *Statistical Learning Theory*. Wiley, New York, 1998.

307. Virage Web Site. http://www.virage.com/.

308. M. Volz, K. Aberer, and K. Böhm. Applying a flexible OODBMS-IRS-Coupling for structured document handling. In S. Y. W. Su, editor, *Proceedings of the Twelfth International Conference on Data Engineering, February 26 - March 1, 1996, New Orleans, Louisiana*, pages 10–19. IEEE Computer Society, 1996.

309. E. M. Voorhees and D. K. Harman, editors. *The Tenth Text REtrieval Conference (TREC 2001)*, Gaithersburg, MD, USA, 2002. NIST.

310. W3C. W3C XML Schema. http://www.w3.org/XML/Schema, 2001.

311. W3C DOM Working Group. Document object model (DOM), 2002. http://www.w3.org/DOM/.

312. H. Wactlar. The informedia digital video library. Available at http://www.informedia.cs.cmu.edu/.

313. R. Weber and K. Böhm. Trading quality for time with nearest-neighbor search. In Zaniolo et al. [329], pages 21–35.

314. R. Weber, H.-J. Schek, and S. Blott. A quantitative analysis and performance study for similarity-search methods in high-dimensional spaces. In A. Gupta, O. Shmueli, and J. Widom, editors, *VLDB'98, Proceedings of 24th International Conference on Very Large Data Bases, August 24-27, 1998, New York City, New York, USA*, pages 194–205. Morgan Kaufmann, 1998.

315. T. Westerveld, A. P. de Vries, A. van Ballegooij, F. M. G. de Jong, and D. Hiemstra. A probabilistic multimedia retrieval model and its evaluation. *Eurasip Journal on Applied Signal Processing*, 2003(2):186–198, 2003.

316. R. W. White, I. Ruthven, and J. M. Jose. The use of implicit for relevance feedback in web retrieval. In F. Crestani, M. Girolami, and C. van Rijsbergen, editors, *Proc. of the European Annual Colloquium on Information Retrieval Research (ECIR)*, volume 2291 of *Lecture Notes in Computer Science*, pages 93–109. Springer Verlag, 2002.

317. M. A. Windhouwer, A. R. Schmidt, and M. L. Kersten. Acoi: A System for Indexing Multimedia Objects. In *International Workshop on Information Integration and Web-based Applications & Services*, Yogyakarta, Indonesia, November 1999.

318. M. A. Windhouwer, A. R. Schmidt, R. van Zwol, M. Petkovic, and H. E. Blok. Flexible and Scalable Digital Library Search. Technical Report INS-R0111, CWI, Amsterdam, The Netherlands, December 2001.

319. M. A. Windhouwer, A. R. Schmidt, R. van Zwol, M. Petkovic, and H. E. Blok. Flexible Digital Library Search. In A. Dahanayake and W. Gerhardt, editors, *Web-enabled Systems Integration: Challenges and Practices*, pages 200–224. Idea Group Publishing, 2003.

320. Wold Wide Web Consortium. Resource description framework. http://www.w3.org/RDF.

321. Wold Wide Web Consortium. Semantic web activity. http://www.w3.org/2001/sw/.

322. Z. Wu and M. Palmer. Verb semantics and lexical selection. In *32nd. Annual Meeting of the Association for Computational Linguistics*, pages 133–138, New Mexico State University, Las Cruces, New Mexico, 1994.

323. J. Xu, R. Weischedel, and C. Nguyen. Evaluating a probabilistic model for cross-lingual information retrieval. In Croft et al. [84], pages 105–110.

324. Y. Xu, D. Sauquet, P. Degoulet, and M. Jaulent. Component-based mediation services for the integration of medical applications. *Artificial Intelligence in Medicine*, 27(3):283–304, Mar. 2003.

325. Y. Yang. An evaluation of statistical approaches to text categorization. *Journal of Information Retrieval*, 1(1/2), 1999.

326. Y. Yang and O. Pedersen. A comparative study on feature selection in text categorization. *International Conference on Machine Learning (ICML)*, 1997.

327. B. B. Yao, M. T. zsu, and J. Keenleyside. XBench - A Family of Benchmarks for XML DBMSs. Technical Report TR-CS-2002-39, University of Waterloo, 2002.

328. M. Yoshikawa, T. Amagasa, T. Shimura, and S. Uemura. XRel: A path-based approach to storage and retrieval of XML documents using relational databases. *ACM Transactions on Internet Technology*, 1(1):110–141, 2001.

329. C. Zaniolo, P. C. Lockemann, M. H. Scholl, and T. Grust, editors. *Advances in Database Technology - EDBT 2000, 7th International Conference on Extending Database Technology, Konstanz, Germany, March 27-31, 2000, Proceedings*, volume 1777 of *Lecture Notes in Computer Science*. Springer, 2000.

330. P. Zezula, G. Amato, F. Debole, and F. Rabitti. Tree signatures for XML querying and navigation. Technical Report 2003-TR-04, ISTI-CNR, March 2003.

331. C. Zhang, J. Naughton, D. DeWitt, Q. Luo, and G. Lohman. On Supporting Containment Queries in Relational Database Management Systems. In W. G. Aref, editor, *Proc. of the 2001 ACM SIGMOD International Conference on Management of Data*, pages 425–436, Santa Barbara, California, May 2001. ACM Press.

Index

Lecture Notes in Computer Science

For information about Vols. 1–2710
please contact your bookseller or Springer-Verlag

Vol. 2744: V. Mařík, D. McFarlane, P. Valckenaers (Eds.), Holonic and Multi-Agent Systems for Manufacturing. Proceedings, 2003. XI, 322 pages. 2003. (Subseries LNAI).

Vol. 2745: M. Guo, L.T. Yang (Eds.), Parallel and Distributed Processing and Applications. Proceedings, 2003. XII, 450 pages. 2003.

Vol. 2746: A. de Moor, W. Lex, B. Ganter (Eds.), Conceptual Structures for Knowledge Creation and Communication. Proceedings, 2003. XI, 405 pages. 2003. (Subseries LNAI).

Vol. 2747: B. Rovan, P. Vojtáš (Eds.), Mathematical Foundations of Computer Science 2003. Proceedings, 2003. XIII, 692 pages. 2003.

Vol. 2748: F. Dehne, J.-R. Sack, M. Smid (Eds.), Algorithms and Data Structures. Proceedings, 2003. XII, 522 pages. 2003.

Vol. 2749: J. Bigun, T. Gustavsson (Eds.), Image Analysis. Proceedings, 2003. XXII, 1174 pages. 2003.

Vol. 2750: T. Hadzilacos, Y. Manolopoulos, J.F. Roddick, Y. Theodoridis (Eds.), Advances in Spatial and Temporal Databases. Proceedings, 2003. XIII, 525 pages. 2003.

Vol. 2751: A. Lingas, B.J. Nilsson (Eds.), Fundamentals of Computation Theory. Proceedings, 2003. XII, 433 pages. 2003.

Vol. 2752: G.A. Kaminka, P.U. Lima, R. Rojas (Eds.), RoboCup 2002: Robot Soccer World Cup VI. XVI, 498 pages. 2003. (Subseries LNAI).

Vol. 2753: F. Maurer, D. Wells (Eds.), Extreme Programming and Agile Methods – XP/Agile Universe 2003. Proceedings, 2003. XI, 215 pages. 2003.

Vol. 2754: M. Schumacher, Security Engineering with Patterns. XIV, 208 pages. 2003.

Vol. 2756: N. Petkov, M.A. Westenberg (Eds.), Computer Analysis of Images and Patterns. Proceedings, 2003. XVIII, 781 pages. 2003.

Vol. 2758: D. Basin, B. Wolff (Eds.), Theorem Proving in Higher Order Logics. Proceedings, 2003. X, 367 pages. 2003.

Vol. 2759: O.H. Ibarra, Z. Dang (Eds.), Implementation and Application of Automata. Proceedings, 2003. XI, 312 pages. 2003.

Vol. 2761: R. Amadio, D. Lugiez (Eds.), CONCUR 2003 - Concurrency Theory. Proceedings, 2003. XI, 524 pages. 2003.

Vol. 2762: G. Dong, C. Tang, W. Wang (Eds.), Advances in Web-Age Information Management. Proceedings, 2003. XIII, 512 pages. 2003.

Vol. 2763: V. Malyshkin (Ed.), Parallel Computing Technologies. Proceedings, 2003. XIII, 570 pages. 2003.

Vol. 2764: S. Arora, K. Jansen, J.D.P. Rolim, A. Sahai (Eds.), Approximation, Randomization, and Combinatorial Optimization. Proceedings, 2003. IX, 409 pages. 2003.

Vol. 2765: R. Conradi, A.I. Wang (Eds.), Empirical Methods and Studies in Software Engineering. VIII, 279 pages. 2003.

Vol. 2766: S. Behnke, Hierarchical Neural Networks for Image Interpretation. XII, 224 pages. 2003.

Vol. 2769: T. Koch, I. T. Sølvberg (Eds.), Research and Advanced Technology for Digital Libraries. Proceedings, 2003. XV, 536 pages. 2003.

Vol. 2776: V. Gorodetsky, L. Popyack, V. Skormin (Eds.), Computer Network Security. Proceedings, 2003. XIV, 470 pages. 2003.

Vol. 2777: B. Schölkopf, M.K. Warmuth (Eds.), Learning Theory and Kernel Machines. Proceedings, 2003. XIV, 746 pages. 2003. (Subseries LNAI).

Vol. 2778: P.Y.K. Cheung, G.A. Constantinides, J.T. de Sousa (Eds.), Field-Programmable Logic and Applications. Proceedings, 2003. XXVI, 1179 pages. 2003.

Vol. 2779: C.D. Walter, Ç.K. Koç, C. Paar (Eds.), Cryptographic Hardware and Embedded Systems – CHES 2003. Proceedings, 2003. XIII, 441 pages. 2003.

Vol. 2781: B. Michaelis, G. Krell (Eds.), Pattern Recognition. Proceedings, 2003. XVII, 621 pages. 2003.

Vol. 2782: M. Klusch, A. Omicini, S. Ossowski, H. Laamanen (Eds.), Cooperative Information Agents VII. Proceedings, 2003. XI, 345 pages. 2003. (Subseries LNAI).

Vol. 2783: W. Zhou, P. Nicholson, B. Corbitt, J. Fong (Eds.), Advances in Web-Based Learning – ICWL 2003. Proceedings, 2003. XV, 552 pages. 2003.

Vol. 2786: F. Oquendo (Ed.), Software Process Technology. Proceedings, 2003. X, 173 pages. 2003.

Vol. 2787: J. Timmis, P. Bentley, E. Hart (Eds.), Artificial Immune Systems. Proceedings, 2003. XI, 299 pages. 2003.

Vol. 2789: L. Böszörményi, P. Schojer (Eds.), Modular Programming Languages. Proceedings, 2003. XIII, 271 pages. 2003.

Vol. 2790: H. Kosch, L. Böszörményi, H. Hellwagner (Eds.), Euro-Par 2003 Parallel Processing. Proceedings, 2003. XXXV, 1320 pages. 2003.

Vol. 2792: T. Rist, R. Aylett, D. Ballin, J. Rickel (Eds.), Intelligent Virtual Agents. Proceedings, 2003. XV, 364 pages. 2003. (Subseries LNAI).

Vol. 2794: P. Kemper, W. H. Sanders (Eds.), Computer Performance Evaluation. Proceedings, 2003. X, 309 pages. 2003.

Vol. 2795: L. Chittaro (Ed.), Human-Computer Interaction with Mobile Devices and Services. Proceedings, 2003. XV, 494 pages. 2003.

Vol. 2796: M. Cialdea Mayer, F. Pirri (Eds.), Automated Reasoning with Analytic Tableaux and Related Methods. Proceedings, 2003. X, 271 pages. 2003. (Subseries LNAI).

Vol. 2803: M. Baaz, J.A. Makowsky (Eds.), Computer Science Logic. Proceedings, 2003. XII, 589 pages. 2003.

Vol. 2805: K. Araki, S. Gnesi, D. Mandrioli (Eds.), FME 2003: Formal Methods. Proceedings, 2003. XVII, 942 pages. 2003.

Vol. 2810: M.R. Berthold, H.-J. Lenz, E. Bradley, R. Kruse, C. Borgelt (Eds.), Advances in Intelligent Data Analysis V. Proceedings, 2003. XV, 624 pages. 2003.

Vol. 2817: D. Konstantas, M. Leonard, Y. Pigneur, S. Patel (Eds.), Object-Oriented Information Systems. Proceedings, 2003. XII, 426 pages. 2003.

Vol. 2818: H. Blanken, T. Grabs, H.-J. Schek, R. Schenkel, G. Weikum (Eds.), Intelligent Search on XML Data. XVII, 319 pages. 2003.